THE

PARABLES OF JESUS

EXPLAINED AND ILLUSTRATED.

BY

FREDERICK GUSTAV LISCO,
MINISTER OF ST. GERTRAUD CHURCH, BERLIN.

TRANSLATED FROM THE GERMAN,

BY THE REV. P. FAIRBAIRN,
MINISTER OF SALTON.

PHILADELPHIA:
DANIELS AND SMITH, 36 NORTH SIXTH STREET.
NEW YORK: ROBERT CARTER AND BROTHERS.
BOSTON: GOULD, KENDALL, AND LINCOLN.
1850.

WM. S. YOUNG, PRINTER.

PREFACE.

THE author of the following work on the Parables, briefly notices in the Preface to the First Edition, that it was not his design, in preparing it, "to give a complete commentary, or to embrace every thing which has been embraced in commentaries on the Gospels at large, or on this select portion of them. Hence it is only on particular passages, where it seemed necessary for grounding more deeply the exposition given, that special remarks have been submitted; but the connexion of the Parable, with its attendant circumstances, has been all the more carefully investigated, in order to arrive at as precise an apprehension as possible of the truth unfolded in each. The practical design of the work seemed to me to require that the citations from other authors should be literally made, for the satisfaction of those who might not have the works cited at hand; and then the numerous quotations from Luther's Postils and Calvin's exegetical writings may possibly have the effect of leading some to give to these authors themselves a more regular and careful perusal. Luther's Postils contain an inexhaustible treasury of Christian wisdom and instruction, so that it is by no means superfluous to point to the exegetical riches stored up in them. And, in regard to Calvin, how much his commentary deserves to be consulted, has been well stated by Tholuck, who, after lauding its eloquence of diction and terseness of expression, its just proportions, and freedom from all extravagant digressions, goes on to say: 'In regard to his method of exposition, we must first of all admire that free and independent tone of thought, which, while it did not prevent him from paying all due respect to what had hitherto been held as of authority in the church, at the same time never constrained him to adopt an exposition which was not justified by the connexion, or which seemed at variance with the grammatical construction. This property of Calvin's mind stands united with the singular exegetical tact which rendered it well-nigh impossible for him to take up with forced interpretations. And there is further to be admired, his multifarious learning, and, finally, his deep Christian feeling. How much this profoundly learned and penetrating man made faith in the Redeemer a heart-concern, how much he sought the salvation of his soul in the way of practical self-denial, all his works bear witness.' "

The sincere regard which the author here expresses for Luther and Calvin,—the frequent quotations he has made from their writings, and the deference he uniformly pays to their judgments, may serve, in some measure, as a security for the general orthodoxy of his views, and the soundness of his principles of interpretation. In the exposition of particular passages, he does not, indeed, slavishly follow either the one or the other, but, throughout the volume, I am not conscious of having met with any thing at variance with the Calvinistic system of divine truth. And, besides this important article of doctrinal correctness, the work is distinguished by much care and discrimination in ascertaining the real scope and meaning of the interesting portions of Scripture which it handles—by much clearness and simplicity in its exhibitions of gospel truth—and by the lucid order in which it presents the train of thought pursued in each parable, and the heads of doctrine, or obligations of duty respectively inculcated. In a few instances I have taken occasion to express my dissent from the views submitted by the author; but these have always been on incidental or subordinate topics, and have never involved either an article of Christian faith, or the leading scope of a parable.

This work is not so much designed for private individuals, to assist them in their meditations on the parables, as for ministers of the gospel, that they might have a suitable help to aid them in discoursing upon the Parables. And, for this purpose, it will probably be found of equal, if not superior, value to any other work on the same subject. In one respect especially it may be of considerable service. For discourses on the Parables not unfrequently run much in the style of loose and disjointed observations on the successive parts of the story or image delineated, without due regard to any prominent idea or leading topic as the heart and centre of the whole. Much important and valuable matter may doubtless be delivered even when they are so handled; but it must be obvious, on a moment's consideration, that for the purpose of bringing clearly and distinctly out our Lord's meaning, such a mode of treating the Parables must be very defective and inefficient, as compared with that adopted by Lisco—according to which every Parable is regarded as one whole, illustrative of some important truth, or obligation, or principle in the divine government, and which the different parts of the Parable only serve, in some respect, to open out and develop. The work, it is hoped, may exercise a beneficial influence in recommending this more excellent way of conducting discourses on the Parables, as also in facilitating the apprehension of what is in each case the real scope and object of the Parable, which is first always carefully investigated, and then, with the train of thought unfolding it, is spread before the eye with all the distinctness of a tabular representation;—while the reflections subjoined from the author himself, and from the most approved commentators on the principal verses of the Parable, suggest the most important and appropriate thoughts for the practical treatment of the subject. Most heartily do we concur with the author in wishing, concerning the translation, what he sought for the original—"That the Lord of the church may so accompany it with his rich blessing, as that it may contribute, in however small a degree, to the right understanding of his blessed word, which in its meaning is deeper than the sea, and in its truth is lasting as eternity."

P. FAIRBAIRN.

MANSE, SALTON,
23 *November*, 1840.

INTRODUCTORY REMARKS UPON THE PARABLES,

AND

THE MANNER OF TREATING THEM.

---

1. NAME AND IDEA OF THE PARABLE.

THE word PARABLE,—similitude,—properly signifies *a placing of one thing together with, or by the side of another,* and most correctly expresses the peculiar essence and intrinsic nature of this form of poetry. For, in a parable, the image borrowed from the visible world is accompanied by a truth from the invisible (spiritual,) and the proper or literal sense of the story, which serves for the image, is only the bearer, the presenter of a spiritual truth and doctrine. In this respect the parable resembles the fable, from which, however, it is essentially different. In both we find a story, which is designed to unfold a truth or inculcate an obligation; but the regions from which these two kinds of inventive composition derive their images, are not the same. The genuine fable does not exercise itself in the province of actual life, but makes irrational and lifeless creatures from the kingdom of nature, think, speak, act, and suffer in a manner suited to their proper nature. The parable derives *its* matter only from the territory of the possible and the true; let the event, which it presents before us, be ever so fully described, it must still be in itself so natural, that no objection can be brought against it; and that the transaction might have actually occurred in real life. The fable and parable are also different in regard to the doctrine of truth itself, which they both seek to render palpable, inasmuch as the parable has to do with nothing but religious truths, while the fable has for its object also experimental sayings and prudential lessons. Poelitz, in his survey of the German language, thus defines the fable, the allegory and the parable: "The peculiarity of the fable consists in the delineation of human transactions and circumstances within the circle of instinct, which is so nearly allied to human freedom. The allegory does not name the object itself which is to be delineated, but makes it appear under an image exactly corresponding to it, and it is a matter of indifference, whether the object delineated be a truth of reason or a moral principle. The parable is the representation of an action which enfolds within itself the emblem of a higher truth of reason, or a moral principle, under the unity of a complete and palpable form. Just as the similitude arises out of a continued and perfectly formed comparison, so does the parable arise out of a complete and full drawn similitude."

2. AGE OF THE PARABLE.

In regard to the age of these two methods of instruction, the parable and the fable, we find both were practised in Old Testament times, and were very common among the people of the East. In the book of Judges, chap. ix. 8—15, we meet with the fable of the trees choosing for themselves a king, which Jonathan spake to the inhabitants of Shechem, in order to convince them of the folly of having elected so vile a man as Abimelech for their king. And of the parabolic method of instruction we are furnished with examples in the second book of Samuel, chap. xii. 1—7, where Nathan charges David with his crime in regard to Uriah; and in chap. xiv. 1, *seq.*, where the woman of Tekoa entreats the favour of David towards Absalom.

3. RESPECT WHICH THE PARABLE HAS TO THE VISIBLE AND INVISIBLE WORLD.

In the general, there is manifested in the parabolic form of instruction a very fine talent of observing appearances in nature and in human life; a delicate feeling, and a susceptible mind for the truths and objects of the spiritual world; a pious, devout heart, which is ever disposed to apprehend the relation in which the temporal stands to the eternal; and, finally, the capacity of selecting the most suitable form, wherein to embody the eternal truth, and depict what is common to the earthly type, and the heavenly antitype. It is the part of the parable to bring the known into contact with the unknown; and cause the latter to be understood according to its real nature and properties in the known; it connects the old with the new; transports us from the visible world into the invisible, that it may present this distinctly before us in a sensible resemblance; the earthly is made the image of the heavenly, the present of the future, the temporal of that which is eternal. In it the whole empire of nature is an image of the empire of grace, and it shows that in the one the same, or at least similar laws of the development are to be found which belong to the other; for example, that a progressively advancing cultivation, seed-time, and harvest, have a place in the kingdom of grace, as well as of nature. It sets out from man's natural experience, and gives us to discern therein God's principles of government toward the whole human race, and every individual. It teaches us to conclude, that if even sinful men act so and so, are so full of love, so ready to help, how much more must God, who is love itself, and is almighty! It derives its matter out ot the inexhaustible province of nature and human life, and throws light upon both, while it employs them as an emblem for representing what is heavenly. Kleuker, in his excellent work upon "the Son of God and of man,"* expresses himself upon the parables of Jesus in this respect, after the following manner: "The lofty apprehension of Jesus chose many parabolic representations of the kingdom of God, the import of which is commensurate with the grandeur of that kingdom. He spake for a new sense, for the eye and emotion of the heart; imagined and allured through new images, new pictures, copies of the living world. When he wished to shoot a ray out of his infinite orb of truth, or to illuminate an entire night, he did it under images, symbols, characters of nature, and of history. The circle of nature and of history, the objects of sense and observation supplied emblems to his thoughts, became vessels for the food of heaven, which eternally satisfies; every thing visible was made by him a symbol of the invisible, for creatures who live and move, are born and must act in the world of visible things. Depth of thought in understanding what *is* and *is done*, was indispensable in Christ; because he chose out of all possible forms of instruction the parabolico-poetical, which, according to the manner it was used, necessarily required that his one eye should see nature and the other history in every present circumstance with living force and reality. Parable is the proof of all proofs, level to the apprehension even of the most sensual men, while the greatest hero of abstraction must admit, if he has not become a mutilated being, that a single image full of significance and power in a present reality gives more light, impressiveness, authority, and conviction to the highest truth, than the most unbroken chain of evidence. All these parabolical comparisons are so admirably excellent, so profound and high, comprehensive and inimitable, that nothing but a mind such as Christ had for *time*, *men*, and *things*, could have so employed them. Were we to consider an object according to its end or design, its cause or effect, its

* Menschlicher Versuch ueber den Sohn Gottes und der Menschen, (Bremen, 1776.)

contingencies or necessaries, and such like, we should never be able to say so much that was *complete*, as is contained in such a parable."

Upon the demonstrative force of the parables, considered in this point of view, Tholuck in his Commentary on the gospel of John, chap. xv. says: "The convincing power of the parable lies in this, that the author of the kingdom of mind is also the author of the kingdom of nature, and both kingdoms develop themselves according to the same laws. For this reason, the similitudes which the Redeemer draws from the kingdom of nature, are not mere similitudes, which serve the purpose of illustration, but are internal analogies, and nature becomes a witness for the spiritual world. Hence was it long ago set forth as a principle, that, 'whatsoever is found in the earthly, exists also in the heavenly kingdom.' Were it not so, those similitudes should not possess that power of conviction, which they carry to every mind, not utterly depraved."

With what observation Jesus looked upon nature and human life, and how he employed both as full of instructive images, for the higher truths of his eternal and heavenly kingdom, we learn not only from the parables, but also from the figures, with which his whole language is replete. Hunger and thirst are, in his hands, the image of insatiable desire after divine things. He is the bread of life: he gives the living water, and accordingly represents himself as the person who is able to satisfy every want of an immortal spirit throughout all eternity. Corporeal poverty is the image of spiritual; corporeal depression of the feeling, which admonishes us of still prevailing deficiencies; earthly treasures bring to remembrance the heavenly, the nobler treasures of a divine nature and a good conscience; splinters and beams are made to indicate the faults which more or less conspicuously strike the eye. The strait gate and the narrow way are emblematic of so many neglecting the right way, and the right gate to eternal life, or shunning them on account of the hardships attending them; the good tree, which bears good fruit, conveys the lesson how truly good words and works can proceed only from a good, a renewed heart; a large harvest-field represents the joyful sight of many souls being won for the heavenly kingdom, and a field growing white unto harvest denotes the happy result of having laboured for the Lord. The serpent brood stand for a false hypocritical race. Whosoever does the will of God is regarded by Jesus as so nearly related to himself, as to deserve the name of mother, brother, and sister. The hand, the eye, and the foot which are diseased, and must be cut off, tell us of the obligation to crucify the most loved, but sinful inclinations; and how utterly incapable the carnal mind, which is ever engrossed with the love of earthly things, is of entering into heaven, we are forcibly reminded by the camel's inability to go through the eye of a needle. As he literally bore the cross, so for his sake we must bear the cross of afflictions. The moral corruption of a people, and the destruction overhanging it, we are taught by the fact, that wherever the carcass is, there the eagles are gathered together. The breaking down of the temple is the image of his death, and the dying of the seed corn, thereafter springing forth to fruitfulness, teaches how in Jesus a new life has to unfold itself out of death,—in his people the divine life of the spirit, out of the death of sin, and how the grand process of development in his kingdom is life out of death. Natural birth admonishes us of the new birth; the throes of a woman in labour, of the painful contests between the fleshly and the spiritual life; the joy of a mother who had been delivered of a child, of the blessedness of that heart which has attained to the new life, that is from God and in God. To be refreshed with food, points to the satisfaction and delight which is experienced by the soul that works the work of God. To eat the flesh, and drink the blood of the Son of Man, is expressive of the full approbation of his death by the exercise of faith. At the grave of Lazarus, Christ named himself the resurrection, because he shall one day awaken all the dead; he is the way that alone can lead to heaven, without whom there is no salvation; his death is his going away to the Father, and the death of his people their entrance into those mansions which he has prepared for us. He himself is the physician, sins are diseases, for sin and sickness are equally a disorder, the one in the soul, the other in the bodies of men.

In the writings of the apostles of Jesus, we find also an exceedingly rich, an inexhaustible treasury of the most noble and excellent images. Paul represents the unity of Christians which binds them together in love, and calls them to mutual acts of kindness, under the image of their being members of a body; Christ as the head of the body, and his people as members to the head, are intimately united to each other; the Christian life is to him a race and a battle, Christians are the soldiers of Christ; teachers are husbandmen, master-builders; the denial of self, and the victory over self, is an enervating and taming of the body, a daily dying; a permanently adhering sin he names a thorn in the flesh; the crown of victory, the crown of life and of righteousness, shall be the portion of all true disciples; and in the sixth chapter of Ephesians there is described at length, the armour of a complete spiritual equipment. Peter sets forth eternal bliss as a heavenly inheritance, names Christians a holy priesthood, describes the common endeavour of all as a building up of themselves into a spiritual house, and their obedience to God in spirit and in truth, as a spiritual sacrifice. John compares with the different ages of life, the degrees of spiritual strength, just as the Lord himself in this respect calls his disciples sheep and lambs. What richness of imagery! and yet only a part of the great whole has been mentioned. Well may we say, that for the sacred enunciation of the gospel, such a multitude of images is given to set forth its eternal truths in living and sensible form, that it is hardly possible to increase their number; at least it will be advisable to learn from the simplicity and transparent clearness of this scriptural imagery how we should proceed in attempting to employ new images.

4. WHY JESUS ADOPTED THE PARABOLIC FORM OF TEACHING.

Since all figurative language, and especially a continued figure, as in a parable, carries with it a certain degree of darkness, because it still remains to be considered what is the plain reality, it may be asked, what could have led our Lord, in addressing such mixed audiences, to use so frequently the parabolic method, and why he does not always rather employ his first and proper address, which of itself was powerful, as he spake not like the scribes and pharisees? The disciples proposed this question to their Master himself with the words, Matth. xiii. 10: "Why speakest thou unto them in parables?" And his answer is given in the five following verses. That the figurative and parabolic form of instruction was one not very uncommon, might possibly have induced Jesus to make use of it; but it appears, particularly from his answer, that there were other grounds, on account of which he opened his mouth in parables. (Matth. xiii. 35.) It was beyond doubt pre-eminently occasioned by the diversified character of his assembled hearers—the various degrees of spiritual and moral cultivation, in which they were found. In capacity of mind and in moral condition they were, indeed, far from being on a footing, but the difference that prevailed, required this method of discourse for the several classes, though upon different grounds. The great mass of the people were extremely rude and unpolished, blunted through fleshly inclination, indifferent to the highest interests of man, and consequently so much the less capable of relishing a discourse devoid of imagery. The small number of those, who were better inclined, especially his own disciples, were in like manner held fast in Jewish prejudices, in false representations of the kingdom of God about to be erected, unskilled in spiritually apprehending the spiritual, and much too weak to look upon all the truths of the gospel, if presented in undisguised and naked simplicity. Then, lastly, the scribes and pharisees, the sadducees and elders, and priests of the people, puffed up with vain pride for the privileges of their nation, with being God's people, jealous of Christ's rising reputation, full of hatred, enmity, and evil designs toward him, could not on this very account bear so much truth, and therefore Jesus gave it to them only under a figurative covering. If the hearers of Christ, upon whom he had to work, were, as we learn from the pages of the evangelist, such as has just now been described, and if we take, besides, into account the doctrines themselves, which he delivered, we readily perceive the suitableness, nay even the necessity of the parabolical style. Certain doctrines, quite peculiar to the gospel, which concerned the development of the kingdom of God upon earth, so intimately connected with Christ's person and history, could not be understood in their full compass and entire significancy, before the historical transactions themselves had taken place, in which they were grounded. Now if Jesus wished to set these transactions and their consequences before his hearers, it was not possible for him to do it otherwise than through such images as are found in the parables. This was the case more especially in regard to his death, and the circumstances growing out of it; his resurrection, ascension into heaven, and outpouring of the Holy Spirit. Before his disciples were, through these transactions, instructed and taught concerning the nature of his kingdom, comparisons were the best means of bodying forth to them these heavenly things, and of representing, by manifold similitudes, their vast variety. Jesus, indeed, spoke often also in plain language, and especially toward the end of his ministry, of the things that were to befall him; but they understood him not, clear as the words appear to us now; they were so blinded that they knew not the things which were spoken to them. (Luke xviii. 34.). If their eyes were so held, and their understanding so blinded, by carnal views of Messiah, and the expectation of an earthly kingdom, that even after his resurrection they put the question to him: "Lord, wilt thou at this time restore the kingdom to Israel?" at an earlier period they were certainly much less fit to apprehend the great consequences of his death,—the gathering together of a holy people, clinging in faith and love to Jesus. And if they did not take in the doctrine of the resurrection when formerly announced to them, still less could they then have apprehended the power of a risen Saviour, overcoming and regenerating the world; begetting through his word and spirit a new and spiritual offspring to himself. But when the Holy Spirit was given to them by the Lord, who is himself the Spirit; when the Spirit led them into all truth, and brought all things to their remembrance, which he had said to them, then did they also begin to understand the images and similitudes of the Lord in their deep significance and manifold application, and though means of these more especially the Spirit announced and disclosed to them the future. The cover dropped off, the veil was taken away, and the divine eternal truth was beheld by them in perfect clearness. Kleuker, in the work above cited, says: "It was the design of the parables of Christ, like the old prophetical delineations of his coming, to describe things, indeed, according to the whole compass and internal truth, yet still, like the former, to carry with them a certain darkness, so that those alone could see into the spirit of them, who sought it with full sincerity of mind; no others understood any thing of it, and what they understood, they made no other use of than to fret themselves and oppose Christ." What Paul says of all human knowledge of divine things, that "we see through a glass, darkly," may be said in a particular manner of the parables. As the object forms itself in the glass, and we, by looking therein, perceive the image of the object, yet still not so clearly and distinctly as when we view the object directly, not through the medium of the glass; so is the knowledge of divine things, truths, and relations for the present connected with the word, and through the word brought to our experience, until the time comes when we shall see every thing face to face. Now the parables of the Lord are as a clearer and more perfect glass, in which he shows us the laws and institutions of his kingdom. But if the weakness of his disciples, who still loved the truth, sought after it and gave themselves up to it, rendered it necessary for him to deliver the truth in a form suited to their power of apprehension; so, when he stood in the presence of his enemies, who hated the truth, which he himself was, it certainly was doubly necessary to communicate it to them in such a way that it might find access to their fore-closed and darkened understandings, and at the same time occasion no new embitterment to their feelings. Jesus had to teach truths, which were in the highest degree offensive to the national pride of the haughty scribes and priests; he had explanations to give them, which could only tend to inflame their hatred and raise them the more violently against him, because they continued, just as they were at first, disinclined to his demands—to exercise repentance, to yield obedience, to lay to heart his warnings, and receive his merciful invitations and promises. To these truths belonged, above all others, that of their judicial hardening, which was such, that they would lay violent hands upon his life, would draw upon themselves the frightful judgments of God, and cause them, and all who were of one mind with them, to be shut out from the blessings of the Messiah's kingdom, while the heathen should be called in their room. It was necessary that such things should be told them, for a testimony against them; but that the truth might be declared to them in the most delicate manner, might give them no unnecessary provocation, might not tend to make them sin wilfully against the truth, and incur an aggravation of their guilt, Jesus clothed these prophecies of future things in similitudes, intelligible enough to every one who had a mind to hear them, and lay them to heart, yet at the same time so covered that his adversaries were spared. In this manner alone, is it possible to have the truth disclosed to its enemies, delivering it to them veiled in images, so that it may be heard without provoking indignation; a sound eye, a truth-loving heart, desires the full light of the truth; but when the eye is evil, it is the part of love also to spare the evil, that it may not turn itself against the truth. The adversaries of our Lord often had strong suspicions that he spoke of them, but because he did it in similitudes, the thorn, which truth ever has for contumacious sinners, was lopped off, and they might still have received its blessings, if they only would. If, as Kleuker remarks, " he would not cast his pearls before swine, it was necessary for him to wrap them up in the sacred drapery of parabolical description; by which means he consecrated the parable to be the casket of his pearls." So that there is, as appears from what has been said, this wonderful peculiarity in the parable, that it is at the same time both an unfolding and concealing of the truth;—an *unfolding*, because the veil is so transparent, that the matter concealed under it could easily be discerned; a *concealing*, because whatsoever looks only upon the cover and the shell, does not perceive the hidden kernel, but yet receives this along with the shell, and may possibly also at a later period come to partake of it.

But if, as we have just said, there were sufficient reasons for our Lord using the parabolical and figurative mode of instruction, in the condition of his hearers, viewed in connexion with the truths delivered by him, other reasons are also to be discovered for it in the peculiar nature of this kind of instruction. Nothing is so attractive to us as history; nothing more awakens our attention and interest than the behaviour and the fate of our fellow men; and are not most of the parables histories from human life? This is what makes the Bible so attractive and full of instruction, that it contains so much history; and, as God, through means of the histories contained in his word, wishes to nurture and form us, as his nourishing grace is represented to have done, in the history of those who are discoursed of in the Old and New Testament; so are the parables of Jesus histories of the divine economy toward us, and as the Father, so also the Son, wishes in this manner to instruct and rear us by the help of history. Besides, for history, at least for short narratives, stupidity itself can command an attention; and they awaken the interests of those who are most unfeeling; whosoever in his levity and folly has shut his ear and his heart against instruction, admonition, threatening, and warning, may possibly be disposed to open them to a narrative, and thus through means of the history, the seed of divine wisdom gains admittance into the heart. And though all the parables are not of this description, yet they are all beautiful images. Their figurative character is made plain to every one, by the intimation, "the kingdom of heaven is like"—and then forthwith curiosity is awakened; or, in profounder minds, the desire of knowledge, and consequent upon that, reflection and inquiry after the meaning of the figure. Are not the parables, then, on this account, singularly fitted for being vehicles of instruction? Even if nothing farther were at first accomplished by this form of instruction, than impressing the truth taught more readily and deeply upon the memory, this were of itself an important benefit, and would greatly recommend its use. But as the figurative language of Christ contains in itself eternal truth, there moves in it a living power, which being faithfully preserved, will sometimes manifest itself to the enlightenment of the understanding, to the improvement of the mind, to the sanctification of the will, and the blessed satisfaction of the whole man. That Jesus was determined, by the condition of his hearers, by the substance and nature of the truth which he delivered, and finally, by the suitableness of the figurative and parabolic method of instruction to its adoption, according to his wisdom in teaching, is manifest from his expressions to the twelve disciples and others who attended on him, and came in a body, to ask him about the meaning of the parable of the sower, (Mark iv. 10.) According to the account in Matthew xiii. 10, the question runs: "Why speakest thou to them in parables?" To them therefore it was a matter of astonishment to hear our Lord speak in this manner, for since they themselves, his confidential scholars, had not understood the parable, they naturally drew the conclusion that the great mass of the people must still less have understood it, and consequently, that the benefit of his teaching was lost, and he was not gaining the blessed object he had in view. Upon this objection of his disciples, and in order to elevate their views to the proper use and design of the parable, Jesus replied; "Unto you it is given to know the mysteries of the kingdom, but to them it is not given." Here our Lord makes a distinction among his hearers; he says, *to you*, that is, to you all who are desirous of your salvation, of knowing the truth, and obtaining further instruction, *to you it is given;* ye do thereby show that ye have linked your wills to divine truth, and have attained to a capacity for having it more fully disclosed to you. But whosoever, as is the case with many, is carnally minded, and pays little or no regard to what is heavenly, he lies on this very account under such an incapacity of heart for farther instruction in the clear light of heaven, that the secrets of the kingdom of God cannot be opened out and communicated to him, according to the righteous judgment, that despisers must not, and cannot be compelled to taste of the divine goodness, (Luke xiv. 24.) The expression in verse 11, Jesus explains still farther in verse 12, the statements of which contain a general principle of divine and human action towards the faithful and the faithless. He says; "for whosoever hath, to him shall be given, and he shall have more abundance: but whosoever hath not, from him shall be taken away even that he hath." That is: It fares in this matter with my hearers, after the principle, that whosoever has desire, and love, and fidelity in regard to the offered salvation, to him shall always be given more grace through his growing acquaintance with divine truth, and he shall become rich in all manner of wisdom and experience; but whosoever does not count the offered grace, and now in particular the revealed truths and doctrines of the kingdom, worth farther reflection and more careful consideration, he shall sooner or later lose every thing, and even the word which he has heard, shall again vanish from his memory. Then he adds, verse 13; "therefore speak I to them in parables;" *therefore*, because the instruction so often given to them in plain language has proved of no avail to them, I shall now try, through means of figures and similitudes, if I can lead them to reflect, and move them to carefulness for their salvation. The sad spiritual condition of so many of his hearers, their stupid insensibility, their careless departure, unconcerned about eternal life, Jesus represents in the following words of this verse; "because they seeing, see not; and hearing, they hear not; neither do they understand;" that is; They understand not my instructions, for although they have the natural capacity, and besides, have also, through my preaching, the opportunity afforded them by God of seeing and hearing, and consequently of apprehending the truth, still they will not use their natural capacities, by reason of the hardness of their heart, nor give themselves to serious application, and the natural, inevitable consequence is, that they remain unenlightened. This experimental truth Jesus confirms, verse 14, 15, by a quotation from Isaiah, chap. vi. 9, 10, which, as it was originally applied to the prophet's contemporaries, so was it also verified in the case of our Lord's hearers, and continually is so in the case of many hearers of the divine word in all ages,—since the same causes produce the same effects in the kingdom of grace, as well as in the kingdom of nature; for in both alike every thing develops itself according to divine laws—in the latter according to inevitable necessity, in the other also according to a necessity not less sure, though of a different kind, just as man, with the freedom still left to him, receives or rejects the help of God. The words of Isaiah, which thus contain the history of the past, and the prediction of the future, therefore import: with the ear ye shall hear, and will not understand; and with the eye ye shall see, and will not perceive—and in like manner shall it be with all obstinate hearers. The groundwork of this unprofitable hearing and seeing lies in the following words of the prophet: "For this people's heart is waxed gross (become insensible,) and their ears are dull of hearing, (they will not properly hear, nor lay to heart what is contrary to their lusts,) and their eyes have they closed, (they have made them slumber, shut them hard, that they might not see;) and the mournful consequence of such inward aversion to the truth, while it is externally received by the ear, is thus declared by the prophet: "that they may not at any time see with their eyes, and hear with their ears, and understand with their heart, and be converted, and I should heal them." The hardening and rejection of Israel does not follow upon an unconditional determination of God, but by way of judgment, condemnation and punishment. Because they would not have the light, therefore they remain in darkness; because they disdain the physician and his help, they therefore die in their sins; because they will not turn, they must therefore receive that death which is the wages of sin. After this description of the one class of hearers, Jesus turns to the other, to his disciples and those who were of one mind with himself. (Mark iv. 10,) and says to them, Matth. xiii. 16; "But blessed are your eyes, for they see, (to be understood both corporeally and spiritually,) and your ears (of body and of soul,) for they hear," because ye have also striven to understand.

The parabolic and figurative mode of instruction, then, was designed to serve the purpose of bringing near the truth to every one; and it was the undoubted aim of Jesus, that all might find the hidden kernel of divine truth. That this was his design, is manifested from the words, which, according to Luke viii. 16, 17, he subjoins to his solution of the parable of the sower, where he says, "No man, when he hath lighted a candle, covereth it with a vessel, or putteth it under a bed; but setteth it on a candlestick, that they who enter in may see the light; for nothing is secret, which shall not be made manifest; neither any thing hid, which shall not be known and come abroad." To these let us add the other words of Jesus, Matth. x. 27; "What I tell you in darkness (in secret and hidden instruction,) that speak ye in light, (openly and to every one,) and what ye hear in the ear (in secret,) that preach ye upon the house-tops, (in the most public places, that the whole world may hear it;)"—and it becomes clear, to a demonstration, that the secrets, which were once so darkly veiled that he could scarcely disclose them to his disciples, were, at a later period, to be disclosed without reserve to all. Of a secret doctrine in Christianity, which must not be made known to all, there is here, therefore, no mention; for he, who is the light of the world, will have all men to be enlightened.*

* [In this sentiment we entirely concur, and grounded as it is upon such clear and explicit texts, as well as confirmed by the

5. PERFECTNESS OF THE PARABLES OF OUR LORD.

If we direct our attention to the beauty of our Lord's parables, we shall find them the most complete and finished models: "apples of gold in pictures of silver." They present the most important, consola-

whole tenor of the gospel, it may well be wondered that the contrary sentiment should need, even in the present day, to be repudiated. Greswell, in his elaborate, but very tedious, and, in many respects, unsatisfactory work upon the parables, has found it necessary, for the vindication of his most arbitrary arrangement of them, to resort to the exploded doctrine of an esoteric and exoteric doctrine in Christianity; one measure of light for the initiated, and another, and much smaller one, for the rude and unlearned. If there ever was such a distinction, it certainly did not derive its authority from the blessed Redeemer, who was ever ready to impart to all his disciples the full knowledge of the truth, and most strictly commanded his apostles, that they should leave nothing undisclosed or unexplained, which they had received from him, even in his most private communings with them. Any view of the parables, or other portion of the word of God, which requires such a groundless assertion for its support, needs nothing more to prove its fallacy. But we have a partial exception to take in regard to the reasons which our author assigns in this section for our Lord using the parable. These reasons, though not distinctly branched out into so many heads, are the four following: 1. That in the age and country in which Christ appeared, this was a common and popular method of instruction. 2. That it was admirably adapted to meet the diversified circumstances of his hearers, especially to serve as a vehicle for conveying more instruction than could otherwise be imparted to minds so carnal as those of his immediate disciples, and hearts so malignantly opposed to the truth as those of the Scribes and Pharisees. 3. That being of the nature of history, it is, in itself, of a most interesting and impressive character. And, 4. That it was resorted to in the way of judgment for the people's persevering and obstinate rejection of the truth, when presented to them in its unveiled and naked form. That these reasons are all valid and proper, no one will be disposed to doubt; and yet we cannot but feel, in perusing what our author has said of them, that the one reason assigned by our Lord himself for his speaking in parables, and which we may, therefore, presume to have been the chief one, as concerns those to whom the parables were first spoken, does not receive the place to which it is entitled, nor, though it is mentioned at the last, is the precise turn given to it which the words of our Lord seem to warrant. That the parabolic style was adopted in judgment to the people for their inexcusable blindness and perversity of heart, tory, and blessed instructions, in the most inviting form; in them there is nothing superfluous and unnecessary; in the noblest language, with the most lively colours, in the most suitable arrangement are these

is the answer which he gave to his disciples, when they put the question to him, "Why speakest thou to them in parables?" And though our author admits this, yet he seems afraid to look at the matter properly in its judicial aspect; and in his remarks upon Christ's answer, tries, as much as possible, to explain away the apparent severity, and to draw out of it a merciful design. But there were all along two ends to be served by the work of Christ, the one displaying the severity, and the other the goodness of God. He was set "for the fall," as well as "for the rising again of many in Israel." "For judgment," says he, "I am come into this world, that they which see not might see, and that they which see might be made blind." And if we look into the 6th chapter of John's Gospel, we shall find a particular example, apart altogether from the parables, of the manner in which he fulfilled the melancholy part of the alternative, the blinding of those who saw. In the dialogue there recorded between him and the unbelieving carnal Jews, he began with speaking to them in figurative terms of imperishable food, which they, in the grossness of their understandings, mistook for something of a fleshly nature; and constantly, as they pressed him for further discoveries concerning it, instead of softening, he continually strengthened the figure; wrapt the truth in a deeper and deeper mystery, until he at last clothed it in language so peculiarly strong and apparently inexplicable, that many, even of his disciples, were offended at the hardness of the saying, "went back, and walked no more with him."

By the conduct our Lord pursued on this remarkable occasion, and in like manner by his resolving during the latter half of his ministry to speak to the people in parables, there was no positive infliction of evil from him upon the minds of his hearers, and to a certain extent it might be proper to say, with our author, that this change in his address should have excited in them a more solemn and awakened inquiry after the truth. But that could hardly be said with propriety to be the purpose or design which led him to adopt such a line of procedure. The veiling of the truth in such a mysterious form was a direct act of judgment for their previous resistance to its power, and in its natural effect on them was very nearly the same with pouring a thicker blindness over the eyes of their understanding. It thereby became to them a more shrouded and impenetrable thing than it was before; and so the adoption of the parabolic style fell upon them as a dreadful visitation for the neglect of former privileges, as it inevitably tended to increase their aversion to the truth of Christ, and lessen their capacity for apprehending it. If Christ's small paintings set before our eyes; they contain nothing more and nothing less, than is just necessary to give clearness and force to the ideas sought to be unfolded; every thing is rendered palpable through means

simple object had been to enlighten them with a knowledge of his truth, there is no question that he could, and we may also say, would, have presented it to them in a more engaging and intelligible form than he had yet done; but, in point of fact, their abiding alienation from the truth did not arise from its having been revealed so darkly, that they could not apprehend it, but from its being so spiritual that they would not receive it; and, therefore, according to those principles of probation, on which the moral government of God is conducted toward men on earth, according to which "he shows himself froward to the froward," as well as "merciful to the merciful," withdraws himself to a greater distance from them, and they obstinately persist in withdrawing themselves from him, abridges their measure of light, or allows it to become more faint to their apprehensions, after they have refused to follow out the convictions it awakened; according to these principles, when the Jews had long heard and refused to profit by the plainest statements of divine truth, our Lord proceeded to veil his speech in the darker covering of parable, and thus rendered it more difficult of access, more palpably obscure to their carnal minds. The lesson furnished in this affecting portion of their history is substantially repeated over again in the history of multitudes of various shades, both in faith and practice, who begin by trifling away their day of grace and withstanding the light given to them, and who often come in consequence to be shorn of many of their Christian privileges, or at least are left to the operation of causes which render them continually less clear in their apprehension, or more insensible to the power, of divine truth.

It is proper to add, however, that though both the design and the effect of Christ's teaching in parables was to remove it in a manner farther from the Jews, and make it less palpable to their understandings, he still longed for their salvation. He wept in anguish of spirit over them, even at the very last, when he knew the things of their peace were for ever hidden from their eyes. And not only so, but no sooner were the things which concerned himself fully accomplished, than he sent his apostles with the message of reconciliation to them first, propounding it in the plainest terms, and confirming it by signs from heaven. But this does not hinder that, in the course of his personal ministry, in which he came to reveal the Father, to disclose his methods of dealing with sinners, as well as the truths which belong to his dispensation of grace, he should have made such a change in his style of speaking, as tended virtually with the mass of his hearers to increase their ignorance and misapprehension of the truth.—*Trans.*]

of the most powerful contrasts, and each individual is, with the utmost penetration, marked according to its characteristic properties. A single perusal of these parables is sufficient to acquaint us with their beauty; but the more frequently and attentively we apply ourselves to consider them, whether as a whole or in their separate parts, the more are we filled with wonder and astonishment at the perfection of their form and matter. They always appear to me like a lovely casket made in the handsomest style, of the most precious materials, and embellished with simple, yet most attractive ornaments; but when the key is put into our hand, and we open it, and see the jewels and finery it contains, these appear to surpass all worth, and make it difficult for us to be satisfied with looking on their glory. However attractive in form may be the parables of Jesus, and however inviting, when considered only as specimens of poetic beauty, the truth contained in them is still more glorious, for it is the truth which makes blessed, truth leading to divine felicity through the hope of eternal life. What Luther said of scripture in general, that it is a garden of God, with many beautiful trees full of the most precious fruit, and though he had often already knocked upon the boughs and got much fruit into his lap, yet did he continually find new fruit, as often as he sought and knocked again, —this may be said more especially of its parables, in which is treasured up an inexhaustible store of instruction, consolation, warning, and admonition. Their meaning is richer than the sea, no one has ever drunk out its fulness; every new consideration of them discovers to us new relations, gives new solutions, spreads new light over the affairs of the heavenly kingdom. Every reader, whether learned or unlearned, polished or unpolished, will understand somewhat of the parables, although the more acute eye sees farther into them than the weaker; they are simple enough for the simple, and deep enough for the most profound thinker; they are, like the whole of scripture, a stream, which the lamb can wade through, while yet it is deep enough for the elephant.

6. MATTER OF THE PARABLES.

The commencement of so many parables: "The kingdom of heaven is like, &c.," shows, as their main scope, what they wish to explain; and those also, which have no such beginning, are equally intended to open up the kingdom of God in its manifold relations. The words in Ps. lxxviii. 2: "I will open my mouth in parables; I will utter things which have been kept secret from the foundation of the world," are applied, in Matth. xiii. 35, to Jesus, and teach us, that our Lord in his parables conveyed information upon the nature, extent, and destiny of his kingdom, as also of those who should be subjects of it, and that in it are disclosed the eternal purposes of God for the salvation of men. They do, indeed, all stand in the most intimate connexion with contemporary characters, with surrounding circumstances and pressing events, were delivered for the most part only as occasions gave rise to them, to show their application to particular cases, yet still they are quite general in their nature, and of perpetual force. For although human nature, in the time of Jesus, manifested its internal peculiarities, as it ever does, only in determinate, temporary, and popular forms, the Searcher of hearts did continually seize upon what was general and permanent, upon which he directed his instructions, and hence the parables reach so far beyond every thing peculiar to one time, one place, or one people: because in the particular he held up to view the general, in the temporary, the permanent and constantly recurring. The heavenly kingdom, which forms the subject of the parables, is God's dispensation of mercy and grace for the redemption of sinners. Because this dispensation was an eternal purpose of the paternal love of God, it is called *the kingdom of God*, and because it was set up in the fulness of time by Jesus

Christ, the Son of God, it is also called *the kingdom of Jesus Christ.* Purposed from eternity, it was promised to our first parents immediately after the fall, and thenceforward proclaimed and described with manifold variety by all the prophets. At first confined only to Israel, this dispensation of grace was, however, latterly, by progressive development, to extend its empire over all mankind, in conformity to the love of God, who would have all to be saved, and in conformity also to the necessities of men, who are universally sinners, standing in need of redemption and eternal blessedness, but in themselves incapable of attaining it. The highest end of the heavenly kingdom is communion with God through Jesus Christ, and in this a blessedness, already begun in time and continued throughout all eternity. This idea of communion with God must be kept in view as the essential point in all the parables, while, at the same time, it is treated of in many different aspects and relations; for sometimes the discourse is of the means through which such communion is attainable, as of the word of God, (in the parable of the sower,) sometimes of its worth, (as in the treasure and the pearl,) sometimes of the company, brought into that state wherein it appears as a church or community in the present world, (as in the tares,) then again of the progress of its development, (as in the mustard-seed,) and, finally, in a number of parables, of the spiritual condition and destiny of those who are willing to participate in this communion, or have already partaken of it. The kingdom of God, in its constitution as a church, in its past and future history, in time and in eternity, *that* is the great burden of the parables of Jesus. Draeseke: "What do we Christians understand by the kingdom of heaven? Sometimes the state of bliss to which the church shall be brought. Sometimes the church itself, which will conduct us thither. But always the communion of souls, which seek and find their salvation through Christ in God. Whether we consider alone, or by many together, as a community united to each other in the bonds of one salvation, the thing itself remains the same. Wherever souls seek and find salvation through Christ in God, there is the kingdom of heaven."

7. MANNER OF EXPOUNDING AND TREATING THE PARABLES.

Upon the principles which ought to be followed in the exposition and practical treatment of the parables of Jesus, there prevails, among expositors and divines, the greatest difference of views and contradictory opinions. As with the exposition of Scripture generally, there is primarily and above all required an application of the parable to one's own heart, as an essential qualification for the deep and thorough understanding of them. From such an application we often learn, in a moment, what has escaped the most diligent investigation. The learned expositor has, therefore, as much to lay to heart the saying—*de te fit sermo*, as the practical divine. As when Nathan said to David, "Thou art the man," the full light of the parable flashed upon the latter, so is it still found to be the case. The truly practical judgment, at which one arrives through such a manner of consideration, is the best safeguard against the error of an allegorical interpretation, which is always more or less arbitrary, and, consequently, in the same proportion false—a rock upon which so many of the older expositors of the parables struck. Hence, the watchword of Luther, "the literal sense," proves itself here also to be the effective instrument; for in that is to be found instruction, power, life, and art. Through this practical judgment we are also prevented from surrendering the traits and incidents to an unbridled and lawless imagination, but are led to understand that the parables and their interpretation must be "profitable for doctrine, for reproof, for correction, for instruction in righteousness, that the man of God may be perfect, thoroughly furnished unto all good works," that both alike must be made to minister to our salvation, through faith that is in Christ.

It is further necessary, as a general rule for the profitable treatment of the figurative matter contained in the parables, to render clear and manifest, in the first instance, the image, which is used to embody the spiritual truth,—without respect to this truth,—merely by itself, in its own proper meaning and relations, after which we may transfer it to the spiritual province to determine the nature of what is signified by the image. For example, Jesus names his disciples "the salt of the earth;" what does he mean by doing so? Salt is of itself a savoury thing, which quality it also imparts to other things; it purifies, it preserves from corruption. Now the disciples of Jesus must be a salt in regard to the world; they are in themselves savoury, lively—there are found in them the noblest properties of the heart, because they have imbibed the gospel, the spirit of Christ; and, in regard to others, with whom they come into contact, and over whom they obtain an ascendency, they are also salutary, since, through the influence of their spirit, which is the spirit of Christ, they are instrumental in purging these others from sin, making them acceptable to God and men, preserving them from moral corruption, from entire perdition in sin and death, nay, helping them to obtain eternal life. Considering things in this manner, we shall hit upon the point of resemblance, the *tertium comparationis*, and discover, in every parable, a rich treasury of truth.

But, since each parable is one whole, made up of several images, there arises the question, which has received very different answers, whether every individual trait in the picture, however small, ought to be interpreted or not? That in the parable, as a finished picture, every part of the image is important, as serving to designate more exactly the characters of the persons introduced, to render the transactions more palpable, and hence forms a sort of necessary part of the parable, as the picture is only rendered complete by means of these subordinate traits, is admitted on all hands. But many are of opinion, that much in the parables was designed merely for ornamental painting, introduced from no other necessity than to produce effect, and ought, in the exposition of the parable, to have no interpretation put upon it, as having no corresponding object. To this view many expounders of the parables may have been led, from the circumstance that the meaning of small, and comparatively unimportant particulars, has often been carried to excess, and because, by entering too minutely into what was particular, the grand design of the parable has often been overlooked or even completely missed, a practice which is certainly deserving of blame. But just as little is the opinion tenable, that much in the parables of our Lord serves the purpose merely of ornament, as is manifest from the consideration, that the several expositors differ very much in regard to what is essential and non-essential; and if we bring together the various expositions, since this part, according to one, and that, according to another, is non-essential, it must follow, as a necessary consequence, that all and every part is, at the same time, essential and non-essential. But, as this latter cannot possibly be the case, we must adopt it as the most correct opinion, that nothing is entirely non-essential, a mere meaningless ornament, and that to every lineament in the figure there is another answering to it in the reality, the spiritual thing thereby represented. It is by no means, however, on this account to be maintained, that we must, in a petty and straitened spirit, give significancy to every word; for there is a vast difference between the import of particular words and of particular, distinct parts of the parable, every figurative word being far from forming by itself a distinct portion of the figurative delineation. The more we confine our attention only to what is general, and leave unnoticed the particular parts of the figure, the more shall we find the life, the grace of the similitude vanish away; whereas, by the contrary method of handling them, the interest increases, and the beauty and truthfulness of it become more deeply felt. Olshausen, in his Biblical Commentary on the Writings of the New Testament, expresses himself, at p. 429, upon the significancy of the parables, in the following manner: "The parable of the sower is one of the few, whereof our Lord has given us an authentic exposition, which is of much importance, not only for the understanding of that particular history, but for the derivation of those principles which should guide us in the exposition of all the parables. We may learn from it, more especially, what is usually the most difficult thing in the exposition of the parables, how far the particular incidents of the parabolical narrative have, or have not, any proper meaning. As a shallow spirit can here get over every thing of a profound nature in the divine word, by declaring this or that to be mere ornament, so can superstition convert every particle of sand into a mountain. The same spirit which framed the parables, must also expound them, and then we are sure of striking the golden mean." And again, at p. 600: "How far particular incidents in each parable are to be interpreted, remains, indeed, always very doubtful; yet, still in the similitudes of Jesus, which open up to us so rich a field of contemplation, we must, on the whole, maintain it as a canon, that no incident is to be lightly passed by, unless by insisting upon it the figure, as a whole, should be manifestly obscured." Farther, at p. 787, on the parable of the rebellious labourers in the vineyard, he says; " But how far the particular incidents may be applicable, that is here, as in the parables generally, a difficult question. In regard to this no certain boundary-line can be drawn, since the penetration required to apprehend the more remote lines of resemblance depends upon the expositor's state of advancement in the spiritual life. Only, a due reverence to the words of our Lord will naturally lead to the most careful application possible of every particular incident, since the completeness of the similitude depends upon the fulness of the parallel resemblances which lie enclosed in it." At p. 799, he also remarks on the parable of the wedding-garment: "It would certainly be the easiest method to say, that these incidents (the wedding-garment, &c.,) are not to be minutely pressed, but they stand in such close connexion with the whole of the similitude, that the entire representation must be void of meaning if particulars of such moment are to be pushed aside as accidental." Lastly, at p. 910, on the parable of the ten virgins, he says: "It is asked how far the individual traits are to be taken into account. The natural fitness of these to symbolize what is spiritual, is the only determinate rule that can be given, and this, applied without violence, will furnish for the parable before us a fulness of interesting resemblances, sufficient to constitute it the finest in the gospel. For the more points of resemblance that a similitude readily and naturally presents, the richer must it be reckoned."

When a parable is to be expounded and applied, we must first of all consider its connexion with what precedes and follows, and determine accordingly, before every thing else, its prominent idea. Until, through repeated attentive consideration of the circumstances and subject, this central point and kernel of the parable has been discovered, and set forth in the most precise and determinate manner, we need not meddle with the import of particular parts, for these can only be seen in their true light when contemplated from that central point. We might compare the whole similitude to a circle, whose centre is the divine doctrine or truth, and whose radii are the several figurative lineaments of the narrative. So long as we do not stand in the centre, the circle neither appears in its perfectly round form, nor are the radii perceived in their order, as all tending to the centre, and in beautiful accordance with each other; but all this is done when the eye surveys every thing from the centre. It is so exactly in the parable, when we have obtained a full and distinct view of its central point, its grand doctrine, the relative position and right meaning of its several parts also become clear, and we shall then condescend upon these, only in so far as the grand doctrine can thereby be more vividly displayed. The most difficult matter, though one of indispensable importance, is certainly to find out the principal idea, since, in each parable, so many individual truths meet us, which, at first, might seem of equal importance; but, on maturer consideration, there is always one which comes out before the rest into the clearest light, while these, on the other hand, fall more into the shade, and serve only to define more exactly the grand truth, which forms the central point; and perhaps, also, in some respects, to illustrate it. When it is our design to illustrate a parable in edifying discourse, this will certainly be effected in the best manner for the hearers, when it is treated as one whole; for the parcelling out of the parables into many separate discourses does unquestionable injury to the impression of the whole, as, however much of excellent matter may be delivered, the unity and completeness of the main idea are still frittered away on the too wire-drawn extension of the parts. When handled in this manner, the parables are regarded, chiefly, as a storehouse of texts; and though they may certainly be so handled, we should, however, at the same time, confess that the parables, as a whole, and in their distinctive peculiarity, are not then handled and explained at all.

8. ARRANGEMENT OF THE PARABLES.

Since the fundamental idea of all the parables of Jesus is that of the heavenly kingdom, it seems proper to arrange them with a respect to this, and to determine the classes according to the particular aspect in which that idea is contemplated by each individual similitude. Scholten, p. 181: "Since the nature and genius of the parables is such that they are bound together as with a strait chain by the doctrine of the heavenly kingdom, it is there we are to seek the principles of sound interpretation. For all the parables which occur in the writings of the Evangelists, although delivered by Jesus on particular occasions, and with a special design, do yet set before us some branch of that doctrine which pertains to the kingdom of heaven, and must be referred either to the *constitutions*, or rather the *principles*, on which it leans as its own proper foundation; or to its *evolutions* during the lapse of ages; or, finally, to the *laws*, which it is necessary for those to obey who wish to be subjects of this kingdom, and the *rewards* which, in this life and the next, are promised to those who do become its true and faithful subjects. Every interpreter, therefore, of the New Testament, applying himself to the interpretation of the parables, has something at hand whereon to ground his interpretation; nor does he need anxiously to inquire, what is the general argument of the parables; but must give the utmost care and diligence to discover to what particular part of this general argument each parable must be referred. And this general argument, drawn from the common nature and design of the parables, whereby they are most closely united to the doctrine of the Messiah's kingdom, may be compared to a guide, who indeed conducts us to the boundaries of some country to which we are going; but, that we may proceed forward through its domains, and acquire an accurate knowledge of its nature, cities, places, and whatever it contains worthy of observation he thenceforth hands us over to other guides."

It is obvious that we have here nothing to do with a close systematic arrangement in necessary sequence, but only with such a classification as may serve to bring more readily under our review what is taught in all the parables, and to point out the place which each parable holds in regard to instruction in the kingdom of God. Gray and Bourns have already attempted such a division of the parables, and in the following manner:

Gray forms them into three classes,—

1. Parables which represent the nature and progress of the gospel dispensation, together with the opposition which it had to receive from the malice of Satan, and from the folly and perversity of men; such as the parable of the sower,—of the tares among the wheat,—and many smaller similitudes.

2. Parables which have for their object the rejection of the Jews and the calling of the Gentiles, events which had an evident connexion with the subject of the preceding class; and to this class are referred the labourers in the vineyard,—the wicked vine-dressers,—the fig-tree and the wedding-garment.

3. Parables which were directly intended to deliver a moral instruction for the improvement of our dispositions and conduct, which forms by far the greatest part of the parables; and this class may again be subdivided into two classes:—

a Such as have it for their aim to illustrate an important truth, or to enforce an indispensable obligation: of which sort are the good Samaritan, the wicked servant, the unjust steward, the rich man and Lazarus.

b Such as are of more extensive import, and convey certain general lessons of wisdom and piety, without being confined to any one view in particular, to which belong the virgins, the talents, the lost piece of silver, and prodigal son, the unjust judge, the pharisee and publican.

Bourns arranges them into four classes.

1. The parables in the 13th of Matthew, which speak of the effects of the gospel, and the future condition of men in connexion with the present.

2. The parables in the 15th and 16th of Luke, which are moral paintings, wherein the Saviour delineates

4

the character, disposition, and conduct both of himself, and of the different classes of those who heard him, in reference also to the accusation which his enemies preferred against him.

3. National parables, which point out the character of the Jewish people, and the different sects amongst them, containing also predictions of their subversion; of which cast are the pharisee and publican, the two unlike sons, the fig-tree, the great feast, the wicked vine-dressers, the wedding garment.

4. Apostolical parables, or such as have for their object, the conversion of the first disciples of Jesus, especially the Apostles, and were intended to qualify them for their future office; the rich fool, the unjust judge, the wicked servant, the kind-hearted Samaritan, the labourers in the vineyard, the ten virgins, the talents.

I would also attempt a division of the parables, keeping in view, while I do so, the constant reference which they have to the doctrine of the kingdom of God, and always making the leading idea in each parable the ground of the particular place assigned to it.

THE FIRST CLASS.

Parables which represent the heavenly kingdom as a divine power, that is, as containing truths and powers, which are divine in their origin and blessed in their effects.

1. Matth. xiii. 3—9. The sower. The different efficacy of the word of God depends upon the different states of the human heart.

2. Mark iv. 26—29. The growing seed. The inherent growth and advancement of the heavenly kingdom.

3. Matth. xiii. 56. The householder. The well prepared teacher of the heavenly kingdom.

4. Matth. xiii. 31, 32. The mustard-seed. The progressive development of Christianity.

5. Matth. xiii. 33. The leaven. The all-renewing power of Christianity.

6. Matth. xiii. 44. The treasure. The internal glory of the heavenly kingdom.

7. Matth. xiii. 45, 46. The pearl. The all-surpassing worth of the heavenly kingdom.

The first two parables bear respect pre-eminently to that upon which the prosperity of the kingdom of God depends; externally considered, it depends upon the state of heart which belongs to those to whom the word is preached; regarded internally, upon the living power inherent in the word. But although human power does not command success to the word, it is still of great importance that they who proclaim the divine message should possess the proper qualifications, —hence follows the third parable. Then, the fourth and fifth represent the power of the word, in its great overpowering efficacy; both in respect to what is without (the mustard-seed,) and, in respect to what is within (the leaven;) and out of the whole come forth the glory and the worth of the heavenly kingdom. So that all the parables of this class have the divine word for their object and subject, in so far as this word is of itself spirit and life, and, through the gracious workings of the Holy Spirit, the germ of life, out of which the heavenly kingdom develops itself in particular individuals, and in mankind at large.

THE SECOND CLASS.

Parables which represent the heavenly kingdom as a community or church, founded on those divine powers of the word of God. In the preceding class, the *efficacious* power, the Word, was the subject of the parables, and now it is that which is *effected* or wrought by the power—the church, as a society of believers in Christ Jesus. But the church may be considered in a twofold respect, either as an already existing whole, or in regard to the entrance of individuals into it. There consequently arise here two subdivisions, for some parables speak of the church, as an existing whole, others treat principally of the entering of individuals into the church.

I. PARABLES WHICH RESPECT THE CHURCH AS ONE WHOLE.

1. Luke xiii. 6--9. The unfruitful fig tree. An admonition to secure sinners to repent.
2. Matth. xxi. 33—44. The wicked vine-dressers. Of impenitence.
3. Luke xiv. 16—24. The great feast. The love of this world is a hinderance to salvation.
4. Matth. xxii. 1—14. The royal marriage-feast. Calling and election are not the same.
5. Matth. xiii. 24—30. The tares among the wheat. The mixture of good and bad in the church.
6. Matth. xiii. 47—50. The fish-net. The final separation in the Christian church.

Since every social union has its origin and progress, its end and destiny, and consequently also its history, these parables, which concern the church or community of God, may be considered entirely in a historical point of view; and they then disclose the history of the heavenly kingdom from the choosing of the Israelites to the very last transactions of that kingdom at the end of time. In the first parable, the secure theocrats of the old covenant are admonished with a threatening of divine judgment; the second manifestly represents the judgment which immediately pressed upon them, their rejection, and the calling of the Gentiles; the third speaks expressly of the gracious call being sent forth to all; the fourth shows how the reception of the gracious call is not sufficient to salvation if one does not also fall in with God's method of salvation; the fifth describes the mixture of good and bad which prevails also in the church of the New Covenant, and the last discloses the final separation that is to be made in the Christian church.

II. PARABLES WHICH RESPECT THE ENTRANCE OF INDIVIDUALS INTO THE CHRISTIAN CHURCH.

7. Luke xv. 1—7. The lost sheep. The vast importance which Christ attaches to the conversion of every lost sinner.

8. Luke xv. 8—10. The lost piece of money. The worth of the lost sinner in the eyes of Jesus.

9. Luke xv. 11—31. The lost son. Of repentance.

10. Luke xiv. 28—30. The building of the tower. And,

11. Luke xiv. 31—33. The war of the kings. A careful self-examination must precede our following of Christ.

12. Luke v. 36. The old garment with new patches. Of a false amendment.

13. Luke v. 37—39. The new wine in old bottles. Of true amendment.

The first two of these similitudes teach what the Lord does in order to bring sinners into his fellowship, for their conversion is to him a matter of much importance, because they themselves possess a great worth in his sight. The third parable speaks of the state of mind which must of necessity belong to those who desire personally to experience the Lord's receiving love. The last four similitudes are concerning continued fellowship with Christ, as what requires first of all a careful self-examination, (No. 10, 11,) and as the result of that, not a false, but a real amendment.

THE THIRD CLASS.

Parables which principally treat of the fellow-members of the heavenly kingdom, according to their state of feeling, conduct, and destiny. And, as the spiritual frame of Christians is described in scripture as made up of faith, love, and hope, we may very properly arrange the parables belonging to this class under these leading characteristics.

I. PARABLES WHICH RELATE TO THE PRINCIPLE OF FAITH IN THE MEMBERS OF THE HEAVENLY KINGDOM.

1. Matth. vii. 24—27. The two master-builders. The right use of the divine word. To this true living faith owes both its birth and continuance.

2. Matth. xx. 1—16. The labourers in the vine-

yard. Humility is the measure according to which the Lord apportions reward to the labourers in his kingdom.

3. Luke xvii. 7—10. The labouring servant. Humility is indispensable.

4. Luke xviii. 9—14. The pharisee and the publican. The conceit of being good, the want of humility robs us of the divine favour, and nullifies our prayer.

5. Luke xi. 5—8. The importunate friend. Of persevering prayer.

6. Luke xviii. 1—8. The ungodly judge and the widow. Motives to persevering prayer. These two parables speak of the fruit of faith, prayer, and the one immediately preceding (No. 4,) forms the connecting link between Nos. 3 and 5, since it speaks of humility, particularly as requisite in prayer.

7. Matth. xxi. 28—32. The two unlike sons. Of insincere faith.

8. Luke xvi. 19—31. The rich man and Lazarus. Of unbelief. The nature and fruits of true faith having been described in the first six parables, these last two treat of false faith, which assumes the appearance of hypocrisy and practical unbelief.

II. PARABLES WHICH HAVE FOR THEIR SUBJECT THE LOVE THAT SHOULD BELONG TO THE MEMBERS OF THE HEAVENLY KINGDOM.

9. Luke vii. 41—43. The creditor and the two debtors. The pardoned sinner's grateful love to Jesus.

10. Matth. xviii. 23—35. The wicked servant. Motives to mutual forgiveness. Both parables set forth the pardoning grace of our Lord as the spring of our love; the spring, first of all, of grateful love to him, and this again the spring of pardoning love towards our brethren.

11. Luke x. 25—37. The warm-hearted Samaritan. Of Christian compassion. The two foregoing similitudes pointed out the origin of true love; and now this love, as compassion, (love to the miserable and the

needy,) is described according to its wide compass and sphere of action.

12. Luke xii. 13—21. The rich fool. Of the deceitfulness of riches.

13. Luke xvi. 1—9. The unjust steward. Of Christian prudence. In the last two parables the want of true love is spoken of; in No. 12, the foolish love of riches is depicted, and in No. 13, a prudent use of riches is recommended in doing works of love.

III. PARABLES WHICH REFER TO THE HOPE OF CHRISTIANS.

14. Matth. xxv. 1—13. The ten virgins. The proper preparation for the coming of the Lord.

15. Matth. xxv. 14—30. The intrusted talents. Exhortations to Christian fidelity.

16. Luke xii. 36—48. The different servants. Of the believer's state of readiness for the coming of Christ. Christ's return to judgment is the object of Christian hope; No. 14 represents the inward readiness of believers for the coming of the Lord; No. 15, the influence of this hope upon outward activity; No. 16, the influence of this hope upon the *spirit*, which is induced to watchfulness, and upon the *conduct*, which is persuaded to fidelity.

17. The concluding parable, Luke xix. 11—27. The intrusted pounds. The kingdom of Christ is a heavenly kingdom. This parable discloses the innermost nature of the kingdom of Christ, with especial reference to the second coming, and final judgment.*

* [The division of the parables here adopted by our author, is certainly better than either of the two which he notices before it, and may perhaps be as proper and judicious as any other that could be devised; but we cannot see what benefit, either theoretical or practical, can arise from such classifications. The parables were delivered without order, as the circumstances occurred which served to call them forth, and were never intended to be reduced into any system of precise and logical arrangement. Besides, every such division must be exceedingly imperfect, and can never exhibit any thing like a full or complete view of the varied and pregnant instruction which is contained in the parables.

9. WRITINGS UPON THE PARABLES.

Campegius Vitringa, Brief Exposition of the Gospel parables. Frankfort and Leipsic, 1717. A work of great power in many respects, in broad dialect, full of constrained and unnatural expositions.

J. G. Palms, Considerations upon the Parables of the New Testament, Hamburg, 1735. Only seven parables are illustrated in 26 Meditations.

Samuel Bourns, Spiritual Discourses upon a few Select Parables of our Saviour, translated from the English, by J. J. Dusch. Altona and Bremen, 1771.

Andrew Gray, Prelections upon the Allegories of our Saviour, (English title, Delineation of the Parables of our Blessed Saviour;) together with a dissertation upon Allegories and Allegorical Works in general. From the English, Hanover, 1783. A work abounding with instruction.

G. Lorenz Bauer, (Prof. at Altdorf,) Collection and Exposition of the Parabolical Narratives of our Lord. Leipsic, 1782. It contains much that is good, only the moral of the parable is not given with sufficient brevity.

John Ehr. Fr. Eck, Religion for Men, or the Value of Christ's Instruction shown from his Figurative Dis-

They all, indeed, bear in one respect or another upon the kingdom of God, and each one may, therefore, be said to illustrate a doctrine, or inculcate a duty, or unfold a prediction concerning it; but from the unmethodical manner in which they were delivered, and the complex nature of the species of composition to which they belong, it is impossible, without some measure of violence, to range them under any specified number of heads, nor can it be of any material service in the practical handling of them. If this may be objected to any general division of the parables, which yet does not involve any special error, the division of Greswell, referred to in a preceding note, into prophetical parables, and such as inculcate moral lessons, the one unexplained, wrapt in mystery, except in one or two instances, to the initiated few, the other level to the comprehension of all, is so expressly contradicted in various respects by the testimony of Scripture, that we cannot but regard it as the most objectionable of any classification we have met with.—*Trans.*]

courses. Berlin, 1797. In the first section—Christ's Figurative Discourse upon some important doctrines of Christianity,—various parables are handled, but only in a practical view. In the second section—On the Importance of Christ's Figurative Discourses, in respect to the Truths of his Religion,—the author speaks principally of the design, the suitableness, the excellence of the figurative discourses of Jesus, and the propriety of imitating them.

J. J. Kromm, The whole Parables of Jesus Translated, Explained, and Handled in a Practico-homiletical style. Fulda, 1823. Is of no value, either in an exegetical or a homiletical point of view. By the same author: Homilies upon the Allegories of our Lord. First Part, containing five Parables, in sixteen Homilies. Nurenberg, 1830.

Storr, Opuscula Academica ad interpret. librorum Sacr. pertin. Vol. I. p. 89, ss.

Ger Annaeus Van Limberg Brouwer, de Parabolis J. Chr. Specimen Academicum inaugurale. Lugd. Batav. 1825. At p. 10, the author says: The comment shall consist of two parts; of which one shall treat in a general way concerning the nature, argument, and design of the parables, and the other concerning the right determination of the sense of the parables, or concerning the rule of interpretation. For I do not wish to write a commentary upon the parables.

Wesselii Scholten, Diatribe de Parabolis J. Chr. Delphis, Batav. 1825. "This treatise consists of two parts, the first of which embraces those things which belong generally to the parables of Christ; the second shall give certain rules or observations, which have more special reference to the interpretation of these."

E. W. Rettberg, de Parabolis J. Chr. Goetting. 1827.

A. H. A. Schultze, de Parabolarum J. Chr. indole poetica commentatio. Goetting. 1827. Two Essays that received a prize from the Theological Faculty of Goettingen, which treat the parables chiefly in a poetical point of view, dwell at length upon principles of interpretation, but contain very little that is profitable for the exposition of the parables.

A. F. Unger, De Parabolarum Jesu natura, interpretatione, usu scholæ exegeticæ rhetoricæ. Lips. 1828. Full of instruction.

J. L. Ewald, The Look Jesus took of Nature, Humanity, and Himself; or Considerations upon the Parables of our Lord. Hanover, 1812. Third edition. Exceedingly attractive, rich, and worthy of commendation.

R. Eylert, Homilies upon the Parables of Jesus, together with a Treatise upon their Characteristics. Halle, 1818. Second edition. There are eight parables illustrated in twenty homilies, which, as also the prefixed treatise, contains many fine remarks.

N. von Brunn. The Kingdom of God unfolded according to the Instructions of Jesus Christ, especially in his Parables. Basle, 1816. It takes in only the greater part of the parables contained in Matthew, and one from Luke.

Schreiter, Historico-critica explicationum parabolæ de improbo œconomo descriptio. Lips. 1803.

David Schulz, An Essay upon the Parable of the Steward. Breslau, 1821.

Chr. Guil. Nieder, de Loco Commentar: Lucæ xvi. 1—13, dissertatio. Lips. 1826.

Jensen, upon the Unjust Steward, in the studies and critiques of Hillman.

Mutzel upon the Design of Jesus in the Parable of the Rich Man and Lazarus; in the latest Archives for the "Pastoral Science" of Boeckel, Vol. 1st.

Meier upon the same parable, in his Pages for a Higher Truth, Vol. 7.

Schleiermacher, four Sermons upon the Parable of the Sower. Magazine of Noehr, Schleiermacher, Schuderoff. New Series, vol. 5. Magdeburg. 1827.

Theremin, Sermon upon the Prodigal Son; in the third volume of his Sermons. Berlin, 1823.

Very instructive hints and excellent remarks upon the Parables are also to be found in the following works:—

Herder's Epistles upon the Study of Theology; in Part 4th. Stutgart and Tubingen, 1829.

Menken, Reflections upon the Gospel of Matthew. Bremen and Leipsic, 1822.

Dræseke, on the Kingdom of God. Bremen, 1830.

Opera Melancthonis pars tertia. Vitibergæ, 1563. Enarrationes evangeliorum dominicalium et evangelii secundum Matthæum.

Harmonia ex tribus evangelistis composita, Matthæo, Marco et Luca cum Johannis Calvini Commentariis. Ed. sec. cur. Rob. Stephano, 1560, Paris. Upon Calvin's exposition of Scripture, Pelt expresses himself thus, in his preface to his Commentary on the Thessalonians: "He must be numbered amongst the best interpreters of all ages—with wonderful sagacity laying open the most profound thoughts, and selecting, with the happiest skill, from a multitude of interpretations, that which commends itself as most probable, at the same time expressing himself with such elegance, that we derive as much pleasure as advantage from the perusal of his writings."

Hugo Grotius, Opera Theologica, Tom. ii. vol. 1. Amstel. 1679.

Joan. Alb. Bengelii Gnomon, N. T. in quo ex nativa verborum vi profunditas, concinnitas, salubritas sensuum innuitur. Tubing. 1759. The following judgment on the spirit of this work is pronounced by Boehmer in his exposition of the Epistle to the Colossians: "That pious theologian, cherishing the most profound reverence for the word of God, possesses at once an accomplished scholarship and the most requisite skill for expounding it, comprised much solid and ingenious matter in a few words, and because his notes indicate what is strictly contained in the words of the original, they received from him the name of Gnomon (Index.")

G. Ehr. Bartel's special Homily for the Historical and Parabolical Homily. Braunschweig, 1824.

I have not had access to the following:—

Krummacher upon the Spirit and Form of the Evangelical History, in a historical and moral respect. Leipsic, 1805.

Conz Eastern Apologues, or the Wisdom of Jesus as a Teacher, in Parables and Sayings. Leipzic, 1809.

Gittermann, the Parables of Jesus, or Moral Narratives from the Bible. Bremen, 1803.

[We have a better work on the parables in English, than either of the two referred to by our author at the beginning of this list, by Dr. Dodd;-which displays, throughout, a sound judgment, and contains a much fuller exhibition of gospel truth than the work of Gray. There is also an older work by Keach, not deficient in excellent matter, but too antiquated, both in style and the manner of handling the parables, to be found of much service now. We have already spoken of Gresswell's recent laborious work; which certainly contains many good things, as it could scarcely fail to do in such a compass. But it labours under the threefold defect of being often fanciful, very prolix, and not a little expensive.—*Trans.*]

EXPOSITION, &c.

I.

THE TWO BUILDERS.

Matth. vii. 24—27. Luke vi. 47—49.

This similitude forms the conclusion of the sermon on the mount, reported at large by Matthew in the fifth and two following chapters. The hearers were his disciples and a great multitude of people, (Luke vi. 17, 18.) The reason of concluding his more lengthened discourse in this manner, lies in the corruption of the human heart, well known to the Searcher of hearts, which finds it easy to hear, but difficult to do; and hence the delusion, that hearing is of itself sufficient; against which error the similitude before us is directed, (as also the passage in Jas. i. 22—25,) and the consideration of it will admonish us regarding the proper use of the divine word.

TRAIN OF THOUGHT IN THE PARABLE.

The right use of the Divine word.

I. What is necessarily required to this?

1. Hearing the word, v. 24: Whosoever heareth these sayings of mine.

2. Doing it, v. 24: And does them; the opposite, v. 26.

II. The blessing it secures; a well grounded salvation.

1. It secures salvation, v. 24: Who *built* his house?

2. And this salvation is well-grounded, v. 25; opposite, v. 27.

Luther in his exposition of the sermon on the mount says upon this passage: "This is the conclusion and end of the whole; whosoever does not merely hear this sermon with the ear, but also does it, he is a wise and prudent man. For though the doctrine is in itself good and precious, it is not preached only that it may be heard, but that it may be done and manifested in the life. When we spare ourselves this, until our glass is run, and death and the devil attack us with their floods and tempests, we have spared too long. Therefore it concerns you, not merely to hear and understand, but to strive and do!"

Ver. 24. *Therefore;* because the external act is not sufficient to give us true fellowship with Christ, v. 21—23; so that the same truth is figuratively expressed in the similitude, which in plain terms is stated in the foregoing verses. Calvin; "Because it is, for the most part, difficult to distinguish between the true and the false professors of the gospel, Christ shows, by a beautiful similitude, wherein they principally differ. He compares the vain and empty professions of the gospel to a spacious, indeed, but not solid building, which, notwithstanding its fair appearance, is every moment in danger of tumbling into ruin, because it has no foundation. For which reason Paul commands us to be well settled and grounded in Christ—to have our roots struck deep into him, that we may not give way before every assault. In short, the sum of the matter is, that true piety is not easily distinguished from its counterfeit, until it is put to the test. For the trials by which we are proved are like billows and tempests, which readily overthrow unstable minds whose levity was not observed in seasons of tranquillity." Luther, as above: "By such a similitude Christ designs to give us good warning, that we be careful, and hold fast his doctrine, and not lose him out of our heart, as our only sure ground and corner stone of salvation, as he is named by St. Paul in Rom. ix. 33; and Peter in his first Epistle, ii. 6; from Isa. xxviii. 16. If we stand grounded and built on this foundation, we shall remain unmoved, and the world and the devil, with all false teachers and corrupters, may rain down hailstones and fire, and every kind of danger and distress may roar and storm about us. This consolation and security cannot be enjoyed by the miserable and foolish people, who are devoid of faith, for they stand not upon the rock, that is, upon the doctrine of Christ, but upon the shifting sand of their own dark and dreaming minds. Wherefore, if the necessity comes, that in this state they must fight with the devil and death, then do they feel that they have placed their confidence upon loose sand, and that their works and devices cannot stand."

These my sayings (words,) every thing contained in the sermon on the mount, concerning the Christian's state of heart, Matth. v. 3; righteousness, v. 20; love, v. 44: confidence in God, vi. 44, ss., vii. 7, ss. —*hears*, or reads, the means and the way of obtaining a knowledge of the divine word. *Does them;* Luther's gloss: "Here also Christ demands faith, (the internal act of the heart, source of all outward action;) for where there is no faith, the command is not rightly done, Rom. iii. 27, and all good works done with a fair appearance, but without faith, are sins. On the other hand also, where faith is, works truly good must follow. By *doing*, Christ means, doing from a good heart. But faith purifies the heart, Acts xv. 9, and such piety stands firm against all blasts, that is, against all the power of hell. For it is built upon the rock, Christ, through faith. Good works without faith are the foolish virgins' lamps without oil."

I will liken him to a wise man: wise or prudent, φρονιμος, in opposition to foolish, μωρος,—is here taken in a good sense. He who takes into account the end and the means, the present and the future, reality, possibility, and probability, weighs them and determines his procedure accordingly, he is the prudent man; the foolish overlooks this, and hence acts beside his purpose. Bengel, Gnomon: "True prudence of its own accord accompanies true righteousness, comp. xxv. 2." *Built his house,* as one builds a house for himself, that he may dwell in it quietly, comfortably, and securely, in the midst of tempestuous weather; so, a house is the image of desired felicity; *building* is the necessary preparation for reaching that end; *building upon a rock,* is a figure indicating the solidity of the work, and under it hearing and doing are to be understood. *Rain, floods, winds,* v. 25, denote the manifold and perilous evils which threaten our salvation, such as divine judgments expressed in various tribulations, persecutions from men, accusations of conscience, terrors of death and retribution, false teachers (Eph. iv. 14,) who seek to draw us away from Christ, and overwhelm us in sadness and despair; but they cannot succeed, (Rom. viii. 33—39,) for we are bound too closely by a living faith to Christ (John vi. 68, 69.) True faith cannot remain without assaults; in this world these are just as inevitable as the many threatening accidents which abound in nature; but, far from endamaging faith, they only serve to preserve it in its steadfastness, and to manifest its glory. (Rom. v. 1—5.) How blessed is the true hearer of the word, in not shunning the labours and applications which are necessary to deny and overcome himself! (Jas. i. 12.)

V. 26. *Built upon the sand.* Sand is in itself loose, and imparts to that which is built on it no solidity. To build upon sand is consequently an image of deficient steadfastness; it denotes the mere faithless hearer, who is without any corresponding obedience, who makes only half work, being grounded upon no real fellowship with Christ. Bengel, Gnomon: "Sand has the appearance of a rock, but it wants consistence." Calvin: "Whosoever do not dig down to a complete renouncement of self, they dig upon sand."

Ver. 27. *It fell, and great was the fall thereof;* the self-delusion vanishes, the man feels it is too late, his past life is for ever fled, his misery is boundless, the more so as he flatters himself with vain hopes; such bitter disappointment arising out of groundless hopes is portrayed by Ezekiel in chap. xiii. 10—15.

Similar prudence and folly is set forth in the parable of the ten virgins, the foolish hearer of the word is painted according to his different aspects in the parable of the sower, Matth. xiii. 4—7; and in the faithless servant, Matth. xxv. 24, 25, as also in the guest who wanted the wedding garment.

II.

THE SOWER, OR DIFFERENT SORTS OF GROUND.

Matth. xiii. 1—9, 18—23; Mark iv. 3—9, 14—26; Luke viii. 4—15.

GENERAL REMARKS UPON THE PARABLE IN

Matth. chap. xiii.

This chapter presents us with a choice collection of precious similitudes. The first four were delivered by Jesus while sitting on a ship by the shore of the Galilean sea. A multitude of people had collected around the spot, fruitful fields stretched themselves before him, and the much frequented highway passed in the immediate neighbourhood. With these local circumstances the parables are closely connected; what life, what truth must they then have carried! How vivid must they have been! And the images chosen were of such a kind, that every one could not but find something in the words of our Lord, connected with his own calling and manner of life, which might solicit and win his attention to the truths presented to his view. The eye of the Lord first of all surveys the multitude thirsting for instruction; it appears to him like a field that must be sowed, and in the first parable he discloses the different fates which are to befall the dispersed seed of the word. How mournful and depressing that the good seed does not thrive every where! But as this might have led the disciples, the future sowers, into error, our Lord, according to Mark iv. 26—29, immediately adds the parable of the seed ripening by the force of its innate vigour, as a consolation, to assure them, that under God's blessing the good seed would certainly bring forth fruit. Next follows the parable of the tares among the wheat, recommending a prudent sparing of the tares, for the benefit both of them and of the wheat, and pointing to the great harvest time, which might serve also to console the saddened hearts, that beheld with grief such a foul mixture in the field of the Lord. The two short similitudes of the mustard-seed and the leaven, represented at the close, the mighty growth and invincible efficacy of the Gospel. Gnomon: "These seven parables, which have a most recondite meaning, v. 35, bear respect not only to the common and abiding states of the kingdom of heaven, or the church, but also to different periods and ages of the church."

Scholten, at p. 127, s., expresses himself thus upon the mutual connexion of these parables, and their relation one to another: "If we may declare what we think by these seven parables in Matth. xiii. the beginning, progress, and final perfectionment of the kingdom of heaven are shadowed forth, and held up as it were to the observation of the eyes. Therefore, in the *first* parable the different effects are described, which the gospel produces upon the different persons to whom it is proclaimed. In the *second*, Jesus informs us, that among those who should receive the gospel, there would be some who should propagate errors, and indulge in vice, and who, both by doctrine and example, should endeavour to lead others into error, and restrain their pursuit after religion and virtue; and these men should be endured and tolerated here by the wise counsel of God, but in the next life should be appointed to bear the fearful punishment due to miscreants and impostors. The *third* parable, as it appears to us, is intimately united to the preceding ones. In these, the subject of discourse had been concerning the world, as the theatre whereon the gospel was to be proclaimed, which gospel was, therefore, to be carried far and wide, through the whole world, even to the most remote nations. But of this the disciples of Jesus were not easily persuaded; for the commencement of his kingdom was so inauspicious, that men, whose minds had hitherto, in common with the rest of the Jews, been possessed by many foolish opinions of the Messiah's kingdom, as if it should be set up with great outward splendour, could hardly be made to think it possible that a time should come when he would extend its boundaries through the entire world, and all the nations that worship him should receive the faith of the gospel. The same, also, is the design of the *fourth* parable, different, however, from the one that immediately precedes, in this, that it has respect to the preconceived opinion concerning the external pomp and kingly power with which the Jews thought the Messiah's kingdom was to be instituted; and showed, that the kingdom, which justly deserves to be called by the name of Messiah, should be set up and grow on every side, but not with outward splendour, nor by dint of force and victorious arms. In the *fifth* and *sixth* parables, our Saviour presents the fact, in a manner, before our eyes, that the true knowledge of the nature of Messiah's kingdom should make its way to men of every rank, learned and unlearned, wise and foolish; that all should acknowledge the excellence of this knowledge for promoting their true salvation, and, with the greatest zeal and application, should endeavour to grow in a more enlarged apprehension and settled conviction of it, as also to bring forth the fruits of salvation, which are inseparably connected with such an apprehension and conviction. Therefore the parable in v. 44, refers to the knowledge of the true nature of Messiah's kingdom, and the internal conviction of its excellence, as about to be received by men the most common and unlettered. But in that which is contained in v. 45, 46, the Saviour seems to inform his disciples, that many also of those who were given to the study of wisdom, seeking after truth as a precious jewel, as soon as they knew the truth concerning the Messiah's kingdom, would acknowledge his excellence to be such, that they should abandon the pursuits they had hitherto followed, and henceforth apply themselves to the study of this alone; Rom. i. 14, 15. The *seventh* parable still remains, which, as appears to us, is closely related to those preceding it. For the disciples were not to be allowed to think that all these would be true and sincere citizens of the Messiah's kingdom, as with the good there would certainly be an intermixture of bad. But this ought not to disturb their minds, for the state of his kingdom, he taught them, would not be always so imperfect, but that a period should some time arrive, when this its initiatory state would be raised to higher perfection; and that at length εν τη συντελεια του αιωνος, as being freed from all pollution, the kingdom of Christ should become perfect and complete in having only such citizens as are in every respect pure, faithful, and good."

Neither in the sower, nor yet in the seed, which he scatters, lies the blame of unfruitfulness, but solely in the heart. If the state of the heart, however, is such as to impede, rather than to further the productive efficacy of the word, this can afford no justification to men. For as bad soil may, through much labour and continued diligence, be improved, so may also the heart; and the word is given us as a means to this end, and possesses such peculiar power, that we both may and ought to be improved by it. Whoever will not employ it for this purpose, or not employ it faithfully, incurs guilt, and is deserving of punishment, for the word works freely upon men, not with mechanical, external force, but simply by moral suasion, to which the agreement of our will is indispensable.

Amid the innumerable multitudes of men, amid the great varieties of temperament and character, and the manifold peculiarities of individuals, there are still no more to be found than these four grand characteristic differences of heart, in regard to the divine word; but these four may be found fully and distinctly formed. The Searcher of hearts has manifested this, and its truth is proved whenever and wherever his word is preached. How the divine word finds the hearts upon which it has to work, is described under the four kinds of ground; all have in them what is sinful, but still one condition is much more favourable to the growth of the seed than another. The ultimate ground of these different appearances lies in the conduct of men under the preparatory grace of God. Just as ploughing goes before and prepares for the seed, so is there much done by God, through means of his kingly government toward nations and individuals, to make them ready for the further manifestation of the word of life, (Israel had the law and the promises.) If men would only employ with fidelity this preparatory grace of God, in the law, the promises, conscience, education, they should be as good soil, fitted for receiving the word.

TRAIN OF THOUGHT IN THE PARABLE.

The different efficacy of the word of God depends upon the different states of the human heart.

I. On many hearts the word of God has no effect at all, Luke v. 12.

A. It has no effect at all;

1. They hear it, indeed, v. 12.

2. But they are nothing the better, *ib.*

B. Why it has no effect;

1. From *internal* grounds, because these hearts are hard and insensible, Matth. v. 4. Some fall by the way;

a) They understand it not, Matth. v. 19.
b) And do not believe it, Luke v. 12.
2. From *external* circumstances, employed by the wicked one to hinder the success of the word;
a) Other impressions overpower the word, Luke v. 5: The seed was trodden down.
b) Hostile powers withdraw it from the heart, Luke v. 5: The fowls of the air devoured it.
II. On other hearts it has no deep-rooted, and hence no *permanent* effect.
A. Proof.
1. It has an effect upon them;
a) They hear it, Matth. v. 20.
b) And presently with joy receive it, Matth. v. 20. Mark v. 5.
2. But it has no deep-rooted or permanent effect;
a) For a time they believe, Luke v. 13.
b) But by and by are offended, Matth. v. 21.
c) And at last completely fall away, Luke v. 13, Mark v. 6.
B. Grounds.
1. Internal grounds;
a) Their inmost being is not moved by the word, Matth. v. 5.
b) Hence the word acquires no fixedness in them, Matthew v. 6: because they had no root.
2. External grounds:
a) Tribulation and persecution, Matth. v. 21.
b) Temptation (of faith, through doubts, raillery and such things,) Luke v. 13.
III. On other hearts, it has no *purifying*, and hence no *strengthening* effect.
A. Proof.
1. It has an effect upon them;
a) They hear it, Matth. v. 22.
b) And it makes an impression on them, Luke v. 7; the thorns grew up *with it*, namely, with the seed of the word.
2. But it has no purifying or strengthening effect.

a) They allow their lusts to grow beside the word, Luke v. 7.

b) And thus the action of the word is again suppressed, Matth. v. 22; The word is choked and becomes unfruitful.

B. Grounds.

1. The cares of this world.
2. Deceitfulness of riches.

} Matth. v. 22.

IV. On other hearts it works with the most blessed effect.

A. On what hearts it works with this blessed effect; on such as,

1. Hear the word, Matth. v. 23.

2. Receive it (Mark v. 20; *i. e.* understand, believe, Matth. v. 23,) in opposition to the first class.

3. Keep it in an honest and good heart, Luke v. 15, in opposition to the second class.

4. Bring forth fruit with patience, Luke v. 15, in opposition to the third class.

B. Its manner of working most productive of blessing; a hundred-fold, sixty-fold, thirty-fold, Matth. v. 23.

Luke v. 5. *The sower*, Christ and every one who brings the divine word to work upon men. *His seed*, v. 11. The seed is the word of God; still more definitely in Matth. v. 19. *The word of the kingdom;* therefore, not merely in the general what God has spoken, but pre-eminently his gospel, his gracious message by Christ, his gift of grace and glory, his testimony and invitations concerning the kingdom of heaven. The seed belongs to the sower, it is Christ's; whoever besides may scatter this seed, he has it from Christ, but it must also have become, through spiritual experience, the possession of every preacher, for it must be taught of faith, Ps. cxvi. 10, 1 John i. 1—3. The *heart* is the understanding, the feeling, the will.

1. The *first* class of hearts, Luke v. 5, 12. Here the heart is like the highway; the surface is hard, nothing can make an impression on it; the seed con-

tinues to lie exposed, and is hence either trodden down or eaten up by the fowls. Of these hard and unfeeling hearts, the leading characteristic is, that the divine word produces no effect upon them at all. The heart is first rendered like a highway through thoughtlessness, levity, indifference to holy impressions; however clear the doctrines of the gospel may be in themselves, however intelligible they may be delivered, and with whatever powerful considerations enforced, such a heart remains unconcerned, is quite negligent and regardless about every thing which concerns eternal life, and the word of God is to it a word destitute of all meaning, from not being able to understand it. Moreover, having given itself up to all worldly impressions, it is thereby filled with prejudices of every sort, which completely prevent the good seed from making any impression. In the hardened smoothness of such a heart, nothing is properly cogitated; hence spring up by degrees gross ignorance, and a disinclination toward all the instruction which it has any how received; the natural, whether less or more important, capacities are neglected, and consequently deteriorated, so that the heart is continually growing harder and more unfeeling, (v. 14.) When the heart is in such a condition, firmly shut against every thing divine, the word of God, as often as it happens to be heard, is in part *trodden down*, vanishing without a trace from the heart amid the bustle of life, the dissipations of the world, which are engaged in with no collectedness of mind, or calm meditation; in part also devoured *by the birds;* the wicked one, (Matt. v. 19,) Satan, (Mark v. 15,) the devil, (Luke v. 12,) snatches the word from the heart. The kingdom of darkness fights against the kingdom of God, which is built up within us through the word of God, and there is still permitted to exist a secret power of Satan, which, through much cunning, and all kinds of wicked artifice, draws away from the heart the preached word, (Eph. ii. 2. 2 Cor. iv. 3, 4.) So it happens, that such hearts do not understand, (Matth. v. 19,) or, which is all one, they do not believe, (Luke v. 12,) and hence do not attain to salvation. "In the first rank," says Calvin, "he mentions the barren and uncultivated, who give no inward reception to the seed, because there is no *preparation* in their hearts. Yet when Christ says the word is sown in their hearts, although the speech is improper, it is not used without reason; because the wickedness and depravity of men does not take from the word its proper nature, which still retains the virtue of seed; and this must be carefully borne in mind, lest we should think there has been any failure in the grace of God, when its effects have not been experienced in ourselves. For, on the part of God, the word is sown in the hearts of men: but the hearts of all do not receive with meekness the ingrafted word, as James exhorts, chap. i. 21. The gospel, therefore, is always fruitful seed, in regard to its divine virtue, but not in regard to its actual effects."

2. The *second* class of hearts—the stony-ground, Matth. v. 5, 6 ; 20, 21. By stony, as Bengel remarks, "we are not to understand stones lying scattered about every where in the field, but a rock or stone, stretching continuously under a thin surface of earth." *And forthwith sprung up;* Gnomon: εξανετειλε, not merely ανετειλε, *sprung*, but *grew aloft;* ver. 20, *instantly with joy receiveth it;* Gnomon; "For much quickness and joy are not always the best sign; for there, commonly, the whole vigour directs itself to outward things, and upon these spends its strength."

From the word heard and believed there unfolds itself a spiritual life, and this, like new-sprung corn, possesses a beautiful appearance, and raises joyful expectations; but, under the surface of quick emotions, of lively feelings, of an easily moved susceptibility, there lies a hard rock concealed, which prevents the seed from taking proper root. This rock is the earthly, sinful nature of man, upon which temptations, trials, and afflictions, for the sake of the word, produce a highly disadvantageous effect. The feebleness of their faith, which is only of a superficial nature, and goes not into the underground of their heart, together with many unfavourable outward circumstances, bring on a withering decay of the tender blade, a falling off from Christ. And with still greater power shows itself here the might of Satan, which is able to undermine the faith that has already been planted in the heart. The scorching heat of temptation is partly the fear of sufferings, which are threatened by external violence; partly the hope of gain, to be derived from apostacy, with which wily seduction cozens and allures; partly, also, the raillery with which carnal wisdom reviles what is holy. Through such means the heart of this class are overcome, because they want the steadfastness, and determinate boldness, which springs out of deep-rooted faith, (2 Cor. iv. 8, 9.) They seek and expect from Christ an easy life, treasure up his word only so far as it provides for them satisfaction, or falls in with their earthly designs, would fain reach heaven, but will make no sacrifice to gain it. With such a manner of feeling they never experience the power of that faith which overcometh the world, and without this blessed power of faith, for which they have no adequate depth of feeling, they sink into perdition. The striking characteristic here is the rapid change from bloom to decay, from the reception of the word to apostacy from it; the divine word produces here no deep or permanent effect, for while the hearts are soft and susceptible, they are, at the same time, weak and inconstant. Calvin: "This class differs from the preceding one, because temporal faith, the conception, in a manner, of the seed, promises some fruit, while yet the heart is not brought into such good and thorough subjection, as that its softness can minister to the seed a continual supply of nourishment. And, indeed, as the sterility of the earth is proved by the heat of the sun, so persecution and the cross detect the vanity of those, who, though touched with some sort of desire toward divine things, are yet imbued with no truly devout spirit of piety. It is found that they are not in reality born again by the incorruptible seed, which, as Peter testifies, (1 Ep. i. 4,) never decays."

3. The *third* class of hearts, Luke v. 7, 14. There are seeds of corruption in every heart, for no one is perfectly pure. The good seed of the word was early cast into the class of hearts before us; they felt themselves drawn and blessed by it, and continued in a joyful frame of mind, while the good seed had found root in them. But, latterly, they entered into the whirlpool of the world, and then sprung up in their hearts all sorts of vain thoughts; they neglected watching and prayer, in consequence of which, also, the corrupt seed makes rapid shoots, draws all the nutritive juice to itself, penetrates the whole soil; step by step the good impressions are worn out; the opposition to sinful lusts becomes continually weaker, the power of evil desires increase in virulence and strength, and the nobler, the more elevated life of the spirit, is imbittered until it becomes quite extinct. How mighty must the power of evil be, that it can here also prevail against the word of God! As principal antagonists to the efficacious working of the divine word, the Redeemer mentions *the care of this life*, care for our present livelihood, the pressure of an earthly existence; and *the deceitfulness of riches*, the glittering side of this life, both with poor and with rich; with those who are in quest of them, and those who already have them, because both look upon them as the highest good, and put their confidence in them. Luke calls this impediment *the pleasures of this life*, including, therefore, the inferior lusts and sensualities of the flesh, which destroy the life of the soul.

In the case of these hearts, which are full of cares and earthly inclinations, the great characteristic is, the contest maintained with the thorns, so that in them the divine word works nothing *pure*. Calvin: "Although evil desires dwell in the heart of man, before the word of God puts forth the green blade, they yet do not appear to have the dominion at the earlier stages; but, by and by, they get the superiority, when the blade is shooting up and is making promise of fruit. Every one, therefore, must apply his care to pluck out the thorns from his heart, unless he would have the word of God to be choked; since there is no heart which is not replenished with a great abundance of thorns, even as with a thick forest."

4. The *fourth* class of hearts, Matth. v. 8, 23; Luke v. 8, 15. They *hear* the word willingly and with attention, and *understand* it, receive it in faith, obey it, and thus experience its powers, and understand it always better and better; in which respects they are distinguished from the first class. They also *keep* it in a pure, good heart, often meditating on it by themselves, and laying it up in the deep recesses of their mind, which constitutes their distinction from the second class. Finally, they *bring forth fruit*, in them are manifested the fruits of the Spirit, Gal. v. 22; 1 Cor. xiii. 4—7; *with patience*, persevering with unshaken steadfastness against opposition and difficulties, under the reproach of the world, in the storm of persecution; and it is precisely in these circumstances that their glory shines brightest, like that of the stars when the sun has withdrawn his light from the heavens. The patience which they exercise, distinguishes them from the third class. *And some bare a hundred-fold, some sixty-fold, some thirty-fold;* none are destitute of fruit, but it is not always precisely the same, neither uniformly beautiful nor uniformly rich, and also in different persons varying according to their respective powers, the relations of life, and spheres of operation, in which the Lord has placed them; in each case, however, the fructifying only proceeds when the internal cultivation and renewal of the heart has gone before it, Gnomon: "ο μεν, ο δε, ο δε; the accusative, in the neuter gender; for the subject ος, expressed here

in the singular number, does not admit of a subdivision, of itself, into three kinds of good hearers of the word, as it is commonly understood. The progress of one hearer from three grains of seed, as it were, as being copious in greater or smaller degrees, is signified by the *hundred-fold, sixty-fold, and thirty-fold.* As the degrees of hearing without fruit were three-fold, so also the abundance of fruit is three-fold. To him that hath is given." Calvin: "Christ compares those only to good and fruitful ground, in whom the word of God overcomes all the obstacles which would hinder its fruitfulness. Should any one object, that nobody can be found utterly devoid of thorns, the answer is easy; that Christ is not here discoursing of the perfection of faith, but merely showing in whom the word fructifies. We are taught by no means to despise those who excel least, since the householder himself, although he prefers some to others, in proportion to their respective abundance, yet dignifies also the least productive with the common appellation of goodness. We must, moreover, note, in passing, that Christ does not speak hyperbolically concerning the hundred-fold return, for such was the actual fertility of some regions, as we learn from the testimony of many historians, some of whom were eye-witnesses."

Luther, in his exposition of Matthew, remarks, on this place: "This is uttered against the reptiles who maintain that the spoken word is unprofitable, because, in the greater part, it brings forth no fruit. The fools! as if they, of themselves, could bring forth fruit, while yet, on this very account, that they make light of the word of God, they are manifestly base reprobates. But here thou seest that the seed upon a good ground does produce fruit, while no fruit is gathered from ground on which seed has not been sown. Therefore, if there were no preached word in the church, neither should there be any fruit in her."

III.

THE TARES AMONG THE WHEAT.

Matth. xiii. 24—30; 36—43.

The preceding parable shows that the kingdom of God must be grounded and built up in each individual through the word of God; and also that, in the peculiar condition of each there naturally exist circumstances more or less favourable or unfavourable to the success of the word. In this parable an advance is made. The word has taken root,—has had effect; the kingdom has obtained its members,—is formed into a society,—exists in the world as an institution,—all which is to be understood of the visible church, as an institution founded by the Lord, in the manner it presents itself to the eye of the believing disciple; and the Lord here discloses the future and final termination of that mixture of good and bad which, during the progress of time, continued to prevail in his church. The kingdom of God, considered by itself, as a divine institution, and as it shall one day be manifested in the region of glory, is something entirely perfect, without sin; a commonwealth of pardoned, blessed, and holy men, together with the holy angels. But the same kingdom of God, in time, considered as an institution for the conversion of sinful men, and their edification in holiness, proceeds upon the supposition of their sinful nature and moral freedom, remains, and cannot but remain, tainted with the pollution of sin, which has a footing in its members, though gradually losing its hold of them; hence the kingdom of God, the visible church, appears in the world, according to a sort of necessity, as a *mixed* society, and hence also the saying of the Lord: "Let both grow together." Calvin: "For although Christ, with his own blood, cleansed the church, that it might be without spot or wrinkle, he still permits it to be disfigured with many deformities. Nor do I speak of remaining infirmities of flesh, to which all the faithful are liable after they have been born of God; but as soon as Christ gathered to himself a little flock, many hypocrites and ungodly persons crept in among them; whence it came to pass, that that sacred company which Christ had separated for himself, became tainted with much corruption. This, however, appears to many extremely absurd, that there should be fostered, in the bosom of the Church, any impious, profane and abandoned persons. And there are many, with a great show of zeal, rigid to excess, who, because they cannot get every thing squared to their mind, and can nowhere find absolute purity, fractiously depart from the church, or with importunate rigour overturn and destroy it. Wherefore the great scope of the parable is simply this:—As long as the church is tabernacling on earth, there shall be in it a mixture of bad men and hypocrites with the sincere and good, that the children of God may arm themselves with patience, and still retain, amid the annoyances to which they are subjected, an unshaken faith in God."

TRAIN OF THOUGHT IN THE PARABLE.

Of the mixture of good and bad in the church of Christ.

I. The rise of this mixture proceeds:—

(1.) Not from the Lord; v. 24, 37. The Son of Man sows good seed.

(2.) But from his enemy; v. 25. Then came his enemy, &c. v. 39. The enemy that sowed them is the devil.

II. The perpetuity of this mixture, v. 26—30; even to the harvest.

(1.) It is represented:

a) According to its becoming manifest, so as to be discerned, v. 26.

b) According to the impression it made upon the feelings of the servants, v. 27.

c) According to the impression it made upon their wills, v. 28.

(2.) It is described as agreeable to the purposes of Christ:

a) Toward the good, v. 29,—lest ye root up the wheat with them.

b) Toward the bad, v. 30. Let both grow together.

(3.) It is limited as to its continuance, v. 30: until the harvest.

III. This mixture shall be made to terminate:

(1.) By means of a *general* separation, v. 30. Gather together first the tares; v. 41, 42.

(2.) By means of a *righteous* judgment, v. 30. And bind them in bundles to burn them; v. 43.

The kingdom of heaven is like, &c. The institution which is set up for the purpose of bringing sinful men into fellowship with the Redeemer, presents the same appearance as a field of corn, in which a man sowed good seed, but afterwards his enemy came and sowed tares. *Sowed in his field;* Gnomon: "In the field in which he himself is; for it is not said, *into a field.*" This expression, therefore, must point to operations of the Son of Man, as being himself present and sowing.

V. 37. *He that soweth the good seed is the Son of Man;* therefore the parable does not refer generally to the contest, ever existing in the world, between good and evil, holiness and sin, light and darkness; but specially to those manifestations of it which have taken place since the divine power of Jesus Christ began to be displayed in the kingdom founded by him.

V. 24. *In his field;* v. 38: *The field is the world,* his property, for it is *given* to him, Matth. xxviii. 18—20; but still not *subjected* to him, as it shall be in the progressive development of the kingdom, Heb. ii. 7, 8. Hence the field of the Lord, till now, is only there, where his word is preached, is believed, has found disciples. The heathen and Jewish world, as a field belonging to the world, became the Lord's field, when his messengers first began, under his blessing, to scatter there the seed of his word, and find faith in the hearers. Calvin: "But although Christ afterwards explains that the field is *the world*, it is yet not to be doubted, but that properly he wished to apply this name to the church, concerning which he had instituted his discourse. But since he was going to draw the plough of his gospel through every region of the globe, that he might cultivate fields for himself, throughout the whole world, and disperse abroad the seed of life, by synecdoche he transfers to the world what properly applied only to a part of it."

Good seed, v. 38. *The good seed are the children of the kingdom;* according to the preceding parable, the seed is the word of God, for only by means of this can men be brought to a state of fellowship with Christ. Here the seed of the divine word, the truth is considered; not by itself, but as it is received into the hearts of men, becomes inwrought and dwells as a living power within them; so that they themselves, through means of the word, and quickened by the Holy Spirit, have been made the children of the kingdom:—have been so changed as to possess the nature of the heavenly kingdom,—the mode of feeling that properly becomes its members, are brethren of Christ, and, as children of God, are *heirs* also of eternal life.

Ver. 25. *But while the people slept;* this incident Jesus has not expounded in the interpretation, but it marks the *favourable time*, which the artful enemy spies out and uses for the execution of his destructive designs and mischievous devices. Since the kingdom of heaven is appointed for sinners, it is unavoidable but that there shall be found something sinful intermixed with it, Matth. xviii. 7; 2 Cor. xi. 19, and hence we must not bring an unconditional reproach of sleepiness against the members of the church, its apostles and teachers. But it is not to be denied, on the other hand, that the kingdom of darkness should not have been able to spread so great and extensive a corruption through the church of the Lord, had not sleep, that is, careless security, spiritual indifference, want of love to Christ, a worthy understanding of the Christian name, provided it with favourable circumstances. Luther, in his exposition on this place, says; "By the *sleeping* he indicates that it is impossible to prevent the entrance of heretics. For while the apostles teach the word as full of joy and consolation, and hope that all will be pure and safe, lo, while they are, as it were, asleep, and never dreamt of any thing of the kind, suddenly arise false apostles and false brethren. Who can prevent it? There are brethren, who will unawares become villains as Cain did towards Abel."

His enemy came, ver. 39: *The enemy who sowed them is the devil,* the perpetual enemy of the kingdom of God, the old serpent. There is a prince of this world, a father of lies, a soul-murderer from the beginning; he holds, with his angels, an organized kingdom, and opposes the designs of God, the advancement of the divine kingdom, by means of falsehood and error. He is the ultimate source of all evil, which lies partly without, partly within the kingdom of God, and is detrimental to its interests. Calvin: "We ought to know, that it is neither from accident, nor in the natural course of things, that many wicked persons introduce themselves among the faithful, as if they were of one and the same kidney; but let us be careful to impute the blame of this mischief to the devil, so as not, through his damnation, to acquit men of guilt, and especially to ascribe no blemish to God, on account of this adventitious evil; neither let us be surprised if we should see the tares, by degrees growing up in the field of the Lord, since Satan is always on the watch for himself."

And sowed tares among the wheat; ver. 38: *The*

tares are the children of the wicked one. Falsehood and error are the proper serpent's brood; the devil's word gives the lie to the word of God, brings it into doubt, or perverts it. But, as falsehood and error were to be described by our Lord, not as something by itself, as a dead thing, as an existence standing apart from the human heart, he therefore says, that *the children of the wicked one* are the tares. The word of falsehood has found an entrance into the heart, it is received as true, it has darkened the understanding, enchained the will, depraved the feelings, and they, in whom this has been done, are now the children of evil, (of the wicked one, the devil;) they have his nature, have become like-minded with him, live and move in falsehood, error, and mischief. "For the parable speaks," says Luther, "not of such false Christians as are unchristian only in the *outward life*, but of those who are so in regard to faith and doctrine, possessing the name of Christians and a glistening appearance, but are in reality noxious. The evil, in their case, lies in the conscience, not in the hand. And they must, indeed, be spiritual servants, who can discern such tares among the wheat."

And went his way; he does not permit himself to be seen, works in darkness, the fruit of his working alone is seen; but he is ever busy in the children of unbelief, Eph. ii. 2, John viii. 40, 41. Luther: "This is the uniform artifice of Satan and heretics, that they strive to avoid the appearance of introducing false doctrines."

Ver. 26. *But when the blade was sprung up, and brought forth fruit, then appeared the tares also.* The good seed was sown beforehand, had already taken deep root, and reached a certain height, and hence was no longer in danger of being checked by the rising tares. What at first did not clearly discover itself as tares, even to the experienced eye, could not conceal itself in its farther progress, when it became more matured. By their fruits the tares were known to be what they really were, though, till then, they had preserved a deceitful resemblance to the wheat. Satan manifests himself as altogether an angel of light. This resemblance of the tares to the wheat is indicated in the name of the first, ζιζανια, which is a sort of after-wheat, cockle, and not easy to be distinguished from genuine wheat.* With this verse begins the more extended bearing of the parable, as describing the continued and permanent nature of the mixture in question. It would be needless labour, and contrary besides to the nature of the parable, to search for those periods in the church's history,

* [Why our author should at once denominate this plant after-wheat and cockle, as if they were one and the same, we profess ourselves unable to understand. Schleusner, on the other hand, expressly distinguishes them, and says, we are not to take it for a kind of cockle, which grows among wheat, but for after-wheat, a sort of inferior or secondary wheat, in appearance very like to genuine wheat, but yielding either no fruit at all, or only bad fruit. That this is the kind of plant referred to, however, under the name of *zizania* or tares, many learned commentators are of opinion; and yet it does not appear that the difference between this secondary, and the genuine wheat, is by any means of such a radical and essential kind as to correspond with the distinction which separates the true people of Christ from the offspring of the wicked one. The language used concerning it in the parable, and especially the application there made of it, seem to imply that it must have been a weed, a noxious weed, incapable of being used for food, fit only to be burned, yet possessing such a general resemblance to the wheat, that it was only by and by, when the field was ripening to the harvest, that the evil admixture became apparent. Now, it is a well ascertained fact, that there is a species of cockle or darnel, which very frequently springs up among fields of corn in Syria, belonging to the same family of plants with wheat, and, when analyzed, found to contain almost precisely the same ingredients, yet so very different in its effects upon the human frame, that when its seeds remain mixed with the wheat, the flour thus produced always occasions dizziness and other injurious consequences. We see no sufficient reason to doubt, therefore, that this is the plant referred to by our Lord,—the more especially when we are further informed, that the name at present given to it by the Arabs is *zulsan*, (not very different from *zizania*,) and that, in several parts of Syria it is customary for the people to pluck out the stalks of this weed while reaping, and bind it in separate bundles.]—*Trans.*

wherein corruption has spread itself more deeply among her professing members. It early began to manifest itself in the church; in Jerusalem we have Ananias and Sapphira, in Samaria, Simon; see also 1 Cor. i. 11; Gal. i. 6, ss.; Phil. iii. 2, ss.; Col. ii. 8, ss.; 2 Tim. iv. 3, 14. And, just as in nature, both the wheat and the tares unfold themselves, each according to their own natures, from the first germ in the seed on till the time of harvest, so is it also in the church; the more *that* in it which is conformable to the spirit of Christ, develops itself in doctrine, and life, in practice and constitution, the more always does that which is unchristian or antichristian, become manifest as such, and appear in more flagrant contrast with the former. And the more the church is sifted with great and severe trials, in the same proportion does the mixture, that existed in her, become more visible, the opposition more marked, and so the first judgment must be regarded as a perfectly correct one.

Ver. 27. *Lord, didst not thou sow good seed in thy field? From whence then hath it tares?* Gnomon: "Tares have a better appearance than thorns and thistles, so that from the one being tolerated, we cannot certainly conclude that the other shall. And often the tares assume the character of wheat, and endeavour to extirpate the wheat as if it were tares." "The servants spake this," says Luther, "because from love to the Word they were indignant against the heretics, and wished that there were none, that all might be like-minded, and a stop put to the devil's rule in the church." The conversation between the Lord and his servants, renders the matter more vivid and lively. The sense of the first question is, we know perfectly well that thou didst sow good seed. The second question exposes in a lively manner their astonishment at the incomprehensible nature of the result. Whosoever has come to know the power of the gospel, and understands how it is adapted to purify and ennoble the corrupt heart, cannot but wonder how a great degeneracy can insinuate itself into the church, and become prevalent even among those who have been favoured with all the means of grace and privileges of salvation.

Ver. 28. *The enemy has done this.* Human nature is indeed corrupt: flesh itself is liable to error; but this experimental truth does not suffice to explain the great corruption in the church, whose divine powers are so utterly unproductive in many of her professing members. The all-seeing Lord keeps a careful watch over the actions of the enemy, who knows so well how to make a skilful use of every unhappy circumstance, in order to restrain the empire of light, 2 Thess. ii. 8—12.

Wilt thou then that we go and gather them up? This is the third question of the servants, and expresses at once their desire and their readiness to serve the Lord. It is good that they ask of him; in the Lord's kingdom nothing must be transacted according to their own will, their private sense and conviction of what is right. His will is the rule of conduct, and becomes also the will of his servants. *To gather* or *root up,* to apply a power of extirpation. Luke ix. 54.

Ver. 29. *Nay;* Gnomon: "The zeal which the pious cherish against the tares is not blamed; it is, however, reduced into proper order." It is the will of the Lord that the tares should for a time be suffered, that the mixture should be allowed to continue; and yet the history of the church shows that those who in courts of inquisition and persecutions, against schismatics, assumed the appearance of faithful and zealous servants, went directly counter to this decided *nay* of the Lord. The Lord converses most graciously with the servants, and shows them the deeper ground on which his remarkable declaration rested.

Lest while ye gather up the tares, ye root up the wheat also. Here is the first ground of allowing the permanency of the mixture, the servants have not the power of making a right division. History proves it to be the case; persons have been persecuted and oppressed, who in the real church of the Lord were children of the kingdom. But the continued intermixture of good and bad, affords these also the opportunity of proving themselves to be true children of the kingdom, in patience, placableness and love towards their enemies; the patience and long-suffering of the Lord in bearing with the children of evil, serves as a means to promote their spiritual advancement; they could not, without the temptations and sufferings which grow out of their connexion with the wicked, arrive at matured excellence and conformity to the image of Christ, and so an essential, a necessary means of improvement, according to the present sinful constitution of human nature, would be withdrawn from them to their hurt. Luther: "There are here two causes; 1. Because some who are still to be converted from among the wicked, should be condemned and destroyed, if they were refused admittance into the church and fellowship with the wheat. 2. If we would suffer no tares, we should also have no church. For since the church cannot exist without tares, if we were to pluck up the tares, it would be all one with rooting up the church."

Ver. 30. *Let both grow together.* This is the second ground of the permanency of the mixture; the intercourse that subsists between the good and bad in the visible Church may, and must be of great service to the latter, as bringing them within the influence of the good example and blissful love of the real members of the kingdom; and from the long-suffering patience of the Lord, it has often happened that in the protracted day of grace, upon this territory, where freedom reigns, a Saul has been changed into a Paul. The tares must not be violently torn up, but this does not hinder that the good wheat should be tended with all care, and its increase constantly sought; does not hinder that error should be exposed as error, and full warning given of it, and that the faithful discipline of the Church, administered in a spirit of love, should so correct the vices that appear as to leave room for repentance, Titus iii. 10. Luther: "The Lord says not that we must *check* the tares, but that we must not *root them up;* nor does he say that we must *sow* or *cultivate* the tares, but speaks only of their being *permitted to grow.*" Melancthon: "He teaches that the Church should not be an earthly kingdom, and does not wish that the apostles should bear the sword, or punish delinquents with the sword. Elsewhere he teaches that flagrant offences should be treated with excommunication. Still, many sins will certainly remain. But here we are told that the Church does not, on this account, cease to exist, for many bad ones have been mixed with the good. This doctrine supplies us with a valuable consolation."

Until the harvest; by this time both the wheat and the tares shall have so fully developed themselves, that no doubt can any longer exist concerning their respective natures, and hence, in the great separation that is then to take place, the righteousness of the Lord will shine forth in the clearest light. Ver. 39: *The harvest is the end of the world,* the completion or fulfilment of the (present) ages of the world; it is therefore a mere dream for any one to expect a spotless visible Church upon earth; where the Church is, there is continually a mixture. Yet still the obligation and the duty remain to have the field of the Church preserved in every respect as pure as possible, that in doctrine, practice, and constitution, she may be conformable to the mind of Christ. Luther: "Just as it is here with the human body, it cannot in this life be perfectly clean; so it is also with Christianity, which is a spiritual body; it cannot on earth be found without filth and impurity."

And in the time of harvest I will say to the reapers; Gnomon: "καιρῳ, then at length there will be a fit season." The Lord here says *I;* and reserves to himself the power of appointing the time for the final sifting. *The reapers are the angels,* v. 39; through the

Lord's power and unerring discernment they are capacitated for the work committed to them.

Gather ye together first the tares, and bind them, that they be burned. This third main division of the parable discloses the final destiny of the two parties, who have hitherto been mixed together. First of all, there is to be the separation of every thing heterogeneous, evil to evil; and then the punishment. Those who formerly were named children of evil, and had also remained such, are at v. 41 divided into two classes: *those that offend, and those that do iniquity.* In regard to the first, σκανδαλα, persons are so named, as Peter in Matth. xvi. 23; it denotes heretics, and hence seducers. The other class comprehends those who have led a manifestly wicked life, and have thereby scandalized the Church, Tit. iii. 11. Calvin: "The former we called σκανδαλα, (offendicula,) because they not only live badly for themselves, but corrupt the faith of many, retard others in their outward course, completely lead astray some, and drive others headlong into ruin. Hence it must be received as a profitable admonition, to beware lest, being surrounded with so many offenders, (σκανδαλα,) we should go on slothful and secure, but rather apply ourselves to the vigorous exercise of caution."

And shall cast them into a furnace of fire, v. 42; an allusion to the vale of Hinnom, where the service of Moloch was, to honour him by burning children. Calvin: "He denounces a terrible judgment against certain hypocrites and reprobates, who appear now principal members of the Church, that they may not lull themselves to sleep with their own vain imaginations. As the infinitude of glory, which is laid up for the sons of God, too far exceeds our loftiest apprehensions to be properly expressed in words, so the punishment which awaits the reprobate, because it is incomprehensible, is shadowed forth in a manner suited to our weak capacity." The misery of the damned shall be most dreadfully severe; *There shall be wailing and gnashing of teeth*, prop. grinding of teeth from anguish of mind, and impotent rage, Matth. viii. 12.

Ver. 30. *But gather the wheat into my garner.* Ver. 43. *Then shall the righteous shine forth as the sun in the kingdom of their Father.* Good to the good, and glorious reward of grace! *The righteous*, those who possess God's favour, because they are what He would have men to be; that they are such is the effect of divine grace. *Shining as the sun*, (Dan. xii. 3,) denotes their glory and blessedness, increased through the far-extending, benignant, blessed and happy influence which they exercise upon others. *In their Father's kingdom;* God is the Father of the righteous, they are his children; an intimate, blessed society, John xvii. 23. Calvin: "Glorious consolation, that the sons of God, who now lie in squalid poverty, or are passed by as things of no price, or are even loaded with reproaches, shall then, as it were, in a serene sky, and overshadowed by no cloud, truly shine forth in refulgent brightness; for the Son of God shall raise his people aloft, and wipe away every spot of pollution which now obscures their glory. True, indeed, it is, that future glory is promised to none but to those in whom the image of God is now reflected, and who are transformed into it by continual advances in glory. But when comparing this glory to the sun, our Lord is not to be understood as affirming its uniform equality; for as here he distributes in various degrees his gifts among the faithful, so also will he crown them with glory on the last day." That the tares are gathered *first*, is a subordinate circumstance, which must not be closely pressed, for in Matth. xxv. 31—46, the reverse order is given.

IV.

THE MUSTARD SEED.

Matth. xiii. 31, 32.—Mark iv. 30, 32.—Luke xiii. 18, 19.

The kingdom of heaven is like a mustard seed; that is, there are to be found in this, and in the Christian dispensation, the same appearances; so that the history of a mustard-seed, which grows and becomes a large plant, is an excellent image of the history of the heavenly kingdom upon earth, and that in a twofold respect. The gigantic effect proceeding from a small and most unpromising commencement; this is the grand point of comparison in the parable, and it finds full application to the heavenly kingdom, whether this be regarded as a society of believers in Christ, an institution for the salvation of sinful men—the visible church; or in its reference to the individual believer, as in him also it rises out of a small beginning to a great and glorious result. For the laws are exactly the same, according to which the divine seed unfolds itself in humanity as a whole, and in each individual. On account of this double reference (of which, however, the first answers most perfectly to the figurative representation, since in it only can the touching incident about the birds of the air coming to lodge in the branches, find its exact signification,) the truth disclosed in the similitude might perhaps be expressed in the most correct manner, if we say that it represents the progressive development of the gospel, or of Christianity,—which on a large scale, and as a whole, belongs to it in the church, as well as on a small scale in individuals. Calvin: "By these parables (Matt. xiii. 31—33,) Christ animates his disciples, lest they should be discouraged and offended at the small beginning of the gospel. We see how haughtily profane men dispute the gospel, and even make it an object of mockery, because it is brought to them by ministers of mean origin and of little note, because it does not meet with an instant and universal reception, but has few disciples, and these for the most part men of little worth in the estimation of the world. Hence it happens, that the weak despair concerning its success, of which they augur according to its commencement. But the Lord wisely prognosticates the successful establishment of his kingdom from small and contemptible beginnings, that its unexpected progress might the better illustrate his power." Luther, in his Exposition: "In this parable, Christ removes another offence out of the way, that, namely, of weakness, which is found to exist in the word, and in the church before the world, and even in the eyes of the pious. For the parable immediately preceding took away the offence arising from ungodliness, and the existence of sects in the church; here he represents even the *external* aspect of the church as offensive when he says: The church is like the very smallest seed, which is looked upon as the most insignificant of things. But out of this one seed, little though it be, there nevertheless grows a church so great, that many peoples, princes, and wise men, come and rest in it through faith. By which he means to inform us, that the world should be converted to the faith in a manner fitted to excite wonder, and give offence, namely, through weakness, in opposition to all power, wisdom, righteousness, &c.; a method of working that may truly be regarded as a divine wonder. For the kingdoms of this world are not established through weakness, but through power as opposed to weakness. Wherefore there is an entire dissimilarity between the manner of planting God's kingdom, and that in which earthly kingdoms are planted. And on this ground alone might it be proved, that the church is the kingdom of God, because all other kingdoms in the world contend with this one, which is continually despised, accounted weak, and reckoned even as nothing, and yet they shall not prevail, but it shall itself prevail at last over all kingdoms, and convert them to itself through the mighty power of God."

TRAIN OF THOUGHT IN THE PARABLE.

The progressive development of Christianity.

1. It is small in its beginning.
2. Gradual in its progress.
3. Great and glorious in its termination.

1. The birth of the Son of Man in Bethlehem, is the small and unpromising commencement of the heavenly kingdom, which, in its manifestation, is identified with him. In the quiet of domestic privacy, the child increases; in his thirtieth year he comes forth into public, teaches three years, and then dies upon the cross, Matth. xiii. 54, 55. Fishermen and publicans, plain and unlettered men, are his first scholars and messengers, and they gathered themselves to him only by degrees, John i. 35—51; besides the twelve, the whole multitude of disciples amounted to but one hundred and twenty, (Acts i. 15.) So small at first was the company of our Lord's followers.

Small also is the beginning of the heavenly kingdom in the human heart; it begins by a word of truth reaching the conscience; a ray of light from above finds its way into the darkness of the inner man, and perhaps some trifling circumstance gives rise to consequences infinitely important. Draeseke, p. 231: "At the first there were *thoughts* of Jesus, which many times flashed upon us, clear thoughts, though still overshadowed with doubts. By degrees, however, the doubts became more rare and feeble; convictions on the other hand, built upon the foundation which has already been laid, find their way into our heart. At first there were *inclinations* to Jesus, which often stirred the heart, pious inclinations, but still intermingled with the love of sin. By degrees, however, we come to crucify the ungodly nature and the lusts of the flesh; attachment, strong and pure, such as he demands, found its way into the heart. At first there were *feelings* for Jesus, holy feelings, but still alternating with impatience, lust, passion, and a thousand interruptions. By degrees, however, the storm was allayed, a calmness, serene as the clear heaven, the offspring of a peace which is higher than all reason, found its way into our heart."

2. The progress, the further extension of the heavenly kingdom upon earth, is gradual. How it was carried on, we learn in the Acts of the Apostles, and in that interesting portion of church history which treats of the spread of Christianity. The mustard seed *groweth up, and becometh greater than all herbs, and shooteth out great branches*, (Mark v. 32.) The gospel spread on all sides from Jerusalem, and, like the increase of that tree, shooting up under the fructifying influences of heaven, so does the extension of the church (especially in the first centuries, and again also in more recent times; in the former of which it owed nothing, and in the latter little, to human power for its progress,) manifest itself as an effect of the power given to the exalted Son of Man, and of his blessed influence, since he accompanies the preached gospel with the gracious workings of his Spirit, and makes it powerful, withal proving here and there openings for the preaching of the gospel. The gradual increase of the church shows itself quite manifestly to be a work of divine grace, for the first preachers had no power or honour from the world. Sprung of a despised and hated people, they had no other means of working but the power of the word, and put to shame the vain, fleshly wisdom of the world, and stood up for one crucified, (1 Cor. i. 25—29,) and made no promise of earthly goods. The lively walk of the first Christians; their constancy under suffering; the blood of their martyrs; the dispersion of their harassed and persecuted members,—all tended to secure only a gradual and steady increase to the church.

It is only a gradual increase, also, that is experienced by the genuine Christian, in faith, in discernment, in love, in hope, in humility, and in all the Christian virtues in his heart. Amid many storms, both of external and of internal temptation, the new creature still grows, and the old more and more decays, (2 Cor. iii. 18.)

3. Great and glorious is the issue! Great—at last one flock, the earth full of the knowledge of the Lord, no people any more in darkness and the shadow of death, the unbelieving Israel converted, the vain idols with their altars and the service connected therewith, vanished away as completely as the gods of Greece and Rome. All this proceeding from the smallest beginning,—but still the time is not fulfilled, and the parable is consequently in that prophetical; on which account, the missionary cause rests its claim upon the Christian world, as a sacred obligation,—an obligation of love to the Saviour of the world, and the miserable beings that still live in sin, an obligation of gratitude for being permitted to enjoy the blessings of the gospel, an obligation of obedience to the clearly expressed will of our Lord, Matth. xxviii. 18—20; Luke xxiv. 47.

Glorious also is the issue; for temporal and eternal blessings flow in rich streams amongst the members of the Christian church; and hence the various peoples of the earth dwell under the shadow of the great tree of the church of Christ, and find rest to their souls under its branches, and imbibe the hope of eternal life; while others are continually coming to receive an interest in the same benefits. The Lord has awakened a desire after his salvation, though still unknown in the heathen world: the latest missionary reports still attest it. So that for this object, the church of Christ must ever strive and pray, "Thy kingdom come," that the parable before us may receive its fulfilment.

The appearance presented by a heart which wholly belongs to Christ, is in like manner great and glorious. What did not a John, a Paul become! And all from the small beginning that the word of God has been implanted in the heart.

The mustard seed is indeed not absolutely the very

smallest seed, but it is so when viewed in relation to the greatness of the plant which grows out of it. In the Jerusalem Talmud it is related; "It happened to a mustard plant at Sichem, which had three branches, that one of them was broken off; and that so large as to cover a potter's tent, and to yield three cabs of seed." Again: "I had in my garden a stalk of mustard, on which I climbed up as I used to do on a fig tree," (Canstein, Harmony of the Four Gospels.) Mustard seed is proverbially used as that to which any thing particularly small may be compared; so in Matth. xvii. 20, Luke xvii. 6. Luther's marginal note: "No word is more despised than the gospel, and yet there is none more powerful; for it makes those righteous who believe upon it; law and works cannot do so."

Vitringa, according to his custom, brings out several more points of comparison, as that the mustard seed has great strength, is healthful to the body, purifies the blood, and destroys what might hurt the body; so also says he, the heavenly kingdom! How is the *tertium comparationis*, with which alone we have to do, stretched here beyond the line of propriety, and contrary to sound taste!

V.

THE PIECE OF LEAVEN.

Matth. xiii. 33. Luke xiii. 20, 21.

The similarity of this parable to the preceding one is not to be mistaken; and yet the leading thought it contains is quite different. The blessed effects of the heavenly kingdom are, according to the preceding parable, first observable, when it has reached a distinguished greatness, then the birds come to lodge in the branches of the mustard tree. But in truth and reality, the efficacy of the word begins as soon as it is any where received. This efficacy concealed from the external eye, but not the less really existent, the Lord represents in the piece of leaven, which begins to work upon the dough the moment it is inserted there. The ideas common to both parables lie, 1. In the small quantity of leaven, therefore in the small beginning from which the effect proceeds. 2. In the gradual, silent, concealed development of the mustard seed and the leaven; 3. In the great result which is produced, the *whole batch* is leavened. But what is peculiar to this parable, lies in the circumstance, that the leaven, by means of its power, assimilates to itself the susceptible dough, imparts to this its own nature and taste, so that in nature and properties, the dough, when completely penetrated by the leaven, becomes another thing, quite different from what it formerly was. The main object of the parable then is, to represent the all-renewing power of Christianity, and that again in a two-fold respect, as it affects single individuals, and as it affects the whole of humanity.

Leaven is often used in the New Testament as a figurative expression for designating an efficient power whether in a good or in a bad sense. In Luke xii. 1, the hypocrisy of the pharisees is warned against as a pernicious leaven: in Gal. v. 9, leaven marks the hurtful effects of false doctrine; and in 1 Cor. v. 6, the corrupting power of bad example is compared to it. But in this parable leaven can only be used as an image of the holy power with which the word of God works, and it scarcely deserves to be mentioned, that Vitringa brings to remembrance the corruptions which have been in the Christian church, and says, that our Lord sought here to warn us of them beforehand. Gnomon: "I would refer this to the propagation, rather than to the corruption of the church." Luther, in his Exposition, says on this place: "Our Lord wishes to comfort us with this similitude, and give us to understand that, when the gospel, as a piece of new leaven, has once mixed itself with the human race, which is the dough, it will never cease till the end of the world, but will make its way through the whole mass of those who are to be saved, and come to all who are worthy of it, despite of all the gates of hell. And, just as it is impossible for the sourness, when it has once mingled itself with the dough, ever again to be separated from it, because it has changed the nature of the dough, so is it also impossible for Christians to be ever torn from Christ. For Christ, as a piece of leaven, is so incorporated with them, that they form with him one body, one mass."

The heavenly kingdom is like unto leaven, as touching the fellowship of men with Christ,—when any one comes to fellowship with him, it is with such a one exactly as with a piece of leaven, which extends its sourness to the whole dough; the whole man, and the whole of humanity, become, through this fellowship, entirely different, and the change is effected through the word of God, as the means whereby the Lord communicates to us the workings of his grace. Luther's gloss: "Leaven is also the word which renews men." Melanch.: "The kingdom of heaven is such, that in it the hearts of men are changed through the word."

TRAIN OF THOUGHT IN THE PARABLE.

The all-renewing power of Christianity.

It is represented:

1. As a renewing power—the leaven leavens;

2. As one all-renewing—the three measures of meal.

3. As one wholly renewing—until the whole was leavened.

The heavenly kingdom is the all-renewing power, the leaven. That it is so, and that nothing else can supply its place, experience teaches. Not art, nor science, nor religion in general, as faith merely in a higher state of being, no, nor even the divine law itself, is able to produce that reformation in man which is wrought by the leaven of the heavenly kingdom. This leaven is that which is more peculiarly divine in Christianity, its divine truth and power, its most spiritual parts, in particular those among its doctrines, of reconciliation through the death of Christ, and of the freer grace of God, which justifies the believing sinner. The form in which it is brought near to us, is the word, the doctrine; and this again comes to us by reason of our communion with the church. But the community of the church may be very ill-regulated as to life, practice, and constitution, and in principle it may possess little that is Christian, be deformed through the corrupt mixtures of superstition, or frittered away by the rash encroachments of unbelief. Nevertheless, the leaven itself is untouched, and must ever remain so; its divine powers cannot be weakened by the sinfulness of men, however much its free and native efficacy may thereby be hindered.

The object upon which the leaven works, is every part of the entire mass, and, consequently, this itself; the individual, and the whole of humanity, with whatsoever belongs to it. It is only when the dough has not already been leavened, that the leaven works; and it is only when the heart has not been fully saturated by the opposite nature and power of the kingdom of darkness with falsehood, error, malice, and hatred of the truth, that the divine leaven can effectually work upon it; such a total want of susceptibility for his word, our Lord ascribes to his hearers, in John viii. 37, ss.

The human heart is the immediate object upon which the power of Christianity works; it enlightens the understanding, purifies and ennobles the feelings, sanctifies the will; the earthly frame gives way to the heavenly, and the man lives no longer for the earth, but even now he lives in and for that life which is in heaven. "The divine power of the gospel," says Draeseke, "works in the human heart after a threefold manner, begetting knowledge of sin, feeling of guilt, longing desire for the Redeemer, who wipes out guilt and takes away sin. As the dough rises from the leaven, so from the divine power of the gospel there rise up in the breast of man thoughts, feelings and aspirations of a divine nature, of which he was before incapable." As every individual who has experienced in himself the efficacy of the gospel, becomes, for the circle in which he moves, a leaven to work still farther, so by degrees the divine power penetrates through the whole of humanity, and every thing connected with it partakes in the renewing change. In domestic life marriage is sanctified, and the education of children conducted in the fear of God; in civil life, equal rights are established, the female sex is rescued from servitude, slavery is abolished, legislation becomes mild, war itself is rendered humane; another spirit is infused into philosophy, science, art, every thing, in short, through the blessed influence of Christianity, which works as leaven, until the whole has been thoroughly leavened. The barbarians that were won to Christianity, at the great period of migration, and the history of the reformation, are proofs of what has now been declared.

And this power works *internally;* concealed from the outward eye it ferments within, and is often working with great power, when every thing, externally, appears still dead and unaltered; the new life proceeds from within toward what is without. The course of development, in the kingdom of grace, as of nature, is generally gradual; working with *a mild efficacy,* so that every thing hostile is subdued, if only it is permitted to have its course; *in various directions,* so that the progress of conversion in the heart is exceedingly varied, and cannot be reduced to determinate forms and methods,—*with a certain triumphant result,* which is unfailing, since the power in question will never cease to work till the whole has been leavened. Hence is it necessary to exercise patience and quiet waiting on the Lord; impatience or violent impetuosity, which would force the leavening process, is perverseness; and for one to think of generating the Christian life, the spiritual renovation, from without, is the height of absurdity.

The relation of the new creature to his former condition is still to be considered. The flour remains flour, only it is leavened; the peculiar temperament of individuals, the distinctive character of nations, is not annihilated by Christianity, but only purged of its sinful intermixture. Christianity does not aim at producing identity of thought, temper of mind, inclination, —not even at producing identity in the forms of life, of government, and constitution; but it does produce a community of saints, one faith, one love, one hope, the same humility and self-denial in all the members of the church, 1 Cor. xii. 4, ss. Acts ii. 42—47; iv. 32—35. What similarity and yet what difference in the apostles! Draeseke: "As the leavened dough still remains dough, but receives from the leaven another spirit, fragrance, and taste, so the man still remains man; but he has become a man of another kind, through the divine power of the gospel. He is no longer the old, natural, fleshly man, sold under sin. He is a new, spiritual, divine man, whose element is the liberty of the children of God."

In figure, this similitude teaches the doctrine of the new birth, John iii., and also, that, in the heavenly kingdom, regard is had, primarily, not to a *doing*, but to a state of *being*, Eph. iv. 22; Gal. vi. 15; 2 Cor. v. 17; and, indeed, to a *new state of being*. Eylert, p. 20, ss. "The divine power of Christ's gospel, though still and noiseless in its workings, does yet penetrate the whole of man. The religion which we derive from Jesus is the most efficacious means of ennobling us, of making us useful and happy;—but it must enter into our inmost souls, must take possession of our whole being,—the righteous direction and strenuous application of our powers, is the great, the indispensable condition, which draws along with it the improving, renovating power of religion; yet still what we do receive from the religion of Jesus, must be reckoned according to the powers we possess, and exactly proportioned to our susceptibility;—every individual is penetrated and ennobled by the religion of Jesus in a separate, peculiar manner, differing, in a thousand ways, from that in which others are affected; but whatever varieties may exist, in this all agree, that the power of the religion of Jesus dwells in the heart, and manifests itself without pomp, with true humanity, in a course of upright and virtuous action.

VI.

THE TREASURE.

Matth. xiii. 44.

After our Lord had withdrawn himself from the people, was come home, and had given to his disciples the desired explanation of the parable of the tares, he went on to deliver this and the three following parables.

In order to excite the imaginations, and to raise in the still carnal hearts of his own disciples a thirsting desire after better things, our Lord makes use of the image of the treasure and the costly pearl, to set forth the incomparable worth of the heavenly kingdom and its glory.

TRAIN OF THOUGHT IN THE PARABLE.

The internal glory of the heavenly kingdom.

1. It is at first concealed from us,—a treasure in the field;

2. It is discovered to us by grace,—which a man found;

3. Manifests itself to be mighty by its influence,—the finder hides his treasure; is full of joy at his good fortune, and gives all for it.

1. The heavenly kingdom is again, as in the pre-

ceding similitude, the internal divine nature and living power of Christianity, with all its revelations, instructions, consolations, its light and blessings,—a glorious treasure; *hidden* in the field, under a covering of unpromising appearance, where one does not perceive it; nay, where one never suspects that so costly a treasure is concealed; and this field is not the world generally, in which, beyond doubt, the treasure has existed since the appearance of Christ; but only that portion of the world of humanity, where Christianity exists as an actual establishment, that is, the visible church. This visible church, as the covering of the divine, as the shell of the precious kernel, is at present existing in such a form and constitution, that one can scarcely discern the efficacious, divine powers, which belong to it; at least the dull, unenlightened eye cannot, in the often very imperfect forms, and the human institutions under which the divine is veiled, clearly discern this according to its true nature and worth. Besides, from our youth we have been walking upon this field, and are so much accustomed to certain influences of Christianity,—so familiar with its doctrines from our ever-recurring opportunities of hearing the word, have so near and ready an access to the institutions of our Lord, that the glory of the divine in Christianity is apt to be concealed from us. The heavenly kingdom is a hidden treasure, presenting itself to us under a covering that serves to conceal it; for its costly blessings are wrapped up in the word and lie infolded in the sacraments.

2. The treasure *is found*. This does not exactly presuppose a *seeking*, though, properly, all acting and striving, on the part of man, is a seeking after a treasure, after well-being, repose, peace; as it is written in Isa. lxv. 1, "I was found of them that sought me not; I was made manifest to them that asked not after me." The Lord pours out streams upon the dry ground, (where there is no longing,) as well as upon the thirsty ground, (where there is a longing;) of

which we have an example in the case of the Samaritans, John iv. The finding is an unexpected good, without any desert and worthiness on our part, but happens according to the gracious purpose of him "who wills that all men should be saved." God manifests to the heart his secret, and the powers of the world to come; where human perversity would never have looked for deliverance from all its wants and necessities, there it finds this, and to the end of leading us there, all the occurrences, joys and sorrows of life, are directed. Gnomon: "Here is at once the application and the prudence of the saints; they find out those things which are hid, and hide those which they have found, Prov. vii. 1." Luther, in his Exposition on Matth.: "We find this treasure without merit, as if it came by accident into our hands; and yet it remains hidden from the ungodly, although it is manifested and declared to them by words and deeds, by the cross and miracles, 2 Cor. iv. 3, 4. He that has it alone knows it; whosoever has it not, he can never know it."

3. The glory of the discovered treasure is represented by the conduct and feelings of him who finds the heavenly kingdom. Both of these were left to himself, they were not demanded of him, but are rather the certain, the necessary consequence of his apprehending the glory of the good he has found; he cannot feel and act otherwise than he does; the discovery of the treasure of itself brings this along with it. Hence the conduct which the finder is here said to have pursued, in order to secure his possession of the treasure, must not be represented, in the general, as a demand or required condition; it helps people, at first, to get the treasure, when they come to know, or at least to suspect, the glory of Christianity as suited to all the wants and trials of life; after that all follows as a matter of course.

He hid it; the hidden treasure has been discovered, and the discovered treasure is hid; so one acts with every jewel. It indicates the *carefulness* springing from a sense of its glory, to preserve, to make sure of it. Divine grace is kept in the heart, Matth. vii. 6; and, when received there, we are silent,—we speak of it only to our most confidential friends; a spirit of levity, raillery, or worldliness, would only soil or plunder the jewel.

Went away for joy; how natural! He has every thing, for he has Christ, righteousness, life, blessing.

Sold every thing that he had. The choice is not difficult; the highest good is possessed; so the mariner in a tempestuous sea readily parts with all, that he may save his life. Whatever there may have been of sacrifice before, there is now no more; self-denial is no longer painful and difficult; it is joy and bliss; what no external violence could have torn from the heart, the love of the world, fleshly wisdom, self-righteousness,—all is abandoned, Phil. iii. 4—11; Luke x. 42; Acts v. 40, 41. Calvin: "He speaks thus, that the faithful may learn to prefer the kingdom of heaven to the whole world, and therefore renounce both themselves and all the desires of the flesh. And we are taught, that the riches of divine grace are not to be estimated according to fleshly sense, or their own external splendour. They only are fit to apprehend the grace of the gospel, who, postponing every other object, apply themselves with all zeal to obtain possession of that. Therefore Christ exhorts his people to the renouncement only of those things which are contrary to piety, meanwhile permitting them to use and enjoy the temporal gifts of God, as if they did not use them." Grotius: "He tells us, that the too great desire of glory, riches, and pleasure, must be laid aside, and, if called to it, that all we have, even to life itself, must be given up, that we may find the word beneficial, not for any brief season merely, but may persevere in obedience to it, even to the end."

And bought the field; now the outward, visible church, is first seen in its true worth by the enlightened and blessed heart, because he has found in it the most precious jewel, and continues to preserve it.

Vitringa and others explain the finding or discovery of the treasure by the shining forth again of gospel truth, before the reformation, among the Waldenses,—a most constrained exposition. It is also very forced to say, that this parable must teach that the gospel is for mean, unpolished, and rude men, while the next one teaches, that the same gospel is equally suited for the polished and refined; which was Scholten's opinion.

VII.

THE PEARL OF GREAT PRICE.

Matt. xiii. 45, 46.

The world is like a great market, where every one can find what he desires; the greater part strive after those goods which gratify the eye; but all cannot succeed in obtaining these; neither are they necessary for life, nay, they cheat and beguile many, and hinder them from seeking the invisible, eternal, real goods, in getting which none may be disappointed. But those often, who have temporal goods in abundance, are first enlightened as to the defective and unsatisfactory nature of these, and led to seek after the better, the really good possessions, when they have come to experience the truth of Solomon's declaration, that all on earth is vanity. So the merchant-man, who seeks goodly pearls; he represents the heart, which is concerned and careful for its true, everlasting salvation. (Simeon, Luke ii. Nathaniel, John i. 45,) but unconscious where it shall find satisfaction to its desire, whether in knowledge, science, and accomplishments. Then while searching he finds *one pearl of great price*, (for God leaves no necessity of his heart unsatisfied.) Because he has sought good, he is favoured to receive the best, and while he has a seeking heart, he instantly perceives that this pearl includes in itself every thing after which he longs, and even more; for its worth is incomparable. Grotius: "The Gospel has shone upon some, who were giving themselves no thought about God, or a new life, or the hope of a blessed eternity, of which kind were most in the Gentile nations, to whom Paul applies that prediction: *I was found of them that sought me not.* There were some also among the Jews and elsewhere, studious of wisdom, who were touched with a certain desire of knowing the truth, who anxiously looked for some prophet or the Messiah himself. The similitude of the treasure respects *the former*, that of the pearl *the latter*." Calvin: "By making merchandise, Christ does not mean, that any compensation is offered by men, whereby they may secure for themselves eternal life; for we know on what terms the Lord invites his people to come to him, Isa. lv. 1. But although the gift of God, eternal life, is bestowed gratuitously, with whatsoever pertains to it, we are yet told to purchase it, since we can voluntarily deprive ourselves of fleshly gratifications, that we may not be hindered in our search after it, Phil. iii. 8."

TRAIN OF THOUGHT IN THE PARABLE.

The incomparable worth of the heavenly kingdom. This is made manifest:

1. From the existence of wants, which no other good could satisfy,—who sought *good* pearls.

2. From the perfect satisfaction afforded by this one good; (1.)—There is but *one* pearl of great price. (2.)—For this he parts with all.

Eylert, p. 48, ss.: "Jesus here shows us the true point of view, from which we must consider Christianity, if ever its holy design shall be accomplished in us. It must be to us a thing of the greatest importance; whence we must apply ourselves above all things to become fully acquainted with it, to know it always more and more thoroughly; and this knowledge, this conviction, will be a thing sought after, will be obtained with labour, application, and perseverance;—the cheering consideration of the glorious and happy result, must strengthen our powers for the work; the sure and well-grounded expectation, that we shall be successful, and not fail to obtain a rich inheritance, cannot but lighten to us every burden, and inspire us with steadfastness;—we must sacrifice all, surrender all, that is incompatible with a Christian frame, Phil. iii. 7—9."

To explain the properties of the pearl, its whiteness, purity, splendour, roundness, size of the heavenly kingdom, were to trifle, and contrary, besides, to the design of the similitude. It is an erroneous exposition, in which the merchant is understood to signify the church, and the pearl Christ. Vitringa introduces much that is improper into his explanation, which serves rather to confuse than to illustrate it.

VIII.

THE FISHING NET.

Matt. xiii. 47—50.

This is a delightful, instructive, direct similitude; for some of the twelve were fishermen, and called to be fishers of men, Luke v. The Lord compares the gathering or calling of men to the heavenly kingdom, with the whole of their business, and not merely with their net; in the one service and the other, there were similar employments and appearances,—a gathering, a mixture, and a separation. Calvin: "The end of the parable is, that he might keep his disciples in fear and humility, lest they should please themselves with the empty title of faith, or with a naked profession, 2 Tim. ii. 19." Luther, in his Exposition on Mathew: "The proper aim and impression of this similitude lies in the last words, that, at the last judgment, the wicked are to be separated from the righteous. It cannot but sustain the hope of believers, that though they are necessitated in this life to bear with the wicked, who are mixed among them, yet they have the firmest assurance that then the wicked shall be finally separated from them."

As this parable is the last of the seven, which here respect the kingdom of heaven, and the Lord has in successive delineations represented the origin, nature, progress, and glory of that kingdom, so it appears, as its position might lead us to suppose, that in this similitude the subject of discourse mainly respects the final completion of the kingdom which is to be ushered in with a general judgment. Hence the gathering together of the church retires more into the background, and the final separation stands forth as the chief and prominent object.

TRAIN OF THOUGHT IN THE PARABLE.

The final separation that is to be made in the Christian Church.

I. It is to take place in regard to all the members of the church.

(1) Who are these members?—All who have been gathered to Christ from the world, (the sea,) by the word, (the net,) v. 47.

(2) Why in regard to all?—Because they are different (which gathered of *every kind*, v. 47.)

II. When it is to take place.

(1) When the gathering of the members is finished.—But when it was full, v. 48.

(2) On the day when all things shall be manifested—they drew to shore, v. 48.

III. The manner it is to be done.

(1.) It shall be exact—*all* the good, and *all* the bad shall be severed from each other, v. 48.

(2) It shall be decisive, v. 50.

Ver. 47. *A net*, a drag-net, which draws every

thing along with it; *the sea*, the new dispensation of grace is not like the old, set up only for one people, but for the race of mankind in its universality. "With the Israelites the theocracy resembled a net which was drawn through a stream, and gathered fish only of that one stream." (Menken, Reflections upon the Gospel of Matthew.) As fish even in the sea are not secure from men, so the grace of God has a thousand means and ways to work upon the hearts of men; and the preaching of the word, of Christ crucified, is pre-eminently that by which the company of believers is gathered.

Of all sorts, according to v. 48, however, only of all sorts of fishes; no one must be excluded through human caprice, or deemed incapable of the heavenly kingdom; wise and unwise, learned and unlearned, old and young, men and women, bond and free, master and servant,—and these one and all without exception or distinction, sinners,—these are the persons of all sorts to whom the word of God, and the invitation to the heavenly kingdom, must be brought. Acts x. 38, 39.

Ver. 48. *But when it was full, they drew it out upon the shore.* The gathering is made through the agency of men, and during the course of time; both shall be continued until the entire number of those, whose names God has written in his book, have been received into the church, to be there sanctified and saved by his grace. But all who are enclosed in the great net of the church, do not employ this communion with the church as they might and should do; hence a separation is necessary, and shall also one time be effected according to God's righteous judgment. So that there is found also in this parable, as in that of the tares and many others, the doctrine of a mixture and separation among the members of the heavenly kingdom. Calvin: "The preaching of the gospel is well compared to a net immersed in the waters, that we may know the present state of the church to be confused."

The bad, dead fish,—men who have never come to spiritual life, or in whom it has again died.

Ver. 49. *At the end of the world*, after the lapse of the present periods of the world, which are certainly fixed, but the continuance of which is unknown to men; so long as they exist, the present constitution of the Church is to stand.

The angels shall go forth, appointed thereto, ordered and capacitated by their Lord, the king of the heavenly kingdom, Matth. xiii. 41. "The separation," says Menken, "is strictly a divine and heavenly thing; an independent, positive act, a free operation of righteousness and love on the part of the Lord himself. Hence we are not to say they shall one day separate; we must say, they shall one day be separated. Scripture teaches that angels have a participation in the events of the heavenly kingdom upon earth; but they must stand back and hold themselves still; no immediate agency is either permitted or required of them for its advancement. As, however, at the first commencement of the kingdom of God upon earth, they had a much greater hand in the transactions belonging to it, (Luke i. ii.; Matth. i. ii. iv. 11; Acts xii. 1, ss.,) so shall they serve the interests of this kingdom in a far greater measure, and on a more extended scale, at the period of its completion. But their service then shall not be that loving service of protection, help and deliverance, but rather that dreadful service of resistless power in the removal and casting away of the unreclaimable and hopelessly wicked; so that it does not properly refer to the impious and wicked. 2 Thess. i. 4—10." As the separation is not made till the wicked have been long patiently borne with, and all means of improvement have failed, its execution will be a matter of the strictest punitive righteousness.

IX.

THE HOUSEHOLDER.

Matth. xiii. 53.

This similitude does not belong to those which open up and explain the nature of the kingdom of heaven. After our Lord had asked his disciples whether they understood what had been delivered by him, and had received for answer, "Yea, Lord," he concludes his whole discourse with this little parable, in which he gives them a direction how they must conduct themselves as teachers in the heavenly kingdom. For a teacher who would proclaim with effect the divine truth of the kingdom of God, must act precisely as a householder. Gnomon: "Jesus speaks concerning the disciples, and what was said at v. 12, in plain words, *that,* now that the disciples had advanced a little, (whence they are called scribes) is confirmed to them by a parable." Luther's exposition; "He concludes with a riddle, or dark saying, which seems strange enough. His meaning is, because ye know every thing, ye are fit for your future office. Whosoever would be an apostle, he must know every thing, just as ye do. He must be like a rich householder, who will have his house full of all goods, that he may be able to serve up, both what he himself wants, and what others want. But the treasure, or rich supply of knowledge, is nothing else than the knowledge of the law and gospel. For in these two the whole wisdom of God is enclosed, and comprised as in a brief extract."

TRAIN OF THOUGHT IN THE PARABLE.

The well-furnished teacher of the heavenly kingdom.

I. His fitness consists in this:

(1.) That he is instructed for the kingdom, has the treasure of divine truth;

(2.) And that this treasure is his property.

II. His activity is represented;

(1.) Wherein it consists—he distributes his treasure;

(2.) How it is exercised—in wisdom; for he gives old, and new, in wholesome and agreeable alternation.

Instructed unto the kingdom of heaven. Luther's note: "He who promotes the kingdom of heaven, teaches others, and brings them to heaven. *New*, the gospel; *old*, the law."

His treasure, that, which through experience has become his. See on the Parable of the Sower, p. 56.

New and *old;* the new, the gospel, as the fulfilment of the promise given in the old; *the message of grace* as opposed to the old *law*. But it was necessary that the old also should be given; for they serve mutually to confirm each other, and so conduce, when viewed together, to make us welcome the change, to awaken attention, to exercise and engage reflection. Moreover, the one eternal, unchangeable, truth of God's love and righteousness, although in itself an old thing, will be announced in a more fresh and agreeable form where the truth itself is in the heart, and has gained possession of the life. Sameness is poverty. Jesus exhibited a pattern for imitation in the very delivery of this parable. Draeseke: "The *old*, in the parables already delivered, has been *nature*. What was known, was thereby more clearly manifested to them; though the images were such as the disciples had seen a thousand times. Now, for the first time, they were taught to connect new thoughts with the old images, and acquired a new advantage from reviving old impressions. And thus the disciples learned, like their master, to look upon nature, and make account both of small and great things; so that the old book imparted to them new wisdom. Like their master, the disciples learned to respect *history*, and judge of experience; therefore the old book here also imparted to them new wisdom. But above all the disciples learned, like their master, to read *scripture*, and understand the law and the prophets in their reference to the kingdom of heaven; therefore again the old book imparted to them new wisdom." Grotius: "The apostles are admonished, that, after the example of Christ, they should endeavour to give a zest to the doctrines of grace, by varying the manner of teaching them." Hess, Bibl. Hist. B. xiii. p. 494: "This last remark is, beyond doubt, designed to show the disciples that, as future teachers, they must not only make use of those images and forms of representation which they had heard from him, but must always study so to address themselves to hearers of unlike capacities and varied conditions, as to connect what is well known with something that may give it the grace of novelty, and skilfully to alter where uniformity would be tiresome." Calvin: "Now the Lord admonishes them, that he had not expended so much labour in teaching them, to make them wise only for themselves, but that they might impart to others what had been communicated to them. And in this manner he stirred them up to more zeal and diligence in learning."

X.

THE UNMERCIFUL SERVANT.

Matth. xviii. 23—35.

The Lord had spoken, v. 15—17, of the brotherly chastisement or correction of those from whom we have received some injury; and as he had done this in a quite general manner, without any qualifying limitation, it appeared necessary to the lively, and indeed fiery Peter, to have some limit set to this mild and placable disposition; for the natural heart, which is still ungoverned by the Spirit of God, feels itself wronged by such a command in its secret desire of revenge, and apprehends it would suffer loss by complying therewith. Self-love also continually fears lest it should go too far, and give too much. On which account Peter came to Jesus, and asked him, vi. 21: "Lord, how oft shall my brother sin against me, and I forgive him? till seven times?" (*i. e.* is seven times enough?) Besides the internal grounds which existed for this question, there may also have been some outward occasion giving rise to it. It may possibly have been a question among Jewish teachers so early as the time of Christ, how often one should forgive his neighbour, which, at a later period, was thus resolved in the Talmud. "If a man commits an offence, he is to be forgiven for the first time; the second and third time he is also to be forgiven; but, if he sins a fourth time, he is not to be forgiven, according to Amos i. 3; ii. 6. Job xxxiii. 29, 30. (Margin.") Now, in extending the forgiveness to seven times, Peter might believe that he did something extraordinary, and sufficiently answered all just demands. But, instead of receiving from Jesus the expected approving answer, that seven times was enough, and that the culprit had no reason to look for any further indulgence, Jesus answered him, v. 22: "I say not unto thee, until seven times; but until seventy times seven." The determinate number stands for the indeterminate, as in Gen. iv. 24; and the meaning is, that we must never, at any time, cease to forgive. Olshausen: "The condition of Peter prevented him from understanding aright the foundation principle of forgiveness, (which is necessarily presupposed in the whole preceding context, about the manner of behaving towards offending brethren;) misapprehending the nature of true love, which can never do any thing but love, he thinks of having a certain measure of forgiveness, conceiving, as natural men must always do, that an unlimited forgiveness must be an impossibility. Here, therefore, the Redeemer sets forth to Peter, by means of a parable, the grounds, on account of which the member of a heavenly kingdom must be continually ready to forgive, because he himself found admission into it only through forgiveness. This must be to all, even to those who view every thing in a legal point of view, a determinate motive for exercising forgiveness; for in that there is only expressed the law of recompense. Whilst, therefore, the question of Peter appears to pre-suppose a right, according to which he might continue, or cease at pleasure, to dispense forgiveness, the Redeemer declares, that such a law does not exist; he who has himself forfeited all has nothing to demand." Luther, in his House-Postills, V. 230: "Forgiveness of offences must have no measure or bounds among Christians; we must always forgive one another, and beware of exercising revenge; this belongs only to God, whose sovereign power and majesty must not be encroached upon."

The answer given, in v. 22, is embodied in the following parable, (which is consequently introduced with *therefore*,) where we have set forth the motives to brotherly conciliation and forgiveness. Calvin: "Because it is difficult to move us to pity, especially when our brethren have many faults to be borne with, our Lord confirms this doctrine by a most appropriate parable, the sum of which is, that those who inflexibly refuse to pardon the offences of their brethren, consult very ill for themselves, and set up a law too harsh and severe, because they will find God equally rigid and inexorable toward themselves. The similitude consists chiefly in three members: for the Lord is opposed to the servant, a large sum to a comparatively small one, singular clemency to extreme cruelty." Scholten, p. 294: "In expounding the parables we must take care not to offend against the analogy of faith or doctrine, which is unfolded in Scripture and discernible by faith. Whence those interpreters are much to be blamed, who, because in such and such a parable they do not find a doctrine, which they conceive to be closely connected with Christ's chief design in propounding the parable, although this doctrine may be taught in other parts of Scripture, forthwith conclude that it is no where else to be found in Scripture, nay, that it does not belong to the true doctrine of the gospel. Yet, in this way it is, that because, in the parable of the prodigal son, no mention is made of an expiation given to the father, but, on the contrary, his guilty son, with a confident mind, and without the intercession of any other, approaches to his father, simply declaring his true repentance and unfeigned desire to return to a better life, therefore Teller concludes that the doctrine of our redemption, through the intervention of Christ's sufferings and death, must not be reckoned among those things which the Saviour properly taught, but rather to those in which he and his apostles wisely accommodated themselves to the prejudices of the Jews. The very same might be gathered from the parable before us;—for there the Lord remits the debts of his servant without any expiation or intercession from another, who might pay in his behalf; he does it, indeed, upon the bare promise of the servant, that he would endeavour, by and by, to pay all. Nor is there any thing in what the Saviour adds, v. 35, which necessarily implies the doctrine of expiation. But it was not the design of Christ to unfold the doctrine of redemption in this parable; he only wished by it to lead his disciples to cultivate a disposition ready to pardon any injuries and affronts they might receive, on the ground that God, though infinitely gracious, will grant forgiveness only to those who follow his benign example."

TRAIN OF THOUGHT IN THE PARABLE.

Motives to brotherly forgiveness.

I. The great goodness of the Lord toward his servant, v. 23—37; which is exhibited:

(1.) In the greatness of the debt, v. 24;

(2.) In the steward's inability to pay, v. 25.

(3.) Through the severe but deserved punishment adjudged to him, v. 25.

(4.) Through withdrawment of the punishment, and the debt, v. 26, 27.

II. The small debt of our neighbour to us, v. 28—30; concerning which we are to consider,

(1.) The smallness of the debt itself, v. 28.

(2.) Its being the debt of the fellow-servant, v. 28;

(3.) His begging for patience, v. 29;

(4.) And his promise of repayment, v. 29.

III. The sorrow and vexation which we raise in our fellow-men, whose esteem and love we forfeit when guilty of harshness, v. 30, 31.

IV. The severe judgment of God upon the unmerciful, v. 32—35; whereon we must remark:

(1.) The remembrance made of the free goodness of the Lord, v. 32;

(2.) The representation given of the abuse of it, v. 33;

(3.) The just and eternal condemnation, v. 34;

(4.) The application to the hearers, v. 35.

V. 23. *The kingdom of heaven is like.* Luther, as above, p. 231: "Such a command to forgive sins we must not carry into the world, as persons and offices are there dissimilar, on which account one always has power and authority over another. There evil must not be connived at, nor must any one be permitted to do what he pleases; but evil must be punished, and people enforced to do what is proper, just, and honourable. Masters and mistresses must punish their servants, worldly governments their subjects, parents their children. But in the Christian church here upon earth,—save when you hold a special office, to which God commits the chastisement of iniquity,—one must always forgive another, and show all compassion and tenderness to his neighbour, where it is necessary, although he may have deserved very differently of us, and we may have had good cause, as the world goes, to inflict upon him all evil." Melanch.: "The ministry of the remission of sins is one thing, private pardoning another. The ministry discourses of God's will, private pardoning bespeaks thy will towards another; namely, that thou dost remit his offence and not demand satisfaction; dost even, with true affection, receive him again to thy confidence for the sake of God. The pious are carefully to be admonished that there is a great difference between self-defence and private revenge, that they may restrain themselves within the bounds fixed by the gospel. *Self-defence*, is to preserve our reputation, life and property, in a just and orderly manner, without any desire thereby to injure another. *Vindictiveness*, is desire to do injury in an irritated mind."

Like a king; just as Christ, in his dispensation of grace, grants forgiveness to sinners, so must these grant it to each other.

Servants; the reckoning, which the king demands is grounded on a relation of dependence; and so, one relation to God is, that of servants to a lord, to whom we are responsible for every thing he has given us, for life, time, powers of body and of soul, opportunities of action, and the word of his grace.

Take account; Luther, Church-Postills, 14. p. 241: "When God takes account, he makes the preaching to proceed out of his law, whereby we come to know what we are guilty of." Such a reckoning is made in serious self-examination, while hearing the word, and in the transactions of life, which make us acquainted with ourselves.

V. 24. *Began to reckon.* As soon as the conscience has been rightly touched by the law, it begins to know its guilt. Luther, House-Postills, 5. p. 251: "Until the king begins to reckon with him, he has no conscience, he is not sensible of guilt, and should always have continued so, contracting more and more guilt, and inquiring nothing about it. So the greater part of men think nothing about sin, go on securely in it, fear not God's wrath; and, even when they confess sin with the mouth, presently go away and make a jest of it."

One was brought unto him; the one is any one, for we have all manifold short-comings. Gnomon: "Every body ought to reckon himself that *one;* comp.

v. 35; xx. 12, 13. For the condition of all is alike." To understand it of the papacy is absurd.

Who owed him ten thousand talents; a terrible sum; for a talent is about a thousand dollars; these are the sins of omission and commission, internal and external sins, in thoughts, desires, words, and actions, Ps. xix. 13. Melanch.: "So large a sum is named to teach us that we have very many aggravated sins before God. If you examine your life, you will readily find that they are many, and great as well as many—that your carnal security is great, your negligence in your calling great, your distrust and doubtings concerning God great. There are also numberless wanderings of desire."

V. 25. *But for as much as he had not to pay;* both are clear, the greatness of the guilt and our incapacity to make amends, to restore.

His Lord commanded him to be sold, &c. Gnomon: "εκελευσεν, the right is shown; however, the Lord does not use his own right, but the servant abuses every right he possesses." Luther, Church-Postills, 14. p. 241: "This is the judgment, which follows as soon as the law manifests sin; for God has not given his law that he might leave those unpunished who do not keep it; it is not pleasant, nor friendly, but brings along with it a violent and painful struggle, and gives us to the devil, throws us into hell, and leaves us in the bonds of punishment; consequently insists upon our paying the very last farthing." God manifests himself in his law through demands and threatenings, pre-eminently as a holy and righteous God. The conduct of the king, as also of the believer, toward his guilty servant, is grounded in Israelitish custom, Lev. xxv. 39; 2 Kings iv. 1. Although very hard, it is still not unrighteous. Gnomon: "His private possessions, which, indeed, belonged to his lord." Scholten: "From the circumstance of the king's commanding not only the steward, his debtor, but also his wife and children, to be sold, some might be disposed to gather, that God intends wives to suffer for the delinquencies of their husbands, children for their parents; which there is no need that we should prove to be contrary to the analogy of faith, and abhorrent to the nature of a most righteous God; and how absurd it would be to determine any thing of that sort, is manifest from hence, that to the wife and children are joined all things that he had," from which it is obvious that the wife and children are here, after the manner of the Orientals, considered as a part of private property, from which, however, it would be utterly absurd for any one to conclude, that the wife and children are to suffer for the debts of a husband and father; whereas the selling of the steward and of all his property, to which, according to eastern fashion, pertained also the wife and children, ought to be considered as the punishment inflicted upon the steward alone."

Ver. 26. *The servant then fell down, and besought him, saying, Lord, have patienee with me, and I will pay thee all.* Gnomon: "Do not deal hastily with me; the feeling of a contrite mind is shown." Luther, House-Postills, 5. 251: "We feel the earnest of God also in our hearts, when our sins are manifested there; when the catalogue of our iniquities is held up before us, then mirth forsakes us. We are forced to exclaim, 'O miserable man that I am; there is none on earth more wretched than I am.' Such knowledge makes a man truly humble, paves the way for coming to obtain the real forgiveness of sin. And where such humility does not exist, there also no forgiveness is experienced." House-Postills, 14. 242: "This has St. Paul rightly expounded in his Epistle to the Romans, iv. 15: The law only worketh wrath; that is, when it manifested to us that we have acted sinfully, brings nothing home to us but wrath and indignation, and causes us to despair.'

I will pay all; Luther, Church-Postills, 14. 241: "The fool thinks that he can still pay, and begs only for patience. This is the plague of all consciences, when sin comes and bites, giving men to feel that they are, on account of it, in an ill case toward God, then have they no rest, but run up and down, seek help here and there, that they may get free from their sins, and still keep promising to themselves that they will yet do much to pay God." House-Postills, 5. 134: "Christ by these words of the servant wishes to show that we (under a sense of the greatness of our sins, when we seek for grace) cannot comprehend such grace, it is so rich and exuberant. We presently think it is too much, God will not be so gracious as to forgive us all; he must also have some payment; it cannot be that we shall get a full and frank forgiveness of all." Humility, conviction of guilt, desires for grace, and resolutions of amendment, deserve not, indeed, the forgiveness of sin; but belong to that scheme of God, in which God dispenses pardon to the sinner.

Ver. 27. *Then the lord of that servant was moved with compassion*, Ps. li. 19. Luther, House-Postills, 5. 234: "This is the true and proper colour wherein most characteristically to represent God and our own heart; whoever would give to him another colour, would depict him in an unjust light, and otherwise than he is in himself. He is a gracious God, and has a fatherly heart; Ez. xxxiii. 10, 11." The conduct of the lord at the first, as rigid and strictly adhering to the law, should serve, therefore, merely to manifest to the heart its guilt, to break and humble it, that to the contrite penitent, and believing (for the prayer of the servant springs from his confidence in the patience and goodness of his lord) there may be granted forgiveness. "As for the means," says Luther as above, "through which God will be gracious toward us, the gospel informs us in other places, when it declares that our blessed Lord Jesus Christ has undertaken for sinners, and by his own death paid the debt of their guilt. Wherever there is such confidence in the Lord

Jesus Christ and his death, there all desire on the part of God to be angry or to inflict punishment, has ceased." Melanch.: "He does not remit on account of our merits, but in infinite mercy for his Son's sake. In him there is such a worth as to exceed our sins. Do not think that your sins are greater and more mighty than the Son of God."

And loosed him, and forgave him the debt; he does more than we ask; glorious reward of confidence in the Lord's goodness! At the first he brings up the deserved judgment or suffering; then he discharges the debt itself, declares him free. Gnomon: "He had sought one benefit, he obtained two." Melanch.: "Our sins are many and great, but grace superabounds, Rom. v. These sins, though so many and so great, God constantly wishes to remit to us. Let faith be here put in exercise, that we may indeed believe this. And in this faith let us approach to God, adoring him with fervent supplication, and giving thanks to his name." Luther, House-Postills, 5. 252: "True Christians, while they feel their sins, have the consolation of believing that their sins are forgiven, and what they believe they obtain in the kingdom of grace. And this kingdom takes its beginning with us in baptism, and increases continually to the end. For to this end are the preaching of the gospel, baptism, absolution, and the supper all directed, that we might have our faith in the forgiveness of sin more and more strengthened; for God has laid up the treasure, forgiveness of sin, in his word and sacraments, and commanded us to believe it." The behaviour of the king is pure *grace,* Eph. ii. 8, 9. Rom. iii. 24.

"The other part now follows, as the fellow-servant must also be brought in; faith is such a possession, that for its sake we might die every hour; for if we believe, we have a gracious God; but if thou must be continued still longer in life, thou must have something to do and act, and that, says Christ, must all be directed upon thy neighbour." Luther, Church-Pos. 14. 246.

Ver. 28. *But the same servant went out:* Gnomon: "Set free from his difficulties. Before the reckoning with his Lord, he treated his fellow-servant more gently. A danger of sinning attends the very joy of restored liberty, health, etc. John v. 14, 2 Kings xx. 13." Luther as above: "How does he go out? Where has he been within? In faith he had entered in, but now he goes out through love; for faith leads people as away from people up to God; (pardon of sin is appropriated by faith in the secret chambers of the heart;) love leads them out again to the people, (pardon truly received must manifest itself in love.")

And found one of his fellow-servants, his equal, towards whom he had not the smallest right to behave as he did; but he overlooks the relation in which he stood to his fellow-servant; this circumstance, therefore, aggravates the harshness and iniquity of his conduct.

Who owed him a hundred pence, denarii, a small debt; which should certainly have been felt as giving additional force to the obligation under which he lay, to mild forbearance and brotherly forgiveness. *And he laid hands on him, and took him by the throat,* which sets before us his passionate violence and hardness of heart. The vehemence of his demand betrays a mind dead to all delicate feelings; he enforces his threatenings through unheard of cruelties.

Ver. 29. A powerful and graphic description. In the same posture, and with the same words, he entreats his fellow-servant, as the latter had just employed toward his gracious Lord. It should have reminded him of the favour he had received, and determined him to exercise the like beneficence. This fellow-servant also promises compensation, in token of his heartfelt repentance, a thing too not impossible in regard to so small a debt.

Ver. 30. "The more this wicked servant is entreated, the more severe and harsh he becomes. This is the common course of the world; when sin is forgiven, one soon forgets the pardoning grace of God, and becomes more arrogant and hard-hearted than before." Luther, House-Pos. 5. 254.—*And cast him into prison,* into the debtor's ward; this right the believer had. He will, therefore, know nothing of remission, stands upon his right, and will act according to rigid justice.

Ver. 31. Luther, House-Pos. 5. 238: "Such a monstrous disregard of equity and compassion cannot remain secret; other Christians will see it and concern themselves about it. And as the intercessions of the pious are not useless and in vain, so neither is the common malediction, the general outcry against the wicked, useless and in vain." The unmerciful forfeits the respect and love of his fellow-men. Calvin: "We must know that there will be so many witnesses against us before God, as there are men now living with us; for it cannot be but that cruelty shall be displeasing and odious to them, especially when every one fears for himself, lest the severity he sees exercised upon another, may alight upon his own head."

Ver. 32. *Then his Lord called him,* this shall be done at the last day.

Thou wicked servant. Gnomon: "He had not been called this on account of his debt. Wo to him whom the Lord rebukes, chap. xxv. 26. Unmercifulness, properly wickedness." Luther, House-Pos. 5. 239: "What hast thou then gained, poor wretch, by all thy fury? Thou shouldst have had a gracious God, and been completely discharged from all thy debt, hadst thou but (from gratitude,) showed compassion to thy neighbour; but now God will not forgive thee, and besides will reckon as strictly with thee, as thou wouldst with thy neighbour."

Because thou desiredst me; out of free grace, without all desert and worthiness on the part of the guilty sinner.

Ver. 33. The design of God, in his gracious manifestations, which the self-willed sinner in his continued hardness overlooks, although it is plainly declared to him. God *first* exercises compassion, and *afterwards* desires and expects it of us; which is also taught in the fifth petition.—*Thy fellow-servant.* Gnomon: "Whom thou oughtest to commiserate; my servant in whom thou hast injured me."

Ver. 34. *And his Lord was wroth.*—God's holy and punitive indignation against the ingratitude of the hard-hearted servant, who renders himself unworthy of the exercise of mercy, and forfeits it. The king does not break his promise; but the ungodly person frustrates the purposes of divine goodness, through his own subsequent obduracy. Gnomon: "Before he had not been angry, cf. Luke xiv. 21. They who have experienced grace ought most of all to be afraid of wrath." Jas. ii. 13; v. 26.

Luther, Church-Pos. 14. 251: "The punishment here spoken of is not for the heathen, or for the general mass, who never hear the word of God, but for those who with the ear receive the gospel, and keep it upon their tongues, but will not live according to its precepts." Mal. ii. 10.—Olshausen: "Upon the hard-heartedness of the sinner the οργη, (wrath,) indignantly breaks out. Where men feel true unaffected sorrow at the sins of their fellow men, (v. 31,) there God manifests himself in anger. Conscience testifies in man, that the root of that sin which he sees in his brother, is also in himself; in God there is a more pure and unmixed hatred of the evil. The idea of the divine wrath is identical with the love of God, the manifestation of which in kindness is χαρις (grace,) the wrath of God is nothing but the manifestation of himself against evil. Hence so far as a being is not the evil itself, but only gives way to it in one respect or another, God, in love to the being, is indignant only at the evil that is in him. So that in the divine wrath there is displayed only another form of the holy activity of God. Where his compassionate activity is misunderstood or abused, as in the case of this servant, there the punitive comes into force."

Till he should pay all; and as he was not in a condition to do this, (v. 32,) he was adjudged to an eternal and righteous punishment. In Matth. v. 26, *till*, signifies also as much as *now* and *never*. Draeseke: "So he forfeited the freedom which was destined for him, because he misunderstood and abused it. But here lay the misunderstanding, and hence also arose the abuse, that he presumed he could expel all compassion from an economy of things, into which he was admitted through the most distinguished compassion; could insult love and still remain in the enjoyment of its blessings. As certainly as there is no kingdom of God without forgiveness being *received* by us, so certainly is there no kingdom of God without forgiveness being *exercised* by us. With the measure wherewith it was meted to us, when we were called by grace, so must we also mete, that we may not fall from grace."

Ver. 35. *My heavenly Father;* Christ does not say, *your* father; for whosoever is so unmerciful, is not worthy to be reckoned a child of God. Here we find the lesson of the parable plainly declared as a threatening of punishment and solemn warning against unmercifulness; Sirach xxviii. 1—11. Col. iii. 12, 13. In this parable two entirely opposite characters are depicted, and through means of the contrast between them the excellence of a placable disposition, and the hatefulness, nay the frightful nature of an unmerciful and avenging disposition are represented in the most striking light. All the circumstances of the narrative are in perfect accordance with the characters described. Von Brunn says upon this similitude, "It contains a clear representation of the most perfect exercise of grace toward the sinner, and also the trials, which serve either to justify him who is the subject of such grace, or to make him an entire reprobate. To the sinner it opens up glorious prospects; the grace of God appears from the first to him almost unlimited; punitive justice completely withdraws; God regards all offences committed against him as cancelled; but the moment grace sees the heart of the sinner unchanged, is unable to soften it, to inspire with feelings of love, to impress upon it its own image, that moment justice resumes its proper place, and the sinner has lost all inheritance in this grace."

XI.

THE LABOURERS IN THE VINEYARD.

Matth. xx. 1—16.

The rich young man, who asked, "Good master, what good thing shall I do, that I may inherit eternal life?" went away sorrowing from Jesus, while he said to him, "If thou wilt be perfect, go and sell that thou hast, and give to the poor, and thou shalt have treasure in heaven, and come and follow me." For he had many goods, which he could not bring his mind to sacrifice, because the demand seemed too hard for him. Upon this Jesus took occasion to direct attention to the important hinderances which the possession of earthly goods raises up in carnal and worldly-minded hearts against their salvation. Then Peter struck in and said, "Behold, we have forsaken all and followed thee; what shall we have therefore?" *We*, says he of himself and his fellow-disciples, manifestly in opposition to that youth who had been frightened away from following after Jesus by the greatness of the sacrifice required; what *he* could not resolve to do, that have *we* actually done; to become thy followers, we have made the greatest sacrifice. "Peter, tacitly," says Calvin, "compares himself and the other disciples with the rich youth, whom the world had alienated from Christ."

In that declaration of Peter, there is displayed, not only a certain self-satisfaction, with which he reflects upon himself and his conduct, but also a vaunting of himself over the young man, and those like him, and a depreciation of others. This manner of feeling gave rise to the question, "What shall we have therefore?" In which there discovers itself the foolish conceit of possessing merits before the Lord, and having righteous claims, grounded upon these merits, which might be made upon him, plainly arguing a selfish thirst for reward. Draeseke: "The natural man must always be a hireling. Peter himself was only a hireling so long as he was Simon. This was betrayed by the question: what shall we have therefore? But by and by Peter laid aside the Simon, and along therewith the hireling, 1 Peter i. 24, 3; iv. 2; 2 Peter iii. 13." And since Peter did not rest upon the external circumstance of his earlier call upon Jesus, and his longer fellowship with him, though in this respect also he was distinguished from the young man in question, but merely upon the sacrifice he had made,—upon his good works, we may hence gather, that afterwards in the parable, the earlier and the later call is not in itself an essential thing, and that the expression *first* and *last*, is to be understood, not so much of an external difference in regard to a longer or shorter fellowship with Jesus, as of men's judgment upon themselves in regard to their personal worth and desert.

To the question of this disciple, our Lord replied, v. 28: "Verily, I say unto you, that ye, who have followed me in the regeneration (Acts iii. 21, at the time of the manifestation of the kingdom of God, Matth. xxv. 31, ss.) when the Son of Man shall sit in the throne of his glory, ye also shall sit upon twelve thrones, judging the twelve tribes of Israel, honour, power, and glory shall be your portion, John xvii. 24.") A peculiarly distinguished and glorious reward is here promised by our Lord to his apostles, and the unfailing certainty with which it should be conferred, is intimated in the *verily*, with which the declaration commences. By such a promise the Lord wished to stimulate and strengthen his disciples to persevering attachment to the faith, and immoveable steadfastness under all tribulations and sufferings which were to overtake them. Calvin: "Lest the disciples should think that they were bound to a fruitless task, or repent of their begun undertaking, Christ informs them of the glory of his kingdom, which as yet lay concealed, but which should one day be manifested. As if he had said: There is no reason why the meanness of your present condition should dishearten you; for I, who scarcely have a place among the lowest, shall yet ascend the throne of majesty; endure therefore for awhile, until the time shall come for the manifestation of my glory." Nor has Christ merely the apostles in view, his eye stretches far and wide over the whole company of his disciples in every age, and hence follows, in ver. 29, the general promise, which belongs to all who should ever attach themselves to him: "And every one, that hath forsaken houses, or brethren, or sisters, or father, or mother, or wife, or children, or lands, for my name's sake, shall receive a hundred-fold, and shall inherit everlasting life." Still more clearly than here we find reference made in the parallel passage of the other Evangelists, Mark x. 29, 30, and Luke xviii. 30, to a twofold reward, an earthly and a heavenly one. Mark says: "There is no man that hath left house, &c. but he shall receive a hundred-fold now in this time, houses, and brethren, and sisters, and mothers, and children, and lands, with persecutions, (nothing without the cross in the fellowship with Jesus, Matth. x. 38,) and in the world to come eternal life." This twofold reward is not to be overlooked, on account of the penny in the parable. *Received a hundred-fold*, Gnomon: "*In this life*, for the future one will repay more than a hundred or even a thousand fold, Luke xix. 16, 17. He shall receive, not politically, and by dint of his own efforts, yet still he shall truly receive, just as he has need of a faithful friend, and in whatsoever other things it is desirable for him to obtain, Matth. v. 5. The word *receive* agrees more closely to the notion of reward, but *in-*

herit implies something far richer." Calvin: "After having raised the minds of his disciples to the hope of eternal life, he supports them also by present consolations, and strengthens them for enduring the cross. For though God may permit his people to be grievously afflicted, he yet never so far deserts them as to leave them without compensation for their sorrows. Nor does he speak here only to his apostles, but takes occasion to direct his discourse generally to all. The sum of the matter is, that they who have voluntarily suffered the loss of all things, for the sake of Christ, shall obtain more happiness, even in this life, than if they had sustained no injury, though still their grand recompense is reserved for them in heaven."

To the promise just mentioned our Lord joins the declaration in v. 30: "But many that are first shall be last; and the last shall be first." The connexion with *but* imports as much as: However sure the word of promise is, and however unfailing the promised reward, it yet may, and will happen, that the promise shall not be fulfilled to all, nor the glorious reward inherited by all,—that many, and of these not a few, even among the immediate followers of Jesus, shall be disappointed in their expectations, and that the actual participation of the reward shall proceed upon quite other principles than men in their blindness and perversity dream. These words contain partly a warning to the naturally proud and supercilious heart, to beware of losing the promised reward through fancied superiority over others, and partly, also, they declare a general principle of government, which shall be acted on in the heavenly kingdom. Calvin: "This declaration was added to make them put away the sluggishness of the flesh. The apostles already grasped at the reward, though they had scarcely begun their course. But Christ exhorts those who had truly begun, to strenuous perseverance, and, at the same time, reminds them that it would be of no avail to have set out boldly on the Christian race, if they did not continue to the end, 1 Cor. ix. 24. Phil. iii. 13."

The first, taken in its proper signification, are such as really have an external precedence over others, according to the parable, the first called disciples, (v. 1, 2,) who had to perform a long, full, laborious day's work, v. 10, do much, suffer much, submit to great sacrifices, continue steadfastly with Jesus, and, according to human apprehension, appear pre-eminently deserving of reward. Such a day's work had the apostles, the first Christians generally, the martyrs, reformers, missionaries to the heathen. But the mere circumstance that one has continued long in fellowship with Jesus, has had to fight with many difficulties, and has overcome them, by no means proves that, before the Searcher of hearts, he is worthy of attaining to the promised reward.

The last, in like manner, strictly understood, stand opposed to those who have just been described according to their external circumstances,—such as have not companied so long with Jesus, have been later in being called, v. 3, 7, have therefore not performed such a day's work, have not laboured, suffered, or sacrificed so much; who, consequently, as compared with the former, occupy an inferior place in this respect, and do not appear worthy of such a reward. And yet, in the actual apportioning of the reward, the first shall be last, shall not receive such a glorious reward as these, must be content to see themselves put behind. The treatment is in the highest degree remarkable, and appears, according to human apprehension, to be not less arbitrary than unjust toward the last. But he, who has to apportion the reward, is the holy, righteous, good, all-wise and omniscient God. He must have grounds for acting as he does, as there can be no caprice in his conduct. All those outward distinctions, which belong to the just, suffice not before God to make them stand also first in the participation of the promised reward, that is, to secure for them a preference before the others, to provide for them a richer inheritance in the rewards of grace.

There must, therefore, be before him, who looks only on the heart, and does not regard the outward appearance, some internal grounds and hinderances, on account of which the first do not remain first. These internal grounds lie in the state of mind belonging to these first labourers, in all outward respects so distinguished, and consist in self-satisfaction, self-elation, contempt of others, conceit of their own merits, presumptuous claims to distinction, consequently, also, in forwardness and want of humility,—these are the secret hinderances which prevent the first from remaining first, and the grounds on account of which the Lord does not think them worthy of distinguishing grace. On account of this state of mind, on account of the precedence which they claimed for themselves, which, in the parable, could be represented no otherwise than through the earlier call and the longer period of labour,—for only such workmen could so confidently extol themselves over others,—they are called the first; and this expression, taken figuratively, is to be understood of the imagined superiority which this class of labourers ascribed to themselves over the others, conceiving that in God's eyes, as well as in their own, they were preeminent in worth,—the first, the best, the most distinguished. The delineation of their heart in the parable, v. 2, 10—12, 15, completely harmonizes with the state of feeling expressed by Peter, v. 27. It is, therefore, a good thing to be one of the first, in regard to what is outward; but a still better thing, and an essential requisite not to know it, not to plume ourselves upon it, as otherwise we shall have our place among the last in the eyes of God.

And the last shall be first; the want of all the outward advantages belonging to the first-called labourers, which do not belong to the last, who, being later called, wrought only for a short period, and had not toiled particularly hard, (v. 3, 7—12,) forms, on the other hand, no sufficient ground, in the sight of God, to refuse them distinguishing grace; and if he grants them a full day's reward, more than they themselves, perhaps, could have expected for their work, he must, as well as in the other case, have grounds for doing so; and discern in them a state of mind which renders them worthy of such treatment. Now, if the formerly described feeling of Peter, which, in the parable, discovers itself in the first-called labourers, rendered them unworthy of a distinguishing mark of grace, on the part of God, and deprived them of it; we are naturally led to conclude that these last labourers, who were so highly favoured above the first, must have possessed an entirely different frame of mind; that, being filled with humility, they thought little of themselves, and judged themselves unworthy of any large recompense; that they knew nothing of personal deserts and claims on God, built not upon themselves, but attributed every thing they possessed of good to their Lord, v. 4, 5, 7;—and all this is represented, in the parable, by the later call. In their own eyes, and the world's, they are last, hence they are the first in God's.

We are, besides, compelled to understand the above expression in this sense, from the place and connexion which the same expression has in Luke xiii. 30, where the subject discoursed of from v. 26, is the arrogant pretensions of the Jews, proud both of their nation and their birth, to the exclusive, or, at least, the preeminent enjoyment of the blessings of Messiah's kingdom, and of the preference to be given to the heathen over them. The discourse concludes with the words: "And behold there are last that shall be first, and there are first that shall be last,"—which, in this connexion, obviously means, that the Jews, in their arrogant and foolish pride, should see themselves disappointed; and that the heathen, who were so much despised by them, and on their part made no such pretensions, should be preferred before them. Gnomon: "The first and the last either differ in kind, so that they are such as are saved, and such as perish; or rather in degree, so that the first also shall be saved, but shall stand far below the last."

Immediately after this dark and enigmatical declaration in v. 30, the parable itself follows in Matthew, which also closes with the same declaration. Not only the commencement of the parable with the connective particle *for*, but also the repetition of the saying in question in v. 16, with ουτως, *so*, *i. e.* in this manner, as the history just recited shows, clearly manifests that the parable was delivered for the purpose of exhibiting the truth contained in the last verse of the preceding chapter, in a specific transaction, wherein the first were last and the last first. The circumstance, that in the first announcement of this truth, v. 30, it is said, "*many* that are first shall be last," has induced the most part of interpreters to bring the universal application of this principle of the Messiah's kingdom into doubt, and to affirm that there may also have been some first, who were not last; but this does not appear to be the meaning, and we are rather led by the design of the parable, and the import of the text itself, to understand the saying in the strictest universality, and to maintain that all the first are last, and all the last are first. This is demanded by the text itself; for while, in v. 30, it is said, in the first clause, "many first shall be last," the converse is stated, quite generally, in the second; "and the last shall be first." And, in v. 16, the sentiment which was expressed in v. 30, with some apparent limitation, is given in the most comprehensive form; "so the first shall be last, and the last first." Hence we must explain the darker saying in v. 30, from the one in v. 16, which is more explicit. Nor can we avoid taking the declaration as universally applicable, if we look to the whole purport of the parable, according to which, in the distribution of rewards, *all* the first were actually the last, v. 1, 2, comp. with v. 10; and there is nothing in the words which opposes this interpretation, for according to Wahl, Clavis N. T. πολλοι signifies, also, *all;* "πολλοι, *a multitudine appellantur, qui sunt omnes,* Matth. xx. 28; xxvi. 28." Wahl, indeed, brings forward the two passages, v. 30, and v. 16, with the view of attaching to *many* its usual, its limited signification, but without a proper regard to the connexion in which the parable stands, and which speaks strongly for the more general sense of the word—*all.* The whole doubt, however, which has been felt concerning the reception of this latter sense, and which some have endeavoured to render probable, by the incontrovertible remark, that there may also have been those among the first who, on account of their humble and confiding disposition toward God, continued to remain first, proceeds, as to its ultimate ground, from an entire misapprehension of the parable; as if the calling of the labourers, at different times, and the longer or shorter period of labour in the vineyard, consequent thereupon, were to be regarded as the main feature in the parable; whereas, first and last have no reference to the earlier and later call, but are rather to be taken as distinct forms for determining and marking the judgment of the workmen regarding themselves; their proud and assuming, or their humble and unpretending disposition.

There is, however, still another way of taking the expression, which is quite allowable. If we make the πολλοι in v. 30, to bear its usual, its limited sense, *many,* we must then supply this to the second clause, so as to give the following sense: And many last shall be first. In this case the *many first* and *many last* are to be referred only to the external circumstance of the earlier or later call; while, on the other hand, the thing predicated of them, *shall be last, shall be first,* must be understood of the judicial sentence of God, pronounced upon the called labourers, and the sense will then be: But many who then (as to the time of their call) were first, shall be last, (as concerns the judgment of God, he does not hold them worthy of distinguishing grace;) and many of the last-called labourers shall be first in the eyes of God, be raised to the highest honours. (The change from the proper to the improper signification in the terms *first* and *last*, in the one and in the same sense, need not appear strange, as we find something quite similar in the word *life*, Matth. xvi. 25.) Ver. 30 is immediately succeeded by the parable, which represents the judicial procedure of God, and which is followed up at the close by the declaration in v. 16. But here the first and last would need to be understood, without regard to the time of the call, merely of the judgment of the labourers upon themselves, and of the contrary judgment of God upon them, and the sense would then be: So, *i. e.* according to the manner just described in the parable, shall the last (*all* the last, for there is no qualifying term there,) be first, and the first last, all those like-minded with the first,—the proud shall be abased; all those like-minded with the last,—the humble shall be exalted. According to this exposition, the possibility in v. 30, grows into a reality in v. 16; in the former verse it is represented as possible that the first might be the last, in v. 16, it is stated to be actually the case; and the parable contains the fundamental principle in the divine kingdom, according to which this reality comes to be established; hence v. 16 is connected with what precedes by—*so*.

DESIGN OF THE PARABLE.

Draeseke: " The grand key to the mystery of the kingdom contained in this parable, lies in the truth, that, although the heavenly kingdom is the gift of God in the souls of men, it yet can neither begin, nor continue, neither manifest, nor develop itself without worthiness on the part of men. And again, though our worthiness is necessary, yet we do not attain to a place in the kingdom of God through " the merit of our works," but through the fulness of grace, and through this alone. In short, the *kingdom longs for labourers, it disdains hirelings*. As the parable primarily applies to that disciple, who wished to know what he was to have for leaving and forsaking all, but in that disciple was personated the whole of Israel and its high pretensions, so it runs counter to *all* pretension, not excepting ours, if we make any. Labourers and hirelings have this in common, that both apply their powers, often even their most strenuous efforts, to the execution of a work, in which they obey the guidance and direction of some other will than their own. But in this they differ from each other, that the labourer being prompted by love, makes his Lord's will his own; whereas the hireling remains as an alien to the will of his Lord, because he is destitute of love. The labourer moves himself with ease and freedom, because he is full of spirit: the hireling is crippled and benumbed, because he has nothing of the right spirit. The labourer finds his pleasure in his work; the hireling is allured only by what he wins. The labourer rejoices in the success also of others, his heart being in the cause; the hireling begrudges every gain in which he has no share. He places the person and the cause in opposition to each other. Hirelings are the servants of their own lusts, and hence the judgment given in Luke ix. 62."

Gnomon: "Peter is taught to exercise modesty in demanding; conf. Luke xvii. 5—10, where we learn, that they who judge themselves unprofitable servants, are of a sounder mind than those who exalt themselves over others." Calvin: "Since this parable is merely the confirmation of the last statement, v. 30, we must now consider how it adapts itself to this purpose. Some interpreters gather this as the sum, that, as the heavenly inheritance is not acquired as the reward of merit, but is bestowed as a free gift, the glory of all will be one and the same. But Christ does not discourse concerning the equality of celestial glory, nor concerning the future state of the pious at all, but simply declares, that there is no reason why *they* should glory, or boast themselves over others, who have precedence in point of time; because the Lord, as often as he pleased, could call those whom he seemed for a time to neglect, and make them to equal, if not to surpass those who had been called at an earlier period. Besides, as we have already said, his aim was to stimulate his disciples with perpetual excitements to go on and persevere. Too much confidence naturally begets sloth; and so it comes to pass, that many, when they have scarcely well begun, fall a loitering in the middle of their course."

In his discourses, answers, and instructions, the Lord constantly deals with the inmost state of the heart; whatever he discerns there sinful and perverse, that he contends with, and brings to light in proper or figurative language, the state of mind, which is right and well pleasing to God; as this is his general practice, so is it in particular here. The sinful disposition, which Peter manifested in v. 27, was the immediate occasion of the parable. Against this it is directed, against the pride and self-elation of the human heart, against a mercenary temper and pretended worth, against spiritual presumption, and such other sinful emotions as naturally arise out of it; in particular, against envy, mutual jealousy, and dissatisfaction with God. It is, therefore, his design to excite a confidential and lowly state of mind, while the mournful consequences of the opposite state of sinful perverseness are delineated in the first labourers. We are compelled to regard the parable in this light by the preceding context; and in the narrative that follows, of the mother of Zebedee's children seeking from the Lord the two most honourable seats in his kingdom for her two sons, the same truth is again inculcated only from another point of view. For whilst in the parable confidence or pride in our doings is combated, and all righteousness of works before God is put to shame, this narrative teaches, that the endurance also of the most painful and bitter sufferings in following the Lord, v. 22, 23, does not of itself make us worthy and deserving of being rewarded with the highest honour and distinction in his kingdom; for though any one should drink, says Jesus, v. 23, of my cup, I am yet by no means necessitated to give him to sit upon my right hand or my left, but shall give it to those for whom it is prepared of my Father. The highest honours in the kingdom shall be distributed by the Son, (as steward, v. 8,) according to a predeterminate purpose of the Father, to those who possess the proper state of feeling, and falling in with God's arrangement shall be counted worthy of distinguishing grace. So that neither works, (according to the parable,) nor sufferings (according to the narrative, v. 20—23,) neither passive nor active obedience toward Christ, can purchase for us merit in his kingdom, and all reward there shall be dispensed according to the determinate purpose of God, though still in a way of desert, *i. e.* in proportion to the faith and humility of each. This truth—that unpretending humility alone is prized before God, and reckoned worthy of the highest honour, is not only thus set forth in the parable and the narrative, but is also, in plain language, enforced in the verses that follow, v. 25—28; and for regarding this as the main design of the parable, something may even be gathered from the epistle, 1 Cor. ix. 24; x. 5, appointed to be read along with the gospel containing this parable, in Matthew, on Sunday Septuagesima; for the last part of the epistle warns us, from the example of the Israelites, against fleshly security, that is, against the delusion of supposing that any thing external, without a state of mind good and well pleasing in the sight of God, can secure for us salvation and the experience of divine favour.

Luther, in his Church-Pos., gives the aim of the parable as follows: "Christ designs to show in this similitude, how it comes to pass, that in the heavenly kingdom, or the church on earth, God judges and acts in a wonderful manner, so as to make the last first, and the first last. And every thing is said to humble those who think themselves something,—that they must have no confidence in any thing but the sovereign mercy and goodness of God; and, on the other hand, that those who are nothing need not despair, but may, as well as the others, confide in the goodness of God. We must observe that the householder insists upon having his gifts exalted above all, works and merits, nay, of having them alone accounted of. Therefore, the main drift of the parable does not turn upon the penny, what it may represent, nor upon the distinction of hours, but upon the gaining and acquiring, how the penny is to be won. This, then, is the sum and substance of the parable,—no man is in himself so high, nor can he become so high, but that he shall still have reason to fear he may be thrust down to the lowest place; and again, no one has sunk, nor can he sink, so low but that he may still hope to reach the highest place. For here all merit is excluded, and the goodness of God alone exalted, while the determination is formed, that the first shall be last and the last first. In saying the first shall be last, he takes away all presumption, and forbids thee to boast thyself over any sinner, though thou didst equal Abraham, David, Peter, or Paul. But when he also says, the last shall be first, he removes all ground for despair, and forbids thee to take refuge under any saint, though thou wert even like Pilate or Herod, like Sodom and Gomorrah."

Bourn understands the parable in the same light, and regards it as directed against spiritual presumption. When it has been considered rather in an external point of view, the calling of the labourers into the vineyard at different times, and the apparent sameness of the reward, all receiving alike one penny, has been regarded as the main thing, and it has not been perceived that all this serves only as a necessary image for representing the different states of mind. Even Luther, at an earlier period, had taken up with this idea, in his House-Pos. 2, 79, regarding it as teaching the truth, that there is no respect of persons in Christ's spiritual kingdom. But that the earlier or later call is only a subordinate point, and the veil of a truth concealed under it, is manifest from this, that the parable takes notice only of the first and the last, and bestows no particular regard on those who were called at the intermediate times, which it should certainly have done, had these separate calls been a matter of primary importance. The expositors who consider the different hours of calling the essential point, hold it for the design of the parable to teach and vindicate the proposed extension of the gospel to the heathen world, and the approaching dissolution of the ecclesiastical state and privileges of Israel, in order to erect a Church in its stead, which should be composed of all classes of men, and extend even to the farthest boundaries of the earth;—so Gray. More spiritual, and nearer the truth, is the view which regards the parable as directed against the national and religious pride of Israel, grounding pretensions to merit on its law and long-tried obedience to God, since on this account Paul so often and so strongly expresses himself in his Epistles against the righteousness of the law, and Israel's presumptuous claims on God. But though we should grant that the parable points to this historical fact, yet this cannot be its immediate and proper reference, for as it speaks only of the heavenly kingdom, and tells us how Christ will act toward *his* labourers, we are under the necessity of confining it to this region. There are still other expositors, holding to the distinction of hours, and the apparent sameness in the reward, who have thought it must teach that the earlier or later entrance into the visible church is a matter of indifference; nay, some have even maintained the unchristian notion, as forming the very kernel of this parable, that it will not signify whether the sinner may have come soon or late to Christ! as if an earlier or later conversion to the Lord were really a thing of no moment. Olshausen, in his Commentary on the New Testament, I. p. 735, says, upon the manifold views taken of this and similar parables: "Such divine narratives resemble well-polished precious stones, which emit a splendour from more sides than one." The same expositors, who have failed to discern the secret grounds upon which the divine procedure and righteous judgment in regard to the first and the last was formed, because they looked only to the long or short period of labour, have sought to justify the apparent arbitrariness displayed by the Lord in the distribution of the reward, by bringing to their help the quite unwarranted supposition, that the first-called labourers may not have wrought rightly and conscientiously, while the last, through redoubled zeal, may have at least equalled, in their short period, the labour of the first. But the parable has nothing in it to justify this supposition; for while the first-called labourers appeal to their long and laborious work, the Lord makes no attempt to deny it, but simply rests for justification on his own free goodness, and it is not so much as hinted, that the last had distinguished themselves by their extraordinary labour. Were the supposition in question right, the leading truth brought out in the parable would be, "according to the work, so is the reward," a sentiment which is directly opposed to the real design of the parable, which rather unfolds the truth, "that the amount of reward is not determined by the labour of the servant." It is, finally, to be remarked, that the sameness of the reward is, after all, only an apparent one. It would have been really so, had there been one period of labour and one service performed. But since both, according to the parable, were very different, the labourers who had wrought only an hour, received in their full day's wages, twelve times more than they deserved, and than was given to the first-called labourers; so that the Lord manifested toward them a quite peculiar, and most distinguishing grace, which was denied to the first. In the parable, both the time of labour and the work done, differs with the different labourers, and the preference of the last-called over the first is marked by the equality of the reward. And, according to the clear import of the parable, when the labourers in the vineyard, the disciples of Christ, wrought for a like time, and accomplished a like work, even then there is to be found an entirely different relation between work and reward, there is to be found an unequal reward. The grace of the Lord, that it is at once free and righteous, and the disposition of the labourers as rendering them worthy or unworthy of distinguishing grace, these are the two leading points upon which we must direct especial attention, and which, in the exposition and practical application of the parable, must be brought most prominently out, and rendered palpable, if it is to be rightly understood.

TRAIN OF THOUGHT IN THE PARABLE.

On what depends the distribution of reward in the kingdom of God? or,

Humility is the only measure for the distribution of reward in the kingdom of God.

I. Negative proof: The reward is not distributed according to *work*,

A. Work indeed is required; for,

(1.) The steward hires labourers, v. 1, 2;

(2.) He repeatedly hires labourers, v. 3, 5, 6;

(3.) He chides the idle, v. 3, 6;

B. But still work is not the measure according to which the reward is distributed; for,

(1.) Neither the length of the time of labour is commended, v. 8—12: "Thou hast made them equal to us."

(2.) Nor the arduousness of the work, v. 12: "We who have borne the heat and burden of the day."

II. Positive proof. The reward shall be distributed only according to the degree of humility; for,

A. The kingdom of God is a kingdom of *grace;*

(1.) Every one indeed receives a reward for his

work, v. 13, (comp. v. 2,) v. 24: "Take what thine is, and go thy way."

(2.) But the gift of eternal life is only of *free grace*, v. 14: "I will give unto this last, even as unto thee;" and herein appears distinctly,

a) God's sovereign power, v. 14: I *will* give, etc.

b) As also his free goodness, v. 15: "Is thine eye evil, because I am good?"

B. And hence the humble are the objects of grace; which is manifest,

(1.) In the case of the first, from the opposite, for they wanted humility, v. 2; They agreed for a reward, v. 11: They murmured.

(2.) In the case of the last; They trust in humility on the Lord, v. 3—5: And they went away, v. 9: They receive a glorious reward.

(3.) From the closing declaration, v. 16: For many are called, but few are chosen.

Ver. 1. *The kingdom of heaven is like unto a householder;* for as a householder transacts with his servants, so will the Lord transact with those who belong to his church, and enter into terms with him. *Householder, lit.* a man that is a householder; by whom we are to understand God.

To hire labourers; man's coming into connexion with God, is from God, according to John xv. 16, the call is of grace, for on this is grounded the salvation of sinners; to *hire* indicates a free compact, God calls and will bestow salvation, the sinner must consent, receive the call; the hiring contains within itself a reward, which is likewise of grace, for God, as Lord of his creatures, is not bound to give any special recompense, but he wishes, through the promise of this, to make men the more ready to accept of his gracious call. Labourers are not merely preachers, but all the called, and they are named labourers, partly on account of their dependence on God, and partly to intimate, that in the attainment of salvation, all must proceed upon the dutiful subjection of man to the will of God.

Vineyard, an image of the church, and of the employment to be performed in it; manifold, laborious, but richly recompensed are the employments in a vineyard; God has established this vineyard according to his great mercy. Olshausen: "The frequent comparison of the kingdom of God to a vineyard, indicates as much as this, that the Redeemer, according to his insight into nature, found in wine and the vine the most fitting analogies in the natural world for shadowing forth spiritual relations. John xv. 1, ss."

Ver. 2. *And when he had agreed with the labourers;* they must consequently have asked after the reward, and the Lord had also made it known to them; they are represented to us as possessed of a selfish, greedy disposition. ch. xix. 27; would confide nothing to the Lord, would not rest in his divine equity. Gnomon: "With the first labourers, the transaction is more a matter of paction and right, with the latter, more a matter of free goodness, even in the hiring, though coupled with the reprehension of these last for their idleness, v. 4, 6, 7. They make up for their idleness by yielding obedience without stipulating for any reward." Calvin: "Here mention is made of a penny, and a hire; but while we quarrel concerning our deserts, and such quarrels draw on many pernicious vices, hatred, self-seeking, pride, wrongs, it happens that the first becomes last, and the good cause is corrupted by ill behaviour." Draeseke: "He gives the called their appointed task. Now they have work. And they set to it heartily, were not hirelings, day-labourers, eye-servants; they were, what they ought to be, workmen, helps, and companions of the householder."

For a penny; a denarius, about sevenpence-half-penny of our money.

Ver. 3—5. *The third, sixth, ninth hours,* according to the Jewish method of reckoning time; the day was divided into twice twelve hours, beginning at six in the evening, so that their third hour of day corresponded to our nine in the morning, and so on. Luther, Church-Postills, 11, says: "This portion of scripture has been applied by some fathers to the different preachers that have been raised up in the different periods of the world; the first hour in Adam's time; the third, Noah's; the sixth, Abraham's; the ninth, that of Moses; the eleventh, that of Christ and his apostles. Such trifling is good enough for filling up the time, when one has nothing else to preach."

Ver. 3. *And saw others standing idle in the market-place;* no activity is right while we are out of Christ, and away from fellowship with him; we must devote to him all our time and powers. Draeseke: "Man may be so busy, in his business he may be so diligent, that the sweat shall flow in streams from his forehead; but until he feels himself called by God to the work, until he knows himself appointed by God in the work, until he begins to exert himself for God in it, and also works in *the kingdom,* he stands idle. Worse even than doing nothing is every sort of working which is not done for the kingdom."

Ver. 4. *Whatsoever is right, I will give you;* he refers them, without any definite promise of blessing, to his justice and equity, and they, simply confiding in this, making no inquiry after reward, go away into the vineyard. How great a difference between these and the first labourers! It is, besides, worthy of remark, that the calling of men, as bodies, to the fellowship of Christ, is done, as in the case of individuals, at different times: one people is called earlier than another, and even in the Christian church, where all enjoy the means of outward fellowship, some come in tender childhood, others in the season of youth, others only in ripened manhood, or even not till declining age, to a living and enlightened fellowship with the Redeemer, when alone they can regard themselves as labourers of the Lord, and apprehend the true design of their being.

Ver. 6. *And about the eleventh hour;* five hours

after mid-day, when there remained but an hour to work. *Why stand ye here all the day idle?* it is reproach.

Ver. 8. Here begins the second division of the parable, the distribution of the reward and justification of the manner of doing it. If, in the first part of the parable, the calling of the labourers at different hours was only the particular form for representing to us the want of a confiding and humble spirit in the first-called, the possession of it by the last, and to lay a palpable ground for the self-exaltation of the former;—if, farther, the different times of labour taken in connexion with the manner of distributing the reward, is only assumed as the form for presenting to our view the truth therein disclosed, that neither the amount of labour nor the imagined desert of the labourer, are the things according to which the Lord apportions the reward; then must the distribution of the reward itself be only the veil of a truth, and we are not to think, in searching for it, of the future transactions of the last judgment. God has so arranged it, that every thing done in his service brings with it an immediate reward, which is even now enjoyed by his servants upon earth, so that it will not be adjudged and given to them for the first time at the final judgment, as we must maintain, if we consider the distribution of the reward in the evening as historically predictive of that judgment. This distribution of reward, and the discourses held concerning it, are only the form, therefore, through which we have made known to us what disposition is most pleasing to the Lord of the vineyard on the part of his labourers, which he pre-eminently blesses, and thereby leads us to regard as right and good. If we are determined to view this, in reference to the last judgment, it can only be done in the sense that there will then be made manifest before all the world, what hitherto was comparatively but little known, viz. those who are blessed of God, and that then also the whole world will be made to understand the supreme justice and goodness of God, in giving or withholding distinguishing grace. The circumstance too should perhaps be taken into account, that through this manifestation of the sovereign good pleasure of God, the last-called, and so highly favoured labourers, shall receive a vast accession to the blessedness they have already experienced.

V. 8. *To his steward,* the overseer of his goods, Christ, according to Heb. iii. 2; John v. 27; Matth. xi. 27. Draeseke: "The labourer is worthy of his reward. So God always reckons. It is not otherwise in the heavenly kingdom. Could the kingdom withhold the promised reward, since the Lord's word is true? But, could the kingdom offer an unsuitable reward since the Lord's ways are wisdom and righteousness? Or could the kingdom fail to afford an adequate reward, since the Lord's dominion stretches throughout all the universe? It is not the labourers alone who receive what is right. The hirelings, also, get their pay. Every one receives his penny. Only the same penny becomes quite a different thing, according as it is the hand, which simply takes it, or the state of mind, which is rightly prepared to receive and prize it. According as thou layest hold of it as a labourer, or as a hireling, by this it is determined what the divine reward may be, shall be, must be to thee."

V. 9. The last called labourers, in receiving a penny, received, perhaps, more than they deserved, or were expecting; that they received the reward first is of importance only as serving, by such an arrangement, to bring out more easily the disposition of the first-called. It was simply their humility and their trust in the promise, v. 4, 7, which rendered them deserving of it, not their labour.

V. 10. *The first thought that they should have received more,* for they were eye-witnesses of the extraordinary goodness of the Lord toward the last called labourers; at the same time there is here intimated their conceit of acquired merits and righteous claims on God's special goodness, the ground of which is given v. 12. Their grand principle is, the more work the more merit, and, consequently, there should also be the more reward. *And they likewise received every man a penny;*—they find themselves disappointed;—God judges and acts differently from men;—he has no particular delight in the conceited labourers. Mel.: "Here the distribution is unequal in regard to merits; therefore it is not merely merits that are accounted of, but Christ wishes to intimate that the mercy of God *must* be more looked to than our merits."

V. 11, 12. The procedure of God is the occasion of discontent to the self-righteous, proud, and presumptuous, (Acts xiii. 44, ss.; xiv. 1, ss.; xvi. 6, ss.; xvii. 11, ss.) and they give vent to their dissatisfaction,—they complain of the unfair treatment they receive. *These last have wrought but one hour,* expresses their feeling of contempt towards their fellow-labourers; *and thou hast made them equal unto us*—hast bestowed unto them such distinguished favour, expresses their envy and jealousy; in their self-elation they wished to have the pre-eminence; and could not, without a grudge, see it awarded to others. In thinking and speaking thus, however, they virtually accused God of acting unrighteously, which they do yet more expressly in the following words; *who have borne the heat and burden of the day;* they look less to the grace which had wrought in them, and through them, than to the confidence which they had in themselves, and therefore praised themselves rather than the Lord. Gnomon: "The *burden,* arising from within, from their own labour; *the heat,* coming from without, from the sun." God must think, judge, act as we imagine to be right: Luther, Church-Pos. 11, 83: "The day and the heat, we must, to interpret them rightly, transfer, from what is outward, to the conscience; so that, by the self-righteous doing long and laborious work, we are to understand their doing it with a heavy conscience and a grumbling heart, constrained and driven by the law; but the short hours indicate the lightened conscience, led by grace, which acts righteously, of a willing mind, and without the constraint of law."

V. 13. This verse contains a justification of the righteousness of God from the reflections cast on it by the first-called labourers, and throws back their reproach. "Didst not thou agree with me for a penny?" Thou hast, therefore, no right to seek for more than what was promised.

Ver. 14. Here comes the punishment of this discontent: *Take that thine is*, despise not what is given thee, but be content with it, no more is due to thee than thou hast received; Rom. ix. 20; Isa. xlv. 9, 10. *And go thy way*, complete proof that there was no hope of obtaining any more. *I will give unto this last even as unto thee*, a justification of the goodness of God, which is grounded in his own gracious will; *I will*, and is consequently perfectly free, ver. 15. *Is it not lawful for me to do what I will with mine own?* And it is only an evil, an envious heart, which begrudges it to the other; *Is thine eye evil, because I am good?* So that God himself ascribes what he gave to the last-called labourers, to nothing but his free goodness, thereby denying all claim to merit on their part. Gnomon: "The *eye*, the mind from the eye."

In regard to their *penny*, we cannot possibly, as some would, understand thereby, exclusively Christ, or eternal life; but it includes all the divine promises and rewards of grace, which differ very much according to men's state and temper of mind, while men, through their different conditions of mind, are rendered capable or incapable of receiving the more or less glorious possessions and gifts of grace. The more heavenly the mind of man is, the more bent upon eternal things, the stronger his faith, the purer his love, the deeper his humility, the more constant his patience, so much the more fitted is he to receive the promised recompense of God in the best and noblest gifts. But if the heart is mercenary, jealous, proud, presumptuous, and full of pretensions, it is on that very account unfit to receive the best gifts of God, and to be rewarded by him with distinguishing grace; it is satisfied with meaner, with temporal goods, Matt. vi. 2, 5. Luther Church-Pos. ii. 82, ss., says, "Therefore, if we would distinguish exactly, we must make the penny stand for temporal good, and the favour of the householder for eternal good. The last continue in grace, and attain to salvation, besides that they also have enough here." Mel.: "The meritorious, afterwards becoming insolent and ungrateful, are cast out, the submissive and grateful are received. The image of this *general rule* is here depicted, nor is it necessary that the rewards themselves should be the same, as there is in this respect a dissimilitude, the penny being given even to the ungrateful. But eternal life is not given to those who are here understood to be rejected. The different parts will not, therefore, correspond, if the penny is interpreted throughout, eternal life. The Jews, since they became ungrateful, are rejected, having previously obtained both present and eternal rewards. Now others are received, that they might gratefully receive the rewards which should be given." Draeseke: "The kingdom, with its gifts of grace for eternity, is the penny which the Lord of the vineyard promises to all whom he calls. However, it is only the labourers, to whom the worth of this wonderful penny is disclosed. In their hands it is the pledge of that complete enjoyment, which never terminates, but always grows and renews itself. Hirelings, on the other hand, go about the kingdom, but are still not in it. Even that which is right in the kingdom, appears to them as a false coinage. They turn the penny up and down in their hand, and know not what to do with it. And yet this penny promised to the labourers, is the noblest prize. Less God could not present to beings whom he made for being transformed into his own image. More God can give to no creature. The perfectly righteous are only made blessed in the enjoyment of his kingdom. And the raising of souls to this final blessedness 'through the Holy Ghost sent down from heaven,' is what the angels themselves desire to look into, (1 Pet. i. 9—12.")

Ver. 16. This is not spoken by the householder, but by Christ, and hence does not form a part of the parable, the design of which, as explanatory of this saying, is once again pointed out, with a manifest reference to chap. xix. 30. After that, in the words "So the last shall be first, and the first last," it had been intimated, that God judges not according to the pretensions of men, and their fancied merits, it is added, "For many are called, but few chosen," as the ground of such a procedure toward the labourers. *To be called* signifies to be invited to a participation in the goods, graces, and blessings of the kingdom of Christ both in this life and the next. Gnomon: Κεκλημενος, is, for example, a labourer, though he may not go into the vineyard; κλητος, one who has received the call." *Chosen* is applied in Scripture to every thing which is the best of its kind, excellently good, and hence of worth, a thing to be chosen and preferred before all others. Now, in Christ's kingdom of grace and before God, the Searcher of hearts, this can only be a state of heart; hence that man is chosen who, on account of a state of mind well pleasing in the sight of God, (full of faith, humble, unpretending,) is reckoned worthy of distinguishing grace. But this worthiness having its ground in a certain state of heart, no arbitrariness of partiality, on the part of God, for the one or the other, can consequently have place, and so these words contain a new reference to the divine righteousness, there having been one already in v. 13. Every thing is done, in the heavenly kingdom, in conformity with the purest righteousness—and even the manifestations given in it of God's sovereignly free grace proceed according to justice and equity—are not at all arbitrary appointments. On his part, God is indeed inclined, where then the sense of this declaration, to bestow distinguishing grace on every one, on all the called, and to bless them with all the blessings of the heavenly kingdom—but the sinful and perverse disposition of many will not admit of it, and hence all the called are not also all chosen. As the judicial procedure of God reaches to all those who are labourers in his vineyard, it is best to understand πολλοι, (many,) here in the sense of *all*, and the opposite ολιγοι, (few,) then signifies *not all*. To understand the saying of an antecedent election, quite independent of the state of the human heart, is utterly indefensible. Luther, House-Pos. II. 84, ss. says; "From this saying the inconsiderate have drawn many impure and ungodly thoughts, as that, he who is chosen of God shall be saved without means, without any co-operation of his own; while, if we are not chosen, it is in vain that we do and purpose. What sort of lazy, secure persons are likely to grow out of such a way of thinking, it is not difficult to conceive. Others take the words thus: God offers his grace to many, but gives only a few to experience it, for there are only a few saved by it. There is, however, another sense, in which the saying may be taken, viz. that the preaching of the gospel is done in an open and general way, so that every one should hear, believe, and receive it to his salvation. But what is the fact? Few are chosen, that is, few give such a reception to the gospel, that God has any pleasure in them."

Vitringa brings from the Jerusalem Talmud a similar parable, in which a king hired many labourers, among whom was one who did his work uncommonly well. What did the king do? He took him to himself, and walked up and down with him. When the evening arrived, the labourers came to receive their pay, and the excellent workman was rewarded equally with the rest, upon which they murmured, and said,

We have wrought laboriously all day, and have received only the same pay with this man, who has wrought but two hours. The king said to them, He has wrought more in two hours than ye have done all day. Right, according to the Jewish notion of self-righteousness.

XII.

THE TWO UNLIKE SONS.

Matth. xxi. 28—32.

General prefatory remarks on this and the two following Parables.

These parables were delivered by Jesus after his entrance into Jerusalem, shortly before his last sufferings. The nearer the time came for their being accomplished, the more clearly he disclosed, in striking images, his own fate and that of the Jewish people; and in them he breathes out the deepest lamentation over the human corruption that prevailed, the wickedness of Israel, the frightful and inevitable judgments of God. He paints, in the liveliest colours, the overflowing goodness, long-suffering, and patience of God on the one hand, and on the other the levity, ingratitude, and increasing wickedness of the human heart, and affirms that, on account of these the punitive righteousness of a holy God would be necessitated to inflict the most terrible visitations. Only, the parabolical covering under which our Lord gave forth the truths, warnings, threatenings, and reproofs, which he delivered, served, in some measure, to blunt their pungent and cutting severity; yet still, the veil, which was drawn around the truth, was so easily seen through, and the application so pointed, Matth. xxi. 43, that his hearers clearly perceived he spake of them, v. 44, 45, and hence thought of new plans for his destruction, v. 46, and xxii. 15, s. The Lord had hitherto not spoken this, but seeing that the mildness he had all along maintained made no impression upon the inveterate depravity of his opponents, he now began to give up somewhat of his meek forbearance, and to speak without reserve, if, possibly, there were some, at least a few, who would be moved to a change of feeling by the solemn earnestness of his words, as there really was, according to Luke xx. 16, a number of his hearers, who were so appalled by the terrible prospect of approaching judgment, as to cry out, *God forbid.*

In the first parable of the two sons, Jesus mainly depicts the hypocrisy of the first, and most influential of the people: in the following one, of the vinedressers, their overwhelming guilt concerning the people committed to their charge is declared, and how their constantly growing wickedness would precipitate both them and the people into destruction. In the parable of the wedding garment, the thought already hinted at, v. 43, of the heathen being called, is more fully disclosed, and a representation given of what was necessary to make them actually partakers of the benefits which God offers to men. All the three parables have primarily a historical reference to the character of the contemporaries of Jesus, to the then existing condition of the people, and to the immediately approaching events; but they admit also, or rather demand, a general reference to the church of Christ, if treated in a proper practical way; they demand it, for the ever-important truths, appearances, and principles in the divine government, lie enclosed in the forms chosen by our Lord. The more determinate, pointed and varied, we take the historical bearing of this, and all similar parables, the more rich and lively becomes their general application; while without viewing them thus historically, we are left with nothing but an abstract truth, which being bereft of every thing special, must exercise little power on the human mind.

The immediate occasion of the first parable was the

following:—The high priests and elders of the people, both bound and authorized to take cognizance of all religious pretensions, (John i. 19—27,) had asked Jesus, while he taught in the temple, "By what authority doest thou these things? And who gave thee this authority?" In answer to which questions our Lord asked them: "Whence was the baptism of John? Was it from heaven or of men?"—a divine or a human institution? The answer to this would have, at the same time, furnished an answer to their own question; but they clearly foresaw the consequence which Christ would draw from the affirmation of the first supposition, v. 25, and the effects which would come to them from the people, were they to affirm the second, v. 26. In this dilemma they considered it better to say, "We cannot tell." They feigned an ignorance which they did not possess, for the two possible cases lay open to their discernment; but, in their depravity, they could not bring themselves to give honour to the generally admitted truth. They speak otherwise than they both think and feel; their internal thoughts and their outward conduct are in discord and opposition to each other, which is the essence of hypocrisy. This master-vice of the high priests, elders, and pharisees, Luke xii. 1, the Lord brings to light, and condemns in the following parable. Calvin: "The clause in v. 32, shows to what the parable is directed, since Christ puts before the scribes and pharisees those who were infamous and detestable. He takes the mask from those hypocrites, that they might no more boast themselves as the peculiar servants of God, and pretend an empty zeal for piety. For although their ambition, and pride, and cruelty, and avarice, were well known to all, they yet wished to be reckoned quite different."

TRAIN OF THOUGHT IN THE PARABLE.

Of pretended faith.

I. Wherein it consists, its nature: want of candour, (v. 27;) this is shown;

(1.) From the opposite, in the first son: who manifests candour,

a.) In his words, v. 28, 29, I will not do it;

b.) In his actions, v. 29, Afterwards he repented, and went.

(2.) Positively, through the representation given of the other son, whose pretended faith consists essentially,

a.) In a fair outward appearance, v. 30; I go, sir!

b.) Without the obedience, v. 30: But went not.

II. Its punishment;

(1.) It is kept out of the kingdom of heaven, v. 31: the publicans and harlots go in before you.

(2.) It hinders repentance and faith, v. 32.

V. 28. *But what think ye?* By this question Jesus brings the following delineation before the judgment seat of the conscience of his hearers, and obliges them to pronounce sentence against themselves, 1 Cor. iii. 19.

A certain man had two sons; the man, or father, according to the explanation given in v. 32, is God, who had caused his will to be declared through John's baptism. The righteousness of the demand is grounded in the relation which a father holds to his children.

Two sons form, on account of their different states of mind and conduct, two very different classes of men; in their immediate reference, publicans and pharisees—more remotely, pretended Christians and genuine disciples. *My son,* an endearing address, which betokens the fatherly affection of God, and with which he would exhort careless sinners to amendment, while self-righteous pharisees look askance upon them with heartless contempt. *Go, work to day in my vineyard.* God desires obedience, the subjection of our will and conduct to the will of God.

Ver. 29. *I will not;* the perverse and evil will of the sinner is the true ground for his disobedience to God, for every thing besides tends to incline him thereto; the love of God, which desires only his salvation, thankfulness for received benefits, the confidence due to a father, all persuade to obedience. *But afterward he repented, and went;* what is represented in the case of this son, actually occurred with publicans and sinners in the time of Jesus. Their exceedingly sinful *conduct* was far removed from all fear of God, and their *heart* appeared also to be completely lost to all that is good, moral, and divine; but John's preaching made an unexpectedly deep and wholesome impression upon these persons; they believed him, v. 32; their moral feelings awoke, they perceived the necessity and importance of a change of heart, and subjected themselves to his demands. The same manifestation is often repeated still; for the vices of excess, extortion, etc., have not immediately such an unhappy effect upon the mind, that they unfit it for better feelings and impressions; and the more that they outrage what is orderly and becoming in external worth and decency, the more readily might the slaves of such vices be brought to feel their impropriety, and acknowledge the necessity of a change of heart; so the prodigal son, Luke xv.

Ver. 30. *And he came to the second, and said likewise;* God's demand is the same to all, and the obligation to obey, is also the same in *all*. *I go, sir,* lit. *I, sir, i. e.* I am ready to do thy will, *and went not;* he is satisfied with fine words and promises, consents to every thing, and does nothing; his carriage and manners are good, better than in the case of the former son, but the main thing is still wanting, real obedience, Matth. xxiii. 3; vii. 21. Calvin: "Christ teaches that this hypocrisy is less tolerable than ferocity, which may be subdued in course of time."

Ver. 31. *They say unto him, the first.* The nature of true piety is therefore obedience to the revealed will of God, and this obedience can be compensated by nothing else. The observance of all devout forms and solemnities, the most religious discourse, the most sanctimonious appearance, the most thorough and extensive acquaintance with scripture, without this obedience, is only a saying yea, but no true fear of God. Here the parable properly ends, the remainder of v. 31, containing a warning admonition upon the sad consequences of hypocrisy, and v. 32, an application of the whole to the two classes of public and pious-looking sinners, who are represented in the parable under the two sons.

Verily I say unto you, an impressive address; however little it may appear to you, and however disinclined you may be to receive it, yet such is the fact, and ye must take it on my testimony.—*The publicans and the harlots go into the kingdom of God before you;* the comparison is, as in Luke xviii. 14, exclusive, and the sense is: They shall be saved, but not you. The ground of this truth is, that the vices of pride and covetousness, of ambition and hypocrisy, do not consist with openness and integrity of mind; they shut up the heart, have immediately a most disadvantageous influence upon true morality, and while their slaves live externally honourable, decent, and becoming lives, the necessity of conversion does not so readily force itself upon them as upon the openly wicked, and they are also much more averse to own their depraved condition, and comply with the demands made upon them to repent; and this refusal to repent is the ground of their destruction, the cause of their perdition. Luther's Gloss: "Much more possible is it for harlots and knaves to be saved, than proud saints, for the former must at least feel their sins, but the latter die in their own righteousness, unless they become wonderfully converted."

Ver. 32. *John came to you in the way of righteousness*, taught you the right way, showed you how a man can be righteous before God, John i. 29; Matth. iii. 1—12, and was himself also a pattern of a holy life.

And ye believed him not, Luke vii. 28--30. *And*

when ye had seen it, &c., a most touching admonition, that Jesus regarded the most worthless and despised men as patterns for imitation to the self-righteous and highly esteemed pharisees.

Ewald makes the following remarks upon this parable, p. 145, ss.: "The leading thought of the parable: To promise much, and perform nothing, to promise nothing and perform much. Whosoever would learn what true wisdom is, wisdom also toward the enemies of truth, he must ponder the discourses of Jesus with the pharisees, or at least this one. The omniscient! How were they constrained by their own answer to set above themselves publicans and sinners, upon whom, as worthless creatures they were wont to look down with so much contempt. Never, indeed, did man speak like this man. Nothing can be clearer than that, in the parable, Jesus primarily delivers the truth, that no father, no master, will hold him for obedient, who promises to obey, but obeys not, and none will hold him for disobedient, who, at last does what his master commands. And yet, what is perfectly manifest in every-day life, is not admitted in matters of religion. What no man, no earthly lord, would be satisfied with, from a child or a subject, with that God, the highest father, the highest lord, must be content. It is thought that the *saying*, the *promise*, may supply the place of true obedience. But Jesus delivers yet another truth, which is not less important and well-known, that harlots and reprobates will sooner go into the kingdom of heaven than pharisees. For many times these depraved characters believe, and the pharisees believed not; and amend their lives on being admonished, and the pharisees do not. So we are here warned against two errors, into which so many Christians fall, and think they are all the while walking upon the true paths of Christianity. 1. Never think that thou rightly bearest the Christian name without Christian deeds, or shalt enjoy Christian salvation, John xiv. 15, 23, ss.; 1 John v. 3; Matth.

vii. 18—28. And, 2d, let no one also think this, that a merely external, or outwardly reputable walk, is sufficient to constitute any one a Christian, Matth. v. 20, ss."

XIII.

THE WICKED VINE-DRESSERS.

Matth. xxi. 33—46; Mark xii. 1—12; Luke xx. 9—19.

In its immediate reference, this parable contains, partly as a narrative of the past, partly as a discovery of the future, the wonderful history of the Jewish church. It manifests the riches of divine love, and the benefits flowing out of it to the chosen people, portrays an almost inexhaustible patience and long-suffering on the part of God toward the refractory and unthankful sinner, discloses at the same time the wickedness and hardening of the sinful heart as rising to a fearful height, and finally closes with a threatening of certain and dreadful, but most righteous, judgments. But when viewed in a more extended reference, this parable speaks also of the general truths, which, in the Christian church, are continually unfolding themselves, and reflected anew in the history of individuals and entire communities. Viewed in either light, the description given of the lord of the vineyard serves to admonish us of the union there is in God's character, of mercy and holiness, of goodness and righteousness, of patience and indignation. If we consider the general truth as represented under the more special forms and lineaments,—how, notwithstanding so many proofs of divine goodness, the Israelitish people in stiff-necked impenitence refused to yield to God the obedience that was due, and thereby prepared themselves for his condemnation, we might say, that the chief object of the parable was, a delineation of impenitence in the history of the Jewish people; but leaving out of view this primary reference of the parable, and considering it in the widest generality and application, the subject of the parable then comes to be simply of impenitence. Calvin: "The sum of this parable is, that it is no new matter for priests and other leaders in the church to attempt impiously to defraud God of his right, for in such a spirit of robbery did they formerly carry themselves against the prophets, and now were ready to kill the son, but they were not to escape with impunity, for God will arise to vindicate his own right. The scope of the parable, however, is twofold, that it might charge ingratitude upon the priests as full of perfidy and wickedness; and that it might take away the offence which would soon be occasioned by the approaching death of Christ. Therefore he fortifies beforehand his weak disciples, and teaches them, that as so many prophets had formerly been killed by the priests, one after another, there was no need for any one now to be disquieted, if such an example should be again repeated in his person." The speech of Stephen, Acts vii., is just an extended historical addition to what is now briefly related in the parable.

TRAIN OF THOUGHT IN THE PARABLE.

On impenitence.

I. Its nature, v. 33—39;

(1.) It does not profit by the manifestations of divine goodness, v. 33, 34; Mark v. 1, 2;

(2.) It despises the riches of divine patience and long-suffering, v. 35, Mark v. 3—5;

(3.) It becomes always more violent and malignant in its opposition to divine grace, v. 36, Mark v. 3—5;

(4.) It frustrates the most affectionate and powerful provisions of divine mercy, v. 37—39, Mark v. 6—8;

a.) Therein acting against its better convictions, v. 38. This is the heir;

b.) And flattering itself with a prosperous issue, v. 38. Let us seize on his inheritance.

II. The consequences of impenitence, v. 40—44; Mark v. 9—11;

(1.) It falls short of its designs, and is punished, v. 41. He will miserably destroy those wicked men.

(2.) It loses the enjoyment of the divine benefits, v. 41. And will let out his vineyard unto other husbandmen, who shall render him the fruits in their seasons.

Ver. 33. *A vineyard;* the Jewish church, an image often used in former times by the prophets, and especially by Isaiah, v. 1—6, where we find many of the particulars mentioned also here. Melanch.: "The sense is: God chose the people, Israel; drew a hedge around it, *i. e.* the law; and made a wine press in it, *i. e.* the ministry of divine truth; and built a tower, *i. e.* gave them a kingdom and a temple; and let it out to husbandmen, *i. e.* the seed of Jacob."

Hedged it round about; separated the vineyard from other lands, the Jewish nation from other nations, Deut. vii. 8, ss., through the law, Eph. ii. 14, the moral law as well as the ceremonial. Such a separation implied that there were particular ends to be served with the people so separated, and that their land should be placed under a special administration.—*Digged a wine press in it;* just as in the wine press the juice of the grape, being pressed out, flows in rich abundance, so this image, if it may be understood to carry a spiritual meaning, must refer to those institutions through which the true fruits of piety had to be sought, as through the manifestations that were given to Israel of the word of God.—*Built a tower;* a watch-tower, from which the whole vineyard could be observed; the means employed for the oversight of the people, that their well-being might be looked after; the introduction of the spiritual and civil government, Ex. xviii. Deut. i. 9—18; latterly judges, kings. Calvin: "By the wine press and tower you may understand the institutions, which had been superadded to the law for the nourishment of the people's faith, such as sacrifices and other ceremonies. For God, like a provident and attentive householder, left nothing undone, that he might strengthen and confirm his church with every help."

Let it out to husbandmen; the chiefs and princes of the people, Mal. ii. 7; Jer. xxxiii. 18; Ez. xxxiv. 2, ss.; Matth. xxiii. 2, 3; they remain answerable to God.—*And went into a far country,* Luke v. 9, *a long time;* either, God no longer manifested himself after the first planting of the vineyard, after Israel's deliverance out of Egypt, after the giving of the law from Sinai, and the introduction into Canaan, in so manifest and extraordinary a manner, Deut. xxxiv. 10—12; or, it indicates the feeling of the vine-dressers, who think that God has no regard to their conduct, Ez. viii. 12; ix. 9; Ps. x. 4, 5; Luke xii. 45. Gnomon: "The time of God's forbearance is intimated, during which men act according to their own will, ch. xxv. 14; Mark xiii. 14."

A people (vineyard) so highly favoured might have brought forth glorious fruits of piety and holiness; God had provided every thing for the accomplishment of this end; it was now the part of the people's overseers, who were invested with particular power, honour, and regard, to enter into God's designs, and, through the faithful discharge of their office, by instruction and example, to press forward the moral improvement of those committed to them. For this God gave them sufficient time, Luke v. 9. Calvin: "When Christ says that the vine-dressers received the vineyard well furnished and provided from the hand of the owner, he shows their guilt to be greatly aggravated, since the more liberally he had acted towards them, the more odious was their ingratitude."

Ver. 34. *And when the time of the fruit drew near;* the patience of God had already waited long for the fruits that might and ought to have been produced; and the farmers had not sufficient ground of justification, wherewith to palliate their faithless discharge of duty, in which they had been less careful of God's honour and the people's salvation, than the gratification of their own avarice and ambition. *He sent his servants*, extraordinary messengers, the prophets, who, as ambassadors of God, had a special commission to preach repentance, to remind men of the obligations under which they lay, to yield obedience to God, and call people, and priests, and rulers alike to the subjection that was due. These extraordinary provisions of God afford peculiar indications of his *love*, testifying how much he desired the sinner's amendment, and how far he is from viewing with indifference the sinner's conduct. Calvin: "By the divine law, priests were certainly appointed from the first, that with wholesome doctrine they might instruct and edify the church; but when, through sloth or ignorance, they neglected the work committed to them, the prophets were sent, as for an extraordinary help, that they might purge away the noxious weeds from God's vineyard, might lop off the superfluous branches, and, in many respects, supply the negligence of the priests; that they might, at the same time, sharply reprove the people, revive the languishing piety, arouse slumbering souls, and bring them back to the worship of God and the way of holiness. But what else was this than to seek the increase that was due to God from his own vineyard?"

Mark v. 3—5. The repeated messages which God sent by the prophets, and the trials of amendment again and again renewed, both indicate the continued patience, long-suffering, and wonderful compassion of God, and also unfold the levity and wantonness, the forgetfulness of God, and general wickedness of the leaders of the people, who sought to be independent, in their blindness entirely overlooked the gracious designs of God, and saw in the prophets nothing but men, through whom they were disturbed in their freedom and enjoyments, robbed of their respect among the people, and restrained in the gratification of their evil desires. The bad reception and horrid treatment which the prophets experienced, is grounded, as matter of history, on Jer. xx. 1, 2; xxxvii. xxxviii. 1 Kings xviii. 13; xxii. 24. 2 Kings vi. 31; ch. xxii. Isaiah was sawn asunder, Jeremiah was stoned, Amos murdered with a club; to all these transactions Jesus refers in Matth. xxiii. 29—37, and Stephen, in Acts vii. 5, ss., and the apostle, in Heb. xi. 36—38. The apostles, at a later period, fared no better, as, for example, John the Baptist.

Mark v. 6. *Having yet, therefore, one son, his well-beloved,* John iii. 16; both the ideas here implied were necessary to represent the invincible love of God to sinners, his solemn earnestness in the demands he makes upon them, and how he leaves nothing untried to secure the accomplishment of his precious designs concerning them. *He sent him also at last;* the sending of Christ was, therefore, the last trial of divine mercy with his covenant-people, *as such. They will reverence my son,* Luke v. 6. *It may be they will reverence him, when they see him;* it expresses the wish and the just expectation, that so great a favour would bring the sinner to himself, fill him with shame, move him to change of mind and submission, but all in vain. Calvin: "This thought is not strictly attributable to God, for he knew what would happen, nor was he misled by the hope of a better issue; but it was usual, especially in the parables, for human affections to be transferred to him. Nor was this added without due cause, for Christ wished to exhibit, as in a glass, how deplorable would be their impiety, of which it was to become too certain a mark, to rise with diabolical fury against the Son of God, who had come to bring them to a better mind. This was the consummation of all wickedness, to kill the son, that they might reign as in a desolate house."

Ver. 38. *This is the heir,* the owner of the property; the manifold testimonies which declare Jesus to be the Son of God and the Messiah, his miracles, holy walk, the power of his teaching, the fulness of his love, and every thing that God did to establish his credentials, actually brought out from many of the first among the people the acknowledgment here made, John iii. 2; and though, in unbelief, they threw all this away, as well as Christ's own solemn testimony, Matth. xxvi. 63—66, it was yet well known to them, that Jesus affirmed himself to be the Son of God. *Come, let us kill him,* Matth. xxvi. 3, 4. John xi. 47—50. *And seize on his inheritance.* Gnomon: "So they thought it would be, when Christ was killed, Matth. xxvii. 63." Grotius: "By these words it is shown, that the priests and elders of the Jews strove with all their might to constrain the divine law to subserve their own interests and ambition; which was all one, as if the husbandman should thrust himself into the possession of his lord. For, by the term *inheritance*, the full title to lordship is expressed." In short, they wished to relieve themselves of the dreaded reckoning, and remain in the undisturbed possession of their honour and their influence, which they were in danger of losing through Christ; for already had the great mass of the people began to pay more regard to Jesus, and attach themselves more closely to him than the priests and scribes, John xii. 17—19. Incredible blindness of servants towards their lord.

Ver. 39. The wickedness reaches the highest degree, and keeps pace in its growth with the renewed efforts of God for their improvement, Heb. xiii. 12, 13. Gnomon: "They disallowed Jesus both before his death, by denying his claims, especially by delivering him up to a heathen judge; and also after his death, by setting a watch upon his sepulchre, chap. xxvi. 66."

Ver. 40. The Lord puts the question to his opponents, so that the answer from their own mouth might serve as a testimony to the righteousness of the punishment that had been so richly deserved by the wicked vine-dressers. The coming of the Lord is the period when the work of divine judgment shall be executed.

Ver. 41. The adversaries of our Lord are still affected with blindness; apprehend not what purpose he aims at in the parable, and answer according to the truth; in Mark v. 9, and Luke v. 16, the judgment pronounced appears as the declaration of the Lord; but the different report of the Evangelists admits of being most easily harmonized, by supposing that the answer given by the persons interrogated (Matth. v. 41) is repeated by our Lord himself, which repetition is omitted by Matthew, while Mark and Luke, on the other hand, have not given the answer itself. The judgment pronounced is twofold: HE WILL MISERABLY DESTROY THOSE WICKED MEN, *i. e.* WILL BRING ALL SORTS OF EVIL UPON THEM; AND HIS VINEYARD WILL LET OUT TO OTHER HUSBANDMEN, WHO WILL RENDER HIM THE FRUITS IN THEIR SEASONS: the despisers of the divine mercies, and those who misuse them, shall be torn away from them, that these may be given to others more deserving. According to Luke v. 16, the hearers struck in here, and said, *God forbid!* They suspected the drift of the parable was against them, and meant either to express their horror, or, through fleshly confidence upon God's promises, their unbelief, and to say: It shall never happen to fare so ill with us. Upon this follows the question from the Old Testament, confirming the judgment pronounced.

Ver. 42. Ps. cxviii. 22, 23. The Truth contained in this scripture is, according to Christ, a prophecy, which was to receive its fulfilment in the conduct of the Jewish rulers, and of the whole people toward himself; the course and issue of the whole transaction was to become manifest as a purpose of divine wisdom and almighty power, for, although the opponents of Christ had no respect but to his destruction, yet still their opposition to him, under the divine government and direction, gave occasion for the foundation of a new covenant of grace, which should extend its blessings to the heathen. *The stone which the builders rejected,* (as unsuitable and unfit for use,) *the same has become the head of the corner;* Jesus, rejected by the high priests, scribes, and elders, not owned and recognised as the true Messiah, is the strong and firm corner stone of the new building of the Christian church, in which those who were hitherto divided asunder, Jews and heathen, have been united into one glorious body, Eph. ii. 13, 20. *This is the doing of the Lord,* not according to the will, nor accomplished through the working of man, Phil. ii. 9—11; Eph. i. 20—23. *And it is wonderful in our eyes;* the exaltation of Christ, the gathering of a new church, and the general extension of this church, is, as a work and manifestation of God's purposes and almighty power, an object for men's adoring wonder.

V. 43. *The kingdom of God shall be taken from you;* announcing, in direct terms, what was spoken, figuratively, in v. 41. Calvin: "Hitherto Christ directed his discourse to the heads and rulers, though in the presence of the people: but now he addresses the people themselves in similar language; nor without just cause, since they were to aid and assist the chief priests and scribes in preventing the grace of God. The evil, indeed, originated with the priests, but the people had already deserved, on account of their sins, to have such corrupt and degenerate pastors placed over them." *Given to a nation bringing forth the fruits thereof,* one, therefore, that should make a better use of the offered grace, and act more agreeably to the mind of God; this nation comprehends the whole people of the new covenant, 1 Peter ii. 3—10, both Jews and heathens, for the former were not excluded; faith in Christ is the general condition; whosoever does not possess this principle, is no partaker of the new dispensation of grace, nor has he a standing among the people of the covenant, although, as a descendant of Abraham, he might formerly have thought himself to have good claims to such a privilege. Calvin: "The Jews thought that the kingdom of God belonged to them by hereditary right, and therefore went on securely and obstinately in their sins; we, contrary to nature, suddenly came into their room; much less, therefore, shall that kingdom be continued with us, if it is not grounded on the root of genuine piety."

V. 44. *And whosoever shall fall on this stone shall be broken,*—an image borrowed from an earthen vessel, which falls upon a rock, and is broken in pieces. The meaning is,—he hurts only himself, not Christ, who is offended at the humble form of the Redeemer, Matth. xi. 3; Isa. liii. 1—3, and, in consequence, turns from him in unbelief. *But on whomsoever it shall fall, it will grind him to powder;* the rock, if it falls upon the earthen vessel, completely shivers it to atoms, Dan. ii. 34, 44. The sense is,—Whosoever falls under the condemnation of the Messiah, who is exalted by God, though rejected on the part of man, he must experience complete destruction. Such is the different fate of those who reject Christ without any special enmity and hatred, and of those who bitterly oppose him,* as did these wicked vine-dressers, and

* [This, though the most common explanation, gives a turn to our Lord's expressions which they can but ill bear, and completely overlooks the distinctive character of the two kinds of punishment referred to. It is not certainly to be doubted, that those who have manifested a spirit of bitter and malevolent hostility towards Christ, shall be partakers of a heavier condemnation than those who have simply disregarded the offers of his salvation,—the guilt of the one being much more aggravated than the other. But the language of Christ does not appear to have any respect to a difference of this nature; it marks two different kinds of punishment, not two different degrees of the same punishment. In the one, the person offending is active, (he stumbles and is broken;) in the other passive, (he is fallen upon and crushed.) Whatever evil is experienced in the first case is self-inflicted by the person who endures it; but that which is experienced, in the second, rushes upon the sufferer with irresistible force, from the offended and now avenging Saviour. Consequently, the one is a punishment only of this life, where alone sinners have the opportunity of stumbling on the rock of salvation; and consists in all the loss of peace, consolation, and blessing, together with all that judicial blindness, bitterness of spirit, hardness of heart and manifold disquietudes of mind, which inevi-

as those also did who are described in the next parable, Matth. xxii. 6, 7, and in Luke xix. 14, 27. Luther's marginal note: "*All* must come into contact with Christ, whether for benefit or for stumbling." Calvin: "They are said to *fall* upon Christ, who set on him to destroy him; not as if they could actually rise above him, but because, in their madness, they are so far carried beside themselves that they endeavour, as from a vantage-ground, to make an attack upon Christ."

V. 45, 46. Most extraordinary effect of the parable, and the solemn threatening annexed to it, the meaning of which was, indeed, understood by the enemies of our Lord, and applied to themselves; but, instead of repressing their bitterness, and withdrawing their enmity from Christ, they only redoubled their malice, and hastened forward the accomplishment of their ungodly purposes. The internal ground of this conduct of theirs lies in the truth, which all experience confirms, that passions, when once they have reached a certain height, and gained a complete mastery of the heart, are excited, brought out, and violently inflamed, by nothing more than by having exhibited before them their own image, and the righteous punishment that is due to them. The most affecting entreaties produce then the very opposite of the effect intended, and

tably blight and desolate the moral condition of those who resist the claims of Messiah. But the other punishment belongs to eternity, and consists in the fearful and everlasting retribution which Christ will inflict upon all his adversaries when he takes to himself his power and great glory, one which shall overwhelm them with complete destruction. So that there is a double retribution flowing from the rejection of Christ; one here, which the sinner receives into his own bosom,—kicking against Christ, he inevitably kicks against the pricks; and one hereafter, which consigns him to final perdition, in utter darkness. We think our author right, however, in explaining the figure employed by the earthen vessel, and discarding the allusion which Lightfoot and others have found here to the alleged mode of punishing criminals among the Jews, by first throwing them over a precipice, and thereafter, if still alive, throwing over a stone upon them.—*Trans.*]

make the bad only more determined and obstinate in their wickedness; their heart hardens itself against threatenings, and they are the more confident in setting at naught the fear of all danger, nay, their self-love flatters itself with the prospect of yet bearing off the victory, and securing a quite different from the threatened result. So did it happen with these wicked vine-dressers, with the pharisees, scribes, high-priests, and elders of the people; so, likewise, did it happen with Judas, and so also with Hazael, whom Elisha forewarned, 2 Kings viii. 12, 13; x. 32. Calvin: "The Evangelists show how little Christ prevailed, that we might not be surprised, if now the doctrine of the cross does not bring all to the obedience of God. Let us learn also, that threatenings cannot but serve to make the fury of the wicked rise higher and higher. For as God seals his own word upon our hearts, so also does he wound, as with a sharp sword, bad consciences; from which it comes to pass, that their impiety is but the more inflamed." Ewald, p. 158, ss: "If we would seek for an admirable example of our Lord's forbearance, and of the abuse of this forbearance, of beneficence and ingratitude, of goodness, which has nothing to excite it and still is excited; if we would have an example of senseless hardihood, which mistakes itself for prudence, of blind and raving folly, taking that for weakness which was nothing but unmeasured patience, we may find it here. Insolence could not be pushed farther than it is here pushed by the vine-dressers, nor could watchful oversight go farther than in the case of the Lord of the vineyard. They were punished with great severity, and yet every one feels that it was nothing but strictest justice. We find here the history of Israel, of all humanity, and of each single individual. Many a germ of good has God planted in thy heart, and preserved there even since the fall of humanity. Many powers have been given thee by God, which thou both shouldest and mayest use for good. How often has God kept thee, and drawn a hedge around thy heart! How often has God upheld thee against the enemies of good! All, that thou mightest bring forth fruit in its season, mightest grow in truth and love, in purity and faith on God, and so become his image. And when the time came for God seeking fruit of thee, how many messengers did he send to thee! Friends, preachers, his blessed word, conscience, what are they all but messengers of God, means which he employs to put thee in remembrance of what thou owest to him? But how often hast thou set thyself in opposition to these messengers of God—slighted, shunned, yea, even hated them! Thou couldst not properly kill the Son, whom God has made known to thee in the Bible, but thou hast wounded him with thy deeds. Truly, God's goodness is not weakness, his forbearance is not indifference. Thy fate will be similar to the fate of the Jews! Still two words of exhortation—one to the secure and one to the doubting. It is clear, from this parable, that the consequences of disobedience are often *distant*, but are always *certain*. There are many to whom God might say: Thou doest that, and I am silent, thou thinkest that I am as indifferent as thyself toward what is good, but I will punish thee, and convince thee by punishment, Ps. l. 21. And though for ten or twenty years, or even through thy whole life, thou dost not experience it, it yet remains an eternal, an unfailing truth, 'Whatsoever a man soweth, that shall he also reap.' But it is just as clear from this parable, that it is not too late to become servants of God, because we have been so long in doing so; that it is not too late to become better, because we have not been so long before. The earlier a man reforms, so much the better for him, but better late than never, therefore, since we still hear his voice, let us not harden our hearts to-day."

XIV.

THE ROYAL WEDDING, OR THE WEDDING GARMENT.

Matth. xxii. 1—14.

Many expositors have taken this parable, and the one given in Luke xiv. 16—24, as one and the same, alleging that the latter is only altered from this in some unimportant particulars; but the small resemblance and strong dissimilarity between the two parables render it impossible for us to agree to this opinion, and we are constrained, both on external and internal grounds, to consider the two parabolical discourses of our Lord as quite different from, and independent of, each other. Not only are the time, place and hearers in the one, quite changed from what they are in the other, but, what is still more material, the scope is entirely different, as a careful consideration of all the circumstances convinces us. The parable of the great supper, in Luke, was delivered by Jesus before the last journey to Jerusalem, in Peræa, in the house of a pharisee, at an entertainment, (for the scope, see No. 26;) the one here recorded by Matthew, in the temple at Jerusalem, chap. xxi. 13, probably on the Tuesday before his sufferings (v. 18,) before the high priests and elders of the people, (v. 23.) The immediate reference of the parable is certainly historical, and according to many expositors, represents in v. 3—6, the treatment *hitherto* given by the Jewish people to the prophets; in v. 7, gives a prophetic intimation of the approaching judgment of God, on account of it, in the devastation of Jerusalem; discloses in v. 8—10, the call of the Gentiles to the heavenly kingdom; and, finally, points in v. 11—14, to the different judgments which shall be pronounced upon its members. It is better, however, to understand the conduct of the first invited guests, v. 2—6, as a prophetic description of the persecutions which the messengers of Jesus, his apostles suffered, who first properly invited men to the heavenly kingdom, to a blessed fellowship with Jesus, and to refer the later invitation, v. 8—10, to the general call, which from that time forward, is always being addressed to Jews and Gentiles, to come into the Christian church. But if we look beyond the nearest historical application, the parable discloses to us the following important general truths, which are receiving new confirmations at every period of the church's history: God provides for the salvation of men through the preaching of the gospel—the conduct of men in regard to the offered grace is exceedingly different—even among those who receive the call, there are found some unworthy—but all shall be treated with perfect justice. The sentiment occurring at the close of the parable, v. 14, *for many are called but few are chosen*, closely connected with what precedes by *for*, contains the ground of the figuratively described issue of the matter, and at the same time the leading idea, which shines palpably out through the whole narrative, namely, that from men's own blame, all shall not be partakers of the distinguishing grace tendered by God. Mel.: "It is much to be regretted that men do not consider such great and undeserved goodness of God toward us; the whole parable is the image of the church in all ages; and although the rejection and punishment of the Jewish church is principally referred to, yet the discourse must be applied to the similar events of every age."

TRAIN OF THOUGHT IN THE PARABLE.

Calling and election are not one and the same; or, all are not partakers of the salvation prepared for them by God.

I. Many are not saved, because they are open despisers of the grace of God, v. 1—8.

(1.) The state and temper of these despisers:

a) Some are perfectly indifferent toward the gracious call, v. 2—5;

b) Others show an open hostility to it, v. 6.

(2.) Their guilt is manifest;

a) From the greatness of the offered grace, v. 2;

b) From the repeated and pressing invitation, v. 3, 4;

c) From the trifling nature of that which they prefer, v. 5;

d) From the hostility showed by them, v. 6;

e) From the punishment executed upon them, v. 7;

f) From the judicial declaration of God, v. 8.

II. Others are not saved, because they will not comply with the order necessary to salvation.

(1.) The state and temper of these guests;

a) They willingly indeed receive the invitation, v. 9, 10;

b) But they do not comply with the necessary order, v. 11;

(2.) Their guilt appears in:

a) Their speechless confusion, v. 12;

b) Their condemnation from God, v. 13.

Ver. 2. *The kingdom of heaven is like;* just as it went at and with the wedding-feast which a king made for his son, so is it also found to take place in regard to the blessed fellowship of men with Christ, to which they are invited, Zeph. i. 7, 8; Prov. ix. 1, ss. *A certain king who made a marriage for his son;* "The king who made the marriage-feast (says Luther, Church-Pos. 14. 189,) is our heavenly father, the bridegroom is his son, our Lord Jesus Christ, the bride is the Christian church, we and all the world, so far as it believes." God's gracious purpose, from eternity, was the salvation of sinners through Christ, and he manifested this gracious purpose after many preparatory arrangements in the fulness of time, Gal. iv. 4, 5. In comparing the saving ordinances of the Christian church to a royal wedding, the essential point of comparison is, not the internal union of the soul in individuals, or in the whole church to Jesus, which is certainly often represented in scripture under the figure of a marriage-union, Hosea ii. 19; Eph. v. 32; 2 Cor.

xi. 2; Rev. xix. 7, xxi. 9; but the *tertium comparationis* of the whole parable lies pre-eminently in the conduct of the invited guests, toward the invitation held forth to them, and in the destiny arising to them out of it. The farther extension of the comparison by many expositors to the fellowship between believers and the Redeemer, however much of what is beautiful, true, and scriptural, may be said upon the subject, only serves to keep out of view the main features of the similitude, and veil its real scope; but still less can we agree with Luther, Church-Pos. 14. 193, in saying: "This wedding is a union of the divine nature with the human." Bauer understands by this marriage-supper, a feast, such as was wont to be given at the commencement of a king's reign, who then married himself as it were to his people, 1 Kings i. 5, 9; 1 Chron. xxix. 24.

Ver. 3. *And sent forth his servants to call them that were bidden to the wedding.* Luther Church-Pos. 14. 189: "To invite to this wedding, God at first sent forth his servants, that is, his prophets, who should bid them to the wedding, should preach and point their faith to Christ. But the persons they invited would not come, that is, the Jews, to whom the prophets were sent, would not hear or receive them. To others he sent out other servants, that is, the apostles and martyrs, whose part it was to call us." Others refer the first invitation to the commission of John the Baptist and of the twelve as first sent out, Matth. x.; but the main thing is the *repeatedly* proclaimed invitation to each. The motive on the part of God to such invitation, is nothing but his *free grace,* without any thing like merit or worth on the part of men, for even in the social relation of life, no one can *demand* of another, that he should invite him, and least of all can the inferior make such a claim upon the more honourable. The point of comparison between the heavenly kingdom, God's institution of grace, in which we are to be safe, holy, and glorious, and a royal wedding, lies especially in the honour, satisfaction, and delight, which such an occasion furnishes to its guests, and the heavenly kingdom to its members; for it is honour, when sinners enter into fellowship with the Son of God, himself, and this fellowship brings with it satisfaction,—pardon of sin, peace with God, righteousness, life, and blessing,—in which and from which they necessarily experience delight. From these three considerations, that the invitation is of free grace, that it comes to us without any merit of ours, and that it brings so great a gift, the criminality of those guests who despise the invitation is clearly manifested.

And they would not come. The first class of the invited, who do not come; it is no want of knowledge of the feast, or of the invitation, but the bad state of their mind, which holds them back; it is just as if they did not hear the call, did not give the slightest heed to it; a dull and stupid insensibility for God's rich grace, which is freely offered to them, has taken possession of so many, that they pay no regard to the gospel, the promises, or the hopes of eternal life.

Ver. 4. From the frequently repeated invitation, we may farther discern God's deep earnestness and fatherly love, who is so bent on helping sinners, and also the high importance of a participation in the gospel feast,—which circumstance brings the criminal conduct of the invited still more distinctly into view.—*Tell those that are bidden,* those who have been already bidden; God's gracious call is given to every one, not once merely, but often.—*Behold I have prepared my dinner; my oxen and my fatlings are killed, and all things are ready.* The invitation is more urgent, through the full representation and description of the proffered grace; in Luke this is expressed by the words, "compel them to come in;" in this feast all salvation is the free grace and gift of God, which he, without any co-operation on our part, has prepared through Christ, so that man's business is only to come, receive, and enjoy, what God's fatherly love presents, Eph. i. 3, ss.—Oxen and fatlings were in olden times the noblest entertainment, 1 Kings i. 9; Gen. xviii. 7, 8. Luther goes quite beside the purpose, in referring these to the nourishment, growth, and exercise of the life of godliness, (Church-Pos. 14. 190.) Others as unnaturally refer it to the sacrifice of Christ, and the enjoyment, thereby purchased and prepared, of all the blessings of salvation.—*Come in to the marriage;* the method in which we attain to the enjoyment, is the coming, and the change of place represents the complete change of condition and frame of mind that must be made by the invited.

Ver. 5, 6. " Luther, Church-Pos. 14. 191: " These are the three hinderances that keep us back from going to the feast. First, *lands*, in other words, the worldly honour, which tends to hinder us from thinking upon Christ and believing on him, to make us fear lest we should suffer shame and be dishonoured; not to confide in God, that he will screen us from shame, and preserve us in honour, John v. 44; xii. 43. Others go to their *merchandise*, that is, give their whole heart to temporal good, to the gains of covetousness, afraid, were they to give themselves up to the word, lest they should lose, and their belly be starved, unable to trust that God will support them. The third class are the worst, that is, the high, the wise, and the prudent, the proud spirits who not merely despise the gospel, but would straightway destroy it, utterly strangle it, that they might retain their names, their honour and their glory. For the gospel cannot but condemn their wisdom and righteousness, and pour contempt upon their arrogance." Mel.: " There are still many called Christians, who, for the sake of their farms, flee from the profession of the faith, and become either avowed Epicureans, or, at least defend the common corruptions for the sake of their belly. Others are led, by their worldly business, to forsake the profession of the faith. Under this class are chiefly comprised princes and courtiers, who though they do not exercise any cruelty, yet neglect the gospel and the church, and think that the care of such things is unworthy of them,—that they have great concerns to mind, necessary to the life of men, namely, the government and defence of empires."

They made light of it. Gnomon: "This already implies more than if it had been said, *they would not come;* they ought to have *understood,* and been watchful." They are not simply indifferent, as at first; the heart turns itself away from the gospel with the manifestation of a stronger dislike, if it has been repeatedly treated with the offer of salvation in vain, and the enmity to this increases in the very same heart, even to open and determined resistance; for enmity and hatred have a far more mournful and hardening effect upon the heart that cherishes them than upon the heart of him who is hated, so that the latter can much sooner be brought to forgive, than the former to lay aside its feelings of hostility. This mournful experimental truth, which manifests the power of sin over the human mind, might also have been pointed at in the parable under the different conduct of different individuals. *Slew them,* John xvi. 2—4. Matth. xxiv. 2. Acts vii. 58; xii. 1—3.

Ver. 7. The servants only entreated, 2 Cor. v. 20. They do not repel violence with violence, nor recompense evil with evil; they leave the matter in God's hands, who is both judge and avenger. From the behaviour also on the part of the servants, and from the friendly message with which they come, we perceive the greatness of that malice and hardness of heart, which the adversaries of the gospel manifest. But they are not left unpunished. *Sent forth his armies.* Every thing must serve the Lord and execute his will, whether consciously or unconsciously. Luther, Church-Pos. 14. 191: "That was done to the Jews by the Romans, when, under Titus and Vespasian, they burned Jerusalem to the ground. However, I would rather understand it spiritually, since the whole gospel is to be spiritually understood, so as to consider the prediction fulfilled, when God set on fire and levelled to the ground the synagogue at Jerusalem, abandoned the Jewish faith, scattered to and fro the people, so that all was torn asunder, and they were deprived both of the priesthood and the kingdom, and now no people is to be found upon the earth so poor, miserable, and deserted as the Jews. So shall it fare with the despisers of God's word." From the punitive righteousness of God, marked by the words—*the king was wroth;* we see once more how sincere is the gracious call of God, and how, in despising it, a guilt is contracted on the part of man; but, at the same time, we can also perceive, that the reception is a free act, and that man is not compelled to it by God.

Ver. 8. *The wedding is ready;* it still continues so, notwithstanding that many have slighted the call to it. The mercy of God is long-continued. The invited guests were not worthy of it; they were in such a state of mind, that they could not receive the grace offered them; here divine grace is justified, and all guilt thrown back upon the guests, (Acts xiii. 46, 47,) so that not even the servants inviting them are partakers in it. Gnomon: "No one is reckoned unworthy, unless he has refused the boon already offered; but, doing that, he finally commits himself." Grotius: "They were not worthy, that is, they were most unworthy."

Go ye, therefore, into the highways, the crossways. Luther, House-Pos. 5. 188: "To the heathen, who lay without upon the paths, having no law or word of God, like the Jews; they were not walled in, but set off as an open vacant space. We still see to-day, that God has appointed his word, his baptism, his supper, for the purpose of giving every one an opportunity to partake who desires to do so." The national pride of Israel is here primarily aimed at, Matth. viii. 10—12.

Ver. 9. *Bid as many as ye shall find,* expressing the universality of divine grace, and the call to the

Christian church, John iii. 16. Matth. xxviii. 18, ss. Luke xxiv. 46, 47. No distinction of people, no grades of intellectual or moral condition, must form an exception, but all must be invited, not excepting even the Jews.

V. 10. *Gathered all, good and bad;* the manifestly wicked, whom all considered as reprobates, and those who had led an externally honourable life, for such were found even among the heathen; for example, Cornelius and the ruler at Capernaum; for, as regards the internal condition, all are alike sinners. To refer the good and evil spoken of to the subsequent condition of the guests, as indicating that all were not rightly and permanently established in the knowledge of the Christian faith, will not suit. Grotius: "That it might more distinctly appear that this gift was entirely gratuitous." *And the wedding was furnished with guests;* although many had slighted the gracious designs and purposes of God, and frustrated them, there was yet no want of such as, with the greatest joy and readiness, appropriated this grace, so that the table was filled, Isa. liii. 12; John xi. 52; xii. 24.

V. 11. *When the king came to see the guests;* Luther, Church-Pos. 14. 192: "This shall be done at the last judgment, when the king will let himself be seen." At least, every one shall then be made manifest before the whole world, according to his internal condition, so that God's dealing with each will be acknowledged as perfectly just; but, even upon earth, the secret state of heart is disclosed, through means of many trials and experiences in life, so that every one, who still wants the wedding-garment, might ponder the will of the Lord, who asks after it, and provide himself with it. Taken generally, v. 11—13, intimate the truth, that the church on earth is not pure, but always made up of good and evil,—of true believers and hypocrites, a mixed society, but shall afterwards be purged of all false unworthy members by the most righteous judgment of God. This work of separation, however, is not the business of the servants, who also could not hinder the entrance of such unworthy guests; and hence no reproach is cast upon them by the king for the appearance which presented itself. The thought, further, is expressed here, that the time of gospel invitation, the day of grace, shall some time cease, and that thenceforth, through all eternity, the fate of each is decided and made manifest.

Saw there a man; Luther, Church-Pos. 14. 192; "That is, not a single individual, but a whole multitude; not clothed with the wedding-garment, that is, with faith. They are, however, pious people, much better than the preceding; for you must understand them to be those who have heard and received the gospel, but still have leaned somewhat upon their works, and not crept wholly into Christ." It is quite an indefensible opinion to consider this *one* to represent those who are described by Paul, 2 Thes. ii. 3, ss.; which opinion is advocated by Canstein in his Harmony. *Who had not on the wedding-garment;* which was wont to be given by rich and honourable entertainers to their guests, that they might put it over their clothes, and so appear in the fitting apparel, Judges xiv. 12; Gen. xlv. 22; Rev. iii. 4, 5. The wedding-garment is the state of mind which is, in itself, right and well pleasing in the sight of God, and that we must have on this wedding-garment, if we would not be shut out from the marriage-feast, is evident from its being the order appointed by God in the work of salvation, with which every sinner must, of necessity, comply, if he would become a partaker, either in time or in eternity, of the blessings proffered to him. To regard moral qualities as a clothing, is an image frequently employed in holy writ, Eph. iv. 22—24; 1 Peter iii. 4; Col. iii. 12; Rev. vii. 13—15. As scripture connects salvation above all with faith, that is, the gracious disposition which, *first of all*, appropriates every thing that Christ has purchased—pardon of sin, righteousness and the several gifts of grace, must be the wedding-garment; (on which account some expositors affirm Christ himself to be this garment, according to Rom. xiii. 14; Gal. iii. 27;) and this gracious disposition, or believing frame of mind, becomes, thereafter, the source of all the virtues that adorn the faithful, of righteousness, of life, and that as the fruit and consequence of the righteousness of faith. This principle of faith is conferred upon us, *i. e.* through the preaching of the word it is rendered possible to every one who has a mind, Rom. x. 9, 10, 13—17. In the practical treatment of this image, it is most judicious not to dwell upon the garment by itself, but upon the state of those who either have or want it. Luther, Gloss.: "The wedding-garment is faith, for the gospel rejects the self-righteous, and takes in the faithful." Calvin: "It is needlessly contended, whether the wedding-garment be faith, or a pious and holy life; because, neither can faith be separated from good works, nor are good works practicable without faith. Christ, however, only meant, that we must so comply with the call of our Lord, as to be renewed in spirit, after his image, remaining constantly in union with him, that the old man, with his defilements, must be put off, and the new life diligently applied to, by which means our garment might become suitable to our honourable calling." Mel.: "The wedding-garment, then, is that regeneration which comprehends within itself the actings of repentance and faith, which receives the remission of sins; and throughout the whole life, cleaves to God for help, and endeavours after new obedience. But there are many in the visible church who have not this wedding-garment. First, there are those who continue in sin against their conscience; then there are hypocrites, like Ahaz, who, though in appearance an upright man, and sound in his profession, yet is without any true light; that is, without repentance and faith, multiplies acts of worship, thinks himself righteous, carries on many operations, but all in confidence on his own wisdom, distrusting God; neither seeking nor expecting aid from him, but searching every where for human help, against the exhortations of the prophets, 2 Kings xvi."

Ver. 12. *Friend, how camest thou in hither? &c.*—Language expressive of the greatest astonishment at the extraordinary circumstance of his presence in such a state. The word *friend*, εταιρε, occurs always in a bad sense, Matth. xx. 13: xxvi. 50; and here, in particular, it designates one who was not sincere in his professions. Luther: House-Pos. 5. 203: "These are false Christians and hypocrites, who seek only their belly and their honour in the gospel; such persons put to shame the bride and bridegroom, in not being better arrayed and having no marriage clothing. If I were the bridegroom, I should also take it for an indignity, and think nothing else than that he designed to mock me." And again, at p. 189: "If thou art already an invited guest, art baptized, hearest the gospel, goest to the sacrament, and still hast on no wedding-garment, that is, dost not believe, art not in earnest in the matter, and thinkest only of enjoying the Christian name—thou art then no Christian for the sake of God or thine own salvation, otherwise thou shouldst act differently towards the world. Never dream that thou shalt slip through in such a state. The king will perceive thee, and drag thee forth, either at the last day, or at thy latter end, and shall say, Do I find thee here, having the name of a Christian, and still not believing what a Christian should believe? During thy lifetime thou wert never in earnest how thou mightest be free from sin, holy, and meet for heaven."

But he was speechless, his mouth was in a manner muzzled. Luther, House-Pos. 5. 189: "Whenever such loose Christians are charged with being such, either in their own conscience, or on the day of judgment, they shall be speechless, that is, they shall have no defence. For what have they to justify themselves withal? God has done what he would." Their silence, then, marks the consciousness of guilt and of the righteousness of God's judgment; the servants, who invite to the wedding, point also to the appointed way of salvation, so that the demands necessary to be complied with remain unknown to none of the invited guests, and every one, besides, must allow, that the possession of the wedding-garment was possible for him. Why did so many decline it? Their own clothing appeared to them good enough, and they think it must also be well pleasing to the king; it is, therefore, presumptuous ignorance, self-righteousness, confidence in their supposed virtue, which prevents many from being saved; others dream of faith in Christ, and rest upon his merit, while yet their faith has no renewing effect upon their heart and conduct. They remain, (says Luther, Church-Pos. 14. 212,) whoremongers, adulterers, gluttons, drunkards, usurers, full of hatred and envy; they remain in the old rags and tatters of their own fleshly darkness, unbelief, security, without repentance and acknowledgment of their wretchedness; console not their hearts with the grace of Christ, nor improve their lives thereby, seek no more, in short, from the gospel than is pleasing to the flesh. For as this wedding-garment must be the new light of the heart, so the knowledge of this abundant grace of the bridegroom and his marriage feast, works in the heart so as to make it hang in close dependence upon Christ, and be penetrated with joy and consolation, consequently to live and act in light and love, as knowing that it is giving pleasure to him, as a bride does to her bridegroom." The warnings so often given through the preached gospel to false Christians, and the repentance pressed upon them, as well as the example of those near and around them, who are adorned with the wedding-garment, renders them the more liable to condemnation. And since they have not employed the long-continued day of grace for the attainment of the necessary frame of mind, it is at last too late when the king comes, and they sink into perdition. "Hence does the gospel carry a very solemn admonition to every one who hears it, to improve well the time of the gospel, and a terrible threatening of frightful punishment to alight, both upon the secure, arrogant despisers, who have slighted the day of grace and set themselves against the preaching of the gospel; and upon the false and frivolous, who, for appearance-sake, shelter themselves under the name of Christ and the gospel, yet never do so in solemn earnest." Luther, Church-Pos. 14. 198.

Ver. 13. *Bind him hand and foot.* Luther, as above: "The hands are the works, the feet the walk, in which he has confided, and so, not having wholly trusted in Christ, he must perish with his works; if thou wouldst, therefore, do good works, thou must first believe." *Cast him into outer darkness.* Luther, House-Pos. 5. 190: "They must be shut out from God's light, that is, from all light, in eternal pain, sorrow, and anguish, where they shall never see one ray of light." Gnomon: "This shall be done a little before the nuptial hour."—*Weeping and gnashing of teeth.* Luther, ib.: "They must, therefore, be bound for ever in hell, tormented with cold and heat, as was taught by the ancients. But the Lord in this expression includes all sort of tortures which can be thought of; as if he had said, Ye shall suffer more than can be expressed in words, or conceived in thought."

Ver. 14. See toward the end of the parable of the labourers in the vineyard. This guest without the wedding-garment makes the truth palpably manifest, Luke xiii. 24. Mel.: "There is both consolation and warning in the words; consolation to the pious, who, when they see many utterly regardless of the faith, are offended, and brought into doubt whether such a society can be the true church. All the warnings of God are announced for the purpose of moving some thereby to turn from their wickedness."

XV.

THE TEN VIRGINS.

Matt. xxv. 1—13.

General prefatory remarks upon this and the following Parable.

This parable stands in very close connexion with the preceding instructions, warnings and admonitions of Jesus. Matth. xxiv. To the question of his disciples, propounded in v. 1—3, our Lord answers in v. 4—14, with general remarks upon the commencement of a very troublous, eventful period, which they themselves should live to see, (v. 5—8) and which was principally to affect them, (v. 9—14.) Then he speaks more particularly of the destruction of Jerusalem, v. 15—28, as the proper commencement of a great and general contest between light and darkness, and especially cautions them against the mistaken notion, that he was to come in his glory *immediately* after the destruction of Jerusalem, v. 23—28. Of his return, he speaks in v. 29, ss., admonishes to carefulness in regard to the sign of approach, v. 32, declares in v. 36, that it was unknown as to the precise time and hour, though still as certain as the deluge was to the ancient world, and that it would be attended with very different consequences to men, just according as their conduct had been, v. 37—41. For this reason he admonishes to watchfulness, v. 42, the happy consequences of which are described in v. 43—47, as, on the other hand, the mournful consequences of which are described in v. 43—47, as, on the other hand, the mournful consequences of false security in v. 48—51. Now, the parables recorded in ch. xxv. 1—30, contain in figure the same admonitions, which, without figure, are given in the preceding discourse of our Lord; they set forth in lively colours the *certainty* of Christ's return, v. 6, 19, though it should be longer delayed, than people would readily believe, v. 5, 6, 19; and that when it arrived, a very different fate should befall the watchful and trustworthy, and the faithless and negligent. If the first parable portrays in more general terms the necessary readiness of the Christian for the arrival of his lord, the latter, as having this event more immediately in prospect, speaks in particular of the fidelity and conscientiousness that are required. This both have in common, that they refer to the same most important event, the return of the Lord to his church, and call our attention to what on our part is necessary for his reception, that we may stand before him with honour and acceptance, and may not be ashamed before him at his coming, 1 John ii. 28. The parable of the ten virgins mainly teaches, that there is required for that purpose a genuine persevering faith, and the parable of the talents shows, that such a faith must not be a dead thing, and wholly separate from the rest of the life, but binds us to make a faithful application of all the gifts bestowed on us by God, and to the conscientious use of all the circumstances of our lot; the former describes the internal state of mind belonging to the true disciples of Jesus, without which every thing external is insufficient to salvation, and in a manner nothing; the latter teaches that according to the will, and to fulfil the design of Christ, there is also necessary a kind of working, proceeding from a right disposition of heart, because it is only through such an exercise of principle in the daily life, that the disposition itself can be preserved and strengthened, which otherwise would languish and die, v. 29. So that faith, and the works of faith, are represented in these parables in their internal union and mutual relationship, and that, in the most impressive manner, in the quite different characters of the prudent and foolish virgins, of the conscientious and faithless slothful servant. The foolish virgins were deficient in the proper frame of mind, although they had what was outward, the lamps; the faithless servant acknowledged himself to be a servant of the Lord, but this testimony was dead, wrought not the effect it should have produced, he is without *living* faith—and so both the one and the other fall short of the hoped for salvation. Calvin: "Although the exhortation here given has nearly the same tendency (as will appear from v. 13,) with that in Luke xii. 35—48, it was yet properly added, that it might encourage the faithful to persevere. The Lord knew how prone the nature of man is to ease, and how it, for the most part, happens, not only that men become languid in process of time, but are even liable, on a sudden, to fall off. That he might correct this disease, he taught his disciples that they were not well fortified, unless their patience could bear up for a long period. The sum of the parable is, that the diligent application of a short time is not sufficient, unless there be also found an unwearied steadfastness."

The more important, in the Lord's eyes, is the salvation of his people, and the more earnest his wish, that none of them should be lost; the more there were of alarming events threatening destruction, to depress the courage of the apostles, and other disciples, in later times; the more the distressing and hampering influence of the temporal life, of its cares and occupations, of its joys and pleasures, tend to mislead and restrain believers in their course toward the heavenly inheritance, and in concern for their souls; finally the more eventful, throughout all eternity, for bliss or misery, is the acquired or neglected preparation, the exercised or not exercised fidelity; so much the more solicitous and careful is the Lord in pointing out to his people every thing necessary, in order to keep them from all that was injurious to their souls; and for this reason he employs such various images, to make them familiar with the right frame of mind, and to work upon them through the manifold motives thereby presented to them. The image of the householder, who, before the thief has broken into his house,

(Matth. xxiv. 42—44,) must be admonished to watchfulness, from a regard to his own well-being; the example of the faithful servant, (v. 45—47,) encouraged by the hope of honour and reward; the fate of the unfaithful servant, (v. 48—51,) through fear of disfavour and punishment; the very same motives, only represented more at large, are also brought forward in the two longer parables, in ch. xxv.; wakefulness or readiness, in general, is recommended, v. 1—13, fidelity in particular, v. 14—30, active benevolence, v. 31—46; all in reference to the advent of our Lord.

According to Matth. xxiv. 3, these parables were spoken upon the Mount of Olives, and only to the disciples; they are the last parables delivered by our Lord.

TRAIN OF THOUGHT IN THE PARABLE.

The proper preparation for the advent of our Lord.

I. Wherein it consists:

(1.) Every sort of preparation is not the proper one, v. 1, 2.

(2.) What then is the right preparation?

a.) It does not stand merely in externals, v. 3: Lamps without oil.

b.) But consists in preparedness of heart, v. 4: The wise have oil, and of that enough.

II. Why it is so necessary; on account of the advent of the Lord; as this shall be an event,

(1.) Long delayed, v. 5; insomuch that even the prepared were asleep;

(2.) Unexpectedly sudden, v. 6;

(3.) Decisive; for it

a) Manifests to all their obligations, v. 7; and their state, v. 8;

b.) Leaves no room for help, neither from others nor from one's self, v. 9, 10.

c.) Determines, for ever, the fate of both, as well the prepared, v. 10, as the unprepared, v. 11—13.

V. 1. *Then shall the kingdom of heaven;* from this close connexion with the instructions delivered by our Lord in ch. xxiv., it is manifest that the course of transactions described in this and the following parable, has its primary reference to the destruction of Jerusalem, as, by this great event, the fate of those who believed on Jesus was to become different, according as they had or had not, in faith upon his word, prepared themselves for it. But since the Lord, in that preceding chapter, had also spoken of his future coming, the parable must also refer to the final advent of the Lord to judgment, and in general to the visitations of God, which are all a coming of the Lord; to such time and transactions as serve to throw *the unprepared* into fear and consternation; to the whole day of grace in life, during which men must be preparing themselves for great future events, since death begins the night, during which no man can work; and the life after death, the moment it begins in each individual, is the day of the Lord, wherein we are called to be sifted and judged. Mel.: "This parable is an image of the church in all ages, but especially in the last, and contains both doctrine, reproof, and consolation. The doctrine is, that there always have been, and will be, good and bad in the church on earth, the latter called hypocrites, because in name and appearance bearing a resemblance to true worshippers. The consolation is, that it foretells there should always be a true church and some wise virgins, who, in real faith and well-grounded hope, look for Christ."

The kingdom of heaven is likened; those who stand in connexion with the Redeemer, shall be found in condition and fate, as different, as this parable represents of the ten virgins. *To ten virgins;* "We would not include in these two classes of wise and foolish virgins, those who revile and persecute the gospel, for such are not good enough to be named even among the foolish virgins." Luther's Miscellaneous Sermons, 18. 241. *Virgin,* says Luther, imports purity, but the farther prosecution of this image, as including that the souls of believers belong to Christ as the bridegroom, John iii. 29, because he has bought them with a great price, 1 Peter i. 18, 19, to make them his own property, Acts xx. 28; 1 Cor. vii. 23, and that, through faith, Christ is united to his people in cordial love, is here out of place, as it would only serve to veil the leading character of the parable and interrupt its design. Calvin: "Christ had no other object in view than to lighten the oppressive tedium which might be supposed to arise from the delay of his arrival; for which purpose he tells us, that he demands of us nothing more than what was wont to be done by friends at a marriage solemnity. It was customary for virgins, (who are tender and delicate,) in honour of a bridegroom, to lead him to the marriage bed; and the main design of the parable turns on this, that it is not enough to be once prepared and ready for the office, but to continue so to the end." Grotius: "The scope is indicated by Christ, in the words, *watch, therefore;* namely, that we ought to be always careful concerning the right ordering of our lives."

Who took their lamps and went forth to meet the bridegroom. The essential thing here is, that the virgins who knew of the coming of the bridegroom, prepared themselves for his reception, in order to participate in the honour and joy of the festive transaction. It is delightful that our Lord here also, as in chap. xxiv. 32, makes choice of an image, which raises such joyous expectations, sufficient to divest of their terror all the frightful circumstances with which his coming is also connected. The believers of the old covenant looked for the coming of Messiah, Isa. lx. 1, ss.; lxiv. 1; Luke ii. 25. The believers who live under the new covenant, look for his second coming, Phil. iii. 21; Heb. ix. 28; Titus ii. 11, ss. This expectation is a powerful means, in the hand of God, for raising and sanctifying the heart; it springs out of faith in the promises of the Lord, Matth. xxv. 31;

John xiv. 3, xvii. 24; Acts i. 9—11, and is at once the proof and the nourishment of love to him: we look for him, because we love him, and could not love him if we were not looking for him; we look for him, because we have already experienced love to him when absent, 1 Peter i. 8; and this expectancy toward Christ's coming and preparation for it, is the leading purpose and main concern of all true Christians, Col. iii. 1, ss.

The image is borrowed from the Jewish custom, according to which the bridegroom had to conduct the bride home in the evening from the house of her parents, to his own dwelling; he came accompanied by young men, his particular friends, and, as soon as the report of his coming was announced, the young friends and play-mates of the bride put themselves in order to meet him, after which they attended the pair, with lamps carried before them, to the bridegroom's house. The lamps were placed on copper dishes, which were fastened from above to long poles, comp. Judg. xiv. 11, 18; 1 Sam. xxv. 42; 1 Macc. ix. 37; Ps. xlv. 15; John iii. 29; Matth. ix. 15.

V. 2—4. Here is represented the different state of these young women; *five were wise*, the number is of no moment to the point in question, the distinction alone is essential; they are called wise, because they kept steadily in view the end and the means, thought of the future with foresight, and, during the present, held in contemplation distant possible contingencies, all which the foolish did not do. Calvin: "It is the part of prudence to take care that it be provided with the necessary helps for the course of life; for, though time be short, it yet appears to be too much prolonged according to the eagerness of our impatience; and then such is our poverty, that we stand in need of help every moment." The difference existing between the members of the visible church is here indicated; a mixture prevails; all call themselves Christians, profess an interest in Christ, would be saved, and have an interest in the blessed joy and glorious inheritance of the heavenly kingdom; but, however uniform in regard to the end they have in view, they are often widely different in regard to the course of procedure they adopt, and the degree of care and application which they give to this important matter, and it is in this that their prudence or folly discovers itself.

The foolish took their lamps, and took no oil in them; they had only so much oil that their lamps could burn well enough for a little time, but nothing in reserve. Lamps denote the outward profession of the gospel, mere external fellowship with the Redeemer, such as going to Church, using the means of grace, waiting on the ordinances of worship, at the same time that all is but dead work, only matter of custom, formal observances. Such people (being hypocrites, formalists, or at most but dead Christians,) want internal, proper, and living acquaintance with Christ; their profession does not proceed from any experience, or full-wrought conviction of the truth and divinity of the gospel; they may, indeed, at times manifest much zeal for it, but they are still destitute of the internal principle of life, Matth. xiii. 21. Luther, Miscell. Sermons, 18. 34: "Scripture calls those persons fools, who will neither sing nor speak. They hear the gospel, but do not follow it, still wish to have their own sentiments in high account. Of which sort, there are some, who possess the highest gifts of God, and are in the ministry. It is not said of wicked, godless Turks and heathens; but of those who call themselves evangelical, though they are still of one mind with Adam." Ibid. p. 244: "There are Christians, who obtain the name of pious persons, can say a great deal about such things, praise the word; but the kingdom of God does not stand in word but in power; the mouth is there, but the heart far off, Matth. vii. 22. When they hear the word, they frame and imagine to themselves some thought or fancy in the heart, which they take for oil, and continue still as before in their wonted courses." Luther's Marginal note: "The lamps without oil are good works without faith, which must all be destroyed; but the lamp of oil is faith in the heart—faith in the grace of God which brings forth good works, that will stand, and since no one here gives oil to another, this tells us that every one must believe for himself." Church-Pos. 14. 481, ss.: "Here the Lord calls all Christians virgins. The foolish virgins are those Christians who have the profession of Christians, hear the gospel, wish to be accounted quite evangelical, and can discourse much of divine things, extol and speak much of the word of God, praising it as a fine thing, according to which every thing must be determined and judged, and many such fair speeches. But St. Paul tells us, 1 Cor. iv. 20, that the kingdom of God is not in the word, but in power. It proceeds, not with speeches, but with the life; not with words, but with works. The mouth is well exercised about it, but the heart is not there; there is no oil in the lamp, that is, no faith in the heart. But this they do not think, or know, nay they reckon their lamps to be even in a state of readiness. Their way is, that they preach and hear about faith, and when they have heard the word, they make out of it, after their own liking, some thought or fancy in the mind; which they take for oil, and proceed onward without any change in their course, as choleric as before, as avaricious, as niggardly to the poor, as rude and unenlightened as ever. This faith or fancy, which they form to themselves, is a production of man; therefore it is just like scum upon the water, or the froth of bad beer, which has no consistence, and soon disappears. The other virgins, the wise, not merely took their lamps in their hands, but had also oil in them, that is, genuine faith, which God has formed and established in the heart, with which they can fortify themselves. For they have God's work in them, and not an imaginary, self-created notion, which has nothing to support it when death appears before them. They are supported by the divine promises, and the Spirit of God works great things through them, so that they would even now rather die than live. Now consider, that this parable will be verified at the last day, and all Christians dealt with as it declares, therefore, as the word is begun and works unequally, it becomes us to think that the last day is not far distant. In fine, this portion of the gospel, by the lamps without oil, represents to us an outward thing, a bodily exercise without faith in the heart; but the lamps with the oil denote the internal riches, together with the external works springing out of a true faith."

Ver. 4. *But the wise took oil in their vessels with their lamps.* Luther, Miscel. Sermons, 18. 34: "This oil is the anointing of the Holy Spirit, 1 John ii. 27; they have an accurate knowledge of God, they live in fear, and are careful, lest God should become angry, and take his grace from them; therefore they entreat his favour when they stumble; they beg and cry for help." This, along with true acquaintance with God, and hearts full of Christ, a living and a spiritual fellowship with the Redeemer, a hearty and open profession of the gospel, the careful use of the means of grace from faith and in faith, this is what characterizes these virgins, Matth. v. 16; Phil. ii. 15. Gnomon: "A burning lamp is faith, such a lamp and oil besides, is rich faith."

Ver. 5. *While the bridegroom tarried they all slumbered and slept.* Both wise and foolish; the delay of the return of Christ is often the occasion of a general diminution of watchfulness, fervour, and activity, and that by degrees, for first they slumber and then fall fast asleep. Calvin: "The sleeping is by some taken in a bad sense, as if the faithful could give themselves along with others to slothfulness, and fall asleep amid the vanities of the world, which is quite foreign to the mind of Christ, and the context of the parable. I understand it more simply, of earthly transactions, in which it is necessary for believers to be involved, as long as they live in the flesh. But, although they should never allow forgetfulness of the kingdom of God to creep over them, yet the distraction of worldly affairs is not unaptly compared to a sleep. For they cannot be looking so intently for the coming of Christ, but that various cares will either distract, or retard, or entangle them; on which account it happens that, through much vigilance, they may in part sleep." Luther's Sermons, 18. 35: "For we fall indeed at times into sin, have occasionally good thoughts of the bridegroom, but are not always burning with desires toward God. Here, however, is the answer and the consolation: Despair not! there are some in the heavenly kingdom who are sleepy, but are not therefore to be rejected, who sometimes even commit flagrant sins. The bridegroom is not always with us, he conceals himself, and lets his people at times fall, but will soon raise them up again." Mark xiii. 27. Matth. xxvi. 41. Rev. iii. 2. But there is a wide difference between the sleep of the wise and of the foolish.*

* [There is here, and in some other places, an unsatisfactoriness in the manner in which our author treats a nice or difficult point—first, throwing out a view of his own, without being at any pains to defend or illustrate it, and presently introducing the sentiments of others, sometimes contradicting, sometimes coinciding with his own. In a single sentence he has here stated his view of the slumbering and sleeping, then he adduces Calvin supporting one considerably different, and then, again, Luther is heard in confirmation substantially of his own. There is certainly a benefit in having the views of different authors thus brought before us, but it is somewhat perplexing to have the matter left in such a state of uncertainty. In the present case, we venture to think that Calvin has, with his usual discrimination, hit upon the right view, and that it was not our Lord's design, as is very commonly supposed, by the slumbering and sleeping of the wise virgins, to represent them as sinking along with others into slothfulness. This would have been to disfigure the image he was drawing of Christian wisdom by a leading characteristic of folly. The trait referred to is simply an indication of the long delay of the bridegroom, which naturally led the virgins to fall into other employments than those immediately connected with the expected festivity. So, in regard to the second coming of Christ, though the great object of the

Ver. 6—10. We have here represented the conduct of all the virgins at the arrival of the bridegroom. *At midnight;* much later, therefore, than was expected, but he is true and faithful, 2 Peter iii. 3. *A cry was made;* Luther, Miscell. Sermons, 18. 35: "If this were not done, all must despair; but the consolation is, that the bridegroom causes a cry to go before him, and calls us to him." Calvin: "Concerning the cry, I consider it as put metaphorically for a sudden coming. For we know, that when any thing new and unlooked for happens, men are wont to give a shout. The Lord, indeed, daily proclaims that he is coming, but then the whole machine of nature will resound, and his terrific majesty fill the heaven and the earth, in such a manner as shall not only awaken those who are asleep, but bring the dead out of their graves." *Behold, the bridegroom cometh!* Such rousing cries in the church of God, and in the lives of individuals, are often found in great outward changes, national judgments, desolations, diseases, extreme dangers, extraordinary deliverances, and other solemn occurrences, through means of which zealous and godly Christians, as well as those who are lukewarm and ungodly, are constrained to think of the coming of the Son of Man as near at hand.

Ver. 7. The impression of this announcement upon all; all think now anew of preparing themselves for

church's hopes, yet it was to be so long deferred, as to render it both allowable and necessary for her members to mingle in employments not immediately connected with his advent. His people, as well as others, must betake themselves to the cares and business of life—must enter into occupations, which, in themselves, are no way connected with Christ's appearing—but, while amidst these, work and business of their Christian calling, it is otherwise with real Christians—the holy oil of divine truth still abides in their heart, and shines forth in their conduct,—and all they have to do, when called to meet their Lord, is just to recall their minds from their other necessary duties, and address themselves more immediately to the work of meeting, in a suitable manner, the presence and glory of their divine master.]—*Trans.*

his reception; all are again manifestly made conscious of their present condition, their calling and their aim.

Ver. 8. But now becomes manifest the great internal difference, that lay under the external resemblance and agreement. The foolish virgins find themselves in the greatest embarrassment, and what should otherwise have been the occasion of the greatest joy and gain to them—the approach of the bridegroom—because they are not in the right condition, and therefore not in a state of readiness, throws them into the most terrible confusion and frightful dismay; which shows itself with much force and impressiveness in their speech; *Give us of your oil, for our lamps are out.* Calvin: "Here is reproved the too late repentance of those who do not perceive their defects before that the gate is shut against all remedy. For they are, on this account, condemned of folly, in allowing a long time to pass away without making provision for themselves, because living securely in their want, and spending the time in mutual converse, they make light of offered help." Luther, Miscell. Sermons, 18. 35: "It is torment to the conscience when we first go to seek for aid at the coming of the bridegroom, and must abandon the good thoughts we had of ourselves, discovering then, for the first time, our failure. There is a disclosure of sin, if we flee from the presence of God, when we should chiefly run to him." Give us of your oil, that is, permit us to have an interest in your faith, to enjoy its benefit and fruit, as we are already one with you in profession; the extinguishment of their lamps bespeaks the feeling and knowledge they had of their own insufficiency. Such shall be the fate some time of pretended Christians and hypocrites. Luther, Miscell. Sermons, 18. 36: "Wherefore do they not cry to the bridegroom that they have no oil? Why do they run to their fellows for oil? The cause is, that they have never truly known the bridegroom, otherwise they would run to him." This characterizes also the cry of the rich man, Luke xvi. 24.

Ver. 9. *But the wise answered, saying, Not so;—* *not so* are not in the original, but must evidently be supplied. Calvin: "We know that the Lord distributes his gifts variously to each according to his own measure, for this reason, that they might mutually assist each other, and bring to the common advantage what has been imparted to each, that thereby the sacred connexion between the members of the church may be strengthened. But here Christ points to the time when all must attend at his judgment seat to receive, according as each has done in the body. With propriety, therefore, does he compare the store, which every one has laid up for himself, of received grace, to provisions for the way, which will not be sufficient for more." The refusal is coupled with the grounds on which it is given; there is no superfluous desert of good works, from which, as an ample treasury, sinners might purchase pardon and supply the defects of their own virtue; the wise virgins are, at the same time, humble in forming a right estimate of themselves, for the true Christian is distrustful of himself, as being most sensible of his imperfections, failings, and crimes. Gnomon: "Every one shall live by his own faith."

But go ye rather to them that sell, and buy for yourselves. Gnomon: "What will appear advisable then, let us now do in time." The sense is: see if it be still possible, with such shortness of time, and in such a desperate case, to make up what has been neglected, to supply what is wanting, to procure what is necessary, Rev. iii. 18. Luther takes these words for irony, and says, Miscell. Sermons, 18. 36: "So must it happen; the just shall laugh at the destruction of the wicked, when it goes ill with them who despise God. You will not buy, you have neglected it, therefore shall all creatures mock your folly, Wisdom, v. 1, ss." Calvin: "It is not an admonition, but a reproach, having this meaning? There was formerly a time of buying, which ought not to have been neglected by you; for then there was oil to be bought, but now the power of recovering it is gone. Therefore there is no other way of obtaining it than receiving in faith what is offered to us. But it is better to find here the counsel of love, than a reproach of indifference and sloth; for the folly of the wicked is far more an object of pity and regret to the righteous, than of cruel mockery and bitter reviling, Prov. xiv. 9. However, the words are still not to be understood as if a sure hope were held out to the foolish of gaining their object; but love hopes all things. Since a *sincere* conversion during the day of grace is never rejected, we must not deny to him, who has been late in turning, the hope of his gracious reception with God, while yet the fate of the foolish virgins manifestly shows how difficult, nay almost how impossible it becomes, when sinners are long in applying themselves to it.

V. 10. *And while they went to buy, the bridegroom came;* for them, therefore, it was indeed too late, they could not now make up for their neglect. *And the door was shut,* as well to secure those who were within, as to shut out those who had allowed the time granted for preparation to pass away; at the same time, the expression indicates the unalterable condition of both kinds of Christians after the arrival of the bridegroom, Rev. xxi. 27, xix. 7. Here also we find the often recurring thought of a general and thorough sifting impending the church of the Lord, and that through him and at his arrival; as also in the parable of the tares among the wheat, the fishing-net and the wedding garment.

Ver. 11, 12. The conduct of the foolish virgins after the arrival of the bridegroom. *Lord, Lord, open to us,* expressing at once their hope and their claim to a participation in the blessedness. The repetition of the address denotes the earnestness of their desire, and that they still dreamed of a relationship to him, as if they had duly honoured him with the obedience of true servants. *Open to us;* so that no one can then claim or take any thing for himself, it must be given him by Christ.

Ver. 12. *Verily I say unto you, I know you not.* The *verily* is impressive, and intimates how only his, and not their judgment upon them is correct; he does not recognise them as fit, nor in the proper condition to be admitted, although they judged quite differently regarding themselves, upon their state and their worthiness. As vain as were the hopes of these foolish virgins, are also the expectations of those who, in fleshly confidence upon the greatness of God's compassion, undervalue his holiness, continue in sins and corruptions, give no heed to repentance and conversion, and notwithstanding the explicit declarations in the word of God concerning the necessity of sanctification in the followers of Christ, yet never apply themselves to this, in the vain imagination that there shall still somehow at last be provided for them an entrance into the abodes of everlasting joy, Prov. i. 24—33.

Ver. 13 contains the words of Christ, not of the bridegroom; they are directed to all the professors of the gospel, for exhortation and warning; they form the key of the parable, and point out its end and subject. *Watch, therefore;* the spiritual watchfulness, or preparedness of the Christian is that state of mind wherein one is truly conscious to himself of his actual condition, of the aim and tendency of his life, of his relation to the Redeemer and the things of this life, and every thing is so applied and used as to be of service to us for our eternal salvation.

For ye know neither the day nor the hour wherein the Son of Man cometh. The ground of the watchfulness just recommended, is our ignorance of the exact time for the coming and manifestation of Christ, which uncertainty or ignorance true believers improve to their salvation. According to this parable, the wisdom, which the world names folly, consists mainly in thinking of the approaching future, of death, judgment, and retribution; and what the world calls wisdom, a mere living for the present, is folly in the eyes of the Lord. Ewald, p. 190, ss.? "Thou must watch, O man, over all that is in thee, and what is without thee, what works upon thee, what can elevate or depress thy spirit, inflame or allay thy passions. Watch over all that tends to withdraw thee from Jesus, or bring thee near to him, to increase or diminish thy faith upon him. Watch over the world around thee, over thine own heart, over those powers of darkness with which, according to the word of God, we have to contend. In every age, in every life, there are periods, which, more or less, resemble the coming of Christ, upon which just as much depends for the individual, which are just as decisive for his future condition, in which he stands fully as much in need of faith and love, of watchfulness and prudence. Every occurrence in which a man either comes much nearer to Christ, or removes much farther from him, where there is no alternative; he must either wholly abandon Christ, or say, I will not decline from thy paths. Every circumstance in our life, wherein we see much on the one hand, that attracts our hearts to Christ, and on the other, much that prejudices them against him; wherein we must choose between Christ and antichrist, must declare for or against the Bible,—for or against virtue; every such circumstance is just as decisive for men as the return of Christ will be for those who live to see it. Then, these circumstances come so unexpectedly, if we are not thinking of them, they will certainly take us by surprise if we feel ourselves secure. We must have been making preparation for them before-hand, gathering strength and faith for the trial, and preparation comes too late for them when they are already present."

XVI.

THE TALENTS.

Matth. xxv. 14—30.

All that is necessary to be said on the connexion of this parable with what precedes, has been already mentioned at the beginning of the former one. Mark has only given a hint of this parable, when he says, ch. xiii. 34: "Like a man taking a far journey, who left his house, and gave authority to his servants, and to every man his work, and commanded the porter to watch." There certainly exists between it and the parable given in Luke xix. 11—27, to be explained afterwards, a strong resemblance, which has led many expositors to the conviction that they are, properly, but one, but besides that the time and place of delivery are different, there appears, even on the most hasty comparison, such important differences in their respective plan, that we are compelled to assign them an essentially distinct aim. Mel.: "This parable must be understood both concerning the public ministry and the use of private gifts."

TRAIN OF THOUGHT IN THE PARABLE.

Admonition to Christian fidelity, derived,

I. From the distribution of gifts, v. 14, 15;

(1.) As dependent servants, we owe fidelity, v. 14: "A man called his servants."

(2.) And because every thing we possess is matter of gift, v. 14; "Delivered unto them his goods."

(3.) And because this distribution is made according to the highest wisdom, in proportion to our powers, v. 15.

II. From the conduct of the servants, v. 16—18.

(1.) The exemplary behaviour of the faithful servant, v. 16: "He went, and traded."

(2.) The immediate blessing granted to his fidelity, v. 16, 17: "And made them other five (two) talents."

(3.) The shameful inactivity of the faithless servant, v. 18.

III. From the righteous judgment, v. 19—30.

(1.) This judgment is certain, v. 19: After a long time; and general, v. 19: And reckoneth with them, (v. 20, 22, 24.)

(2.) The joyful reckoning of the faithful servants, v. 20, 22.

(3.) The rich and gracious reward of the Lord, v. 21, 23, wherein we have to notice,

a.) The praise given them, v. 21, 23: "Well done," &c.

b.) The enlarged sphere of action, *ib.*: "I will make," &c.

c.) The promised bliss, *ib.*: "Enter thou into," &c.

(4.) The matter of the faithless servant.

a.) The wicked accusation, v. 24: "Lord, I knew," &c.

b.) The groundless justification, v. 25: "I was afraid," &c.

(5.) His melancholy fate, v. 26—30.

a.) The exposure of his secret wickedness, v. 26: "Thou wicked and slothful servant."

b.) The refutation of his subterfuge, v. 27: "Thou oughtest, therefore," &c.

c.) The withdrawment of the lent gift, v. 28, along with the ground of such treatment, v. 29.

d.) His banishment to final misery, v. 30.

V. 14. *As a man;* we must evidently supply from v. 1: *Then shall the kingdom of heaven be.* The Lord of this kingdom will act toward those who have come into connexion with him, just as a rich man does with his servants, to whom he has committed his goods, whom he afterwards called to account, and dealt with according to their desert. *Travelling into a far country;* so has the Lord withdrawn his presence from the church. *Called his servants, and delivered unto them his goods;* divided these amongst them. So also has

Christ bestowed many gifts upon his servants; in particular, he assigned to his apostles an appointed sphere of labour, and still now gives life, health, powers of body and of soul, many talents, capacities, spheres of duty, and opportunities for action.* There is here indicated the relation of entire dependence in which we stand to Christ, as servants to their Lord; which is overlooked by many, because the Lord is not visibly present; but his word teaches us the certainty of this relation, the approaching judgment, to which he will call us before him, will make it fully manifest, and faith is continually acting in conformity to it.

V. 15. The different numbers of talents that were committed to each of the servants, represent the different degrees of power and influence,—of means and capacities, which are distributed among men in so diversified and dissimilar a manner. *To every man ac-*

* [It might have been desirable, had our author specified here more exactly what we are to understand by the goods or talents committed by Christ to his people. They are not, we conceive, the natural powers or capacities belonging to us as men, for the goods in question, we are told, were distributed according to these,—according to every man's ability; so that their natural ability formed no part of the talents themselves, but only the sort of measure after which the bestowment of them was proportioned. The talents are such things only as are bestowed by Christ as the head and dispenser of a kingdom of grace; and we may comprise them under three divisions. 1. Our stations of life and spheres of duty,—which are all marked out to us and appointed by Christ,—and the various advantages therewith connected, the means and opportunities of usefulness, the events and circumstances of life, all so many talents put into our hands by Christ, to be used in obedience to his will, and for the promotion of his glory. 2. Our standing and privileges in his church, whether as pastors, elders, or deacons, parents, teachers, or as private members of the church. 3. Our gifts of grace or measure of the Spirit's power, divided severally to all, as every man has need. And that need, in every case, is determined by his ability,—by his reach of intellect, his extent of obligation, his sphere of rank and usefulness. Christ himself had the spirit above measure, because the work given him to do required infinite resources of grace, but his people have it according to "the measure of the gift of Christ;" that is, in other words, according to their need, the Spirit being given to every man to profit withal.]—*Trans.*

cording to his several ability; that is, the different distribution of the different gifts is not done by the All-wise, as it seemed good to him, according to arbitrary pleasure, but rather according to his foreknowledge, by virtue of which he knows how zealous, active, and faithful each will be in laying out what is committed to him, that it may be employed with profit, and he distributes more or less accordingly. Through the unequal distribution of manifold gifts, the church of the Lord appears like a body composed of many members, every one of which must contribute to the good of the whole, according to the part assigned, and the capacity bestowed on it, 1 Cor. xii. 4—30; Rom. xii. 4—9. Luther, marginal note: "The talents are the written word of God, whosoever uses which well, he has much himself and teaches much to others; whoever lets it carelessly lie, he is possessed of little; for, while it is one and the same word, it accomplishes through some much more than through others; therefore it is named now five, now two talents." This is obviously too straitened an interpretation, and, besides, not sufficiently profound in the dissimilarity of the gifts.

Ver. 16—18. Here is described the different manner in which the servants employ the trust committed to them, two being conscientious and faithful, and one entirely the reverse. The first two servants thankfully acknowledge the trust placed in them by the Lord, and the gifts bestowed on them, the obligation under which they lie to serve him, and the honour and blessing it would bring to them, if they acted agreeably to the will of the Lord; and they acted accordingly. Their gain and increase of goods stand in exact proportion to the sums committed to them; experience also teaches us the same, and hence we perceive the wisdom and the righteousness of the rule, according to which the Lord continually judges, and which is also confirmed in the parable, v. 21, viz. that to whomsoever much is given, of him much shall be required. (Luke xii. 48.)

Ver. 18. *Went and digged, and hid his lord's money.* Thus he acted, in whom the Lord had placed least confidence, and to whom he had given only one talent; which enforces on us the important truth, that the possession of few and small gifts is before the judge of all the earth no sufficient justification for the misuse of what we have, and that we must consequently employ this little with the greatest fidelity if we wish to obtain his approbation. It was not a sinful prodigality, or a bad use of the lent talent, which served for the condemnation of this servant, but only his slothful indifference, that he had not employed it either for himself or for others; from which we may draw the double reflection, that they are culpable in the highest degree, who misspend any divine gifts in vice and wickedness, but that they also are exceedingly culpable, who squander or leave unemployed many and great gifts.

Ver. 19—30. These verses describe the reckoning which the Lord held with his servants, and the judgment he pronounced. *After a long time,*—directed against the error, which looked for Christ's return as immediately to happen. *Reckoneth with them;* that thereby his sentence might appear before all the world as conformable to the strictest principle of righteousness.

Ver. 20. Such is the language of a good conscience, of a peaceful mind, of an exercised fidelity, and to the same effect also is the declaration of the other servant, v. 22, who had received the two talents.

Ver. 21, 23. The judgment of the Lord on these two servants is expressed in the same words; from which we may learn that, in distributing his commendations, the Lord looks more to the honest heart, the approved fidelity, and tender conscientiousness, than to the greater or less result of the activity of his servants, 2 Cor. viii. 12. Both have been equally faithful, and hence both receive the full, unqualified approbation of their Lord. *Well done, thou good and faithful servant;* the Lord looks primarily upon the heart, from which all action proceeds, and because that is good, he commends also the work itself. He names the servant faithful, because he had justified his lord's expectations, and the confidence placed in him.—*Thou hast been faithful over a few things;* the Lord calls even the highest, the richest and most honourable gifts, which he bestows here, a few things, in order to raise our expectations the more concerning the much greater and more glorious things which he has reserved for his people hereafter, and so to fill our hearts with blessed hopes, as well as admonish us to a conscientious fidelity. Grotius: "Christ does not weigh the works themselves, for the performance of which all have not equal power, time, and opportunities, but the faithful application. Therefore it often happens, that labour spent on what is little brings great glory."

Ver. 24. The faithless and unconscientious servant feels, when called to give his account, his guilt and liability to punishment, though hitherto he could not be brought to the proper conviction of this, either through the example of his good fellow-servants, or through the knowledge he had of his lord's will. He sees now that he cannot slip through, and, in order to palliate his unrighteous conduct, he betakes to a plea, which involves the lord himself in accusation. So wicked is sin, that it will rather cast all the blame on a holy God, than confess to its own unrighteousness. Grotius: "Christ has given the example of negligence in that servant to whom least was intrusted, lest any one should hope that he would be excused from working because he had not received the highest gifts. More, indeed, shall be demanded from him to whom much has been given, as Luke tells us, and he, therefore, who has received little, does not owe no return, he only owes less,"—*Lord, I know thee, that thou art a hard man;* an avaricious person, who allows himself to be drawn away by avarice and greed into unrighteousness; but the conduct of the lord towards him, v. 15, was an indication of good feeling, and therefore manifested the groundlessness of his subterfuge. It is the tendency, however, of a heart, that is given to wicked and ungodly passions, to conceive of God as being like to itself, Ps. l. 20.—*Reaping where thou hast not sown, etc.* Spoken proverbially, and meaning: Thou takest by force what does not belong to thee; distributest small gifts, and expectest a return disproportionately great.

Ver. 25. *And I was afraid* of losing the gift committed to me, and of the hard treatment then to be apprehended from thee.

Ver. 26, 27. *Thou wicked and slothful servant, thou knewest, &c.;* granted that thy speech and the accusation thou bringest were well grounded, and that I really was thus minded. *Thou oughtest, therefore, to have put my money to the exchangers;* what the slothful and wicked servant had contrived for his justification, the lord applies to his confusion, and draws from it the quite opposite, but just conclusion, that he should then only have felt he had to do the more, in order to give such a master at least some satisfaction. If thou hadst but given it up to the usurers, then it would have yielded to thee and me some interest. Olshausen: "Because he was afraid of losing the confided good, he durst not lay it out in independent activity for the interests of his Lord; that is, the dangers which are connected with active exertions for the kingdom of God upon earth, on account of the manifold persecutions and oppositions of the world, keep many back, who want confidence in the supporting help of God, from applying in faith and energy to the work. Persons of such timid, straitened dispositions, being unfit for bold, independent action in the affairs of the kingdom, are only requested to connect themselves with other persons of more powerful minds, under whose wing they might apply their talents profitably in the service of the church."

Ver. 28. *Take therefore the talent from him, and give it to him that hath ten talents;* this was part of the appointed punishment, taking away from him the neglected gift; the other part is mentioned in ver. 30. This man acted at first, ver. 14, as lord with his talents, now as judge.

Ver. 29. The ground of this treatment; *whosoever hath,* having rightly employed what was committed to him, exercised his gift with the required diligence, fidelity, and conscientiousness, *to him shall be given,* more shall be put into his hand; as is wont to be the rule among men, so shall it be in the highest degree with God; the proper use of all divine gifts multiplies them to their possessors; *and he shall have abundance,* a more extensive sphere of action, and therewith more opportunities for the exercise of his fidelity. *But whosoever hath not,* wants diligence and carefulness, therefore has not rightly executed the trust committed to him, *from him shall be taken away even that which he hath,* the just desert of his guilt, Luke xvi. 10—12, and a judgment demanded alike by the wisdom and the righteousness of God.

Ver. 30. See on Matth. xxii. 13.

There is subjoined from ver. 31 to v. 36, a description of the final judgment, which the Lord will hold concerning all according to the strictest justice. There the blessed of the Father are declared to be such as have given themselves to labours of love, and the cursed, who go into everlasting pain, such as are punished for their negligence and shortcoming in regard to these; so that we may consider the whole of the following section as a farther illustration and confirmation of the doctrine delivered in this parable, manifesting how important in its consequences, even throughout eternity, shall be found the faithful application, or the careless neglect of the gifts conferred on us by God, according to our sphere of labour and opportunities of usefulness; and while this issue discovers the necessity and importance of works of love, it teaches, at the same time, that all the gifts of God are bestowed only for the purpose of being laid out for the best interests of our fellow-men, 1 Cor. xii. 7. The reference of our Lord's words in ver. 27, primarily to the application of the gifts conferred by him to beneficent purposes, might be still farther confirmed by calling to remembrance the mercy which is exercised by the pious, but neglected on the part of the ungodly. We cannot, however, take this section ver. 31—46, for a parable, although it represents, under images well known, and borrowed from earthly transactions, the alike good and righteous conduct of the judge of all the earth, forming an admirable illustration of the words in Rom. ii. 6; 2 Cor. v. 10. Calvin: "Christ follows out the same line of instruction, and what he had already described under parables, he now sets forth in plain and simple language. The scope of the whole is, that believers should stir themselves up to the work of a pure and holy life, by looking with the eye of faith to the heavenly life, which, though now hid, shall be fully disclosed at the final advent of Christ."

XVII.

THE GROWING SEED.

Mark iv. 26—29.

The position which this parable occupies according to the account of Mark, throws some light upon its design. The impression which the parable of the sower produced upon the hearts of the hearers, and especially of the apostles, could scarcely be otherwise than sad and discouraging, for if a sower, with all diligence and fidelity, had yet to find that so much seed should fail to bring forth fruit to perfection, therefore his labour had been in vain, he was bound to a heartless task. But in order to prevent such an effect, and strengthen his apostles, as well as all teachers of the gospel, with joyful hopes, stimulate them to continued fidelity, and direct their eye to the happy result in which their labours were certain to issue, the Lord delivered this parable. He shows, in the seed, which makes increase through its own internal vitality, and the progress of which the sower must leave to the blessing of God, the success of the preaching of the gospel, which is equally under the care and superintendence of God, and is a living seed; from which the reflection is to be drawn, that the announcement of the gospel should always be made in joyful confidence on the fruitful operations of the Holy Spirit, Mark xvi. 20. Calvin: "Christ appears to direct his words to the ministers of the gospel, lest they should apply themselves more coldly to their work, when they do not immediately perceive the fruits of their labour. Although the seed of the word may lie for a time to all appearance choked, yet Christ commands his pious servants to be of good courage, and not allow distrust to diminish their alacrity."

TRAIN OF THOUGHT IN THE PARABLE.

The self-advancing progress of the divine kingdom. This self-advancement shows itself,—

I. At the very commencement:

(1.) The word must, indeed, be sown and received, v. 26;

(2.) But it carries within itself a living, divine power, v. 26: It is good seed:

II. And in the progress:

(1.) It must, indeed, have time for development, v. 27; The seed springs and grows up.

(2.) But it develops itself without human aid, and that gradually, v. 27, 28.

III. And in the termination:

(1.) In the ripe and abundant fruit which it yields, v. 29: When the fruit is brought forth.

(2.) Which man, however, must gather and appropriate to himself, v. 29: He putteth in the sickle, because the harvest is come.

Ver. 26. *So is the kingdom of God;* it is exactly so with the extension of the church upon earth, and with the progress of the divine word in the heart, *as when a man casts seed into the ground.* In the parable of the sower, it is said that the sower sows *his* seed, but here the word is only named seed, in general; we must, therefore, by the sower understand Christ himself, the author and proprietor of the word, while here Christ cannot be represented under the man spoken of; what is said of him can only be understood of the human teachers of the divine word; and then the carelessness and inactivity of the sower, described in v. 27, can admit of no application to the ever active Lord of the church, without whose power and grace nothing succeeds, and who, with his all-seeing eye, continually discerns the progress of the divine seed, while, of the man in question, it is said, that he knows not how it grows up.

Ver. 27. *And sleeps, and rises night and day;* after having fully finished the work of sowing, he sleeps by night quietly and without care, and rises up by day to look after his other business, patiently expecting that what is sown may, through the blessing of God, grow, and bring forth fruit. The expression is of a proverbial nature, as in Ps. iii. 5. Our part is only to plant and water, the increase is from God, 1 Cor. iii. 6. *The seed springs and grows up,* a gradual process of development. *He knoweth not how,* on what day it properly began, and how, from time to time, it makes progress; so is the progress of the divine word concealed from the eye of the labourer, that he may continue sowing, and do so in the exercise of confidence in God, and a spirit of humility.

Ver. 28. *For the earth bringeth forth fruit of itself;* the earth is the heart that has received the seed; the word works in the heart, which has a capacity to receive it, as the earth has for the seed; and without which neither could the earth bring forth a good crop, nor the heart yield any fruit from the word of God implanted in it. Gnomon: "*Of itself* is put in opposition to human care; husbandry, with the rain and suns of heaven, are not excluded." *First the blade, then the ear, after that the full corn in the ear;* the process of development, in the kingdom of grace, is one and the same with the kingdom of nature, slow, gradual, and progressive; hence in knowledge, holiness, humility, and all the graces of the Christian life, there are many degrees, 1 John ii. 13, 14. Rom. xv. 1. Eph. iv. 13.

Ver. 29. *But when the fruit is brought forth;* properly, when the fruit gives up, namely, itself—when it is ripe, and has reached the full development. *Immediately he putteth in the sickle,* the reaper comes with the sickle and cuts it down. Under this figure is represented the believing appropriation, and the enjoyment of divine things, which can only be found then, when the gospel is allowed to unfold itself without restraint. *Because the harvest is come;* when the word of God has wrought in the heart all that it was designed to do, and the heart has become ripe for another state, it is translated into that state; and this shall also be done with the church at large, with the whole dispensation of grace; the present order of things will entirely cease when the gospel has been preached to all nations, and accomplished in them, through God's blessing, the purpose for which he sends it.

XVIII.

OF THE OLD GARMENT AND THE NEW PATCH.

XIX.

OF THE NEW WINE AND THE OLD BOTTLES.

Luke v. 36—39. Matth. ix. 16, 17. Mark ii. 21, 22.

THE occasion that gave rise to these two parables is most distinctly related by Matthew. When Jesus was at table with the publican Matthew, whom he had called to be his disciple, and the pharisees saw it, they said to his disciples, (manifestly by way of reproach, as in Luke xv. 1, 2:) "Why eateth your master with publicans and sinners?" Jesus justified his conduct with the words, "The whole need not a physician, but they that are sick." But if the conduct of Christ, in companying with sinners, was extraordinary in the sight of the pharisees, the circumstance appeared quite inexplicable to the disciples of John the Baptist, who now drew near, and who, without any bad design, merely for their own information, for the solution of an incomprehensible difficulty, or rather for the removal of a ground of offence, put to him the question: "Why do we and the pharisees fast oft, but thy disciples fast not?" To which Jesus, in the first instance, replied, v. 15: "Can the children of the bride-chamber mourn, as long as the bridegroom is with them? But the days will come when the bridegroom shall be taken from them, and then shall they fast." Then, as a further reply, he delivers the two parables before us; the general sense and connexion of which is well explained by Neander in the following passages, taken from some occasional pieces, chiefly of an exegetical and historical kind; in No. V. of these, (p. 143 of the edition published in Berlin, 1829,) on the various methods which God takes in the work of conversion, he says: "The Lord answers first:

Now is the time to my disciples for child-like unrestrained joy, on account of my being present with them; nor will I damp them in this child-like joy, I will not force upon them what, in their present state of mind and feeling, would not be suitable to them, what consequently could only be to them a matter of hypocritical observance, or of sickly constraint, interrupting the natural development of their religious feelings. This child-like joy had certainly, however, no firm or abiding ground. It would of itself pass away into sorrow, sorrow on account of their external separation from the Redeemer, until they should again be united to him for ever in their internal fellowship with his life and spirit. In such a time as that, all the expressions of sorrow, such as fasting, would be natural, proceeding out of the inward state of their minds, and not merely formed from without, consequently false. Our Lord might here also refer to the manifold privations which the calling of the apostles afterwards laid upon them, and which were matters of feeling with them, since through love to their Saviour and his divine work, they cheerfully and resolutely bore these privations. Now to this very naturally attaches what the Saviour expresses in the two parables, that it is in vain to think of improving man by any sort of bodily asceticism, binding him to an external severity of life; that by and by the new spirit of life shall transform the old nature of man, from the internal to the external, and that from this inward fundamental change, every thing belonging to the renewal of the outward course, shall of itself come into operation." Luther, in his Exposition on Matthew, says here: "It is now not time for fasting, they have other things to do. Your fasting does not stand simply in the act, nor in a consideration only of the time, but also in a consideration of the person, the kind, and the manner. Therefore he rejects them with their fastings, just as he had rejected them above, v. 12, 13, with their repentance. It must all be nothing. In short, it is no use to mend an old coat with a new patch. Thus we are accustomed, in German, to say of a worn out coat thus: Ah! the coat must now be mended with a new one, patches can no more help it; that is, we must lay aside the worn out coat, and get a new one in its stead. In like manner, we may say of a too much used wine-cask: Ah! hoops and girds are of no service here, we must bind it with a new cask; that is, we must make a new cask for it. Therefore the meaning here is, all your fasting, and repentance, and righteousness, must be improved by a new fasting, and repentance, and righteousness; that is, all your doing must be thrown away, and every thing made new. Your old doing does not constitute this new one. The righteousness of the law, and the righteousness of faith, cannot stand together, or coalesce with each other. Because there are now quite different people, every thing is quite changed, other times, other works, other words, etc."

TRAIN OF THOUGHT IN THE PARABLE OF THE OLD GARMENT AND THE NEW PATCH.

Of false improvement.

I. It is something merely external: A patch in a garment.

II. It is not lasting: The patch rends again from the garment.

III. It is hurtful to the soul: The rent is made worse.

TRAIN OF THOUGHT IN THE PARABLE OF THE WINE AND THE BOTTLES.

Of true improvement.

I. It is the acquirement of a new sense: New wine.

II. It reaches from within to the outward conduct: Put the new wine into new bottles.

III. It is lasting and full of blessing: Both are preserved.

IV. It meets with hinderances in the hankering that is felt after the old, Luke v. 39.

V. 36. *Piece of a new garment*, Matth. *cloth;* new, unfulled, undressed, which will afterwards contract, run together, and so make a greater rent; it is not to be understood as if any one were to cut off a piece from a new garment, and mend an old one with it; the meaning is, simply, that no one is to bring together old and new cloth. *If otherwise, then the new maketh a rent;* if any body should still do so, the new piece will certainly make a rent. *And the new piece agreeth not with the old*, there is no proper assimilation between them, and it is, therefore, the merest folly to think of uniting them. Luther's marginal note: "That is, we cannot comprehend these new doctrines with old fleshly hearts, and where they are preached to carnal people, the matter is only made worse. As we constantly see now, for when spiritual freedom is preached, the fleshly lays claim to a freedom for its own lusts, 1 Peter ii. 16." Neander, as above: "It is of no service to patch up the old garment of a corrupt nature with any single pieces of new cloth; where the whole has not been made new, where the new birth has not sprung up within, the improvement in particulars does not last, the pieces tear again from the garment, and the rent becomes worse."

V. 37. The new wine, like the new cloth, represents the new spirit of Christianity. Neander, as above: "A new manner of life prospers only when the whole nature has been renewed, when a new principle of life has been received into it. If a new mode of life were to be enforced from without, while there was any remnant of the old nature, this would but strive the more against the constraint, the evil would become the greater through hypocrisy, or the fresh rejection of the unwilling yoke." Other expositors limit the sense, more historically, thus: the old additions of fasts and other external self-appointed things, suit not the new doctrine of the gospel, which, as a new doctrine, will cause the old forms to vanish, and introduce new ones in their place.

V. 39. *No man, also, having drunk old wine*, being accustomed to drink of this, *straightway desireth new*, he is averse to the change; *the old is better*, milder. Gnomon: "Their own ancient doctrine was more agreeable to the pharisees than the general doctrine of Jesus, which they thought to be new, though it was far more ancient, Gal. iii. 17; 1 John ii. 7, 8; at once *new wine*, Zech. ix. 17; and yet *mild*, Matth. xi. 30." Calvin: "I understand it simply to be an admonition to the Pharisees, that they should not ascribe more than was meet to received custom." Neander, as above: "Man still clings to his old course of life, until his mind has become entirely new, but then all his dispositions change of their own accord, and he feels himself constrained to abandon his earlier course of life for that which his new state of mind requires."

The relation of the two parables to each other might be explained thus: The first tells us, that the improvement must not be begun externally, leaving the state of the inner man untouched; the other shows, inversely, that the internal renovation must reach to what is outward, and give to this a suitable direction. Olshausen, in his Commentary, remarks here as follows: "What Christ says here, (Matth. v. 15,) is concerning all his disciples, of every age; now they rejoice, and now again they fast. It is manifest that the bodily presence of Christ cannot be so much referred to, as his internal, spiritual presence in the soul, for to Judas, for example, the former was not the occasion of festive joy. But the other was still more glorious and powerful after his resurrection than before it. Understood of this, the words of Jesus involve the deep, spiritual thought, that even with believers there is an alternation in their spiritual state, an interchange of light and darkness (Jas. i. 17,) at one time festive joy filling their hearts, at another, sorrow, mourning an absent bridegroom, and according to this difference their outward life naturally assumes a different aspect. Still, under the New Testament, the joyful tendency is represented as the prevailing one, while, under the Old, it is the sighing, longing disposition; on which account also a deeper spirit of penitence appears to reign in the piety of the Old Testament. Both comparisons certainly indicate the same thing, but they are taken from different points of view; from this difference in the point of view, is the difference to be explained, which is manifest in the comparisons themselves. In the first, the New is a subordinate matter, arising from the necessity of repairing the Old,—so the Pharisees, from their limited point of view, must needs look down upon the gospel; in the second comparison, on the other hand, the New appears as the essential thing, the Old as the mere form? so that the relation they have to each other, is according to the truth. By combining together the two comparisons, divine mercy, graciously accommodating itself to human weakness, satisfies the necessities of all. The second comparison is as simple and intelligible, as it is wonderfully deep, and full of meaning. In particular, the comparison of the gospel principle of life to the ethereal, physical power of production in nature, is profound, and gives rise to many thoughts. The circumstance added in Luke v. 39, is very characteristic, and leads back to the pharisees. The gracious Redeemer apologizes for those hearts which had grown accustomed to the nature of the old, and finds it not unnatural that they should feel it difficult to depart from the regular and wonted course, and venture into a new and fermenting element of life. The old, though in itself less pleasant, is yet, through custom, more acceptable; the new will not go down at first. At the same time, this expression also intimates, though mildly, the necessity of entering into the new life of the spirit, brought in by the Lord of humanity."

XX.

THE CREDITOR AND THE TWO DEBTORS.

Luke vii. 41—43.

This parable stands in closest connexion with the history of the female sinner, who anointed our Lord. Jesus was invited to an entertainment by a pharisee, and while he sat at table in his house, this woman, who in v. 37 and 39, is named a sinner, brought a box of ointment and anointed him, with every manifestation of profound joy, gratitude, and admiration. The behaviour of Jesus, who allowed the woman to proceed, and offered no interruption to her manifestations of affectionate gratitude, was to the pharisee in the highest degree offensive, as, according to his judgment, (which from Luke v. 30; xv. 1, 12, we learn, was the prevailing one of their sect,) it was quite unseemly for a pious man to come into near contact with persons known to be of profligate character, and hence he drew, from the behaviour of Christ, the not less erroneous than harsh conclusion, that he could not be a prophet, v. 39. The conclusion thus arrived at by the pharisaical Simon, besides implying that all intercourse with sinners is in every respect blame-worthy, proceeded, moreover, upon the false presumption, that the prophets must have known the entire condition of the persons with whom they were conversant, which indeed they did, in some particular cases, (1 Kings xiv. 6; 2 Kings i. 3; v. 26,) but not generally; and then Simon improperly took the woman for what she was at an earlier period, an open and abandoned sinner, which she no longer was, since, according to v. 47, she had already obtained the forgiveness of her sins. That she was still designated by the name of sinner, v. 37, is no proof of the continuance of her former state, and against her having already in part experienced divine grace, for Matthew is styled a publican, Matth. x. 3, long after he had become a disciple of Jesus, and had abandoned his earlier vocation. Simon, however, concluded Jesus to be no prophet, from the two circumstances mentioned above, in the following manner—either, he knew not who this woman was, and then he could be no prophet; or, he did know, and held fellowship with her, in which case also he could be no prophet. Against this false conclusion, though affecting himself, and doing despite to his proper dignity, Jesus did not immediately direct himself; but the object of the refutation which he brought against it, was only designed to justify the conduct of the woman, together with his own, as quite natural, agreeable to the actings of the human heart, and here in particular flowing from the woman's inward experience; but at the same time it was intended to press on the pharisee, by way of application, the impropriety of his behaviour, and of awakening him, if possible, to more profound knowledge of himself. Calvin: "The sum of this parable is, that Simon erred in condemning a woman whom the heavenly judge had acquitted. It proves her to be righteous, however, not because she had pleased God, but because her sins were forgiven her; for otherwise the parable would not be applicable, as in it Christ expressly declares that the pence were freely remitted to the debtors who were unable to pay. And it is indeed wonderful that many commentators should rave so absurdly, as if this woman had merited forgiveness by her tears, &c. For the argument which Christ employs is drawn, not from the cause, but from the effect; as the reception of a benefit is in point of order before giving thanks, and a gratuitous remission is here assigned as the cause of reciprocal love."

TRAIN OF THOUGHT IN THE PARABLE.

Of the forgiven sinner's grateful love to Jesus.

I. The source of it is, the grace of Jesus forgiving sins; which,

(1.) Is both great, taking away all guilt; v. 41:
The five hundred, as well as the fifty pence;
(2.) And entirely free; v. 42; remitting the guilt of those who have nothing to pay.

II. Its necessity, it is quite certain: v. 42: Who will love him (most?)

III. Its strength; v. 43: I suppose he to whom he forgave most:
(1.) Internally—by intensity of feeling;
(2.) Externally—by outward manifestations of gratitude.

V. 40. *I have somewhat to say unto thee;* it demands thy whole attention, is applicable to thyself, is important for thee, but, at the same time, perhaps not agreeable. By this request Jesus makes himself known, with reference to the pharisee, speaking within himself, v. 39; as the Searcher of hearts, while, at the same time, he sought to work with the greatest friendliness upon the cold heart of the pharisee. Grotius: "He is going to show that it was well known to him, both what the woman and what Simon were, not merely as to what is outward, but in the most secret recesses of the mind."

V. 41. *A certain creditor*, a usurer; a man who is accustomed to lend. *Five hundred pence*, denarii, each worth about four groshen, (or seven pence three farthings;) the determinate numbers *five hundred*, and *fifty*, can only be meant to indicate the great inequality of the debt of these two persons, and, at the same time, to teach that sinners in the eye, and according to the judgment of God, are not equal, but have different degrees of guilt. Luther, House-Pos. 6. 345: "This is the condition of all men, who are sinners in the judgment of God, not merely, however, on account of the sins which each individual commits in his daily walk, but also in regard to nature, for we are all sprung from a father and a mother who had sinful flesh, were sinners, and under the wrath of God on account of sin. Now, though there is a difference between these two kinds of sinners, yet it is of no moment. For in the main thing they are both alike, inasmuch as they are both debtors, and can pay nothing. And so, though there be some distinctions among us, in respect to the outward life, in that some hold themselves more in check than others, and all are not thieves, adulterers, murderers, yet, let the difference in this respect be ever so great, when we come before God in judgment, we have all alike to make this confession: We have nothing to pay, and must remain debtors; and this, whether we have been guilty in a smaller or a greater sum."

V. 43. *And when they had nothing to pay, he frankly forgave them both;* so that on the part of the debtors two things are indubitable,—the certainty and greatness of their debt, and their perfect incapacity to make restitution; while on the part of the creditor there appears correspondingly in the remission of the debt,—1. a very great goodness; and that, 2. perfectly free, depending simply on his own will, quite undeserved by the debtor, and never to be sued for by him as a matter of right. Such also is the relation of the sinner to God, that all sins require an exercise of grace, that is perfectly free, and this also it is possible for them to find.—*Tell me, therefore, which of them will love him most?* This question of Christ obviously implies two things; 1. That such a manifestation of love infallibly begets love in the heart of the receiver; 2. That the degree of this reciprocal love will always be determined by the apprehension entertained of the greatness of the received benefit. From the first of these statements, and from experience, there may be drawn the further consequence, that the debtor, before the gracious remission of his debt, experiences no love to his creditor, but is only conscious of the oppressive feeling of a heavy burden resting upon him, and at the same time afraid of meeting from the creditor the severe treatment which the law warrants and empowers him to use. It is entirely the same in the heart of the sinner; he learns, from the divine law, both his guilt and his liability to punishment; so that nothing but fear of God can take possession of him. But the sinner, in such a state, is met by God in the gospel with the gracious message of pardon for his sins, and this, in the believing heart, which appropriates to itself the word of God, becomes the means of rooting out all fear, and implanting a principle of love, Rom. xv. 1, 8, 15; 2 Tim. i. 7; 1 John iv. 18, 19. The application of the parable, therefore, leads to the following conclusions of doctrine; 1. Love to God cannot precede the pardon of sin; 2. And hence it cannot deserve this pardon of sin; 3. But infallibly marks an act of forgiveness, already past and experienced.

V. 43. *I suppose*, it follows from the differently related circumstances of the two debtors, *that he to whom he forgave most*, will love him most in return. And now follows the application of the parable, in which (v. 44—46) the Saviour compares the conduct of the woman with that of the pharisee, and shows the latter how he had failed to afford the common and ordinary manifestations of love, while the woman, on the contrary, had given the most uncommon and extraordinary marks of love. This comparison, drawn so much to the advantage of the woman, must have put the pharisee to shame, who had judged so harshly of her conduct, as it placed him behind the person he had so thoroughly despised. Then comes at the close, the judgment pronounced by Christ: *Wherefore, I say unto thee, to her many sins are forgiven, for she has loved much; but to whom little is forgiven, the same loveth little.* The *wherefore* must not, as in the Lutheran translation, be coupled with, *I say unto thee*, but with what follows; so that, *I say unto thee*, should be placed in parenthesis. The *wherefore* also does not indicate the ground or efficient cause of pardon, but rather the demonstration, from which the certainty of the given and received pardon may be inferred; so that we may translate, *hence, for this rea-*

son, has she loved so much, given such great and manifold proofs of love, because her many sins have been forgiven her; and the sense is: From this woman's manifestations of love to me, thou mightest have drawn the conclusion, that her many sins have been forgiven her. Mel.: "He loves much, to whom much is forgiven; as if he had said, the more thou dost apprehend forgiveness, the more wilt thou apprehend the greatness of the benefit conferred on thee; the greater, therefore, is the flame of faith and of love that springs up, and the more always that one loves, the more in turn is he loved of God. On the other hand, the pride of the pharisee is reproved, Christ signifies that he is ignorant of the remission of sins, and is consequently without love. The correctness of this exposition, according to which pardon of sin is the first thing, and mutual love only its consequence, appears partly from the application of the parable, (see on v. 42,) partly from the second declaration contained in v. 47: to whom little is forgiven, the same loveth little, and partly from the analogy of faith throughout the whole of Scripture. Luther, in his disputation upon this verse, says: "There are three things in this passage, which forbid us to hold that the forgiveness of sin is obtained through works or love. The first is the speech which Christ addressed to the woman in v. 50: Thy faith hath saved thee. He does not say, Thy love hath saved thee. The second is the speech of Christ in v. 47, in which he declares, that the forgiveness of sin goes before love, and that love follows upon the forgiveness of sin, as gratitude for a received benefit. For he does not say here, To him little is forgiven who loves little, but the opposite: He loves little, to whom little is forgiven. This manifestly confirms, that the forgiveness is done gratis, without desert, but that love is a fruit or acknowledgment of the bestowed gift. The third thing is, the parable itself, and the whole matter which Christ here treats of, with which parable and matter the speeches just mentioned must not war, but consistently agree. We shall be justified only through the grace of him who pardons, because we cannot discharge the payment of the debt. For if we, as debtors, could, by any merit of our own, have obtained the forgiveness of sin, we should then certainly have had something wherewith to pay. But the text says explicitly, v. 42, that when they had nothing to pay they were freely forgiven. The kindness experienced is not a thing due to the debtor who receives it, but a boon from the merciful and indulgent creditor." Also in his House-Pos. 6. 344: "What, then, is the conclusion from this syllogism in v. 47? Nothing else, than as the Lord very nicely and exactly puts it together: I say to thee, to her are many sins forgiven; the proof of which is, that she loves much. But to thee and thy associates there are no sins forgiven; you as yet stand in them up to the very ears, and shall die and be destroyed in them. For no trace is to be found in you of true love to me; but this love must follow, whenever people hold and believe that they are set free from their sins by me. Papists bring this text against our doctrine of faith, and say, that because Christ affirmed, "To her is forgiven much, for she loved much," that forgiveness of sin is obtained, not through faith, but through love. That this, however, is not the meaning, the parable puts beyond a doubt." As the forgiven debtor naturally loves his gracious creditor, and the woman here testified her love to Christ, the conclusion readily presents itself, that Jesus wished to make himself known as the person who could forgive sin, which also appears from the declaration of pardon, announced again to the woman for her satisfaction, in v. 48, and is farther confirmed by the astonishment of the guests, in v. 49. The whole matter amply justifies Christ as to his knowing well with whom he was transacting, namely, that she was a pardoned sinner. But the inference drawn by many, that this pharisee is to be understood by the other debtor, must only be applied to his guilt as a sinner, but by no means extended so as to imply his having experienced any act of grace from Christ,—because the pharisee gives no evidence of his having the feeling of a pardoned sinner; because his invitation to Christ is sufficiently explained as a very common civility paid to distinguished rabbis; because the setting up of two debtors, and the twofold declaration in v. 47, is done only for the purpose of explaining the very extraordinary indications of love given by this woman, and, if the closing sentence, in v. 47, can be supposed to have any respect to Simon, it must mean, To whom nothing is forgiven, the same loves nothing.

XXI.

THE COMPASSIONATE SAMARITAN.

Luke x. 25—37.

When the Lord pronounced his disciples specially blessed, and said,—Blessed are the eyes which see the things that ye see!—referring, not to the corporeal sight, but to a believing acquaintance with himself and his doctrine;—a lawyer stood up, and, tempting him, therefore, with an ill intention, not for the sake of receiving instruction, proposed to him the insidious question, upon which there was so much discord among the Jewish doctors; Master, what shall I do to inherit eternal life? The question, in itself commendable, (Mark x. 17, and Acts xvi. 30, 31,) because it refers to the subject most important to man, sprang here out of a wicked heart, for it appeared to involve Christ, either in a contradiction with himself, v. 23, or with the divine law, which, as a revelation of God, must be regarded as pointing out the way to salvation, Deut. viii. 1; John v. 30. Luther, House-Pos. 5. 51: "The Lord has before him a proud saint, a lawyer, who will not only have it to be seen how pious he is, but will also play a trick upon Christ, and show that he is a better doctor than Christ. For, while the Lord praises his own preaching so highly, and says; Blessed are the eyes which see the things that ye see, this the lawyer thinks too much; reflects with himself. We have still the law of Moses, to read, teach, and advocate, and surely this Jesus can teach nothing better or higher than Moses has taught. Therefore they are not alone blessed who hear thee; those who hear and abide by the law of Moses are also blessed. Thou goest too far. It were quite enough that thou wert a doctor, like Moses, but that thou shouldst cast aside Moses, as an imperfect preacher, who does not point out the right way to salvation, and wilt be a better preacher, that is arrogating too much." And again, at p. 67, "Upon the question of the lawyer, how one might be saved, there were many opinions, especially among the Jews; however, none of them knew the way of salvation, how and by what man might be righteous before God. At bottom, they were all as one with each other, teaching that salvation must be attained by works, just as in the papacy the monks have done. But there was still a difference among them in this respect, that some laid particular stress upon sacrifices, washings, ceremonies of meat and drink, and such like external works. Some, however, were more strict, and said, This was to do it, to love God with all the heart, and our neighbour as ourself. Such, also, was the opinion of this lawyer, but no more a matter of earnest with him than it was with the others. For they were all mockers, who had the word merely in their mouth, but did it not themselves, nay, made no account of it."

TRAIN OF THOUGHT IN THE PARABLE.

Christian compassion.

I. Its sphere of action;

(1.) On whom it is exercised,—on those who stand in need of it, v. 30;

(2.) How far it reaches,—to all, Samaritans as well as Jews, every person is our neighbour.

II. Its nature; it is,

(1.) A feeling, v. 23: had compassion on him;

(2.) And manifests itself in deeds, v. 34, 35.

III. Its working:

(1.) It gives help instantly and without delay, v. 33, 34.

(2.) And that unsolicited, voluntarily;

(3.) Does what is required, and as well as it can, v. 34: Bound up, &c.

(4.) Is full of self-denial; for,

a.) It fears no dangers, comp. v. 30.

b.) And no trouble, v. 34;

c.) And no cost, spending oil, and wine, and gold, and time thereon, v. 35;

d.) And no labour, going on foot.

(5.) It is indefatigable, and completes the work, v. 35, begging also the help of others.

V. 26. *What is written in the law?* By pointing to the law, as an acknowledged and valid authority, our Lord cuts off all farther occasion for subtle inquiries, and no justification is needed for any of its declarations; but he asks, expressly, after the written law, in order to put aside the contradictory sentiments and human ordinances of oral tradition. Luther, Church-Pos. 14. 23: "For, without scripture, he cannot reach and instruct their darkness."

How readest thou? Probably pointing to the phylactery, on which, according to Jewish custom, the word in Deut. vi. 4—9, ought to be written, and which was to be repeated morning and evening. Calvin: "It is certainly prescribed in the law to men, how they ought to direct their life, so as to obtain salvation to themselves before God. But, because the law can do nothing else than condemn, and is therefore called the doctrine of death, and is said to multiply transgressions, (Rom. vii. 13,) this does not happen from any fault in its doctrine, but only from the impossibility of our doing what it requires. Therefore, although by the law, no one can be justified, the law itself, nevertheless, contains the most perfect righteousness, inasmuch as it is not false in promising salvation, if any one should perfect himself in its requirements. Nor ought this manner of teaching seem absurd to us, because God, first of all, requires the righteousness of works, then offers it gratuitously to us without works, because it is necessary that men should be convinced of their own just condemnation, that they may fly to the mercy of God. But, in this answer, Christ accommodated himself to the lawyer, and kept in view the interrogation, which inquired, not whence salvation was to be sought, but by what works it might be obtained."

V. 27. The lawyer is ready with his answer, in which he couples together two passages, Deut. vi. 5, and Lev. xix. 18. Luther, Church-Pos. 14. 51: "Such he leaves it to be thought is the real kernel and main doctrine, since no one can point out any thing better. And, indeed, it is true that Moses taught nothing better or higher." Matth. xxii. 35 —40.

V. 28. *Thou hast answered right; this do and thou shalt live*, Lev. xviii. 5. The exercise of true love to God and our neighbour, in complete perfection, will indeed conduct thee to salvation, but thou shalt discover, if thou wilt impartially inquire, that perfect obedience to these demands is impossible to the corrupt nature and sinful condition of the human heart, so that the way to God through one's own righteousness, worth, and merit, is inaccessible. Luther, Church-Pos. 14. 25: "Here, indeed, the law is preached, and a good strong election given in it. The doctrine, says Christ, is sound and precious, only let it also be practised,—I would fain see the doer of it; be thou master, and let thine art be seen, for you have all spoken and written it, and know well about it; but the misfortune with thee and with others is, that you fail also to do it,—think it is enough to say the words and think of them. Yes, this word of Christ, *Do it,* is the perpetual lesson and sermon that must be preached to all men, even to the saints, and which makes them feel the impossibility there is of resting, before God, on their righteousness and worth; but that they must, whenever they rightly understand how it is between them and God, condemn themselves and their life, since no saint has ever been able to stand upon this, either in the Old or in the New Testament; all must see themselves alike reflected in this word,—*do it,* which is as much as to say, Lo, thou hast never done, or fulfilled it; Ex. xxxiv. 6, 7. Isa. vi. 5, 6. Dan. ix. 18. Acts xv. 10, 11; xiii. 38, 39. In the answer of Christ there is concealed the secret charge, that the lawyer was more concerned about knowledge and book learning than to exercise himself unto obedience, and that he had almost wholly neglected this. Luther, House-Pos. 5. 52: "Christ says: Do it; as if he had said, the doctrine is sound and correct, but no help is thereby brought to thee and to others." Church-Pos. 14. 5; "Do it; that is, in plain German, Thou art a mere babe, thou hast never, all thy life-long, done it, nay, thou hast never held so much as a letter of it, and it therefore only testifies of thy wickedness. The poor ninny thinks that he must be honoured, for he is wonderfully pure and beautiful, and that he would more fitly be sitting among angels than here among men." Mel.: "Christ shows the pharisee the vanity of his arrogance, that he might acknowledge his sin. Christ had enjoined him to hear the Scripture, leads him to the word, but the pharisee knows nothing excepting the law, neglects the promises, and brings forward a law not understood. Christ rejoins, as a reproof to his ignorance, This do, and thou shalt live, intimating that he could neither do the law nor live, but was oppressed with sin and death. For the meaning is, If thou hast done it thou shalt live; but neither is it done by thee, nor by others, and therefore life must be sought elsewhere. The sentiment is correct, that he who doeth the law shall live; for, if there were no sin, there should be no death. So he reproves the pharisee as being ignorant what a law is, what sin, what death; which death is a terrible evil sprung from sin, and is not abolished by the law, because the law is not performed by sinful human nature."

Ver. 29. *But he, willing to justify himself;* Gnomon: "They, who ask many questions, are not the readiest to do many actions, and would rather withdraw themselves from the law. He who curtails the righteous things that are to be performed, and the persons to whom they are to be performed, creates for himself an easy righteousness." The scribe felt the secret accusation of Jesus, that he had not kept the law; and, if his conscience convicted him, at the same time, of many violations of the command to love his neighbour, by its being said he wished to justify himself, we may understand as much as,—he wished to justify himself, in regard to these violations of law, and push aside the blame from himself, on the ground that it might be laid upon the law itself and its divine author, who had not sufficiently explained what he meant by the term neighbour, and had hence given occasion to disobedience against this command. Luther, House-Pos. 5. 52: "Such (the reproof of Christ) the scribe deeply feels, is conscious of shame on account of it, for he cannot say that he has done it, and yet he will not confess this, but throws out another question: Who is my neighbour? Thereby he plainly admits that he had not loved his neighbour, since he had not yet come so far as to know his neighbour. What benefit does he, then, derive from Moses and his law?" It is possible, however, that the scribe, while he felt the reproof of Christ, wished to show its groundlessness and falsehood, and to say, I am not conscious of having ever violated the command to love my neighbour, so that thou must take the word in some different sense from that which we are accustomed to understand, and therefore he asks further, *Who is my neighbour?* Luther, Church-Pos. 14. 8: "He does not ask, who is my God? As if he would say, I owe God nothing: in regard to God there has been no fault; in regard to man, also, I was willing to think that I had left nothing unfulfilled; however, I should like to know exactly who my neighbour is?" Gray says: "Being much disposed to set out his own merit in the most favourable light, from the exact obedience he had given it, according to the public and approved doctrine of the Rabbins, he asked this question, probably expecting an opportunity of returning such an answer as the young man did upon a similar occasion, Matth. xix. 20." Grotius: "Christ was anxious to bring the lawyer to a confession of his own impotence, that having seen how much God required, and being conscious to himself how far he had come short of such a full and constant love, he might implore the aid of the Holy Spirit, without which such love could not be entertained in the soul. But he, persevering in the Jewish obstinacy, wished to vaunt himself before others as righteous and good. And, there is no doubt, that he would have had himself believed to have had sufficiently loved God, from his exact observance of all the ceremonies."

The parable which our Lord spake in answer to the question,—who is my neighbour? certainly teaches the universality of brotherly love, and unfolds the truth, that *every* man is our neighbour; but the design of it, as appears from the circumstances in which it was spoken, is no other than to lead, first of all the scribe, and then mankind generally, to the more profound and thorough knowledge of the law and of themselves, that so every one might be convinced, that through the law and the works of the law he cannot be saved. For, viewing in this light the design of the parable, we are manifestly supported by the epistolical passage, which is appointed, along with this parable, for the thirteenth Sunday after Trinity. In that epistle, (Gal. iii. 15—22,) the leading idea is, that the inheritance, (v. 18,) the promised salvation, is not, and could not be won through the law; also, that the law was not given for the purpose of enabling the sinner to acquire, through its fulfilment, merit, and claims, since the law no way empowers the sinner to yield a perfect obedience, (v. 21;) but the real purpose of the law is, to manifest to all their sins, that all may apprehend how the inheritance is to be won, and salvation attained only through faith, (v. 22.) This leading object of the parable must be held constantly in view, and the practical treatment of it so directed, as to make the whole bear on that one point. While the obligation of love to man is taught by the parable in its widest generality, it, at the same time, combats the limitations with which the Jewish doctors in the time of Jesus, and at all times the proud and selfish heart, has sought to narrow and disfigure the precepts of brotherly love; for, according to the Rabbins, this precept was to be considered binding only toward those who belonged to the same nation and professed the same religion; all besides, they taught, were to be hated and despised, nay, as enemies of God and of religion, were to be rooted out, as formerly had been done to the inhabitants of Canaan. Blind religious zeal and wild fanaticism has constantly, even in the Church of Christ, discarded the precept of love, and thus brought reproach on the gospel, which neither here, nor in Luke ix. 51—56, nor any where, either justifies or countenances feelings contrary to love in the disciples of Jesus. Calvin: "Christ might simply have taught, that the word *neighbour* is to be applied indiscriminately to any one, because the whole human race is bound together by a kind of social chain. And doubtless, the Lord made use of this word in the law, for no other reason than that he might more sweetly engage us to mutual love. The precept had been more distinct if it had run: Love every man as thyself;

but because men are apt to be so blinded by pride, that in their self-satisfaction they will scarcely think others worthy of being accounted of the same grade, and withhold from them the offices of friendship, the Lord purposely pronounces all to be *neighbours*, that the very affinity might conciliate men toward each other. But Christ wished to elicit from the pharisee an answer, which might serve to condemn himself. Nor may we doubt that Christ delineates the cruel neglect of charity, of which the Jews and priests were conscious." Mel.: "Our *neighbour* is any person in distress, standing in need of our kindness, and especially he who is conjoined with us in a society under the sanction of God, who is one of the people of God. The flesh, on the other hand, desires to account those neighbours, who are flourishing and powerful, but shuns those who are in distress. As has been elegantly said by Menander: 'Fortuna varie pingit amicos.'"

Ver. 30. *A certain man;* some, without sufficient ground, have thought they discovered here a history, which had shortly before occurred, and was now made use of by Jesus.—*Went down from Jerusalem to Jericho;* Jerusalem stood on mountains, and was surrounded by mountains—was consequently higher than Jericho, which lay on the plain, hence *went down;* the distance between the two places was about ten miles.—*And fell among thieves;* the way was reckoned unsafe, from its being frequented by robbers, which renders the circumstances very probable. The description of the unfortunate accident, of the miserable state, the necessitous and helpless condition of this man, given in a few leading traits, is quite sufficient of itself to move every human heart, and fill it with compassion.

Ver. 31. *And by chance;* Gnomon: "Many good opportunities are concealed under those events which appear to be *fortuitous*." Scripture describes nothing rashly as fortuitous; here it is opposed to matter of necessity. Ewald: "If we happen to come in view of a man in distress, that is just the intimation of God that we must help him as much as we can. Matth. x. 30. And so, not to regard such an intimation, is not the humane and childlike disposition which our Lord so highly prizes."—*There came down a certain priest that way;* as many priests and Levites lived in and around Jericho, who had to march to Jerusalem, whenever it was their course to wait on the service of God, and return home again when their work was completed; so this way was seldom quite clear of such persons, which gives to the story additional veri-similitude and new life. Now, whether the priest was travelling to discharge his office, or returning from the performance of its duties, we are unavoidably led to expect, on account of his standing and office, that he would be disposed to manifest a compassionate feeling, Mal. ii. 6, 7. But although he saw his countryman and fellow worshipper, it moved in him no compassion; he passed by cold and unconcerned, without so much as coming near to help or even to console the unhappy sufferer.—*He passed by on the other side,* αντιπαρηλθεν, marks an intentional turning away and going past on the other side, in order not to permit himself to be moved by a nearer view, or to suffer any sort of detention. Grotius takes it differently: "He passed in the opposite direction, namely, hastening from Jericho to Jerusalem. Although Christ had chiefly designed to teach, that the word *neighbour* had a more extensive meaning than the Jews thought, he was yet desirous, by the way, of showing that they often did not give to those whom even they allowed to be *neighbours,* what belonged to *neighbours,* that is, to *friends.*"

Ver. 32. *Likewise a Levite, when he was at the place, came and looked on him;* curiosity led him near, to look upon the unhappy object; but though he obtained a more exact knowledge of his helpless position, he yet passed by without helping him, and thus manifested a still more inhuman heart, a still more criminal conduct. Fearful characteristic of the priests and Levites in the time of Jesus! drawn, as it unquestionably was, from the truth, like all the other parts of this parable; and these were the people who were so zealous for the law, Matth. xxiii. and were wont to call themselves merciful. As experience teaches that those, who according to their office and calling, ought to be best, if they are bad, are not merely in their depravity similar to others, but go beyond and exceed all others; there is disclosed in the choice of these persons a truth, not only historically, but also psychologically confirmed. Luther, House-Pos. 5. 50: "But the stock-holy, like the priests and Levites here, are those who think much and highly of themselves, have naturally no compassion for the poor, but are hard, cruel persons. For they deem that the Lord is glad because they serve him, and therefore think that they must do nothing to other people, nor serve them. The priest here was holy on account of his office and his birth, for which he prized himself so highly, that he asked after no one besides. Upon what do these saints rely? Upon nothing else than their holiness, for they think, if they but attend to the letter of the law, they have performed it all. These are the stock-holy, and the stone-holy, nay the devil-holy, who would have it to be thought that the Lord is indebted to them, but that they are indebted to nobody." If the robbers showed in what they did, much inhumanity and cruelty, the priest and the Levite manifested the same disposition in what they did not do; so that the same sin appears in the one case as an act of commission, in the other as an act of omission, and all the three parties are placed on a footing of equality, to the greater confusion of the lawyer.

Ver. 33. *A Samaritan;* the Samaritans sprung from the mixture that took place at the time of the captivity, between the Jews who still remained, and the heathenish Assyrians and Babylonians. National hatred kept them still apart even at the time of Christ, John iv. 9, 20; Sirach l. 27, 28. Samaritan was among the Jews a word of contempt and reproach, and designated a heretic, John viii. 48. That a Samaritan is here represented as the deliverer, was directed against this national hatred, and was meant to teach, that one often finds in men, utterly despised, and from whom nothing was expected, more humane feeling and truer love, than in hypocritical believers; for which see also Luke xvii. 11—19. This circumstance manifestly declares the truth that as the command of brotherly love ought to be taught and enforced, it must lead us to regard every man as our neighbour, and permit no distinction of a national, religious, or speculative nature to keep us in alienation, even from those who are counted for enemies, but to exercise toward them active love, and in general to cherish no such enmity in the heart. If our Lord had introduced a Jew or a Samaritan as acting in this manner toward his countryman and fellow-worshipper, this truth could not have been placed in so clear a light; and still less, if a Jew had been represented as acting thus toward a Samaritan, for then the Jewish lawyer might have said, that the conduct was certainly very noble and magnanimous, but that no one could expect this from another as a matter of obligation, and thus his party-spirit would have found here a refuge. But since the Lord represents the Samaritan as helping the Jew, he puts to silence the selfish party-spirit, and compels the lawyer, who could easily transpose himself into the place of the injured man, at least to admit in his heart, that this humane feeling and affectionate manner of acting was as excellent in regard to the moral law, as in itself truly worthy of love and respect.

Had compassion on him; a natural emotion of the human heart, implanted by God, existing when no malformation, party-spirit, and enmity have deadened the heart towards it; serving to lighten the obedience, which God, besides, requires in his word in regard to the duty of love. The spring of love must, therefore, be found deep in the soul, and from thence it flows out in acts of love towards external objects, as is seen in ver. 34, 35. Love, compassion must already have existed as a feeling, before it has become an act, and where the feeling does not exist, it will never come into act. Grotius: "The sincere emotion of the mind precedes, and this is followed by deeds conformable to the state of mind."

Ver. 34. In the Samaritan's work of love, all the circumstances are so chosen by the Redeemer, that on the one hand every thing is kept away which might have lightened the performance of such deeds, or brought suspicion on their pure origin, while on the other hand the greatest hinderances and difficulties had to be conquered, so that the source of his love could only be the purest love of God and man, 1 John iv. 20, and his work appears even as one of perfect morality. He makes no account of the danger to which his life was exposed, in a road so frequented by robbers, which was doubtless well weighed by both priest and Levite, and would be ready to be produced in vindication of their heartlessness; neither does he make any account of the loss of time and delay in this journey; troublesome, laborious, and but little accordant with the more delicate feelings, were the acts of relief, which he discharged to the object of his compassion, while he washed his wounds, bound them up, and raised him from his half-dead condition. And the person to whom he does all this belongs to that nation which the Samaritan hates and abhors; and, doing it in the wilderness, he could derive no impulse from the approbation of men, nor could he look for any gain, or even for the compensation of his loss; yet he gives also oil and wine, and performs the journey on foot, and with toilsome labour; he provides for the completion of the begun recovery with a fresh sacrifice; he takes leave at last of the unhappy man, as soon as he knows him to be in a state of safety. It was not a temporary ebullition of excited feeling, but a fixed principle of love, which led him to act as he did. And such pure love Jesus attributes to the human heart, describes it even as the property of a Samaritan, it must, therefore, be a possible thing, and will, indeed, be actually found there, where the heart has been moved and animated by the love of God in Christ.

He poured in oil and wine; with wine he washed out the wounds, and soothed the pain with oil. Wine and oil were, and still are, in the East, a well-known means both of allaying pain and of healing, Isa. i. 6.

V. 35. *Took out two pence,*—denarii. Luther's House-Pos. 5. 50: "This poor man, thinks the Samaritan, is my neighbour, for he also is a man, has a body and a soul like myself, nay, has the same God that I have; therefore he is more nearly related to me than an irrational beast, and for that reason I will not abandon him." *And whatsoever thou spendest more.* Mel.: "Here men prattle about works of supererogation, as if the parable referred to private works, not commanded by God, whereas it refers to works which a friendly solicitude requires, and which are commanded by God."

V. 36, 37. *He that showed mercy on him;* Luther: "The polite hypocrite will not name the Samaritan by his proper name." Church-Pos. 14. 31: "It sounds rather strange, that he must be called neighbour, who loves and does well to another; that he also, according both to scripture and the nature of this precept, is to be called neighbour, who stands in need of a kindness, or to whom we must manifest love and do good; but it refers equally to both, and comprehends all alike as in *prædicamento relationis,* in a state of relationship, binds us all together, so as to make each one the neighbour of another. But to be such neighbours to each other, is twofold, either to be so in name only and in word, or in deed and in reality."

Go, and do thou likewise. Gnomon: "Και συ. When once the love of popularity or party spirit is removed, there is then a readier access to free and common grace. Did the Samaritan, then, he would inquire, by this deed of his, attain to *eternal life?* Comp. v. 27—29. It may be answered from Rom. ii. 26." Luther, House-Pos. 5. 52: "As if Jesus had said; Thou art just such a pious saint as the priest and Levite, not willing to help thy neighbour with a penny, though he may be upon the point of death; and dost thou still inquire what thou must do to obtain eternal life?" And, at p. 60: "This portion of Scripture, then, supplies us with a beautiful and very profitable lesson, as to how we must order our life if we would be found among the number of those who truly love God, namely, that we must love our neighbour, and manifest all kindness to him in the time of his necessity. God will accept that, as if we had done it to him." In v. 36, 37, is contained the answer to v. 29, and the application of the parabolical narrative to the scribe.

Many expositors, without sufficient ground or warrant derived from scripture, have thought they discovered here another and hidden sense, and explain the whole allegorically; so Luther, Church-Pos. 14. 9, ss.: "This Samaritan, here, is certainly our Lord Jesus Christ himself, who has manifested his love towards God and his neighbour; he came unbidden, and fulfilled the law with all his heart. The man who lies here half-dead, wounded, bruised, and plundered, is Adam and all mankind. The robbers are the devil; we make some efforts at resistance, but cannot extricate ourselves; here the similitude is strongly verified, and strikingly represents what we are and what we can do with our high reason and free will. The priest is the representative of the holy fathers, who lived before Moses; the Levite, of the priesthood of the Old Testament; but neither of them could prevail any thing with their works, have passed away even as this priest and Levite did. The Samaritan, Christ, pours oil into the wounds, which he does when grace is preached; for as oil softens, so does the sweet, gentle preaching of the gospel, act upon me so as to beget a soft and gentle heart toward God and my neighbour. But wine is pungent, and represents the blessed cross, which soon follows the other, 2 Tim. iii. 12. Thereafter the Samaritan lays the wounded traveller upon his beast, that is, Christ himself, who carries his people. The stable or inn is our present Christian condition, in which we can remain only for a short time; the host corresponds to the ministers of the gospel, whose office it is to care for and wait upon us." Melancthon allegorizes the parable much in the same manner, but with some difference in the particulars; understanding, by the wine, the preaching of repentance; by the oil, the gospel and the Holy Spirit; by the setting on the beast, giving the penitent believer a place in the church and the privilege of the ministry; by the two pence given to the host, the preaching of the law and the gospel, and by the promise to pay whatever additional expenses might be incurred, the readiness of Christ to supply whatever was lacking for the labours and trials of the Christian life. It is obvious, that in such a method of interpretation, every thing is regulated by the greatest capriciousness; because there is no foundation for it in the scripture itself, and hence we find very important differences in the allegorical interpretations just cited, which, however, are all equally groundless. The real aim of the parable,--which is to produce a conviction of having transgressed the law, and the unsatisfactory nature of a mere external compliance, without the spirit of genuine love, which never springs but from faith in Jesus Christ,—is completely lost sight of in such a fanciful mode of interpretation, and therefore it is not to be applied in this way, nor is such an application of it to be justified.

XXII.

THE IMPORTUNATE FRIEND.

Luke xi. 5—8.

The Saviour, on being asked, by one of his disciples, to teach them to pray, as John also had taught his disciples, proceeded to teach them the Lord's Prayer, and went on to give them further directions upon prayer generally, both in the short parable of the importunate friend, and in the direct admonitions that follow, v. 9—13; and the design of the whole passage, v. 5—13, is to give instructive and comforting explanations, partly upon the nature, and partly upon the fruit or consequence of prayer. There are, particularly, two thoughts which the Saviour unfolds in the parable; 1. That we must pray perseveringly; and 2. That persevering prayer is certainly not fruitless. Persevering prayer and entreaty is again recommended, v. 9, by the exhortation to ask, seek, and knock, for seeking and knocking is, in a sense, also begging; and contains within itself the notion of perseverance; and by the promise, subjoined to the exhortation; and once more by what is said in v. 10, when the wisdom of acting thus is represented as a matter of well-known experience in daily life, which is equally verified on the higher ground of faith. The blessed fruit of prayer is still farther illustrated in v. 11—13, by the reflection that a father, who really loves his child, will not answer his request by giving him any thing useless, (a stone,) much less any thing hurtful, (a serpent or scorpion;) and then follows the inference from the less to the greater: since men, notwithstanding that they are sinful, are yet led to give good gifts to their children, how much more will our heavenly Father, who is love itself, give to those who ask him the best gifts, the holy Spirit. Gnomon: "Scripture, with great frequency, exhorts us to prayer. And wherein stands the nature of this duty? In beseeching with earnestness."

As in the Lord's prayer, which immediately precedes, all the petitions are, at the same time, intercessions; and, as the friend does not properly beg for himself, so the leading purport and design of the parable, perhaps, is to show the efficacy of persevering intercession; but if we take the unexpected visit only as a cover for the thought, that an unexpected necessity or occasion should drive us to prayer, we may consider the design to be, in general, the efficacy of continued prayer; yet the former view appears preferable, because then the parable becomes distinguished from the similar one in Luke xviii. 1—8, not merely by the form, but by an essential point of difference. And, as the thought, in v. 13, stands as a conclusion, so we find the same concealed in the parable; for, if a friend, whose kindly feelings and dispositions were so contracted that he would not undergo a trifling inconvenience in order to assist his friend, yet, through persevering prayer, is overcome, and gives the required help, how much more must God (Eph. iii. 15,) be ready and willing! Calvin: "The sum is: That believers should not harass their minds, if they are not immediately gratified in their requests, or if it should seem a matter of difficulty to obtain what they ask; for, if, among men, importunity in seeking extorts what would not be voluntarily done, we have no reason to think that God will be inexorable to us, if we persist in entreating him, and do not allow our minds to flag through delay or difficulty."

TRAIN OF THOUGHT IN THE PARABLE.

On persevering intercession.

I. The ground of this: Confidence in his friend, v. 5.

II. The occasion of it:

(1.) The unexpected circumstance, v. 6;

(2.) The benevolent disposition toward the visiter; v. 6: My *friend* is come to me;

(3.) His own inability, v. 6; I have nothing to set before him.

III. The efficacy of it:

(1.) It overcomes the unwillingness, v. 7, 8.

(2.) It accomplishes its object, v. 8: He will rise and give him as many as he needeth.

Ver. 5. *Shall have a friend*, from whom he has experienced love, and in whom he has confidence. *At midnight*, therefore at an unseasonable time; Olshausen: The time of the greatest internal darkness and necessity.

Ver. 6. *For a friend of mine*, &c.; the first ground of his entreaty; the unexpected visiter, and the quite unlooked-for call thereby occasioned; *and I have nothing*, another ground, his own inability.

Ver. 7. The disinclination is represented and excused by the trouble which it would cause to him, and the disturbance it would occasion to his household.

Ver. 8. Though feelings of affection could not move him, *yet, because of his importunity, he will rise up and give him*, so that he grants the request only on account of his incessant begging; 2 Kings ii. 17: The sons of the prophets urged Elisha, with importunate begging, till he was ashamed. Matth. xv. 21—28. Ewald, p. 237: "Since Jesus has so represented the Father, so human, so paternal, so exactly as we conceive of a father in heaven, I reckon that we should always view him so. Who should give us more correct ideas of God than he? No one knoweth the Father but the Son, and he to whom the Son may reveal him, Matth. xi. 27. Man must not be what he now is,—God must not be the father of man, if it did not become him to pray, and if God were not to hear his prayer. If it were not the part of man to pray, he must either have fewer necessities, or be able to satisfy them all. He must become either more *straitened*, or more *powerful* than he now is. There are many intimations in nature, that its author has appointed prayer, and the hearing of prayer, as a resort in creation, and wills its mutual attraction. The animal, which cannot support or aid itself, has something of an imploring character. The feeble helpless sex, the female, can also beg in the most urgent and irresistible manner, and often prevails more thereby than the strongest with all his might. What, in former times, took place between Samson and Delilah, between David and the woman of Tekoa, (2 Sam. xiv.) has many a thousand times been transacted. As the consideration of nature leads us to apprehend God, and as Jesus here reveals him, he has always manifested himself in the Bible. He has always heard prayer, and listened to the voice of entreaty. Never was he inexorable, for that indeed never has been and never can be the case with supreme love, Gen. xviii. 22, ss. Ps. cxlv. 19. Gen. xix. 18, ss. Isa. xxxviii., and particularly Ps. cvii."

XXIII.

THE RICH FOOL.

Luke xii. 16—21.

This parable was occasioned by one of the multitude saying to Christ, v. 13: "Master, speak to my brother, that he divide the inheritance with me." This unreasonable demand manifestly sprung out of a contention which had arisen between the two brothers, concerning their proper shares in the division of their common inheritance; but, whether the one who made this application might be the injured or the injuring party, (though it is less probable that he was the latter,) the unbrotherly strife was, at any rate, the indication, that a covetous, selfish disposition had so taken possession of his mind, as to have weakened his brotherly love, and laid his mind open to the feelings of envy and hatred. Our Lord declined his solicitation with the words: "Man, who made me a judge or a divider over you?" That is, I am not sent for the purpose of settling earthly transactions; and then he spake to those who were around him: "Take heed, and beware of covetousness; for a man's life consisteth not in the multitude of things which he possesseth." *Covetousness*, avarice, the insatiable desire of more, springing out of ungodly love and too high an estimation of earthly things. Calvin: "Christ first dissuades his people from avarice, and then, that he might completely rid their minds of this malady, he denies that our life consists in abundance; in which declaration he indicates the internal origin and fountain head, from which the mad desire of possessing issues. For, as people commonly judge, that the life of any one is happy just as he possesses much, and riches are supposed to be the cause of a happy life, hence arises that intemperance of desire, which, like a burning furnace, at once gives forth its own heat, and yet never ceases to be glowing within." The previous entreaty had given occasion to this warning, and from it we may warrantably infer the covetous disposition of the person who presented it; the ground of this warning lies in the words: for a man's life, &c., or rather, a man does not live, &c. In the original text it must be construed in this manner: Οτι 'η ζωη αυτου ουκ εστιν τινι εν τω περισσευειν, (infinitivus pro substantivo,) εκ των 'υπαρχοντων αυτου. Schott: "Since, though a man abounds in possessions, yet his life does not at all depend upon his possessions." And also, if a man lives in affluence, his prosperity does not ensure his happiness. The word ζωη is to be taken in its twofold meaning, according to which it marks a happy state of being in time and in eternity, so that the sense is, Riches by no means secure for us, of themselves, a life of satisfaction upon earth, nor do they ensure us of eternal blessedness; or; Real well-being is no necessary consequence of the possession of riches. But this is precisely the error and delusion in which great numbers live, and hence they are drawn with an insatiable desire after riches, because they continually promise themselves at least a quiet, satisfied, and pleasant life on earth from them. And because this error is so general and wide-spread, and is besides so natural to the carnal heart, our Lord warns us, in this declaration, against such self-deceit, and, with much earnestness, introduces the warning with the words: "Take heed, and beware;" which Schott renders: "Cavete vobis diligenter." Now, the parable of the rich fool is added to inculcate this warning still farther, and expose, in more vivid colours, the mournful deceitfulness of riches. As it closes with the words: "So is he that layeth up treasure for himself, and is not rich toward God," it intimates that he shall also be poor and miserable hereafter, who has not here learned to know, and seek, and appropriate the better things, the riches, which respect God and eternity, but has allowed himself to be completely carried away and deluded by the possession of earthly goods, or his endeavours to obtain them. In the parable itself there is, indeed, no respect had to the other life, but the folly and unreasonableness of *avarice*, and the love of earthly things, is represented only in reference to this present life, which riches can neither prolong, nor of themselves render blessed. There is a very close and beautiful connexion between the parable, in this view of it, and the following words of our Lord, v. 22—34, in which he admonishes to Christian indifference toward earthly things, with childlike confidence towards our heavenly Father, enforced by many and powerful motives, and then to a striving application to the things of God. The structure of the parable, and the portraiture of the rich man, is in full accordance with the end in view; for if the thing to be shown was, that riches of themselves do not give happiness, nothing could be more suitable to this than a very prosperous man, in whose state of mind, also, there appeared not one trace or apprehension of any thing higher or better, whose whole felicity was annihilated by a sudden death, and over whose future fate the closing words, in v. 21, threw a faint but mournful light. Calvin: "This parable sets before us, as in a mirror, a lively representation of the sentiment, that men do not live of their abundance. For, since life may be extinguished in a moment, even with the richest, what avails it for them to have heaped up wealth? To us is shown here, first, the fleeting shortness of life; then, the unavailing nature of riches to protract it. A third consideration must be added, which is not expressed, but may easily be gathered from the two former, that the best policy for believers, whether they be rich or poor, is to repose entirely upon the providence of God, seeking from him their daily bread."

Although earthly riches cannot make us truly blessed, and it is the part only of those riches which are in God, to make us partakers in the heavenly kingdom, Rom xiv. 17, there is no need, at the same time, for denying that they contribute to the agreeableness of life, and are benefits for which we should render God thanks; while yet the temporal life of the rich is then only blessed, when they are also rich toward God. What danger attends the possession of riches, we are also admonished in the parable of the sower.

TRAIN OF THOUGHT IN THE PARABLE.

Of the deceitfulness of riches.

Riches deceive the worldly-minded:

I. In regard to their earthly felicity; for,

(1.) They fill the heart with cares, v. 17;

(2.) They occasion much trouble and solicitude, v. 18, (obstructing the quiet, harmless enjoyment,)

(3.) They prove but a short-lived possession, v. 19: Soul, thou hast (and will also keep) many goods; on the other hand, v. 20: Whose shall they be?

(4.) They delude with the hope of a long life, v. 19: Laid up for many years; on the other hand, v. 20; This night, &c.

II. In regard to true felicity; for

(1.) They can provide no true satisfaction to the soul, v. 19: Take thine ease;

(2.) They sink it into utter sensuality, v. 19; Eat, drink;

(3.) They foreclose the heart against any solemn care for salvation, v. 19: Take thine ease;

(4.) They prevent the inheritance of better goods, v. 21.

V. 16. *A certain rich man*, he was already in the possession of many goods, and received besides a considerable addition, for *his ground brought forth plentifully; ground*, χωρα, may denote a large territory, or property in land. Gnomon: " A way of becoming rich the most harmless, and yet the most dangerous."

V. 17. With his riches his cares at the same time increase; he is in difficulty how to get the fulness of his crops stored up; in the most urgent terms he expresses the solicitude of his soul; many thoughts, purposes, plans, had passed through his mind; the worldly-minded have much to fill them with trouble and anxiety, so that they enjoy neither quiet nor repose. Calvin: "*What shall I do?* Therefore the ungodly are perplexed in their designs, because they have not known the true and legitimate use of what they possess; then, because intoxicated with a false confidence, they forget themselves." Grotius: "Behold, how care grows with increasing wealth."

V. 18. The result of his reflections is, that he forms the purpose of building new granaries, (in the East, subterranean repositories,) which purpose, however, brings upon him new cares, troubles, and all manner of vexations. His language is full both of pride and vanity, he says, *my goods*, and forgets that all is only lent him, thinks nothing of the author of his riches, flatters himself in his folly, with the secure and inalienable possession of his goods, if he had them but once laid up in his new barns, and consequently overlooks the thousand accidents which threaten to interrupt, and often completely destroy all temporal possessions. Gnomon: "He makes no mention of the poor." Grotius: "*My goods;* this is not added without cause. For persons of that sort call riches *goods*, not simply from falling into the popular mode of speaking, but because they consider these the chief good."

V. 19. *Soul, thou hast much goods laid up for many years;* because he has *much* to enjoy, he flatters himself with the hope, that he shall have *long* to enjoy it, and promises himself a great age; in his folly he thinks as little of the possible loss of life, as of his goods, nay, he looks upon his riches as conveying a sort of right to a long life, and regards them as a proper good for the soul. However praiseworthy frugality is, as not suffering any of God's gifts to go to waste, (John vi. 12,) it does not render less blameworthy the purpose here expressed, of applying every thing for one's self, in the gratification of selfish desires.

Take thine ease. Grotius: "From the very torture of anxiety and care, he feels how sweet rest is, which he is unable to provide for himself." Cease to gather and be careful any more, withhold thyself from any further pains and applications; so must it ever be with the covetous,—poor in the midst of their overflowings, they enjoy it not, for they think with anxiety on some possible future want, and hence strive and labour without getting satisfaction. This rich man, however, is not of such a covetous disposition, as desires only to have, and keep, and handle wealth or other possessions; he is bent upon enjoyment, he has been working only for future satisfaction, now he counts himself quite sure of attaining his end; and hence he goes on to say: *eat, drink and be merry.* His design is to gratify all sensual desires and appetites, to have daily entertainments, and welter in the lowest kind of enjoyments; this is his delight, and the use which he wishes to make of his wealth. And, while he imagines that his soul could be filled with satisfaction through such enjoyments, he manifests that he never once thinks of any higher necessities of the soul, and knows nothing of the nobler enjoyments of benevolence; in his selfishness he thinks only of himself, and instead of saying: God has blessed me, now I shall make myself a blessing to others, he merely says: My soul, eat, drink, and be merry. Calvin: " Now since he exhorts himself to eat and drink, he forgets that he is a man, and proudly boasts himself of his abundance. And of this haughtiness, we daily perceive the most striking examples among profane men, who set up their mass of wealth, as nothing but a mighty barrier against the attacks of death."

Ver. 20. *But God said unto him;* God's purpose was quite different from the far-stretching hopes and projects of this rich man. The sudden overthrow of his temporal prosperity through unexpected death, and the greatness of his folly, is most vividly represented in the opposite address. *Thou fool;* so is he styled who complacently praised his prudence, and said to himself, This I will do, &c.—*This night thy soul shall be required of thee;* in contrast to v. 19: Thou hast much goods laid up for many years. Calvin: " The allusion made is in regard to the soul. The rich man formerly addressed his soul as the seat of all affections, but now the matter concerns life itself, or the vital spirit. The word ἀπαιτοῦσιν, (they seek,) although it is in the plural number, yet, because it is indefinite, signifies nothing else, than that the life, which the rich man thought to be in his own hand, was the property of another."—*Then, whose shall those things be which thou hast provided,* in contrast to v. 19:

Take thine ease, &c. Not only is death frightful, but, to the selfish heart, which has been always seeking its own, and paid no regard to others, the thought is peculiarly painful, that it must leave to others all the goods which it cleaves to with so much love, without being able to enjoy them itself, Eccles. ii. 18, 19; Ps. xlix. 16—20. Gnomon: "The rich have many things, which, however, are not for the rich; the rich possessor knows not whose they shall be, certainly they shall not belong to himself."

Ver. 21. *So is he that layeth up treasure for himself;* such a fool is every one who thinks and acts after the manner of this rich man; since he is not rich in God, he is much more to be pitied and commiserated than to be envied; and notwithstanding his riches in the account of the world, he is still poor in the eyes of God, Rev. iii. 17, 18.—*And is not rich toward God*, *εις Θεον*, in respect to God and divine things, these riches consist in the imperishable blessings of faith, love, and hope, Eph. i. 3, ss. Calvin: "They are rich toward God, who, not trusting in earthly things, place their sole dependence upon his providence." In this verse, as in verse 15, a warning is contained against the error of placing one's highest good in earthly possessions and enjoyments.

Vitringa gives to the parable the following signification: The rich man represents the higher classes among the Jews, who, in point of disposition, were Epicureans; the rich produce is God's blessing upon the Jews, especially in the time of Herod Agrippa; the judgment of God is that which, through the Romans, was executed upon the Jews.

XXIV.

THE DIFFERENT SERVANTS.

Luke xii. 35—48. Matth. xxiv. 42—51.

THIS parable is much the same as related by Matthew and Luke, only that the latter has it more extended; but it is introduced by the two evangelists in a very different connexion, so that it must either have been delivered twice, or the exact order of time must not have been observed in the one narrative or the other. The purport of the discourse remains in each case the same, recommending watchfulness and fidelity, on the ground that an account shall some time be demanded, and the reward distributed according to what has been manifested in the conduct, of praiseworthy or blameable. The parable, as reported by Matthew, in whom it has not so much unity as in the other evangelist, has an immediate reference to the Lord's return to judgment, which is there (chap. xxiv. xxv.) discoursed of; in Luke the reference is quite different. Our Lord had been exhorting (see the preceding parable) to think more of the kingdom of God, and its more excellent and desirable possessions, v. 31—33, and concluded with the declaration: "For where the treasure is, there will the heart be also;" in which, as the ground of the preceding admonition, the truth is contained, that all the inclinations and energies of man are concentrated on that which he reckons to be his highest good. And in order strikingly to represent the importance of a state of mind directed toward divine things, and of a faithful, conscientious discharge of the trust reposed in us, Christ gives us the portraiture of two different servants, whose dissimilar conduct led, on the one hand, to the most blessed, and, on the other, to the most unhappy consequences. The rich fool, in the preceding parable, was designing to act with the money committed to him in a manner as arbitrary as it was selfish and unprincipled, gave himself no concern about a day of reckoning and judgment, —while yet the mournful consequences of his perversity were indicated only in one brief notice, v. 21. But now the consequences, as reaching to eternity, of fidelity, or the reverse, form a prominent feature in this parable, which hence serves to the essential elucidation and extension of the other; for if here the worldly disposition and misuse of the earthly goods, without respect to a future life, is marked as folly, here, on the contrary, the reference to eternity is the main thing.

The question of Peter, ver. 41, divides the parable into two sections, the first of which speaks of the duty in general of being wakeful or ready in regard to the coming of our Lord, but the other treats principally of fidelity and its consequences, and enlarges most, indeed, upon the mournful consequences of a faithless conduct.

TRAIN OF THOUGHT IN THE PARABLE.

Of the believer's readiness for the coming of Christ.

This readiness, stands in, I. Watchfulness. II. Fidelity.

I. Watchfulness.

(1.) Its nature, v. 35;

(2.) Its ground, v. 36: The servant's relation of dependence toward his Lord;

(3.) The motive to it, v. 37; The glorious reward;

(4.) The difficulty of it, v. 38: The long delay;

(5.) Its necessity, v. 39, 40: The uncertainty of the time.

II. Fidelity.

(1.) Motives to it.

a.) The confidence reposed in him by the Lord, v. 42;

b.) Who intrusts to him a large sphere of operation, v. 42;

c.) In which much good may be done, v. 42.

(2.) Its nature.

a.) That it deals justly, v. 42: Gives them their portion of meat;

b.) And in proper season, v. 42.

(3.) Its consequences;

a.) The internal joy of a good conscience, v. 43;

b.) The Lord's approval and recompense, v. 44.

(4.) Exhortation to fidelity from the mournful consequences of the opposite.

A.) Source of faithlessness, v. 45: Security and unbelief, (v. 39, 46: Portion with the unbelievers.)

B.) Its nature:

a.) Abuse of power, v. 45: Begin to beat, &c.

b.) Ill use of the means intrusted to it, v. 45: To eat and drink, &c.

C.) Its mournful consequences:

a.) He finds himself surprised in his security, v. 46;

b.) He is severely punished, v. 46;

c.) And the punishment, whether more lenient or more severe, is perfectly just, v. 47, 48.

V. 35. *Let your loins be girded about;* the long garments were a hinderance to quick walking, or to the expeditious discharge of business, and they had, therefore, to be tucked up with a girdle. The meaning is: Remove the entanglements.—*And your lights burning;* an image of watchfulness, for one does not so readily sleep when there are lights burning. Both admonitions are addressed to the servants mentioned in the next verse. Bengel: "He wishes his own people to be in a state of readiness." Draeseke: "Be not merely looking after him; dress yourselves for him. Be ready for his service, provided with what is necessary, that you may wait upon his bidding. But the preparation does not stand in the first garment, which may be taken up at random; but in the good garment, which is put on, in *his righteousness*, Eph. vi. 13—15; Rev. xvi. 15. Without light, however, the holy girding about of this garment is neither suited to the service, nor used in the service. The light is faith. Clear-burning faith does not permit sleeping. It illumines our highest relations, duties, and possessions, as it withholds nothing from us which belongs to salvation."

Ver. 36. *Men*, as much as, servants. Weddings were in the evening, (see Parable XV.) hence the temptation to sleep was the greater for the servants; but they must wait till the Lord came, keeping themselves in readiness for his reception, and not then set about the work of preparation. Olshausen: "The similitude of the wedding always brings us back to the relation of Christ to his church. Now, to the church, in the more extended sense, belong all the members of Christ's body, as well as the apostles; but individual members may be apprehended according to a certain prominence of this or that direction in the circumstances of their condition; sometimes more as active, (δουλοι,) sometimes more as receptive or contemplative, (παρθενοι,) and, accordingly, the figurative ways of expression are variously modified, (Matth. 1, ss.) Here the apostles are represented as active labourers, and they therefore appear as stewards of the house of God, in the absence of the Lord, until the celebration of the divine wedding, that is, until the time of union with the society above, of which the union that is to take place at the return of our Lord (his coming to the wedding) with the company of saints upon earth is analogous."

V. 37. *Whom the Lord shall find watching;* in whom he beholds the proof of love and fidelity.—*He will gird himself*, &c. The meaning is: He will richly recompense, and gloriously reward them. Draeseke: "And now let the blessedness, which every stroke of this image breathes, blow upon you. The Lord girds himself to do service to those who have served him. Love for love! That is the first stroke. The Lord conducts his servants to table, goes up and down before them, and serves them with the promised repast. Gift for gift! That is the second stroke. The Lord sets his servants over all his goods, and will withhold nothing more from them. Fulness for fulness! that is the last stroke. They gave him what they had; he, in return, gives them what is his;—the freedom of God's children; a region of knowledge, of action, of enjoyment, of love, of glory, of honour to fill and occupy, Rev. xxi. 4." Olshausen: "The form, under which the self-denying love of the Saviour, towards his people, is here represented, is borrowed from the promise, pervading all scripture, of a great feast, which, at the erection of the kingdom of God, the Lord will hold with his people. This marriage-supper of the Lamb, (Rev. xix. 9,) was foreshadowed by the last meal of Jesus at which he instituted the supper; and, according to John xiii. 1, ss., he acted then precisely as here represented; he acted as the servant, and treated his disciples as lords. What was there done, was an external image of that which the Lord will do at the end of time to those who have faithfully kept his commands, even unto death, (Matth. viii. 11; xxvi. 29.")

V. 38. The Romans divided the night into four parts, which were called evening, midnight, cock-crowing, and morning. This division was made, also, by the Jews, in the time of Christ, because they were under Roman supremacy; though, at an earlier period, they divided the night only into three parts, each consisting of four hours, Matth. xiv. 25. However, the Jewish division appears to be here adopted as the common one. The design of the figure is to represent to us the continued watchfulness of the servants who victoriously overcome all the hinderances and difficulties which are connected with the protracted absence of the Lord. Draeseke, otherwise: "The first watch is the period of childhood, when others watch for us; the fourth watch is the time of old age, whosoever has watched till which, is safe, and is in no great danger of falling asleep. But the second and the third watch, the seasons of youth and manhood, are the most dangerous stages of life on earth. Therefore must we, who are passing through these, least of all remit our watching. Besides, watching is peculiarly difficult. Not because watching continues all our life-long, and in so far, length here also adds to the burden. On the contrary, he who has fairly entered on the duty of watching, has become habituated to it, overcomes sleep, and is the longer the livelier. It is with him as with the thinker, whose deep cogitations keep him from sleeping, or as with the child, who cannot sleep for joy, when he goes to Christ. To Christ, also, each one of us must go. And great joy holds him awake who waits for the kingdom, and the glory of Christ. Where the treasure is, there the heart is also, v. 34; Eph. v. 14."

V. 39. Matth. xxiv. 43. A new image is here introduced, which, through the representation of a threatening danger to the sleeping, admonishes to watchfulness; still the main point of comparison is the unexpected arrival, as v. 40, shows. Olshausen: "With the image of the Lord removed from his servants, but constantly expected by them to return, while they were left in charge of the household concerns, there is here joined another, for characterizing, more vividly, the unexpectedness of his return—the image of a householder who guards against the expected inbreaking of a thief, and being ignorant of the hour when he is to come, must continue always on the watch. That this similitude should have no further meaning than simply to express the idea of suddenness, is not at all probable. It is used, in the first place, too commonly of Christ's return, (Matth. xxiv. 43; 2 Peter iii. 10; Rev. iii. 3; xvi. 15,) not to carry a special reference, nor can we conceive why, for the indication merely of suddenness, some nobler comparison should not have been adopted, since so many might be found; and finally, the minute detail of the figurative description in some places, as here and in Matth. xxiv., according to which the householder prepares himself for the thief, and the breaking in of the thief is formally represented, is not done so as to countenance the idea, that it was to produce no effect upon the similitude itself. It is rather to be remarked, that very often figurative expressions are used by our Lord, which are taken from a hostile point of view. In the present case, the image of the thief is chosen with a reference to the feeling of those who give themselves to the life and business of the world, as to the affairs of their proper home. These are frightened for the coming of the Son of Man, as for the attack of a thief, believing that their (supposed) property is thereby to be wrenched from them."

V. 40. Application of the figure to the disciples of Jesus, Matth. v. 44.

V. 41. The question of Peter proceeds from the rashness of supposing, that he had done something of great account in the kingdom of Christ, and hence deserving above others to be referred to under the promised rewards, v. 37. Draeseke: "The command to watch, is for all the servants of God. Servants of God are of all classes. But because greatness chiefly attracts observation, we naturally apply the expression pre-eminently to those who are princes and nobles, magistrates and governors, parents and guardians, teachers and preachers, as those who must watch for many souls, (Heb. xiii. 17,) and among these, and besides these, to men, to whom God has granted, or whom he has chosen to great honour."

V. 42. The reply of our Lord, without giving a definite answer, manifestly carries this meaning, that he had directed his admonition pre-eminently to those to whom there was committed a peculiarly great, important and distinguished sphere of action, v. 42, such as the apostles and other teachers, without, however, excluding other believers. But at the same time, he shows how the distinguished position, which is assigned to any one, brings along with it also an obligation so much the stronger, and a responsibility so much the heavier, so that the possession of an extensive sphere of action, apart from fidelity, by no means justifies the expectation of a glorious reward, which is rather apportioned according to the measure of fidelity, Matth. ver. 45. Calvin: "This, indeed, is the purport of Christ's answer, that, if it is proper for the commonest person to watch, much less is it to be borne, that the apostles should be asleep. He admonishes them, that they were not elevated to an idle dignity for the purpose of enjoying themselves with security; but that, by how much there was of excellence in the degree of honour they had attained, so much heavier was the burden that lay upon them, and that faith and prudence ought especially to be exercised by them." Draeseke: "The answer affirms as little as it denies. It instructs; it awakens reflections; it points the inquiring disciple to the main thing he had overlooked, upon which more depends in the case of the householder than upon the extent and importance of his trust,—that is, his fidelity and prudence, the devotedness of his heart, and the intentness of his eye, toward his master. Fidelity and prudence must be shown by every servant, whether in a high or low situation. But neither the one nor the other can be without watchfulness."

Faithful and wise steward, 1 Cor. iv. 2. Such domestic stewards were commonly slaves; Eliezer with Abraham, Joseph with Potiphar. *Whom his lord shall make;* Gnomon: "*Shall set*, future tense, because *fidelity* renders a servant worthy of being set over the household. The expression occurs again in v. 44, where the gradation is from the family to all possessions."

Ver. 43—46. Matth. xxiv. 46—51. In v. 44, the more extended sphere of action is represented as the reward of fidelity. Ver. 45. *If that servant*, the same servant, in whom the lord had placed so much confidence, and whom he had set over others: *say in his heart, My Lord delayeth his coming*, the speech of folly, which believes the day of reckoning and judgment to be far distant, only to abandon itself to the more unrestrained indulgence of its lusts; *and shall begin to beat the servants,* laying claim in arrogance and hard-heartedness to a right belonging to the Lord; *and to eat and drink, and to be drunken,* revelling upon that which has been withdrawn from others, and, at the same time, wickedly squandering the goods of his lord.

Ver. 46. False security sees itself confounded, by the unexpected arrival of the Lord, and is severely punished. *Will cut him asunder,* quarter him, indication of a very hard punishment. *Appoint him his portion with the unbelievers;* Matth. v. 51, *hypocrites;* that is, he shall have the same fate.

Ver. 47, 48. Grotius: "When Christ had delivered his twofold parable, the one part of which relates to Christians in general, and the other to the rulers of the church, he shows now wherein the things spoken agree, and wherein they differ. They agree in this, that common people as well as rulers are beaten, unless they discharge their duty; they differ in this, that the latter are beaten more severely, as persons to whom, for the most part, is given a larger and more accurate knowledge of all that either immediately or remotely pertains to salvation." The different punishments bear proportion to the different degrees of criminality, manifesting the utmost impartiality and integrity in the judge. With v. 47, comp. Jas. iv. 17; all the bad servants, indeed, are punished, but those who had most committed to them, and who, against their better knowledge, and convictions of duty, had left their obligations unfulfilled, were visited with heavier chastisements. But even sins which are committed in ignorance, are punishable, for ignorance itself is guilt. All the subjects of a kingdom are under an obligation to make themselves acquainted with its laws, and misconduct arising from neglect is punishable guilt. Calvin: "It must be borne in mind, that those who are set to govern the church do not sin through ignorance, but perversely and impiously defraud their Lord. From which, however, the general doctrine may be gathered, that men in vain flee to the cover of ignorance, to free themselves from guilt."

Vitringa explains the bad servant, ver. 45, of the Pope, and thereby deprives the parable of its general reference and applicability to all the servants of the Lord.

XXV.

THE FRUITLESS FIG-TREE.

Luke xiii. 6—9.

THE immediate occasion of the deliverance of this beautiful parable, was afforded by the report being brought to Jesus of the murder of some Galileans, whom Pilate had caused to be put to death, while they were employed in the temple offering sacrifices. But it is expressly intimated, ver. 1, that the persons who related this to Jesus had been present while he was delivering the instructions and warnings which are recorded in the preceding chapter, and we cannot but think they must have found some occasion in the words of our Lord to mention the circumstances at this particular time; so that it is necessary to investigate the connexion of the parable with the preceding context still more closely, which is besides of importance for the proper determination of its design. After that Jesus, ver. 49—53, had spoken of the inevitable and necessary contest which the preaching of his gospel should awaken in the sinful and perverse disposition of the human heart, he blames his hearers, that they failed to observe and improve the singular appearances of the present time, in order to prepare themselves for the still more important and eventful future, ver. 54—57. Luther's Comment on ver. 56 says: "When you can see how it goes with the creatures, why do ye fail to perceive where ye yourselves are wanting?" In order to place their blameable and criminal, as well as dangerous, misemployment of time in a still clearer light, Jesus delivers the comparison contained in ver. 58, 59, the meaning of which is: If it is unquestionably a matter of prudence for a debtor to come to good terms with his creditor, before he is dragged by him into judgment, where every thing will be determined only by the strict rule of right and justice: so assuredly would it be the highest wisdom for you sinners to become reconciled, through a true repentance, to your creditor, the merciful and righteous God, before the time comes for a strict and rigorous judgment. Here also are declared the following thoughts—that men are, as sinners, debtors of God; that an impartial judgment threatens them; that, before it comes, it is possible by a sincere repentance to escape the final condemnation of God; but that the time of grace, which may be used for repentance, must not be misspent in security or carelessness, for when past it is too late, and the destruction is inevitable. Now it is precisely the same thoughts which return in the parable of the fig-tree, so that its connexion with the preceding context is rendered obvious. (It is besides to be remarked, that in Matth. v. 25, 26, the similitude used in these last two verses of the twelfth chap. of Luke, is also introduced, but in a quite different connexion, and for an entirely different purpose.)

It was after having listened to the declarations contained in v. 49—59, that some present mentioned the fate of those unfortunate Galileans; with what design, appears from v. 2, where Jesus discovers the bottom of their hearts, and their perverse thoughts, and where it is remarked by Luther in his Comment: "The Jews held, that whosoever was prosperous in this world, was acceptable to God, but that he who was unfortunate, was a sinner, John ix. 2, 3." Gnomon: "Do you think that you are guiltless, and shall escape with impunity? We ought not to look so much to what has happened to others, or why it has happened, as to what might happen to us, and what must be done by us." Since the mention of the fate of these Galileans, in the opinion of these narrators, was to be taken as an example of the punitive righteousness of God, while at the same time they manifested the perversity of the human heart, which, though it is ready enough to judge others, is equally ready to overlook its own guilt and liability to punishment: Jesus, therefore, v. 3, makes a general application of this particular case to the Israelites at large, and says: Except ye repent, ye shall all likewise perish. Here again we find the previously declared sentiment concerning moral corruption, liability to punishment, imminent danger, still abiding season of grace,—concerning repentance as the only means of deliverance, and impenitence as the real ground of an irrecoverable perdition. Jesus farther reminds them, v. 4, of a similar destruction, and repeats over again the asseveration he had already made in v. 3, as to the necessity of repentance to save them from the like sudden and overwhelming judgment of God, and then proceeds to deliver the parable of the fruitless fig-tree, directed against secure and careless sinners, to teach them the necessity of repentance, if they would escape destruction. For that this is the design of the parable, is manifest from the close connexion in which it stands with v. 5, and from the whole context. Calvin: "The doctrine taught may be thus summed up: That many are tolerated for a time, who are deserving of destruction; but that they shall be no gainers by the delay, if they persist in their contumacy. For hence arises the corrupt flattery with which hypocrites harden themselves, that unless compelled, they do not bethink themselves of their own misdeeds; and therefore as long as God connives and suspends his judgments, they imagine that they are on good terms with him. And so they indulge themselves with the more security, as if they had obtained a covenant with death and the grave, as Isaiah speaks, (conf. Rom. ii. 5.) We are besides taught, since the Lord does not immediately avenge himself of the wicked, but delays their punishment, that the best reason exists for his forbearance. So that human temerity is restrained, and no one can charge the Supreme Judge with blame, if he does not always execute his judgments with undistinguishing equality."

The immediate reference of this parable is to the Jewish nation and church, whose deep and wide-spread corruption, notwithstanding the many provisions made by God for their improvement, is here described, and whose rapidly approaching overthrow, in righteous vengeance for their inconsiderate and obstinate impenitence, is predicated. Hence this parable is of a similar tendency with the two formerly explained, of the wicked vine-dressers, and the wedding-garment, in so far as these are to be viewed in their immediate historical reference, as descriptive partly of the past, and partly of the future fate and times of the Jewish people; and that there is actually such a reference here, is manifest, as well from the two historical transactions mentioned in v. 1, 4, with which the parable stands closely connected, and which our Lord represents as types of what would befall the whole Jewish people, as from the parable itself, as shall be farther shown below. Pilate had permitted some Galileans to be murdered in the temple, while they were actually engaged in offering sacrifices, so that their blood was mingled with the blood of their victims; which horrible crime of the Roman governor appears still more frightful and deserving of abhorrence on account of the circumstance, that it was committed in the temple, and while they were engaged in an act of religion. Now the Redeemer says prophetically: Ye shall all likewise perish, (ωσαυτως, in the same manner) as if this murderous transaction was to be only a small omen of the general carnage that was to come upon the Jews, and that too from the same party, the Romans, to which also the declaration in Matth. xxiv. 28, seems to refer; and this divine judgment upon the Jewish people was rendered still more dreadful and shocking, from the circumstance of its having been executed at the time of the passover, when such vast crowds were assembled in Jerusalem, and were employed in offering up sacrifices. Not less significantly typical was the other event mentioned by Christ himself, ver. 4, in which eighteen Jews were suddenly destroyed by the falling of a tower in Siloam; for while our Lord in connexion with it says again: Ye shall all likewise perish, (ομοιως, *similarly*,) the intimation seems to be given, what the history of the destruction of Jerusalem also confirms, that they would some time be buried amid the ruins of the temple and their own dwellings. The resemblance between these transactions is too great and striking to admit of our supposing that the one class of events was not intended to be typical of the other. Gnomon: "ωσαυτως is more than ομοιως; and the event corresponds, for the Jews were punished by the nation to which Pilate belonged; at the season too of the passover, when sacrifices were offered, and with the sword." Grotius: "See how exactly every thing corresponds. For they were killed on the day of the passover, a great part of them in the temple itself, like sheep, for the same crime of sedition, which men of flagrant impiety hid under a false show of piety."—But this immediate application of the parable to Israel's fate is by no means exclusive: for as God still manifests the riches of his compassion to one and all belonging to the church of his Son, as he did in former times to the members of the old covenant—as in his patience and long-suffering, in his holiness and justice, he is the same yesterday, and to-day, and for ever—as in the naturally corrupt state of the human heart, the same levity and inattention to the manifestations of divine grace is ever and anon repeated—as proper repentance is at all times in the divine economy the means of deliverance, but impenitence is perpetually ruinous; therefore the parable possesses a much wider and more general application, and shall have its divine truth made manifest in the great day of final account. Olshausen: "The severe and stringent discourse of Jesus is closed with a parable, in which the loving Son of Man again displays the operations of grace. He appears as the advocate of man before the righteousness of heaven, and obtains room for repentance. This thought of postponing the day of judgment, to give man time for repentance, runs throughout the whole of Scripture, Gen. vi. 3; xviii. 24, ss. The destruction of Jerusalem did not take place till forty years after the ascension of Jesus, and his return to judgment is delayed on account of God's long-suffering, 2 Peter iii. 9."

TRAIN OF THOUGHT IN THE PARABLE.

An admonition to secure sinners to repent.

I. The admonition is directed to secure sinners, who are represented under the image of the fruitless fig tree;

(1.) They are capable of improvement, ver. 6: Had a fig tree, (which, according to its nature, must bear good fruit;)

(2.) Nor are external aids wanting to produce this, ver. 6: It was planted in his vineyard;

(3.) Demands also are made upon them for it, ver. 6: He came and sought fruit thereon;

(4.) And yet they make no progress, ver. 6: He found none.

II. The admonition is accompanied by the threatened judgment of God: Cut it down, ver. 7; And this judgment is,

(1.) A righteous one; both on account of the abuse of divine patience and long-suffering, ver. 7: Behold, these three years, &c.; and also on the account of the adverse influence upon others, v. 7: Why cumbereth it the ground?

(2.) Yet admitting of delay, ver. 8: Lord, let it alone this year also; to which delay the motive is just this prayer of the vine-dresser; and the design of it is to give a new opportunity for amendment, ver. 8: Till I shall dig about it and dung it; and to produce an actual improvement, ver. 9: If it bear fruit, well;

(3.) A certain one, ver. 9: If not, then after that thou shalt cut it down.

Ver. 6. *A certain man had a fig tree planted in his vineyard;* in the parable of the wicked vine-dressers, (Matth. xxi.) the vineyard denotes the whole Jewish people, as also in Isa. v.; but here the vineyard must be understood generally of the whole earth, and the fig tree of the Jewish people; and in the general application of the parable we can understand by the fig tree the Christian church, and also each individual Christian. As the fig tree is a fruit tree, which should bear fine fruit, and besides was planted in a vineyard and treated with special care, this represents the favourable circumstances and relations which the mercy of God had granted to Israel, his design to obtain fruit from the tree, and the just expectation of the same. So is it exactly in regard to the Christian church as a whole, and to each individual Christian, both alike not only possessing the natural means and capacity of being improved, but being placed also in the most favourable circumstances by their God, so that they might bring forth the fruits of piety and holiness. Gnomon: "Fig tree, a tree which does not properly belong to a vineyard. God chose Israel in perfect freeness.—The Father has the vineyard, and Christ cultivates it, comp. ver. 8, or Christ has the vineyard, and his ministers cultivate it." Grotius: "The vineyard here, is the whole human race, in which was the fig tree, that is, the Jewish people giving promise of great things."

And came and sought fruit thereon, but found none, —a description of the ingratitude and impenitence of those for whom God has done so much; Israel was actually, at the time of Jesus, in the condition of a deep moral corruption, excessive wickedness and hypocrisy reigned almost in every heart. The circumstance related in Matth. xxi. 18—20, of Jesus having blasted the fig-tree, from which he had in vain sought fruit, affords a palpable and striking proof of this; for it is very easy to see, in that action, a visible and affecting type of the sudden overthrow and irrecoverable destruction of the Jewish nation, and to regard the miracle wrought by Jesus as symbolical of it.

Ver. 7. *Then said he to the dresser of his vineyard;* in the figure of this verse the divine purpose toward Israel, and all impenitent sinners, is described. *Behold, these three years I come, seeking fruit,* a lively representation of the numerous attempts and movements of God to remind sinners of their obligation to comply with his gracious designs; he comes always anew in his word, by means of conscience, and so forth. Along with this, however, we have here depicted the patience and long-suffering of God, which waits for the expected fruits, 2 Peter iii. 15; Rom., ii. 4. This patience, exercised so long to no purpose, gives so much the more ground for the painful lamentation: *And I find none,* (see v. 34;) and also for the judgment: *Cut it down,* Luke xiii. 35; xix. 41—44. Isaiah v. 5, 6. Matth. iii. 10; vii. 19. The command primarily refers to the subversion of the Jewish church, Ps. lxxx. 9—15, and in it we see the union of love and holiness, of grace and righteousness, Rom. ii. 5, 6. Gnomon: "In this word there is great severity, the great power of the master of the vineyard." And not merely does the abuse made of God's patience show the righteousness of this judgment, but there is a still farther ground for it intimated in the question, *Why cumbereth it the ground?* While the fruitless tree draws to itself the nourishing moisture out of the earth, and extends its shadow far and wide, nothing can flourish in its neighbourhood." This we may refer to the hurtful influence which Israel's pride and hypocrisy exercised upon the nations, Matth. xxiii. 13, 15; and every sinner is, where he lives, a pernicious example to others, and often a great hinderance to their attainment of salvation. Grotius: "The Jews, though treated by God with the highest favours, were not so useful to other nations by the example of their piety, but that they might, on the other hand, by their life, alienate many the more from true religion." The three years are not to be referred to the three periods in the Jewish history, of Moses, David, and the prophets; more than any of them we should have to include the time of Christ's public ministry; but the determinate period is put for the indeterminate, and the image points only to the grace and long-suffering of God. Gnomon: "The Lord was now entered upon the third year of his ministry, as the true harmony of the evangelists manifests." Grotius: "Those who refer these things to the three years in which Christ taught, seem to pay little regard to what follows concerning the one year, in which further trial was to be made. For God did not, in answer to the prayers of his saints, delay the punishment of the Jews for one year only after Christ's triennial ministry, but for forty years. So that it is better to consider the three years spoken as mentioned because the fig trees which do bear fruit, always do so within that period. And to these three years corresponds the whole time before the Baptist and Christ, during which God most patiently waited for the amendment of the Jews." The vine-dresser is manifestly Christ, to whom the judgment is committed, John v. 22, and the destruction of Jerusalem is described as his coming to judgment, Matth. xxiv. 29, ss. Luke xix. 14, 27.

Ver. 8. The intercession of the vine-dresser marks the still longer protracted patience, and still farther delayed judgment, until the time of grace was expired; it breathes the most heartfelt love, and such love was felt by Jesus toward the people, of whom, according to the flesh, he was sprung; he is also expressly named the advocate or intercessor, 1 John ii. 1. Heb. vii. 23; ix. 24. *Let it alone this year also;* therefore, there is only a short and determinate period given for repentance; love hopes all things; *till I shall dig about it and dung it,* marks the renewed endeavours of grace to bring about the necessary change of mind;

the digging, or turning up of the soil, indicates the removal of the hinderances, and the dunging points to the application of new juices of life, which, when the former is done, can operate with so much more freedom and effect. Without figure: I will try every thing which can possibly be of advantage to make the tree yield the desired fruit, and save it from destruction. Grotius: "Those gifts, which the apostles and their fellow-labourers exercised for the conversion of the Jews, may seem to correspond to this."

Ver. 9. *If not, after that thou shalt cut it down;* the very good vine-dresser yields to the determinate and righteous judgment of the Lord of the vineyard, Rom. xi. 22. Gnomon: "The vine-dresser does not say, I will cut it down, comp. v. 7, but refers the matter to the lord; he ceases, however, to intercede for the fig tree." What might be the consequence of these labours and the fate of the tree, is left undetermined by the parable. And in this appears the great inclination to spare in the mind of the Lord, who wished thereby to awaken in the hearts of his hearers the hope of a favourable issue, and admonish them so much the more impressively to repent; it is not till after this that he first disclosed the inevitable overthrow of the Jewish nation, and the history of that of course supplies the real issue of the parable. What befell the Jewish church, has also happened to particular Christian churches, as a fulfilment of divine threatening, and as a proof of the truthfulness, goodness, patience, and righteousness of God, Rev. ii. 5.

We might also give the substance of the parable, were we to say, that Jesus represents to *blinded* sinners their mournful state of mind under the image of the unfruitful fig tree; points *secure* sinners to the long-suffering they have already received, and the approaching judgment of a righteous God: and admonishes the *thoughtless* to the conscientious improvement of their still remaining day of grace.

XXVI.

THE GREAT SUPPER.

Luke xiv. 16—24.

Of the relation of this parable to that of the wedding garment, we spoke formerly under Section XIV. and there also remarked, that the present parable was spoken by Jesus before his last journey to Jerusalem, in Peræa. Its immediate occasion appears from the narrative in the preceding context. Jesus had been invited by a chief person among the pharisees to eat bread on the Sabbath, v. 1. Having entered the house, he first of all healed a man of dropsy, and justified this work of love, to the great annoyance of the pharisees, who were outwardly legal, but internally quite estranged from the spirit of love, (which, however, is the soul of the law,) by pressing the question in v. 5, so that they were put to shame, could not but acknowledge in their heart, at least, the righteousness of his conduct, and did not venture, against the testimony of their own conscience, to declare him to be deserving of punishment, v. 6. Hereupon our Lord took occasion to animadvert upon the vanity and immoderate pride of guests, pressing forward to the chief seats at table, and thereby showing how covetous they were of vain honour, v. 7—11. Then he disclosed to his host the selfishness of his heart, who had so selected his guests as to manifest that he had given his feast in order to be invited back again, and to be recompensed, v. 12, at the same time recommending a compassionate regard to the poor, and pointing to the recompense which is to come from God, v. 13, 14. The persons, therefore, before whom and to whom this parable was delivered, were self-righteous, proud, ambitious, selfish, cold-hearted, and the words of admonition spoken by Christ could not be pleasant to them. The moment, therefore, that he touched upon the resurrection of the just, one of the company laid hold of his words, as affording a welcome opportunity to turn the conversation into another channel, and expressed a great desire to participate in the blessedness of that day, of which, however, his heart knew nothing, so that he only feigned this stroke of piety with his lips. To derive the exclamation of this guest, "Blessed is he that shall eat bread in the kingdom of God," from so bad a source, and not rather to take it in a good sense, to which at first sight we might be inclined, we are justified, nay, necessitated by what was previously intimated of the moral condition of the guests, and still more by the whole structure of the parable, in which it is manifested by means of the guests first invited, how an earthly disposition, and the love of this present world, withheld so many from a blessed participation in the great supper, and how those only made their appearance there, in whose case no such hinderance existed. Calvin, however, remarks on this place: "But, although it is scarcely credible that the friend and guest of the pharisee uttered this exclamation from any thing of truly pious feeling, it does not at the same time appear to have been done in mockery; but, as men possessed of a little faith, and not openly profane, are wont to talk in their cups with an air of confidence concerning eternal life, I conceive that a word was thrown in by this man concerning future bliss, for the purpose of eliciting something from Christ, who thence took occasion of charging ingratitude upon the Jews." The connexion, then, between the exclamation in v. 15, and the parable would be: Thou dost indeed pronounce those blessed who shall eat bread in the kingdom of God, but I say unto thee, although this blessedness is prepared for all, and is freely offered them, there are many who still despise it; and all who resemble thee in spirit, shall, from their own fault, lose the offered salvation. The parable, consequently, is not to be viewed as a more extended representation of that eulogium, and of the blessedness mentioned in it, but as a rebuke, which the omniscient Searcher of hearts (John ii. 24, 25,) gave to that hypocrite, and a discovery of the perverseness of the human heart in relation to the kingdom of God. For this construction of v. 15, and the whole parable, there may still farther be produced the analogy of other parables; for the parables of the wicked servant, of the labourers in the vineyard, of the good Samaritan, of the unfruitful fig tree, and some others, are in like manner directed against sinful perversity of heart, which the Lord rebuked in them, as he does in the case before us. Luther remarks upon this, House-Pos. 4. 223: "After hearing such things, one of them rises up, who would show himself much more learned than Christ, and says, 'Blessed is he that shall eat bread in the kingdom of God;' as if he would say, in his greater wisdom, Thou profitest not much with thy preaching; if the question comes to be about that, I can also do it well, and even better than thyself; for this I reckon to be a very superior discourse: Blessed, &c. To this Jesus again replies: Nay, I will tell thee how blessed thou art, and such as are like thee, v. 16—24. The reproof given him is to this effect: Oh, thou art no doubt in deep earnest, as thou art a very excellent man, one, namely, of those who are invited, and still come not." And he gives, at p. 235, the design of our Lord thus: "The Lord wishes to admonish us in this parable, that we must count the gospel excellent and precious, and separate ourselves from the multitude, who think that they are prudent, wise, great and good." And this design is so far accomplished, that an earthly disposition is represented as a hinderance to salvation, while poverty of spirit (Matth. v. 3,) is essential to the attainment of real bliss; and, accordingly, the narrative makes known the method in which man desires the salvation proffered to him, and shows the inexcusable guilt of thoughtless and inconsiderate despisers. Since the Jewish nation showed themselves peculiarly hostile to the gospel, and many of them slighted the Messiah, and rejected the invitation given them to his fellowship and salvation; since, on the other hand, the Gentiles manifested more readiness in receiving the message of salvation and peace: the parable readily admits of a historical reference to these transactions, though it would be far from exhausting its depth and compass of meaning, to make the rejection of Israel and the calling of the Gentiles its chief and only design. It rather speaks of the ultimate ground of the melancholy fact, that so many despise the gracious call of the gospel to salvation, which fact has always been recurring anew during the progress of centuries, and will be still further continued,—that the love of the world breeds contempt of the love and grace of God, and disinherits itself of the great salvation. Mel.: "It is a reproof for contempt of the gospel; but though Christ spoke concerning the rejection of the Jewish people, yet he does not speak of them alone, but his discourse has respect to all times, and blames contempt of the gospel in teachers, governors, and the more influential part of the people."

TRAIN OF THOUGHT IN THE PARABLE.

The love of this world is a hinderance to salvation.

I. Reasons, why the love of the world is a hinderance to salvation,

(A.) On account of its power over the heart, v. 16, 17.

(1.) It is not attentive to the greatness of divine grace; v. 16: *a supper*, in which it is matter both of honour and enjoyment to take part:

(2.) It disregards the means of this grace, through which the sinner must be brought to the fellowship of it; v. 16: *And bade many;*

(3.) It hardens the heart against the repeated invitations of God; v. 17: *And sent his servant*, &c.

(4.) And does despite to the free grace of God, which has at once provided every thing necessary for our salvation and invites us to partake of it without any personal desert; v. 17.

(B.) On account of its nature, v. 18—20.

(1.) It is directed to what is earthly, perishable;

a.) To goods and pleasures, v. 18;

b.) To honour, influence, and consideration, v. 19;

c.) To ties and connexions, v. 20;

(2.) It prefers that to what is heavenly and eternal, v. 18, 19; *I pray thee have me excused;*

(3.) It lays claim, in doing so, to a right frame of mind, v. 18, 19;—considering itself to have a proper excuse, and thus manifests its ingratitude, its levity, and its obstinacy.

II. Proof that the love of the world is such a hinderance;

(1.) From the consequences resulting to the despisers:

a.) They draw upon themselves the anger of God, v. 21: *Then the master of the house being angry;*

b.) They forfeit the offered salvation, v. 24;

(2.) From the subsequent procedure of God, who still manifests his mercy and grace;

a.) In that he continues to invite men to the blessings of salvation, v. 21: *Go out quickly*, &c.

b.) And even the most wretched of men, v. 21: *Bring in hither the poor*, &c.

c.) And all, without exception, in the most pressing manner, v. 22, 23: *Compel them*, &c.

V. 16. *A certain man made a great supper;* Luther, House-Pos. 4. 223; "The man is our Lord God himself, a great and rich lord, who has prepared a feast according to his glorious majesty and honour, and such a feast as is truly great and glorious, not only in respect of the host, who is God himself, but the provision is also unspeakably excellent and precious; that is, the blessed gospel, nay, Christ our Lord himself. This proclamation of Christ is the great, glorious supper, wherewith he entertains his guests, sanctifying them through his sacred table; consoling and strengthening them through the sacrament of his body and blood; so that nothing is wanting to a full enjoyment, (John x. 11,) and every one is satisfied. For it is an everlasting food, and an everlasting drink, on which a man never hungers or thirsts any more, but is perpetually satisfied and full: and not one man merely, but, large as the world is, were it even ten times larger, there would be enough for all. And to believe on the Lord Jesus Christ is to eat and to drink at his supper." The great supper is, therefore, fellowship with the Redeemer, in whom there is to be found spiritual blessings and heavenly gifts both in time and in eternity. The word *supper* is not to be pressed, because in the original it is δειπνον, *banquet;* and, therefore, Luther gives a false reason for this word, when he says the gospel is so called from being the last word of instruction that was to be delivered to the world. The preparation of the supper, an apparatus of salvation for sinners, has its ground in the love of God; the greatness of it points to the universality of grace as offered to all.

And bade many; Luther, as above: "The many, who were invited to the feast, were the Jews, who, as sprung from Abraham, were specially invited thereto by the prophets; for to that patriarch was the seed promised, through which the blessing was to come; accordingly, the prophets carried it forward, and showed the people that there was no failure in regard to the Lord's will, and pressed on them his invitations." The invitation comes from the free grace and love of God; on the part of the invited there is found no worth or desert; the invitation is still always made through the proclamation of the blessed gospel in churches, schools, families, by all who communicate its truth to others. A participation in the supper brings honour, joy, blessing, and satisfies all the necessities of the soul and of the spirit. From the greatness of the benefits provided, we can easily infer the severity of their punishment, who despise them, and the worthlessness of their excuses. That there were many invited, shows how comprehensive the grace of God is.

The representation of the blessings of Messiah's kingdom, under the image of a feast, was very common, (Isa. xxv. 6; Matth. viii. 11,) and was here, besides, partly occasioned by the exclamation of the guest in v. 15, and partly also, by the entertainment itself, v. 1; during which the parable was uttered. Gnomon: "*Called;* the link of connexion between two convivial discourses, inviting to blessedness. Call the poor to thee; follow the vocation of God."

V. 17. *And sent his servant at supper time;*—sends, according to the eastern custom, to bid the guests a second time,—first, on the day before, or very early on the morning of the same day, and then at the meal-time, when the messenger announces that they might now come, because every thing was ready. Gnomon: "*Now,* is indicative of present time in the New Testament." Luther, House-Pos. 4. 225: "When it was about the time that our Lord was born, and must suffer and rise again from the dead, then went forth servants, John the Baptist and the apostles, and said to those that were bidden, to the people of Israel: Dear people, now is the time, come." The *coming* denotes the necessary internal change and readiness for receiving what was prepared, just as corporeal coming implies a change of place. The *repeating* of the invitation manifests the earnest desire and gracious purpose of God to do every thing on his part, to bring men to a participation in the offered salvation, and, at the same time, also, the utter invalidity of the alleged grounds of excuse.

Ver. 18. *And they all began with one consent to make excuse;* after απο μιας either γνωμης or φωνης must be supplied, *with one voice,* unanimously they excused themselves; παραιτεισθαι, *to make excuse,* properly, to decline under the pretext of inevitable and invincible hinderances. Gnomon: "They had before cast it up in their own minds that they were to have an invitation." Luther, House-Pos. 4. 225: "This reads a lesson to the guests, who sat at meat with Christ, and especially to the vain talker, ver. 15, who thought to gain the mastery over Christ at table. Nay, says Christ, ye would not merely remain without, and leave the householder with his large and sumptuous feast, but would even excuse yourself and be clear. There is therefore a two-fold sin, in that, while ye despise the gospel, ye would maintain every thing to be rightly done, and would still be reckoned wise, pious, and excellent. This is a most heinous sin." And in his Church-Pos. 13. 19: "You must not suppose that these men, who here excused themselves, were chargeable with gross sins or unrighteous actions. No, they had maintained a very good appearance. For it is not an unrighteous thing, if a man buys, and carries on business, walks honestly, or marries a woman and lives in matrimony, but for this reason would they not partake of the prepared entertainment, because they would not part with these things, clave to them with their whole heart. Whereas we must be ready to part with all, if the gospel demands, Matth. xxii. 37; x. 39; xix. 29." The different excuses offered by these persons manifest in them all one and the same perverse state of heart, only the object of their sinful love is not uniform; but there appears in them all a slighting of the Lord's offered goodness, a want of proper regard for his divine person, a misapprehension of the worth of this spiritual repast, of their own spiritual necessities, and of the things of salvation. It is the things of earth only that influence and attract them; these alone appear to them important, and are accounted much more precious, desirable, and necessary, than any thing they can get by partaking of the supper.

I have bought a piece of ground; Gnomon: "The word *bought*, twice used, (v. 19,) indicates desire, as is customary in a recent transaction. To a worldly man, when the divine call comes, all vain things are fresh and delightful." In the merely historical exposition, this is referred to the fondness of the Jews for Canaan, which appeared to them a certain pledge of their participation in the blessings of Messiah's kingdom, so that they, being filled with such a prepossession, despised the gospel, which called them to a depreciation of every thing earthly. Luther, House-Pos. 4. 227: "These are the most honourable and esteemed, as among the Jews the priesthood and the highest orders in the government. Their language is, We must labour, cultivate, and reap our land; that is, we must govern the people, (as Christ also calls his ministers husbandmen, who sow the gospel, John iv.,) and attend upon the priesthood committed to us by God."

I must needs go and see it; Gnomon: "Times most seasonable for grace, and most urgent calls of worldly business, often meet together. One pretends necessity; another a mere liking for other things, v. 19; a third, mistaken impossibility, v. 20. The first, therefore, denies that he *could;* the two others deny that they *would*, but express it by a polite circumlocution. That holy hatred, mentioned in v. 26, would cure them all. For the variety that appears in the refusal, does not stand so much in the affection as in the object—the field, the oxen, and the wife." The groundlessness of such a justification becomes manifest, when we reflect that the wedding-feast was held at a late hour, and prolonged often through the night; so that the time in question was at once the most unusual and the most unsuitable for looking after such things, and must be regarded as the most unavailing ground of excuse.

I pray thee have me excused; Wahl, Clavis: "Have me excused, not only now, but always." He, therefore, feels himself the groundlessness of the pretext, the worthlessness of the excuse, the impropriety of remaining away, the guiltiness of his conduct, hence his prayer; and in this too is the greatness of his perverse, worldly state of mind, represented. The apology contains, at bottom, a self-accusation, and gives testimony to previous guilt.

Ver. 19. *I have bought five yoke of oxen;* some explain this of the fleshly confidence of Israel upon his external observances, and of the unbelief and contempt of the gospel thence arising. Luther, as above: "When they justify their refusal with the oxen, it indicates that they were occupied with affairs of government, for oxen represent the rulers of the people, Ps. xxii. 13, 14." If, therefore, in the first class it was earthly goods and pleasures, in this class it is earthly honour, power, and consideration, which keeps men back from the gospel, John v. 44; xii. 43. Mel.: "That human blindness is to be acknowledged and deplored which leads men to care less for God and the concerns of eternity, than any other temporal affairs. As in country places people are, for the most part, more concerned about the cow-herd than the shepherd of souls, and, when interrogated, answer, that they have more need of the cow-herd."

Ver. 20. *I have married a wife, and therefore I cannot come;* this is the most hopeless of all, he does not beg to be excused, but thinks he acts according to the fullest right: it comprehends those who, through the manifold relationships of life, permit themselves to be constrained, contrary to the will of Christ, from his alone truly blissful fellowship, v. 26, 27. The manners of the East forbid women from appearing any where in public, on which account, combined with his love to his wife, this person conceives his remaining away to be a thing so proper and natural, that it requires no justification. Calvin: "In these verses, v. 18, 19, 20, Christ intimates that men were so given to the world and earthly affairs, that no one could find leisure to come to God; as while we are entangled with the cares of the world, there are so many avocations to withdraw us from the kingdom of God. But though all are not infected with the same disease, each one is drawn away by his own lust, and so it happens that all wander about after one course or another."

Ver. 21. *So that servant came, and showed his lord these things.* God knows minutely the conduct of each one, in regard to the gracious invitations offered to him, and this ought so much the more to prevent people from lightly despising these. Gnomon: "Ministers ought to make mention to the Lord in prayer, both of the obedience and disobedience of their hearers." *Then the master of the house being angry;* the righteous displeasure of God toward the conduct of the guests, shows once more his earnest desire for their welfare, the unsatisfactoriness of all their excuses and the justness of his expectation, that the invited would receive the invitation. *Go out quickly into the streets and lanes of the city;* historically this refers to the proselytes from the heathen, or the heathens living among the Jews, John vii. 49. Acts x. Matth. xiii. Without figure, the invitation is now addressed to others. *Bring in hither the poor, and the maimed, and the halt, and the blind;* outward want, and corporeal wretchedness, are easily apprehended by the eye and the mind; hence, under this description are meant all such as feel the necessities of their soul, and their spiritual wretchedness, Matth. v. 3. Bodily distress, also, often opens the heart to the consolations of the gospel, and hence to those, who had experience of it, the gospel was especially preached, Luke iv. 18; Matth. xi. 4, 5, and among them, for the most part, is found the most cordial and extensive reception, 1 Cor. i. 26—29. Earthly riches, on the other hand, very readily become a hinderance to the reception of the gospel-call, as it is apt to blind the internal eye to the wants and necessities of the soul, Matth. xix. 23—26. Luther, House-Pos. 4. 229: "According to this word of Christ, whatsoever among the people has been esteemed wise, holy, rich, mighty, is thrown away, and foolish, simple, insignificant persons, such as Peter, Andrew, Philip, Bartholomew, poor fishermen and needy beggars are chosen, whom no one thought deserving of being made priests and princes among the people." Gnomon: "The poor form the genus; three species are presently named; the *maimed*, whom no woman would choose, v. 20; the *halt*, who cannot walk, v. 19; the *blind*, who cannot see, v. 18." Comp. also Matth. xviii. 9, s.; John ix. 30.

Ver. 22. *Lord, there is still room;* since now the will of the Lord has been executed, the invitation held out to others, and by them accepted, the greatness of divine grace is expressed in these words, as is also its universality in v. 23.

Ver. 23. *Go out into the highways and hedges;* seen on Matth. xxii. 9—*And compel them to come in.* Calvin: "He seems to allude to the nature of the gospel invitation, in which the grace of God is not simply proffered to us, but along with doctrine we have the stimulants of exhortations; in which is manifest the wonderful goodness of God, who, when he sees us slumbering over the call which he has voluntarily addressed to us, eagerly plies our sloth, and not only stimulates us by exhortations, but also compels us with threats to come near to him." Luther, Church-Pos. 13. 21: "This is to be understood of weak desponding consciences, who are not disposed to go to the supper, but must be driven into it. It is not, however, an external, but an internal driving, a spiritual one, and is done after this manner: When the law is preached, and sin is opened up or exposed, so as that the man comes to the knowledge of himself; when his sins are so pressed upon his conscience, that he recognises himself to be nothing, sees all his works to be sinful and worthy of condemnation, and thus becomes troubled in conscience, dismayed in heart, goes out of himself for confidence and help, and never seeks any more for consolation in himself, then he is said to be driven and compelled. Now, when this is done, thou must help him out of his depression; and the way to do that is to comfort him with the gospel, to tell him how he is let free from his sins, to say to him, "Believe in Christ, that he has delivered thee from thy sins; and so thou shalt be freed from sin." Mel.: "It yields a most delightful consolation, that God orders men to be compelled, for it intimates that he *really* seeks our salvation, and *really* wishes us to be saved; as when a father is seriously concerned about the government of his son, he not only employs cold admonitions, but also a certain severity of discipline towards him, and constrains him to do what is required." It is not meant, therefore, that people should be brought to receive the gospel by means of any violent treatment; the compulsion to be used stands in entreaties, representations, counsels, as in Luke xxiv. 29; Gen. xix. 3. An internal constraint, through means of powerful motives, which are pressed upon the heart, 2 Cor. v. 19; Gal. iv. 19. Gnomon: "Every sort of coercion will not do, for he who is pulled or dragged does not *enter*. Saul, when mad for the law, used one sort of compulsion, Paul, the servant of Jesus Christ, a very different one."

That my house may be filled, so that it is only God's design of mercy to save sinners, Eph. i. 3, ss. not any proper merit on the part of men, which is the ground of the invitation; it must not be that his grace has been prepared in vain, and, notwithstanding the many despisers that exist, there are found at all periods an unnumbered multitude, who, with the greatest joy and readiness, receive the gospel-call and promise of salvation as the highest boon. Gnomon: "Neither nature nor grace can endure a vacuum. There shall be such a multitude of redeemed, from one extremity of the world to the other, as shall constitute a main part of its fulness."

V. 24. We have here the judgment pronounced on despisers. Luther, House-Pos. 4. 235: "The moment must come, when they shall be compelled to leave their oxen, lands, houses, or wives, and when they would be very glad to taste of my supper. But I must then say to them: Friends, I am now not at home, I cannot wait for guests. That will be to them indeed a hard, frightful, and intolerable judgment, when his supper shall be found to be all one with eternal life, and their lands, oxen, and houses, with hell-fire." There is here again manifest in God the union of his compassion and his righteousness, in that he causes all to be invited of free love, but judges despisers according to their conduct, and excludes them from eternal life. Ewald, p. 277: "It might be said, it were no great misfortune for sinful men to be shut out, they could still enjoy themselves in their own way, and if such joy may be somewhat gross in its nature, it were still joy to *them;*—but we must take into account the consequences. No earthly enjoyment lasts always—and if it did continue for ever, it could not continue as enjoyment, but would pall at the last, and fail to yield satisfaction. Man is impelled to seek after the highest, purest enjoyment; for that he pants, his internal being sighs after it. For a long period this impulse may be stifled, and man may imagine that the possessions, honours, and pleasures of the world can satisfy him. But he awakes by and by, and then often it is too late, or he at least feels, that that in which he has hitherto been seeking satisfaction, can never satisfy him. Indeed, where there is no enjoyment of God, there in the long run is no enjoyment at all; and where there is no enjoyment, there must be suffering. Ay, frightful, excessive suffering! Eternal hunger, and no nourishing food; eternal thirst, and no refreshing drink; the perpetual feeling of a void, without any thing to fill it up! It is, therefore, the highest wisdom *to possess, as though we possessed not,* because all earthly enjoyment vanishes away."

XXVII.

THE BUILDING OF THE TOWER.

Luke xiv. 28—30.

XXVIII.

THE WAR OF THE TWO KINGS.

Luke xiv. 31—33.

These two parables stand in no immediate external connexion with the preceding one; for the Saviour delivered them when on his journey to Galilee, to the people, who in great numbers pressed upon him, and appeared to seek his fellowship; yet a certain internal relationship may be recognised. While the parable of the marriage-supper points out the carnal mind and the love of the world as the main hinderance, which stands in the way of the sinner's salvation, these similitudes represent the believer's connexion with Jesus to be a difficult thing, which demands the greatest sacrifices, so that the most careful and solemn inquiry must be made, whether we feel sufficiently strong, and so much animated by a spirit of love to him, to stand prepared for such sacrifices. It is, accordingly, the same carnal disposition against which all the three parables are directed; in the first, it is represented in its proper, distinct form, and pernicious influence, as preventing many from coming into fellowship with Christ, and leading them utterly to despise it: in the second and third it is shown, that where this love of the world is cherished, it is not to be expected that there shall be a continued attachment to the Redeemer amid the storms of adversity and trial, as such professors soon fall away, to their own shame and confusion. Here, therefore, we have substantially the same thought which is brought out in the parable of the sower, that continued fellowship with Christ is disturbed, and with the children of this world completely broken up, by some sort of external or internal hinderances.

It is said, in v. 25, that great multitudes went with Jesus; had he been concerned only about a numerous attendance, and not about a true and approved discipleship, he would not have spoken as he did in v. 26, 27. The Searcher of hearts saw that the great multitude, who were really disposed to own him for the promised Messiah, flocked around him merely to have their earthly hopes concerning the Messiah fulfilled in and by him, and that they most looked for nothing else and nothing higher than carnal enjoyments, temporal prosperity, power, and honour. The Saviour would flatter no such vain and groundless hopes, nor were persons of such a disposition prepared for following him; and therefore he declares to them, first of all, that it was necessary to reckon upon the greatest and most difficult sacrifices in his service, that the dearest ties should need to be broken, trouble and persecution encountered, and life itself parted with, without laying their account to which they could not be fit for his kingdom. Then, he relates the two parables, and closes with the words in v. 33, which declare self-denial to be a chief prerequisite on the part of his disciples. How necessary these are, is further expressed in the similitude subjoined in v. 34, 35. The disciples of Jesus were appointed to be as a salt to the world, Matth. v. 13; from them must the new divine powers of life, which they themselves had first received when brought into connexion with the Redeemer, be diffused among their fellow-men. Now if the disciples and followers of Jesus did not possess such principles of life (restrained by their carnal inclinations)—if they could not be to the world what they ought to be to it, they were then good for nothing, and by such disciples he could not be served. In the whole discourse, therefore, from v. 25 to v. 35, our Lord certainly had it for his design, to draw off the frivolous and earthly-minded of his followers, to drive all to serious self-examination, and so divide the righteous and unrighteous followers from each other. Calvin: "Lest any one should think it hard to follow Christ on such terms, which require the renouncement of all his lusts, a proper admonition is given to meditate before-hand what a profession of the gospel really requires. *To build* is a matter full of weariness and trouble, and, from the expense it occasions, by no means an agreeable one; war, also, because it brings so many evils in its train, and may be said almost to threaten the extirpation of the human race, is not willingly undertaken by any one; and yet the advantage of having a house to dwell in is so enticing to men, that they do not hesitate to pour out their wealth for that purpose;—necessity also compels them often to go into the most expensive wars. But a far more excellent reward awaits the builders of the temple of God and the soldiers of Jesus Christ, for it is not a temporary edifice which they labour to erect, nor for a short-lived triumph that they contend."

TRAIN OF THOUGHT IN THE PARABLE.

Those who would follow Christ, should first subject themselves to a careful examination.

Necessity of such an examination; it is called for,

(1.) By the greatness of the occasion; v. 28: Building a tower; v. 31: Going to war;

(2.) By the difficulty attending it; and that

A) As well at the beginning of a Christian course, when we have to consider:

a.) The sacrifices required, v. 26, 28;

b.) The strength of inclination; v. 28: Whether he hath sufficient to finish it;

B) As also in the continuance of the same. Concerning which we have to consider:

a.) The battles to be encountered in maintaining our connexion with the kingdom; v. 31. Sitteth not down . . . . . twenty thousand, v. 27.

b.) The strength we have for continued patience; v. 31: Whether he could meet him with ten thousand.

II. The benefit arising from that examination; we are kept from suffering injury.

(1.) Our sacrifices (costs) have not been made *in vain*, v. 29.

(2.) We are not hurt by the raillery of the world, v. 30.

Ver. 28. *A tower*, a lofty palace, a pompous edifice—the fig tree indicates the undertaking of something great and glorious.—*The cost*, as applied to the knowledge of Jesus and fellowship with him, denotes, 1st. What he demands of his disciples, ver. 26, 27, 33.—*Whether he have sufficient to finish it;* the requisite means; by which we are to understand strength of mind, resolution of will, self-denial.—*Sitteth down first, and counteth*,—the reckoning up, and careful comparison of the costs and the means, represent the preparatory trial and thoughtful considerations which ought to precede the determination of following Jesus. Gnomon: "*Sitting*,—space being allowed him to take a considerate view of his circumstances."

Ver. 29. *After he has laid the foundation*,—the commencement of the building designates the begun attachment to Christ, which was found in so many, ver. 25.—*And is not able to finish it*, defection from Jesus, John vi. 66—69.

Ver. 30. The meaning is: The neglect of self-determination is the real cause of defection from Christ, and in it is manifest the great folly of all those who lightly, and without solemn reflection, begin to follow Christ. Calvin: "But there is no reason why the knowledge of our wants, which the Lord is ever ready to relieve, should depress our minds. I confess, indeed, that if we come to a reckoning, we are all so destitute in ourselves, that we cannot even lay one stone, or so much as offer resistance to the enemy. But since the Lord will provide both arms and treasure from heaven, the difficulty is not such as to furnish any pretext for our sloth and inactivity. The design of Christ, therefore, is to admonish his people, in taking up the cross, to gird themselves with fortitude."

Ver. 31. The first similitude appears to refer mainly to the difficulties which are experienced in the mind, on account of which we are not strong enough to sacrifice all other loves to the love of Jesus, for our love to him must be more and deeper than the love we bear to any thing besides; we must not love father, or mother, etc. more than him, nay, must put our love to these behind the love we feel to him. The other similitude appears to be directed chiefly to the hinderances that arise from without, ver. 27, through which so many are withdrawn from following Christ. But we can perhaps discover a different connexion between the two, namely, that there is a progression manifested in them. If the first speaks of the difficulties which present themselves at the beginning of conversion, the other sets forth the perpetually recurring, the daily contests, which must be fought and won in following Jesus; and, consequently, if people would determine upon following him, they must carefully ponder both the nearer and the more remote difficulties, those which are to be met with at the beginning, and those during the progress of their course, so that they may not fall away from Christ, but may attain to the promised kingdom. Scholten: "The parables coincide with each other, the particle η being interposed between them, whence it appears, that our Saviour evidently wished to enjoin in both the same admonition, which farther appears from αποδοσει, which is subjoined to each parable; at the same time, we cannot deny that there are certain smaller points, which involve ideas in each image, somewhat different from one another, though still very closely connected with the leading idea or admonition contained in both. Thus, the ideas of *building* in the first, and of *warring* in the second similitude, indicate a variety and difference in the labours of the disciples of Christ, as those on whom it was only incumbent to *build* the church of God, and lay, as it were, its foundations, itself, indeed, a matter of great labour, and possessing considerable diversity; but also to *fight* with the greatest dangers, and prosecute their work even amid the constant jeopardy of their life, to say nothing of the struggles they would also have to maintain with the most tender feelings and affections of the mind, ver. 26, 27, 33."—The image of the king, who would go into war, marks something at once important and difficult, doubtful and dangerous; but the following of Christ is this only when viewed in reference to frivolous and carnal minds, which, in apostatizing from such a cause, incur the greater guilt, that they have omitted the preceding self-examination. Gnomon: "Christianity is a great and arduous thing; it is compared with things great and arduous, as in a private concern, an expensive building is; in a public one, war. The first parable declares the necessity of hating father, mother, etc. the other, of one's own life, v. 26. The Christian warfare is a sort of royal thing."

Ten thousand and twenty thousand—the power of the enemy, and one's own strength, or ways and means to meet it. To refer to the ten commandments, through the external fulfilment of which men would demand eternal salvation of God as a right, but only to their own confusion, as God demands also an internal fulfilment of them through a spirit of love, is quite untenable. We are rather to regard the twenty thousand as denoting the enmity of Satan, the hatred of the world, persecutions, afflictions, which, according to Christ's purpose, must be overcome, if we would be true disciples.

V. 32. *Or else*, that is, if, on deliberation, he is of opinion that he cannot cope with the more powerful enemy,—cannot reckon on a successful issue. *He sendeth an embassage*, &c.; he cannot and will not hazard a battle, seeing that he should afterwards be obliged to abandon it, which every thoughtless disciple will also do in regard to his following Christ, and that to his great shame. Calvin: "But what Christ says of a king sending a message of peace, when unfit to sustain the attack of war, that he may not be put to an ignominious defeat, ought not to be accommodated to the matter in hand, as if we might have any reconciliation with our spiritual enemy, when our own strength and confidence fail us. But our Lord simply means, that we ought to be in such a state of readiness as not to be taken by surprise, and be led, with shame, to renounce his cause." Luther's note: "No one shall be able to stand before the divine judgment, he shall then despair of all his resources, and seek grace, and beg for help in Christ." Olshausen: "The consciousness of our own incapacity should lead us to seek for a higher power, to join ourselves to the great empire of light and its prince, which, in all circumstances, contends against the empire of darkness. So that the similitudes, when viewed in connexion with v. 26, 27, virtually says:—Ye undertake, when ye begin to follow me, a battle, from which ye cannot retreat; come first to a conviction of your own weakness, and seek the higher power of the Spirit, for then only can ye be fit for the kingdom of God."

XXIX.

THE LOST SHEEP.

Luke xv. 1—7. Matth. xviii. 12, 13.

General Introductory Remarks on the Parables in the 15th Chapter of Luke.

THE five parables which stand recorded in the fifteenth and sixteenth chapters of Luke appear to have been delivered at the same time, and before the same hearers, as was the case also with the eight parables in the thirteenth of Matthew; and, if the latter delineate, in general figures, the nature and destinies of his kingdom, as also the power of his word, the former do not so much refer to the heavenly kingdom, as a whole, as they point, in particular, to the endeavour of Christ to bring the sinner into blessed fellowship with himself, describe the moral condition of those who would participate in the benefits of his kingdom, and make known the demands which must be complied with, in order to the attainment of this end.

The fact that these parables were delivered immediately after each other, renders it probable that they were all addressed to the same hearers; and, among these, there were, besides the twelve, who always accompanied our Lord, others also of his disciples and followers, who, in xvi. 1, are expressly designated as his hearers,—some publicans and sinners, who drew near to him, xv. 1,—and, finally, scribes and pharisees, who blamed the fellowship of Jesus with the publicans and sinners, v. 2; according to ch. xvi. 14, these also heard the parable in xvi. 1—8, and in continuous discourse, without interruption, the Lord speaks to them again the parable in v. 15—31.

Since there is found to be an external connexion of this sort, among these parables, it becomes probable that there will also be a corresponding internal relationship, viz.: that, individually, and as a whole, they shall have an exact reference to the very different kinds of hearers to whom they are fitted to administer instruction, correction, improvement or consolation, as the respective conditions of the different classes of hearers might require; and this we should expect to appear as prominently as their regular progression and natural growth out of each other, by which their intimate connexion is rendered manifest. The publicans and sinners must have received a new impression of Christ's love and solicitude for their salvation, must have been filled with new confidence in his grace, confirmed in their desire after fellowship with him, comforted under the cold-hearted judgment of the scribes and pharisees concerning them, and especially in the last parable, made acquainted with the proper state of mind in which one may and ought to approach the friend of sinners. The scribes and pharisees had to be opposed, the harsh and unrighteous character of their judgment and procedure laid open to their view, and God's gracious disposition toward them unfolded; the Redeemer had to hold up to them a mirror, in which they might see their own image, their relation to God, and God's judgment concerning them. Finally, the disciples had to learn, from the example and parables of Jesus, the kind of procedure and conduct they had to pursue towards sinners. And as the characteristic traits which were peculiar to publicans and pharisees lay deeply grounded in the nature of a sinful heart, and are continually reproduced, though under different forms and in different relations, the force and application of these parables may justly be extended to all ages of the church of Christ.

The accusation which the scribes and pharisees brought against the conduct of Jesus, in regard to publicans and sinners, furnished the occasion of his delivering the first three parables in justification of himself, that he might put to silence so heartless a ground of accusation. In the first two, he does this by pressing the conclusion, that if it were quite natural for a sheep and a piece of silver to be sought with so much trouble, how much more ought a man to be, in like manner, sought for! And in the parable of the prodigal son, he defends his conduct by disclosing the state of mind which belonged to those sinners to which he showed so much love. The whole three represent a loving disposition; for it is love which moves the man to seek his sheep and the woman her money; and love, also, which prompts the father to take back his lost son; but there is an essential difference among the parables, in this respect, that the love unfolded in them is delineated under different aspects. The first two delineate *a seeking love*, the third *a receiving love;* in the former, the matter to be represented was what the Redeemer must do to bring back the sinner who has wandered from the way of eternal life, to true piety and blessedness; but in the latter, what the sinner, who really desires to be blessed, and has in him something of a penitent and believing spirit, has reason to expect of him, viz. a ready and most welcome reception. In the first two, the chief character is the seeking shepherd, the seeking woman, that is, the Redeemer, deeply concerned for the accomplishment of the sinner's salvation, Luke xix. 11; in the third, it is the sinner, under the image of a lost son, seeking and finding grace. The two former are explained by the words contained in v. 2; "This man *receiveth sinners* and *eateth* with them," in which the affectionate concern of Christ for the salvation of sinners is blamed; the last has to do, in the person of the lost son, with the precise characteristic of those who, in that verse, are named sinners. There can be no doubt as to the proper meaning of the different parts of these parables. The secret motive of the conduct of the shepherd, the woman, and the father, is benignant love; the helpless condition of the wandering sheep corresponds to the misery of the prodigal son:—the joy of the shepherd and the woman recurs also in the father, v. 23; the call to friendly rejoicing is described in v. 6, 9, 23, 32; the heartless disposition of the scribes and pharisees is, in its nature, source, and manifestations, depicted under the image of the oldest son.

As it is the object of Jesus to justify his own conduct, so it is he who is to be understood under the shepherd, the woman, and the father, for the train of thought pursued in the parables, in reference to ver. 1 and 2, is this: Ye blame my conduct, but if it must be allowed that the conduct of a shepherd, etc., is as natural as it is good and beneficent; ye must cast no reflections upon me, for such precisely is my bearing to sinners. And as it is pre-eminently the receiving love of God toward sinners, which is justified in the third parable, it naturally lay out of the way to say any thing of the work of redemption through the death of the Mediator; but the silence maintained here can be no refutation of the numberless other passages, in which the favour shown to the sinner is made to depend upon the sacrificial death of Christ. And the objection taken from this parable of the lost son against the doctrine of redemption that the sinner returns immediately to God, and, without any regard had to a Mediator, is received and blessed by him, falls of itself to the ground, because Christ is the Father, who receives sinners, v. 2, (as father he is also represented in Isaiah ix. 6,) nor is the image of the father at any rate the principal idea, but only *his receiving love.* The correlative object in all the three parables, the sheep, the piece of money, the son, is the sinner, the individual sinner; for though the departure of the prodigal son from his father might well be understood in reference to the transactions of the fall, or rather, can be applied to these, inasmuch as the same appearances manifest themselves in both; yet, to make this application of it is not admissible, since, from the want of any corresponding object to the older son, it cannot be carried through the entire parable. Some expositors, indeed, to make good this application of it, have maintained, that as the prodigal son signifies the whole of humanity, so the holy angels are to be understood by the other son, but it is impossible to attribute to the blessed angels so unfeeling and envious a disposition, as is ascribed to the oldest son in v. 28—30, and it would besides run counter to what is said in v. 7, and especially in v. 10, where our Lord speaks of the joyful sympathy of the angels and inhabitants of heaven. By the prodigal son, therefore, we are to understand only individual sinners, and the eldest son is consequently to be identified with the pharisees and scribes; the objection which is taken against this from v. 29, that no one could boast of so perfect an obedience, is without any weight, since the son merely spoke what he himself judges to be true, that he had conducted himself in a blameless manner, and so as pre-eminently to deserve the approbation of his father—and this was precisely what the pharisees judged of themselves. That the father makes no reply to the arrogance of his speech, but passes it by in silence, affords no support to this objection, much less is it a confession to the truth and justice of the affirmations made in the speech. This silence is very naturally explained from the chief design of the parable, which would have suffered violence by entering any farther into the words in question. And, indeed, the expression in v. 29, carries a reference to those who, according to v. 7, needed no repentance, for the older son was such a one as thought he had no need of repentance, and thus the difficult words in v. 7 derive no doubtful illustration from the sentiment of the older brother, who, like the pharisees in regard to Jesus, murmured against the love of his father, and consequently showed that he still did stand in need of repentance.

In Matthew, the parable of the straying, sought, and again found sheep, must be viewed as designed not so much for the justification of Jesus, as for the farther illustration of the sentiment contained in v. 11, viz. that the Son of Man came to save that which was lost; and v. 14 then contains a conclusion drawn from the comparison, to the effect that even as the shepherd did not wish the loss of any of his sheep, as little did God wish any of his little ones to perish, and therefore did it behoove Christ, as sent by the Father, and come into the world, to save sinners. Calvin: "In Matthew the parable proceeds farther, and intimates not only that the disciples of Christ must be tenderly cherished, but that their faults must be borne with, so as that we may be the more successful in winning them back, when they have gone astray. For although it is possible that they may sometimes wander, yet because they are sheep, over whom God has appointed his own Son to be shepherd, it is proper that they be gathered from their wanderings; and it is the less to be permitted that they should be inhumanly driven away. The purport of what is contained in Luke is somewhat different, and goes to show, that as the whole human race belongs to God, those who have wandered must be brought back, and the same sort of rejoicing must be held when the wicked have been reclaimed, as is wont to be experienced by him who unexpectedly recovers what he had given up for lost."

Ver. 1. *Then drew near unto him all the publicans and sinners;* that is, all who were in that neighbourhood. Luther, Church-Pos. 13. 31: "Those were formerly called publicans, who took from the Romans a city, custom, or bailiwick, paying for it a certain revenue; and because this was a large sum, such officials must needs flay people with their exactions, that they might make good their own; hence were they every where so notorious for their exactions, that no one expected to find among them much piety or worth. On this account they are named along with sinners, the crowd of wicked and abandoned persons, who lived in open profligacy and licentiousness."—*Drew near to him*, ησαν εγγιζοντες; it expresses a confidential and continued concourse of such persons about Jesus, proceeding from an affection of mind toward him, with the design of listening to him. Luther, as above: "There is still a spark or two of virtue and piety in them, since they seek after Christ, and are desirous to hear him preach, and to see what he would do, for they well knew that he was a pious man, and that in his words and deeds they should find nothing but what was good; and although their disposition was far from according with his life, yet they are not hostile to him, so that there is still hope of their possibly being improved by him." Comp. ver. 17—20.

Ver. 2. *And the pharisees and scribes murmured.* Luther, as above: "Those who were reckoned the best and holiest were such poisonous reptiles, that they not only hated Christ and refused themselves to listen to him, but they could not bear besides that poor sinners should come to him that they might be profited."—*This man receiveth sinners, and eateth with them.* Luther, again: "See, say they, is this your excellent, pious man? Who will say now that he is of God, seeing that he takes up with such knaves and reprobates. Nay, he is a glutton and a wine-bibber, the associate of publicans and sinners, Matth. xi. 19. Such names must Christ have from the pious, not that he ate, drank, and revelled with them, but only because he suffered them to come to him, and did not despise them or push them away from him. They lord it over Christ, and would prescribe rules to him, how he should conduct himself and live holily."

The judgment pronounced by them denotes their want of love, (comp. ver. 30)—for these publicans and sinners were not so bad as the pharisees supposed—and bespoke their heartless indifference toward the improvement and salvation of sinners. But it is also perverse, for how else could sinners be delivered? and malicious in respect to Christ, who in his fellowship with sinners acted as a physician; (Matth. ix. 12,) neither sick himself, nor liable to be sick, nor delighting in the sickness of others, but loving the sick so tenderly that he would deliver them from their sickness, which he cordially dislikes. Luther, in his House-Pos. 4. 248, says, concerning the origin of this perverse judgment upon Christ's converse with sinners; "The pharisees interpreted it very ill, as if it had been an indication of peculiar levity, seeing it becomes a pious man to take up and associate with pious people. But they knew nothing more of God's word than is taught by Moses and the law. And because the language held there is, that God would be gracious to those who were holy and kept his commandments, but would punish the wicked who do not keep them, the scribes and pharisees therefore concluded, that it did not become men to act otherwise toward sinners than God did towards them. Because he is angry at them and will not receive them, neither must we receive them, but drive them away. Thus also does our reason judge. Our blessed Lord, however, forms another judgment, and makes no account of such reasoning as that of the pharisees, nay, comes precisely to the opposite conclusion, viz. that God is not an enemy to sinners, nor has any desire for their death, therefore could he, Jesus Christ, not be an enemy to them. This is a different doctrine from that of Moses and the law,—a doctrine which does not grow up in our hearts, but is brought down to us from heaven by the Son of God." Whenever, therefore, from want of Christian feeling, the reception of sinners is blamed, we must support ourselves by taking up the Christian position—*this Jesus receives sinners.* Mel.: "Christ, however, so receives and gathers a church even from those who have lived without the restraint of godly discipline, only if they repent; he does not receive those who persevere in sin against their conscience, as is plainly declared, 1 Cor. vi. 9, 10. 1 John iii. 8. Let us therefore understand that repentance is necessary."

TRAIN OF THOUGHT IN THE PARABLE.

What a value Christ sets on the salvation of each sinner.

This is discovered:

I. From the pains taken by him for the salvation of the erring sinner;

(1.) The ground of this being done:

a.) Because every sinner belongs to Christ; v. 4: What man is there having a hundred sheep.

b.) Because, being full of love, he wills the salvation of every sinner; v. 4: If he lose one of them.

c.) Because the misery of the sinner is so great, v. 4: It is a lost sheep.

(2.) The outward manifestation of it:

a.) He applies to each sinner a special attention; v. 4: He leaves the ninety and nine in the wilderness.

b.) He willingly undertakes all trouble, in order to save him, v. 4: Goes after that which is lost.

c.) And is indefatigable in his efforts to save, v. 4: Until he find it.

II. From what takes place after the salvation of the sinner, and that,

(1.) In reference to himself:

a.) He does not treat him with deserved punishment, v. 5.

b.) He facilitates his safe return to the good, v. 5.

c.) He gives expression to his heartfelt joy, v. 5.

(2.) In reference to others, who are called to a participation in the joy:

a.) Because he rejoices himself, v. 6. Rejoice with me:

b.) Because the salvation is so happy a circumstance, v. 6. For I have found, &c.

c.) Because the inhabitants of heaven show that they gladly participate in the joy, v. 7.

V. 4. *Who has a hundred sheep*, he is a rich shepherd; *if he lose one of them*, the care and oversight, which he directs towards all, does not lead him to neglect any part, he is equally attentive to all, Matth. x. 30,—even the individual sinner is not beneath his notice, though the pharisees could look upon all sinners with indifference. Gnomon: "The largeness of the flock discloses the concern of the shepherd for one sheep." The shepherd is proprietor, Luther, House-Pos. 4. 252: "Our blessed Lord says: Sinners are my purchased, dear-bought property, for I have bought them to myself by my sufferings and death; so that, should they again escape from my hands, and go out of the way, it is impossible for me not to grieve and to be deeply affected, since they have cost me so dear, and have become so much an object of concern that it would indeed pain me were they still to fall into the hands of the devil." This is the first ground of love, and the next is set forth in the miserable condition of the lost sheep. "Nothing (as Luther says,) can be more miserable; for when a sheep has wandered from the flock into the wilderness it cannot help itself, but is every moment in danger, without being able to uphold or defend itself. Even so is it with the sinner. There remains for us just this one consolation, that we have a shepherd, one blessed Redeemer, who himself undertakes for us and seeks us. The multitude (he elsewhere says, Church-Pos. 13. 52) must not be reckoned the lost sheep, who live on securely in their sins, and are alike indifferent whether God smiles or frowns; but they are the erring, lost sheep, who are touched with a sense of sin, and stand in the conflict of faith, in doubt and concern, whether God will be gracious to them." In this state, according to v. 2, were the publicans and sinners who were received by Christ.

Doth not leave the ninety and nine in the wilderness, properly, upon the pasture-ground, in the pin-fold, where they are well cared for. Luther, House-Pos. 4. 252: "Just as a mother, who has many children, that are all equally dear to her, and would not have one of them taken from her, should it happen that one of them falls sick and comes into jeopardy, this makes a difference among the children, the sick one becomes now the dearest, and she can neither interest herself much in any thing besides, nor pay much heed to it. If any one would judge of love by the diligence applied, he would say,—the mother loves the sick child, but not the others that are in health. So, the Lord here says, it is with me in regard to the sinner." The first manifestation of love to the sinner, is that he becomes the object of such special care and attention.

And go after that which is lost—in order to seek it; to apply all care, love, and faithfulness toward the recovery of the sinner, for of his own accord he would not come back to enjoy the blessed fellowship with God, but would go into a state of endless perdition—hence a divine plan of salvation is necessary. Gnomon: "In recovering the soul, it is not man but God who labours, as it were, v. 8." Luther, as above: "Such seeking proceeds, when Christ everywhere causes his word to be publicly proclaimed. In it we hear how dreadful an evil and burden sin is, which brings us down to everlasting condemnation, (the law;) but there also we hear, that God's paternal love has been moved, that he has given us his dear Son, and cares for nothing but that we thankfully receive the gift, rest in faith upon his word, and become willingly obedient to him, (the gospel.)" The second manifestation.

Until he find it; this marks the continued, unwearied endeavour of the poor shepherd to effect the deliverance of the sinner; he leaves nothing untried, through parents, teachers, conscience, providences, (v. 14, the scarcity has an effect on the resolution of the prodigal son,) in order to work upon the sinner, and beget in him the desire of amendment. Third manifestation of love. Luther, as above: "Such finding takes place when the wandering sheep, the poor sinner, from the word preached, comes in confidence to God, thinks and resolves within himself; Quick, quick, return and cease, ere God's anger overtake thee, while he would still be gracious to thee, if thou only wouldest not, through such wayward sinfulness, sink deeper into guilt." Gnomon: "Therefore did Jesus Christ follow sinners even to their meals and tables, where the sin principally manifested itself."

V. 5. *He layeth it on his shoulders, rejoicing,*—the first manifestation of joy at having found the sheep, the other is given in v. 6. Instead of venting reproaches, he lightens the sinner's return by this exercise of love, helps him to overcome hinderances, removes difficulties, strengthens weakness with divine power, v. 20—23. Luther House-Pos, 4. 254: "He forgives them their sins and takes them under the wing of his protection, that they may be secure from the wolf and other wild beasts." "He deals with the sheep, not by law or force, as he well might, driving it before him like other sheep, and letting it go itself; but he takes all the labour and trouble upon himself, that the sheep may have ease and rest, and does it heartily. And so the sheep is safe from all error and delusion, danger and destruction. This is, indeed, a refreshing picture, full of love and consolation. This bearing secures that we be kept safe, and have nothing to fear, just as the sheep on the shoulders does not concern itself, should the hounds be bellowing, or the wolf prowling around. Therefore we also, so long as we abide in faith, need not be afraid of becoming lost, for we are not then pursuing our own course, not even walking upon our own feet, but hang upon the neck of our beloved shepherd,—else were we indeed poor sheep, ready to perish." Gnomon: "He might have used the service of a menial, but love and joy make the work pleasant to himself." Mel.: "The text contains a sweet intimation of the passion of Christ; he places the found sheep upon his shoulders, that is, he transfers our burden to himself, becomes a victim for us; thence bearing us, he carries us to his own flock, bears, feeds, sustains and governs us."

V. 6. This demand occurs in v. 28—32, and has reference to the pharisees. Such mutual joy has its ground in true love to Christ and sinners as our brethren; it is justified by the pains of the shepherd, and the good fortune of the sinner, as having attained to salvation; it is the will of our Lord Jesus Christ, and in its own nature a feeling that has place in heaven, as we learn, from v. 7, while, on the other hand, the mode of thinking adopted by the pharisees, v. 2, and by the elder brother, v. 28, is ungodly, wicked and devilish. Luther, House-Pos. 4. 253: "The heart of our Lord Jesus Christ is here represented so full of joy and love, that it were impossible for any one to make him appear more kind and joyful." Gnomon:

"Jesus Christ at his ascension plainly returned home, for heaven is his home, John xiv. 2, and then especially did he certify the heavenly inhabitants of what he had done on earth. Hence εσται, *will be*, the future in v. 7, but γινεται *is*, the present in v. 10. Interchange these words for a little, and you will perceive the difference." *Friends and neighbours*, Gnomon: "The different orders of heavenly beings, not excepting the angels, v. 10. *Neighbours*, those who inhabit not the same, but an adjoining house; *friends*, those who from good-will take part."

V. 7. The practical application of the parable. *Joy in heaven*, before God with Christ, the holy angels and all the saints, showing that the heavenly inhabitants participate in such transactions occurring on earth, as have an important bearing on the divine kingdom, and thereby implying a new, a primary obligation on the part of the good to receive sinners, as also a justification of the conduct of Jesus. Gnomon: "*Unto you*, most sharply rebuking, by this joy, the murmuring of the pharisees. The shepherd, Jesus Christ, has many friends and neighbours, but especially the spirits of the just, who may the rather participate in this joy, because they are more closely allied to men. In v. 10, a rise is made to the angels, who are there more especially named, because *the man* Christ is not contemplated as present. Nor are the angels said to know the event from intercourse with men, for they cannot all be with any one man, but from its being revealed by the Lord, which it may equally be to the spirits of the just. Thus, in Rev. xviii. 20, the other inhabitants of heaven are distinguished from the angels."

One sinner that repenteth. Luther, House-Pos. 4. 255: "It is not called repentance, if men merely in outward behaviour become holy, but when they trust in God's goodness through Christ, and believe in the forgiveness of sins. Such sinners will Christ receive, v. 2, 17—19. He would also gladly receive others, but they will not come to him, and so he must let them go." Repentance, accordingly, includes faith in itself, takes its rise in a change of mind, and leads to amendment of life, both outwardly and inwardly. *Over one sinner, more than over ninety and nine just persons,*—the greatness of this joy arises from the difficulties attending conversion, and its unexpectedness, just as one is disposed to prize health more highly after sickness, and life, after a remarkable deliverance from danger. Grotius: "It is said there is more joy, because things unlooked for, or well-nigh despaired of, affect us more deeply. But it is much more difficult to break off the habit of sin than to continue in an approved course of life, without open backsliding." The sense of the expression, however, as in Luke xviii. 14. Matth. xxi. 31, is this,—There is great joy over such sinners, but none at all over those who think they are righteous, though they are really not so. To understand by the righteous, persons of such supposititious piety is quite necessary, on account of the reference which this parable carries to the pharisees, and the description given of the old brother. Grotius: "Christ opposes ninety-nine just persons to one sinner, not because the fact actually stood thus, for very few live according to strict rule, but because, although matters had so stood, even for the sake of that one, great labour would have been undertaken; how much more when in this degenerate world, there was such a multitude of sinners, such a scarcity of righteous men! *Who need no repentance,*—is therefore the course of such as hold themselves for righteous. It might be granted that they do not need such a repentance or conversion as the prodigal son, but daily repentance, daily increase and growth in what is good is needed by every one. Our Lord here then accords no actual righteousness to the scribes and pharisees, Matt. v. 20. Gnomon: "They do not need repentance, because they are with the shepherd, and have already repented. The righteous man is in the way,—the penitent returns to it."

Calvin: "The word *repentance*, is especially restricted to the conversion of those, who having been wholly alienated from God, are raised as from death to life. For otherwise there ought to be a purpose of repentance through the whole life; nor is any one exempted from this necessity, since the faults and imperfections of all urge them to strive after daily advancement."*

* [In the concluding remarks on this parable, the same thing occurs, of which notice has been taken in a previous note. Our author throws out a certain opinion regarding the comparatively little rejoicing which is held over the ninety and nine righteous persons, and presently introduces quotations from other commentators, who express themselves in favour of a different opinion. We think our author has not displayed his usual discrimination in the view he has himself adopted on this occasion. It gives a very jejune turn to the sentiment to make it mean, "There is great joy over repenting sinners, but none over those who think they are righteous, though they are really not so." None! certainly not, less than none—they are in the very opposite condition to that which can be the occasion of joy to holy beings. But in this way the sentiment loses all its point,—it would be much the same as to say, that the woman in the next parable who had found the lost piece of silver, rejoiced greatly on account of that one, but did not rejoice on account of some other nine pieces she possessed of counterfeit coin. Such a shallow sentiment was not worth being uttered, and if it had, would not have served the purpose our Lord had in view,—it could not have justified his peculiar solicitude for the recovery, and his peculiar joy at the repentance of profligate sinners. The ground of the one, was the extreme peril in which they stood, while still sinners; the ground of the other, the safe and blessed condition on which, through repentance, they had just entered. The transition from the one of these conditions to the other, is that which constitutes the grand peculiarity in the case of the repentant sinner, and gives rise to feelings in Christ and the holy angels, concerning him which are not called for in the case of the righteous—those who really are such, not in their own estimation merely, but in the mind and reckoning of God—they are established in the possession of life and blessing,—they are basking in the sunshine of divine favour, secure of every real and substantial good, and on that account they are indeed the objects of complacent delight to the inhabitants of heaven; but the farther they are from the condition of sinners, the more secure they are from the danger of eternal ruin, there is so much the less call for exulting over them with the singular, extraordinary joy at present in question. Our Lord, therefore, is not thinking here of such pretenders to right-

XXX.

THE LOST PIECE OF SILVER, (DRACHMA.)

Luke xv. 8—10.

On Christ's design in delivering a second parable, so very similar to the preceding one, Luther says, House-Pos. 4. 257: "That our Lord did not stop with the one parable of the shepherd and sheep, but went on to give another; he showed therein his will that others also should follow his example, not vilely casting away sinners, but seeking to bring them to repentance. But what he says further in this parable may be thus, perhaps, explained. The first parable bears respect solely to our blessed Lord himself, who is the only true shepherd, and is not hostile to the sheep, but lays down his life for it, that it might be delivered and set free from the devil. But the other parable of the woman bears respect to the Christian church, which has committed to it the office of preaching, that poor sinners may be shut up to repentance, delivered from condemnation, and made eternally blessed."

TRAIN OF THOUGHT IN THE PARABLE.

The value of the lost sinner in the estimation of Christ. This is made to appear:

I. From the dignity which belongs to man even in his lost condition;

eousness as the scribes and pharisees, but of those who, whatever they may once have been, are now settled in a state of peace with God, and blessed enjoyment of his favour. He is bringing out a great principle of the divine government in regard to others, who are just entering into this state, from one entirely the reverse, and his object is simply to tell us, that while still unreclaimed, they are, like the lost sheep, the objects of a special solicitude—when recovered, the occasion of a special and quite peculiar joy; and this, not because it was a better thing in itself to exercise the repentance which brought such a happy change, than to be in a condition which did not need such a change to be wrought, but only because a condition so fraught with peril, had been exchanged for one so unspeakably better.]—*Trans.*

(1.) He is, indeed, lost to the original end of his being,—a lost coin;

(2.) But he can be restored to this again,—the lost money can be recovered.

II. From the pains taken by the Lord for the lost sinner.

III. From the joy experienced on account of his deliverance, and which discovers itself;

(1.) Both in regard to the Lord himself, v. 9; Rejoice with me;

(2.) And also in regard to others, v. 9, 10.

V. 8. *Pieces of silver,*—the coin mentioned is the drachma, of the value of sevenpence half-penny. Gray: " Here the primeval dignity of the soul, in its original state, is compared to a piece of silver, having the image of the great Sovereign of the universe stamped upon it. " God made man upright," bearing resemblance to himself in his intellectual and moral attributes, capable of an endless progress toward perfection. But man, being left to the freedom of his will, degenerated from the rectitude of his nature, so that his original glory is departed from him. In this state of moral corruption, he is compared, here, to a piece of beautiful coin, for a time lost in the dust of the earth, where its former lustre is miserably tarnished, and its value diminished. Such is the fatal influence of sensual passions to deface the divine image after which we were created." Similar images are to be found in Lam. iv. 1. Isa. i. 22. Jer. vi. 30.

Light a candle, and sweep the house,—an image of earnest desire, and of the great trouble, prompted by love, which was taken to recover what was lost, v. 9. *Friends and neighbours,* (female,) Gnomon: " The angelic hosts have not the distinction of sexes; they are considered, however, as remaining at home or going abroad—abroad, in manly attire, prepared for war; at home, in the domestic and peaceful garb of females."

XXXI.

THE PRODIGAL SON.

Luke xv. 11—32.

Upon the incomparable beauty of this parable, Lavater, in his reflections upon the most important passages of the gospels, thus remarks: "What would not Christ have deserved of humanity if he had done nothing else than delivered this parable or history, with its meaning? I may boldly say, where is there any thing to be found like this parable? What human teacher has placed the folly of human nature, and the consequences of this folly, in such simple, clear, and graphic colours before our eyes; and, in contrast therewith, has given of the long-suffering and compassion of God so inexpressibly rich an exhibition, as is done in this discourse, which, also, has no parallel for its adaptation to the capacity of all! Had Christ only come to the earth for the purpose of delivering this parable,—on that account alone should all mortal and immortal beings have concurred in bending the knee before him, and confessing with their tongues, that he is a Son immeasurably superior to all others, to the glory of God the Father." Theremin, in his Sermons, vol. iii., says of this parable: "Is there any instruction concerning the state of human nature;—is there a warning to recall us from the path of destruction;—is there an assurance of divine grace and compassion which is not contained in these few words, and unfolded there to our view?"

It is certainly wrong in Vitringa and others, to understand this parable of the reception of the heathen to the fellowship of the gospel, and the envy and dislike with which this was regarded by the Jews. For, as the occasion of the parable had no reference at all to this, and its comprehensive import is quite lost by such a reference; so it is undoubtedly better and more agreeable to the design of Jesus, to understand it of the gracious reception, which the sinner may expect from the mercy of God, whenever, with true contrition and childlike confidence, he turns from his evil ways, and yields himself to God. Calvin: "This parable is simply a confirmation of the preceding doctrine. And, under the person of this young prodigal, Christ describes all sinners, who, wearied with their own folly, throw themselves on the grace of God." Mel.: "Although the parable may, with propriety, be referred to the Jews and gentiles; yet, under the prodigal son, men are universally to be understood, who live, without restraint, in open abandonment. And, on the other hand, the more prudent son represents those who are decent and upright in their lives."

The parable divides itself into four chief heads; 1. ver. 11—16, representing the falling away of the sinner from God, and the great misery consequent thereupon to himself; 2. ver. 17—20, describe the change of mind which he underwent; 3. ver. 20—24, relate the gracious reception which he met with from his father; 4. ver. 25—32, exhibit the feelings and behaviour of the elder brother.

TRAIN OF THOUGHT IN THE PARABLE.

Of repentance.

I. The necessity of repentance is grounded:

(1.) In the state of preceding sinfulness;

a) Origin thereof, v. 12: Give me, Father, &c.

b) Nature of sin, v. 13: And not long thereafter, &c.

c) Manifestation of itself, v. 13: And there wasted his substance, &c.

(2.) And in the misery consequent upon sin;

a) The man still has a desire after blessedness, v. 14:

b) And feels his miserable condition, v. 14:

Began to be in want.

c) And seeks in vain for relief, v. 15: Went and joined himself, &c.

d) And sinks, the longer the deeper, v. 15: Sent him to feed swine;

e) And never finds the longed for satisfaction, v. 16.

II. The nature of repentance is described, v. 17—20:

(1.) The sinner comes to a right understanding, v. 17: Came to himself.

(2.) Perceives the exceeding greatness of his misery, v. 17: How many hired servants in my father's house, &c.

(3.) Forms good resolutions, v. 18: I will arise, &c.

(4.) Recognises his guilt, v. 18: Father, I have sinned, &c.

(5.) Humbles himself, v. 19.

(6.) By faith actually returns, v. 20: He arose, and came to his father.

III. The blessed result of repentance is set forth, v. 20—32:

(1.) In reference to a compassionate God, v. 20—24.

a.) God desires the repentant feeling, v. 20: When he was yet a great way off, &c.

b.) Graciously receives the sinner, v. 20: Had compassion, &c.

c.) Facilitates to him the execution of his purpose, v. 21.

d.) Heaps upon him marks of love, grace and goodness, v. 22, 23.

e.) And calls for a general expression of joy, v. 24.

(2.) In reference to the self-righteous, v. 25—32.

a.) Their cold-hearted envy is thereby excited, v. 28: He was angry, &c.

b.) They accuse God of unrighteousness, v. 29, 30.

c.) They overlook God's goodness to themselves, v. 31.

d.) And violate the obligations to mutual love, v, 32.

V. 12. *Father, give me the portion of goods that falleth to me,*—a speech of self-sufficient, and wayward selfishness, originating in a feeling, that man has something to be regarded as his own, and manifesting an unchildlike, ungodly state of mind. Mel.: "The son is guilty of a twofold error, first seeking his inheritance before the time, while his father was still living, then withdrawing himself from the authority of his father, and going where he should not be checked by paternal admonitions. Thus in our wantonness we all seize upon the inheritance before the time,—the gifts of mind and other things, which God has bestowed upon us for his service, transferring to ourselves and wickedly abusing, so that our mind is not made the dwelling-place of God, our body is polluted and rendered an instrument of the devil, and our goods are expended upon base pleasures. Mark here also grammatically, επιβαλλον μεϱος is a geometrical term, and is used to denote a certain proportion." *And he divided unto them his living*, he gave it up, without any restraint upon its free use; God deals with man as a free being, subject to no compulsion.

V. 13. *And not many days after, the younger son gathered all together, and took his journey into a far country,*—the essence of all sin, separation and departure from God. The design of the son is to be happy, and independent of his father—perfect freedom appears to him to be an indispensable condition of happiness: hence he regards his dependence upon a wise and good father, as a hinderance to his enjoyment, and chooses a state of separation from him, as the only effectual means of accomplishing his design, and making good his hopes. In this there was manifested a want of confidence in the love and wisdom of his father, and an ungracious, insolent slighting of the comfort he had hitherto experienced under his father's roof. The removal to a distant place, shows the unchildlike heart of the son. Grotius: "Appropriately in regard to the thing signified, for they are said to remove themselves far from God, who lay aside all fear of him, Ps. lxxiii. 27."—*And there wasted his substance with riotous living.* When withdrawn from fellowship with God, man sinks continually deeper, so that all the powers and faculties of his soul are misapplied and squandered upon what is worthless, and the gifts bestowed upon him are lost to their proper destination. The necessity of divine guidance, and of childlike subordination, the incapacity of man to govern himself, and the rashness of his foolish levity, are here depicted. Calvin: "Nor is it to be doubted, that under this picture, the extraordinary goodness of God, and his incomparable long-suffering toward us is disclosed, lest the excessive magnitude of our guilt, might deter us from the hope of obtaining pardon." Theremin, as above: "What avail us the high endowments with which the goodness of God has enriched us, even in our banishment, since the love to him, which ought to have directed all their use, is wanting, and selfishness, with all the desires it naturally gives rise to, has obtained the supremacy! We do often but misemploy our reason, to gratify our lusts, —we destroy our good by indulgence."

V. 14—16. The mournful consequences of departure from God are here depicted. Mel.: "For the most part, temporal punishments regularly follow, even in this life, contempt of God, and that for three reasons,—on account of God's justice, for the restraint of men's passions, and as calls to repentance." *His having spent all,* marks the internally degraded state of the sinner, his ignorance, his unbelief, Eph. iv. 18, 19. Rom. i. 21.—*There arose a mighty famine,*—the desire of good, the longing after bliss is never wholly extinguished in the human heart, however far sinners are from rightly understanding it; and, if at times it seems quite gone, and sinners think themselves happy, other times again come, when they *begin to be in want, i. e.* to have a keen feeling of their necessities, their misery, and the unsatisfying nature of all that is temporal; for he hungers, or seeks after what can afford a better and truer satisfaction to the wants of his nature.

V. 15. The greatness of the sinner's misery must soon remind him of the heart and house of his father; but still he is so proud as to think that he will succeed, that he can help himself, and possibly may find aid elsewhere, so that he shall be spared the necessity of humbling himself before his father. "*He went and joined himself to a citizen of that country*,—the sinner seeks enjoyment among the children of this world; worldly wisdom, worldly cares and labours must provide him with the necessary and wished for help. Gnomon: "Although he was not made a *citizen* here. He who is on the way of amendment is often held fast in his error, by something thrown out to him from the men of this world." Theremin: "Instead of that freedom which is only to be found in God's service, who always commands what is best, most honourable and blessed, we have sunk into the most wretched and despicable slavery. That principle in our nature, which makes it painful for us to deny ourselves to feelings of honour and of shame, is now laid hold of by sin, which reigns over us; and we continue to live in sin, because we want courage to break up all our relations, because our pride will not bear that we should declare our past life to be error and sin." *He sent him into the fields to feed swine*, according to the Jewish notions, which regarded swine as impure, this is an image of the most stringent necessity, of the deepest wretchedness, of the most depressed condition. Once a son, now a slave; once in his father's house, now in that of an alien; once with a most affectionate parent, now with a hard master. Such is the sinner's miserable state.

Ver. 16. *And he would fain have filled his belly with the husks*,—things without value, power, or substance, quite incapable of satisfying his desire,—vain wisdom and such like things he seeks after.

Gnomon: "The greater the vanity of the things, the more his desire grows."—*And no one gave to him*,—he does not find in them what he hoped and wished, cannot appropriate them for the satisfaction of his soul. What are here called *husks*, are properly a kind of pods—the pods of the carob tree, with which swine are fed.

Ver. 17. *When he came to himself;* Gnomon: "Food for the dissipation of his mind, (in French not inaptly expressed by *se divertir*) had failed. His return takes its beginning in the depth of his misery, which had so far allayed the fever of sin, that he can first come to himself and then to his God, penitence, conversion." When his necessity had reached its highest pitch, and all endeavours to help himself or obtain deliverance from men had failed, he arrives at last at a clearer and more perfect apprehension of his state, which hitherto the intoxication of pleasure and the binding influence of life had prevented him from seeing. Necessity, therefore, was and still is often the means, which our Heavenly Father uses to awaken sinners to the perception of the one grand necessity,—to occasion it is the part of the seeking shepherd. Calvin: "We have here described to us the manner in which God invites men to repentance. If they were wise in themselves, and would yield to instruction, he would draw them more gently, but because they will not become obedient unless subdued by discipline, he deals with them more severely."

How many hired servants of my father's have bread enough and to spare, and I perish with hunger,—a plain confession of the exceeding greatness of his misery, represented in the contrasted circumstances, servants and son,—they possessed of all abundance, he perishing for want. In this comparison appear the first traces of a change of mind on the part of the son; living in the father's house has come again to be an object of desire, dependence is salutary, and what he once so contemptuously slighted, he now recognises as a real good; he thinks, judges, feels and perceives now, quite differently, nay, in a precisely opposite manner to what he formerly did, and feels sensibly drawn to what he once had an aversion.

V. 18. From this pre-existing change in thought and feeling, comes the purpose—*I will arise, etc.*—and finally the execution of this purpose by actually going; so that repentance is here described in its leading features as a complete revolution in knowledge, sentiment, will and consequent behaviour.—*Father, I have sinned against thee, and before thee.* By the term Father, he expresses his confidence in the still unchanged and loving disposition toward him of his much wronged parent. Genuine repentance, as it is not without knowledge of its fault, so it is not ashamed to confess its iniquity, viewing this in its real magnitude, as a violation of the obligations toward God and our neighbour, by acts of sin. There is to be found no excusing, no palliating or diminishing of past transgressions, but much self-reproach, where repentance is sincere and earnest,—and at the same time a self-condemnation, as the words in ver. 19 show, in which the deep humility is expressed, wherewith the repentant sinner acknowledges, that he has only to do with grace, altogether irrespective of the outward standing that may belong to him in consequence of his good or bad behaviour; hence the son would be content with the place of a servant: and this affords decisive proof of the genuineness of his repentance, in that he experienced godly sorrow more on account of sin itself, than the sad consequences it had occasioned. Grotius: "He does not cast the blame upon his youth or upon his ill advisers, but without excuse of any sort he makes naked confession of his guilt." Scholten: "The things recorded in ver. 17—19, may be regarded by some as the returning of a man to a better life, or the beginnings of his conversion, thenceforth aided by God, and through his grace brought to a happy issue, so that the man thus attains to a fully converted state. But not only the entire doctrine of the gospel, as taught by the apostles and evangelists, but even the story of this parable itself, will not allow us to speak thus. For the publicans and sinners did not of their own accord enter upon a new life, but through the mighty power of our Lord's doctrine upon their minds, whereby they were convinced of their own depravity, of the misery thence arising to themselves, of the wrath of God, and their liability to future punishment, if they did not renounce their sinful ways; and these representations, aided by the miraculous deeds of Christ, which convinced them of his divine origin. By comparing this parable also with the preceding ones, it manifestly appears, that the first rise of conversion in the soul is not from man himself, but from God, who begins the operation in a way suitable to reason, sometimes by other means, but especially by the word of the gospel rendered effectual by the grace of the Holy Spirit. For the sheep, which had wandered from the flock, returned not to the shepherd of its own accord, but the shepherd carefully sought until he found it; and the piece of money which the woman lost, needed to be diligently searched for, and only thus was recovered. But why these things? To show, that the conversion of men to God, from whom they have revolted, must be ascribed only to God himself."

V. 20. *And he arose, and came to his father.*—The execution of his purpose lets us see into the heart of this lost child, how faith wrought there, *i. e.* firm and cheerful confidence in the still unchanged, abidingly affectionate and gracious feeling of the father towards him, though a sinner,—and also hope, *i. e.* an unshaken confidence in the exercise of love, which he expected of his father,—namely, pardon and acceptance. Without faith and hope he would not have returned; without them, therefore, he should not have been saved, —he would have sunk into despair, and there perished. The source of this faith could not be his state, his misery, but only the early acquired experience of his father's love, (v. 12.) Every repentant sinner has now, besides, God's word of promise, upon which he can rest in faith. Matth. xi. 28—30, and even this faith is salvation begun.*

*[The connexion between repentance and faith, and their mutual action and re-action in the case of the prodigal, is so happily expressed by Draeseke in the following remarks, that we cannot forbear quoting them here. "In the deep abyss into which his own waywardness had plunged him, his eyes were opened, and he becomes capable of the walk of repentance and faith. 'How many hired servants . . . . I will arise and go to my father.' He had left, in folly, his father's house. It is still far from him. Return to it seems impossible. Yet it stands before him, as if he actually saw it in all its glory, and it wonderfully captivates his soul. There, indeed, was faith, that he did not see the father's house and yet saw it. It was the spirit of faith, which made him capable of calling him, whom he had so lightly abandoned, so grievously vexed, by the name of *father*, and confiding in his fatherly heart. That faith he assuredly had, 'which is the substance of things hoped for, and the evidence of things not seen.' And repentance has he not less than faith. The more he believes in his father's love and the possibility of regaining a place in his father's house, his alienation and misery press the more heavily upon him. He cannot bear them, and, in the pain he experiences, behold repentance stirring.—The more he believes in his father's love, and the possibility of regaining a place in his father's house, the more he feels himself unworthy of being called a son. 'Father, I have sinned, &c.' See there the self-knowledge in which repentance proceeds, the self-condemnation which it produces, the self-humiliation which it carries along with it. The more he believes in his father's love, and the possibility of regaining a place in his father's house, the more does he heave the wish, Would that I were there! and strengthen himself in the resolution, 'I will arise and go.' See there the new principle of delight in God's favour and active consecration to God's service, with which repentance shines forth as a tree covered with blossom, in which it approves itself as a good tree, yielding good fruit, and perfects itself through the Holy Spirit, in the walk of a regenerated life.—Now, from all this, learn the inseparable connexion between faith and repentance. They mutually depend on each other. Without faith, no repentance. For how can one return who knows not of a home? Without repentance, no faith. For how can the home be reached, if no return is made? Both work in each other. Faith opens the kingdom to the heart,—repentance opens the heart to the kingdom. Both also succeed through each other. Faith without repentance were self delusion. Repentance without faith were self-torture. Faith

But when he was yet a great way off, his father saw him.—The gentlest motions in the sinner's heart are known to the all-seeing God. Calvin: "This is the main point of the parable. If men, who are both naturally prone to revenge, and too tenacious of their own rights, are yet so much alive to paternal affection that they generously pardon their children, and readily receive them after they have miserably ruined themselves, it is impossible that God, whose infinite goodness so far exceeds all the affection of parents, should deal more hardly with us. Before they call, says he, I will answer, Isa. lxv. 24. Ps. xxxii. 5." Mel.: "On this place it is said by Basilius, You have but to wish, and God anticipates. The father here looks upon his son approaching, though still at a distance,—so we draw near to God with slow and trembling step, and bring with us no merits, but a polluted conscience and great filth. Although we are such, however, yet the Father meets us; if we only come, he sees us from afar, that is, he knows our misery, cares for us, calls us, is moved with compassion, and sincerely desires to save us."

And had compassion,—the feeling of righteous indignation against the sinner's guilt vanishes before the compassion of God; the misery of his child, his sorrow and regret, his thirsting desire after grace, his good purposes and resolutions, which were proved to be genuine by his actual return,—all this goes so deeply to the father's heart, that he feels only the tenderest compassion for him.—*Ran, and fell on his neck, and kissed him.* Mel.: "*Ran,* that is, while

is the restoration of the heart to a new sphere of vision, so that it sees what before it saw not, thinks what before it thought not. Repentance is the restoration of the heart to a new sphere of action, so that it wills what before it willed not, does what before it could not do. And both together in the heart of a sinner, are even as two divine sisters sent from heaven, to quell at once the evils in his condition, and the tumults in his breast, and like true guardian angels, to conduct him through the dangers of a troublous ocean, into the haven of rest and peace."]—*Trans.*

we languish, he draws us by his holy word and Spirit; *he falls upon our neck*, embraces us, supports us in trouble and distress; for we should be overwhelmed with grief and sorrow, were we not aided and upheld by God. *He kisses us*, that is, he intimates to us the remission of sins, and assuages our pains and fears by new light and consolation." These tokens of paternal, deep-seated affection disclose the truth, that the all-seeing and merciful Jehovah, who discerns the inmost emotions of the sinner's heart toward amendment, crowns and blesses it with the feeling and consciousness of his grace and good-will in the heart of the sinner, so that the sinner, who really is in that state of mind described in v. 17—19, possesses a blessed experience of the affectionate disposition of his Father, and becomes established in his faith and hope. What, therefore, was before the conviction of faith, is now the conviction of experience. Calvin: "Christ compares God to the human father, who voluntarily meets his returning son; for he reckons it not enough to pardon those who entreat his mercy, but seeks to anticipate them by his paternal goodness."

V. 21. The resolved confession (v. 18) is now carried into effect; for we must confess our sins, 1 John i. 9, and the father's love facilitates to the son the work of unbosoming his heart. Grotius: "It is proper for man to make acknowledgment of his guilt, even after pardon has been announced to him." Since the father has already acted toward him as a child, and done more than he could ask, the words—make me as one of thy hired servants—are naturally dropped. Calvin: "Here another part of repentance is marked, namely, a sense of sin conjoined with sadness and shame; for he, who does not grieve for having sinned, will do any thing rather than think of turning to a better course." Mel.: "The son submits himself to his father, confesses his fault, and acknowledges his double crime, viz. that he has acted offensively toward God and his father. In this acknowledgment and reconciliation stands regeneration or spiritual reformation."

V. 22, 23. Even if we would not keep the individual in view here, we must still keep by the ideas contained in the figure, viz., that the father applies the riches of his compassion to his son, and by marks of love not less numerous than certain and explicit, assures him of his fatherly love, and the son's restoration to the standing of a child,—marks which shall be to him now and henceforth dear pledges of paternal affection, and not only retain, but ever and anon confirm him the more in grateful love and childlike obedience. So that all the blessed experiences of heart are here indicated, which are undergone by the penitent and believing sinner, and a confirmation given, at the same time, to the words in Ps. cxxx. 8—12; Ez. xxxiii. 10, 11. But that the significance of the particular traits is not alien to the mind of Jesus and the nature of the parabolical style, is admitted even by Grotius, who remarks on the place, " Besides the general resemblance, there seems to be also, in the several parts, what admits of being allegorized. For the kiss is beyond doubt the sign of reconciliation—so that we have here declared to us the remarkable goodness of God, who is so moved by the late repentance of the sinner, as to pardon his sins from the mere promptings of divine mercy. Although allegories are not anxiously to be sought for in the single members of comparisons, yet there are some here not to be overlooked, as they are suggested by the collation of other Scriptures. The *robe*, then, appears to signify that continued purity of life, which, through the grace of God, a grateful heart yields in return for the great goodness it has experienced. A *ring*, among the Romans, was the sign of nobility, among the Orientals, of peculiar dignity or vast wealth. But as rings were also used for sealing, the ancients did not think amiss in understanding by the ring the gift of the Holy Spirit, whereby we are sealed, 2 Cor. i. 22.

Shoes are also granted by God to penitents who are received into favour, that they may be fitted for teaching others, if not by words, at least by example." Calvin: "We shall not be torturing the plain letter of scripture, if we say that our heavenly Father not only pardons our sins, so as to bury them in forgetfulness, but also restores to us the gifts of which we had divested ourselves." Mel.: "The *ring* signifies the gospel and faith, through which, the one receiving the other, the son has the honour of a place in the family, has his pristine rank restored to him. For the gospel is the word of reconciliation, and faith is the apprehending and applying of this word, just as if the bestowment of some honour were marked by a ring. In fine, the ring is a mark of any sort of treaty. But he that has been reconciled enters anew into covenant with God, and this is done by the believing reception of the gospel. A *robe* every where signifies a good conscience. *Shoes* mean the works of our calling, in which our faith ought principally to shine. But mention is made of *the fatted calf*, that there might be a reference to the death of Christ, through which we have been redeemed, and whose life provides for us righteousness, the Holy Spirit, and eternal life; and by this Redeemer we are fed, as is said in John vi., that is, we come to God and receive consolation, we are truly made alive."

The *garment* may be understood to intimate the spiritual adorning, the sinner's state of mind, now well-pleasing to God, his righteous condition; the *ring*, an image of freedom, may be taken as significative of the deliverance brought to the sinner, through divine grace, from the vile yoke of sin, and his future standing as a son given to him of love; the *shoes* may be referred to the strength, which, through divine mercy, is imparted to him for the walk of a new obedience; and the *feast* may be understood of the full enjoyment of peace, and comfort, and blessing, which is experienced by the pardoned sinner. What these outward marks of favour were to the son, we have, through the goodness of our Lord, in the sacraments, which are visible pledges of invisible divine grace, appropriated by faith. Mel.: " Hitherto, in this long description of the return of the prodigal son, we have set before us the most attractive image, drawing us to repentance, testifying that we are received, and skilfully embracing both causes and effects. Wherefore it must be often and carefully meditated, that we may be stirred up to repentance and godliness."

Ver. 24. The ground is here intimated of the general rejoicing. *This my son was dead, and is alive again*—all life, even when most prosperous, without fellowship with God, is but death and misery, Eph. ii. 5, 6. *Was lost, and is found,* marks deliverance from the condemnation of sin.

Ver. 25. *The elder son was in the field*—busied about earthly things, and, in the experience of his own heart, far removed from the feelings of a pardoned sinner, he knew nothing of this joy, which, however, was not concealed from him, for the sound of it breaks upon his ears. Calvin: "This latter part of the parable accuses those of inhumanity, who seek maliciously to restrain the grace of God, as if they envied the salvation of miserable sinners. For we know that the pride of the pharisees is here levelled at, who thought that due consideration was not had of their merits, if Christ admitted the common herd of publicans and sinners to the hope of eternal life." Mel.: "The reproof of the hypocrite is added. Here now he shows that outward discipline, although it was spoken of above with approbation, cannot satisfy the law of God. Orderly behaviour, the careful avoidance of scandals, and a due regard to the public peace, is a becoming and necessary thing, but in hypocrites there are great internal vices, such as self-righteousness, arrogance, vanity, contempt of others, who are reckoned beneath them, and envy of those who appear to prosper, as Saul envied David, and the elder brother here, in his frugality, thinks it hard that the prodigal should be received and made equal with himself. For hypocrites, because they conceive themselves to be alone eminent in virtue, wish to reign alone. But true love rejoices when those who have wandered from the way are brought back, desires the good of brethren as well as its own, rejoices in examples of mercy and kindness, takes pleasure in the improvement of the bad, and unites itself to them that their degradation may be screened."

Ver. 28. *And he was angry*—from envy and heartlessness toward his brother, full of indignation at the tender love of the father, into whose state of feeling he could not transport himself, because of his cold, selfish, and contracted disposition. *And would not go in*, would not participate in the joy. *Therefore came his father out and entreated him.* What a contrast between a loveless and loving heart! Calvin: "In these words he chides the intolerable pride of hypocrites, seeing they must be entreated not to envy the exercise of mercy to their brethren. Moreover, though God did not ask, yet by his example he exhorts us to tolerate the errors of our brethren."

Ver. 29. *Lo, these many years do I serve thee*—pride of desert—thinks he has something to claim for his righteousness. Gnomon: "I *serve*, a confession of servitude. He does not add, *father*. Never *gavest*, not to say *killed; a kid*, not to say a *calf; friends*, as opposed to harlots." *Neither transgressed I at any time thy commandment*—blindness at the state of his own heart; for even now he manifests a very unchildlike disposition; it is the pride of virtue in those who boast themselves of their honour and integrity in social life, but know nothing of the spirit of love.—*And thou hast never given me a kid*—he represents the good things granted to him as very small when put in comparison with those which had been afforded to his brother, ver. 27: but not in accordance with the truth, as we learn from ver. 31. The ground of the representation lies in the proud heart and lofty pretensions of those persons who are never content with that which the grace of God gives to them, overlook it and believe that they are treated with contempt, whereas they would judge quite otherwise had they a truly humbled spirit. Ver. 30. *But as soon as this thy son was come,* the fine hypocrite cannot prevail upon himself to call his brother by the name of brother, and thereby discovers his want of love. *Who hath devoured thy living with harlots*—he thinks the worst of his brother, and describes his guilt in the grossest manner, so that the kindness showed him by his father might appear the highest injustice, partiality and unfairness toward himself.

Ver. 31. The meaning is, the goods and gifts which thy brother has received are also for thee, and I will by no means hinder thee from enjoying them. But for the enjoyment another heart certainly is necessary than this son possessed. Gnomon: "The father speaks to him affectionately—*son,* and does not immediately drive from him the envious brother. *Always,* and, therefore it was not necessary that there should be any special rejoicing; *with me,* it is better to be happy with a father than with a multitude of friends; *mine,* it is not necessary to seek for friendship abroad; *are thine,* for the younger brother had received his portion, and the elder was sole heir to his father's goods. Many things may belong to the sons of God, in the full enjoyment of which they do not delight. So that the elder brother ought not to have complained that a kid had never been given to him." Calvin: "This answer has two heads; the first is that the elder son has no reason to be angry, seeing that his brother had been received without injury to him; but the second that he was mortified at the joy expressed on account of his brother's return, because he had no regard for his brother's welfare. This comparison does not intimate, however, that he would grieve for those who had always been pious, being received as penitents into favour, but rather implies that this would furnish him with no just ground of complaint. Besides it is a concession. For neither had the scribes and pharisees lived up to the requirements of the divine law, but since they wished to appear as having done so, Christ granting this, as it were to them, shows, that still there was no reason why they should envy pardon being given to the penitent, since nothing on that account was taken from them."

The ground for the call of rejoicing stands partly in this, that the individual recovered is a brother, and partly in the recovery itself from so deep a misery. Scholten, p. 301: "The Saviour argues from what was granted, as we say, although he by no means allowed that which for the sake of conviction he had yielded.—It is not by any means to be concluded, that the common people of the Jews were altogether and in appearance such pharisees as they professed themselves to be; nor must it be supposed, that Jesus acknowledged their piety and virtuous endeavours, (Matth. v. 20.) But that Jesus might convince them the more of error, he grants, as it were, that they did excel in every virtuous pursuit, but, that even this being granted, it was improper and unjust to pursue with malevolent and bitter feeling, publicans and sinners, when they became truly penitent and returned to a better course."

XXXII.

THE UNJUST STEWARD.

Luke xvi. 1—13.

General Remarks upon the parables in the 16th Chapter of Luke.

The two parables contained in the sixteenth chapter, were delivered immediately after those recorded in the preceding chapter, and before the same hearers, as has been already remarked (No. 29.) The parable of the godless householder is connected simply by the words, *And he said also to his disciples;* by whom we are to understand not the twelve merely, but the other followers of Jesus, especially those publicans and sinners, Luke xv. 1, some of whom might have been once as faithless as this steward, though they now were concerned for the salvation of their souls. Gnomon: "The Lord speaks now more solemnly *with* his disciples who had been publicans, and more severely than he had done *for* them to others. The son received back with joy, is not to be every day regaled with music, but is taught to return to duty." If the publicans and sinners, who drew near to Jesus, really were penitent and sincere in their purpose, the parable will then equally serve for a justification of the Saviour in receiving them; but if they were in any respect of the disposition of those who wantonly abused the goodness of God to sinners, as represented in the three foregoing parables, placing a sinful confidence upon the greatness of the divine compassion, and thinking to abide without true repentance in their sins, then would this parable warn them against all misunderstanding and abuse of those contained in chap. xv. But our Lord might still farther have had a special regard in this discourse to the pharisees, who, if not so openly, yet not less really, were given to covetousness, to a shameful self-seeking, and hence to many acts of deceit and unrighteousness, ver. 14, also Matth. xxiii. 14, 25. By the picture of the unfaithful steward he sought to warn them, holding up to them their own image; admonished them by *his* prudence to a better improvement of their riches, pointed them to the time of reckoning, and the danger therewith connected, and taught them how they might be able to meet this through unfeigned repentance. But the wicked disposition of these hypocrites disdained the earnest and faithful warnings of Jesus, and as they possibly felt themselves especially aimed at in the parable, in order that they might conceal their uneasiness, spite, and indignation, they betook themselves to contemptuous looks and marks of insolence, —"they derided Christ." This led Jesus to say, v. 15: "Ye are they who justify yourselves before men, but God knoweth your hearts." Gnomon: "This is the link of connexion with the next discourse; justification of one's self before men, and pride of heart, feeds avarice, and smiles at heavenly simplicity, v. 15; despises the gospel, v. 16, and destroys the law, v. 17; which is shown to the pharisees in v. 18, by an example most needful to be insisted on. The whole is embraced in the parable of the rich man and Lazarus." Calvin: "The cause of our justification should not be referred to the judgment of men, but to the tribunal of God, where no righteousness is accounted of but what gives a perfect and complete obedience to the law. And when men stand at the tribunal of God, one and all are conscious of guilt."

In the passage in question, v. 15, Jesus exposes and reproves mainly the hypocrisy of the pharisees, for the meaning of his words is, Ye are concerned only about this, that ye may be accounted in the judgment of your fellow men righteous persons and favourites of Heaven, but the all-seeing Searcher of hearts knows the inmost state of your corrupt hearts, and ye are any thing but in favour with him. In the following words, "For that which is highly esteemed among men, is abomination in the sight of God," our Lord censures the self-conceit of the pharisees, which was so closely connected with their hypocrisy, and declares, that as God holds that feeling of self-exalting pride, and every one who cherishes it, in abhorrence, this was their position before him, he had no pleasure in them how high soever their esteem was of themselves, or they were esteemed by others. "Whosoever," says Lavater, "affects a standing of righteousness before men, and is unconcerned about the internal improvement of his heart, he is a pharisee. Whosoever seeks more the praise and approbation of man than the praise and approbation of God, he is a pharisee. Whosoever lays claim to the favour of God on account of his regular outward behaviour, while he neglects his internal state of thinking and acting, he sticks fast in pharisaism. Pharisaism is pedantry in religion and virtue,—a neglecting of the essential for the accidental, of the end for the means, of the spiritual good for the outward ceremony."

Their self-elation of mind, which led them to prefer themselves before others, and to seek that they might be regarded as the favourites of Heaven, the pharisees founded upon two considerations; the first of which was a conclusion which they drew from Deut. xxviii. 1, to the effect, that he who is rich and prosperous upon earth, is a favourite of God, a man of piety, and sure of attaining to eternal life; but that whosoever, on the other hand, is poor and wretched, is hated by God, without piety, and an heir of eternal destruction. Besides this, they reckoned much upon their zeal for the law, the ceremonial observances required by which they most punctually kept, on account of which they were generally esteemed pious, although the weightiest part of the law, (Matth. xxiii. 23,) love, they unscrupulously disregarded, and thus manifested their real unbelief. The false conclusion above mentioned is rebutted in the first part of the parable of the rich man, who, though prosperous upon earth, still fell into condemnation, and therefore could not be a child of God, however pious he may have seemed; while the poor Lazarus, the object of the rich man's contempt, attains to salvation. The self-elation of the pharisees on account of their supposed, but still only outward fulfilment of the law, the Saviour rebukes in the latter part of the same parable, in which the condemned rich man is directed to Moses and the prophets, with the assurance, that if he had heard them, he would not have come into condemnation; so that, though he was well acquainted with them, and highly esteemed them as a divine revelation, he must not have valued and used them in the right manner, that is, must have had no true faith in them. And that is just the nature of practical unbelief, which poisoned the life of the pharisee, pluming himself upon the law and the knowledge of God, while still he allowed them no influence upon his walk and conduct. Calvin: "Comp. Rom. ii. 21. As this reproof formerly applied to the Jews, who, trusting to their mere knowledge of the law, lived no better than if they had been without the law; so we must take heed lest now it should be directed against us. And indeed it is but too applicable to many, who boasting themselves of a superior knowledge of the gospel, abandon themselves to all manner of impurity, as if the gospel prescribed no rule of life; lest, therefore, we should trifle thus securely with the Lord, let us remember what sort of judgment hangs over such babblers in words, who only in their much talking show their regard for the word of God." This practical unbelief, the real kernel of the parable, stands forth there in the semblance of faith, pays respect to the word of God as a revelation, while the heart remains thereby unimproved, the love of the world unsubdued, bowels of compassion unknown. Precisely as the rich man is here represented, the sadducees lived, and were besides tainted with a theoretical infidelity, receiving only the books of Moses, but rejecting the further development of the divine will through the prophets. Indeed, as the behaviour of the rich man is represented quite saddusiacally, many expositors have been of opinion, that the parable is chiefly aimed against the sadducees; but the untenableness of that opinion is manifest from no mention being made of the sadducees on the occasion of this discourse being delivered and especially from the circumstance, that our Lord could not well have called in against them Moses and the prophets, as they would not have owned the force of this argument, which, as directed against the pharisees, is of great weight, since their practical unbelief was rendered the less excusable on account of their theoretical faith.

That the rebuke of the practical unbelief of the pharisees is the main design of the parable of the rich man, receives an additional confirmation from the internal connexion that is brought out by this view of it between the parable and v. 16—18, whereas, in most expositions upon these verses, no such connexion is recognised. It is said in v. 16, that "the law and the prophets were until John; since that time the kingdom of God is preached, and every man presseth into it." The law and the prophets have a reference to the times of John the Baptist; what in them is announced prophetically, namely, the appearance of Messiah and his kingdom—this was proclaimed by John, and afterwards by Christ himself, as the gospel or glad tidings of what was actually taking place. Whosoever then really considered Moses and the prophets as a divine revelation, he ought to have given proof of this by a believing reception of the testimony of John and Jesus, which perfectly accorded with the predictions of the Old Testament. This, however, the pharisees did not; they rejected the preaching of John and of Christ himself, and thus manifested their unbelief in the prophetic portion, at least, of the Old Testament; and as they would not comply with the call to repentance, proceeding both from John and from Christ, whilst even publicans and sinners were doing so, they showed at the same time their unbelief in respect to the moral part of the Old Testament. Their unbelief in both respects is rebuked by Jesus, in the asseveration he makes, v. 17, regarding the inviolable sanctity of the entire law: "It is easier for heaven and earth to pass than for one tittle of the law to fail," (Jas. ii. 10.) And, as a proof of the arbitrary manner in which they dealt with the law, he refers, in v. 18, to the law of marriage, in regard to which the pharisees, according to Matth. xix. 1—9, were accustomed to make regulations, which in effect destroyed the divine command concerning the indissoluble nature of the marriage-bond. By all this the real unbelief of the pharisees upon Moses and the prophets is in plain language manifestly declared, not less in regard to the predictions contained in the scriptures, than to their requirements and obligations; and as what had been in plain terms declared, was often immediately afterwards repeated and made more palpable in a figure or parable, so it is the case also here, and hence, in the parable of the rich man, we cannot fitly represent any thing else as its chief aim and subject-matter, than a reproof of practical unbelief, of which the manifestations in this life, and the destiny in the world to come, are depicted to our view.

When a delineation of heartlessness, or want of compassion, and its disastrous consequences, is held, as very commonly is done, to be the central point of the parable, there is certainly much in appearance to justify this; but the ultimate ground of that cold-hearted indifference is unbelief, and to that the latter part of the parable points, as its connexion with what precedes, warrants and justifies a much farther extension of meaning than the view just mentioned. As in the parable of the unjust steward, the possibility and the means of escape are pointed out, even when there has been a heavy load of guilt contracted, so this of the rich man shows the certainty and the dreadfulness of that condemnation which awaits those whose unbelief has led them to despise that first warning. The faithless management of the steward corresponds to the selfish luxury of the rich man; the debtors of his lord, whom the former makes his friends, stands opposed to Lazarus, for whom the rich man cared not a pin; the reception into everlasting habitations has its counterpart in the help which the rich man fruitlessly implored from Lazarus, and the praise accorded to the prudent steward is put in contrast to the judgment of condemnation recorded in v. 24, 25. By these undeniable references of the two parables to each other, their internal connexion and application to the same character is made manifest.

Not one of our Lord's parables has received so many and such different interpretations, as that of the unjust steward. That the connexion in which it stands has not been sufficiently considered, is the chief cause of this variety of interpretations, and of their often erring so far from the right view both of the leading design and of individual parts. The centre-point of the parable is PRUDENCE, for the Lord praises the unrighteous steward as having acted *prudently;* and the recommendation of prudence for all who would inherit the kingdom of heaven is its main scope. The words in v. 8, "For the children of this world are in their generation wiser than the children of light," contain a truth but too frequently exemplified in daily experience, and show, through the connective particle *for*, that in this matter the recommendation of prudence as a necessary quality was abundantly required. Because the Saviour wills that all men should be saved, but because many, even of those who have some desire for salvation, do not manifest the proper prudence in pressing the important work of their salvation, and many more neglect the work altogether; on these accounts our Lord relates this parable, that he might urge on all the requisite prudence. Prudence is that property, or capacity of the soul, which, for attaining an end, finds, selects, and applies the most fitting means,—without, however, condescending upon the nature of the end or the means, whether they are morally good or bad. That the Redeemer recommends to his disciples a prudence only of a moral kind, appears from the proverb in Matth. x. 16: "Be ye therefore wise as serpents, and harmless (simple) as doves." Christian prudence must, therefore, according to this injunction, be always coupled with a simple, honourable and true heart; and hence the end, which Christian prudence proposes to itself, and the means which it chooses and applies for the accomplishment of this, must always be morally good and harmless, agreeable to a holy God, and the mind of a blessed Saviour. This remark is of much importance for the parable, as many have stumbled at the circumstance that, in commending the steward for a pattern, Jesus has not discountenanced the use of unrighteous means; and hence did the Emperor Julian employ this parable for the purpose of attacking and vilifying the moral character of Christ. But we must take our starting point from the holy mind of Jesus, to which every thing unrighteous is an abomination, and from which a recommendation, not of the unrighteousness, but only of the prudence of the unjust steward could proceed: so that the application which our Lord makes of the parable in v. 9 to his hearers, can have no other meaning than this: Even so do I recommend prudence to you. Just as this steward, for the attainment of his earthly object for securing his future support, laid hold of the most suitable and appropriate means, and thereby showed his prudence,—so must you also do in regard to a higher and better object, the securement of your eternal well-being, employ the best means best adapted to the end, and manifest therein a similar prudence. In earthly designs it is possible that the most suitable means may be in their nature bad, though still conducive to the end in view; but in regard to heavenly things, this is quite impossible, only such means as are morally good and well-pleasing to God can here be of any avail to reach the desired end; and in this undeniable truth, we find a new testimony to the fact, that Jesus could not possibly think of commending the unrighteousness of this steward to our imitation.

As prudence of itself is only an ideal thing—the mere notion of fitness in the soul's discernment and bent of purpose, while the Redeemer continually gives and teaches essential truth, so he must be understood as recommending, through the temper and conduct ascribed to the steward, not prudence alone, but also the worth and exercise of this prudence in respect to the use of earthly goods,—since he says in v. 9, "Make to yourselves friends of the unrighteous mammon, &c." As Christian prudence manifests itself in a moderate use of earthly goods to purposes of kindness and beneficence, this should therefore be regarded as the main idea of the parable, and the recommendation of such prudence its chief aim, as may be made manifest by the following train of thought:—The unjust steward was prudent while he applied the goods intrusted to him to the purpose of making friends to himself, and thus securing his future temporal support; Christians must apply their temporal goods in acts of kindness, in order to make to themselves friends, and to secure their future eternal well-being. The conclusion to which the parable and its practical application leads recommendatory of the prudence in question is this: If the prudence shown by the steward for an earthly object is praised, how much more will God commend a prudence directed towards a heavenly object, and crown it with his blessing! Since the steward's giving up the goods committed to him by his lord was perceived by him to be the means best suited for accomplishing his end, and was that wherein pre-eminently his prudence stood: the point of comparison on which the recommendation of genuine prudence hangs, can be nothing else than the free sacrifice of earthly goods to beneficent purposes. Beneficence, therefore, is beyond doubt recommended, but not, as many expositors think, as the great end of the parable, but only as the means and as the mode of acting, in which the quality of prudence practically manifests itself. If the exercise of beneficence, and, in connexion therewith, a warning against luxury and niggardliness were regarded as the leading idea of the parable, then no account could be made of many circumstances in the conduct of the steward, which serve to bring out clearly his singular prudence, and they must only be viewed as figurative embellishments. But the moment we take prudence, as it manifests itself in general, and particularly in the use of temporal goods, as the leading point and subject of the parable, all its subordinate parts and circumstances find their proper and full significance, as will be shown more at large in the sequel.

To the right understanding of the parable belongs the whole of the practical application, which closes only with v. 13; the consideration of which still farther proves, that not beneficence, but prudence, which in this part alone is discoursed of, is the prominent idea of the parable. For the thought contained in v. 10—12, is this: It is contrary to prudence to be unfaithful in the application of temporal goods, for one thereby sustains injury, losing in consequence of such unfaithfulness the benefit of having better goods committed to us. It is always a matter of prudence to compare the present and the future, the end and the means, the cause and the effect, in a word, the necessary inevitable consequences and connexions of things, and determine our course of action accordingly. This connexion between time and eternity, in reference to the consequences which stretch into the latter, is pointed at in v. 11 and 12, for the purpose of admonishing us to a suitable line of duty, to a prudent course of behaviour, which, so far as earthly goods are concerned, consists, according to Christ's instruction, in making to ourselves friends of the unrighteous mammon, so that we may reach the everlasting habitations, obtain the true riches, and be endowed with that which is to constitute our eternal inalienable property. Luther has given this view of the parable, for he says in his House-Pos. 4. 418: "In this unjust and faithless steward our Lord sets before us a twofold instruction. The first of which is, that we must learn from him, and from the men of this world, to be prudent." And again, at p. 407, "The Lord's meaning is not that we must act unrighteously toward each other, cheating one another of their own goods, and laying it out in alms. No, but his meaning is, that we must imitate the steward in his foresight, activity, and prudence, applying our money and goods so as to provide for ourselves blessings in another and better life." Once more, at p. 411: "Our Lord desires that, in a good cause, we should use the earnestness and diligence, which this steward did in a bad one, for his own profit, and the hurt of his master." For the farther elucidation of the matter he notices how, in Rom. v. 14, Adam and Christ are only in part compared with each other, in respect merely to their root and origin, —something being taken from both which they had in common, but not in respect to their work and the fruit growing out of it, for the one procured for those connected with him death and condemnation, the other righteousness and salvation; "In like manner," says Luther, "Jesus compares here the righteous and unrighteous, that even as the unrighteous act prudently in deceit and knavery, so the righteous must act prudently in uprightness and piety." For the sake of illustration, he employs another comparison: "See how an unchaste woman for the prosecution of her sinful purposes, decks herself out in the finest manner, the gold, the velvet, and the silk which she employs, having no power to testify against their misapplication to such a purpose. But I may even boast of it, and say to thee, Seest thou how this woman knows to adorn herself for wantonness? And why dost thou not use similar diligence for the sake of pleasing our dear bridegroom Christ Jesus? In saying this, I commend not a wanton behaviour, but only the diligence, foresight, and care which it behooves *us* to use in a good, honourable, and righteous cause." The most improper characters, such as the steward before us, have always something good and praiseworthy about them, which may be held up for our example and imitation; and in this way it is that Christ has commended to us this man on account of his prudence. But that the prudence recommended is not to be understood of prudence in its entire compass, as it may then manifest itself in a great variety of ways, (Matth. vii. 24—27; xxv. 1—13,) but specially in regard to the right employment of earthly goods, Luther has also acknowledged, and says at p. 407: "It is a sermon on good works, and particularly against covetousness, to the end that we should not abuse our money and goods, but employ them to help poor, needy people."

The expositions of this parable which are known to me, although in particular parts very wide of each other, yet all agree in this, that the means adopted by the steward for his future support, were most shameful and utterly to be reprobated, and that he crowned his earlier iniquities by an act of surpassing deceit. A view of the parable, however, quite different on this point from the common one, is to be found in an Essay by David Schulz, on the parable of the steward. The method which he strikes out is designed to represent the conduct of the steward as laudable, as being without unrighteousness in regard to the means chosen; and it is certainly not to be denied, that this exposition, if it were well founded, and could be proved, would be most deserving of acceptation, although all misgivings in regard to the representation of an immoral conduct on the part of the steward, may be quashed by the reflection, that it is only in the prudence that the point of comparison stands, and that this alone is recommended. Schulz grounds his exposition mainly upon the notion of steward (οικονομος,) who is not to be regarded as a man that must account to his master for all receipts and expenditures, small and great, and whose books are from time to time overhauled by his principal; such modern conceptions must be banished, as quite unsuitable here. In his judgment the steward is such a person as has full power to dispose of what is committed to him, as the Apostles in their ministrations of the gospel, were named stewards, (1 Cor. iv. 1, 2; Tit. i. 7,) and yet manifestly had the greatest freedom in the use and distribution of the word committed to them. Then he properly takes notice of the image, which the relation of the steward in the parable to his lord, affords of the relation in which the man stands to his God; and as in this relation no one can deny that the fullest liberty is granted to man, and that he may act entirely as he pleases with the goods committed to him, only subject to a day of reckoning, so a similar duty must be demanded, for the more limited relation which forms the figure in the parable. Now, to this liberty granted to man by God, in the employment of the earthly goods committed to him, it manifestly belongs as a part, that the man have something to bestow, freely to give away, in order thereby to make friends to himself, consequently the giving away in the parable, would be but a part of the steward's liberty, and not be chargeable with unrighteousness or deceit. And it is further alleged, that the expression in v. 8, οικονομος της αδικιας, (steward of unrighteousness,) does not mean an unjust, but an ungodly, wicked steward, not indicating any thing like deceit; and indeed his wickedness had shown itself at an earlier period, in the lavish expenditure, the selfish, extravagant use he had made of what was confided to him, while now (v. 8) he is praised for having at last prudently made a better use of his stewardship by the exercise of beneficence, and for the sake of his future welfare.

But granting even that the means employed were as righteous and laudable as Schulz would make them, still the motive of the liberality exercised by the steward, must be regarded as selfish, and consequently deserving of blame, since he acted only out of regard to his own self, and not from pure love to the creditors. Hence, according to this view also, prudence in the use of earthly goods, for the purpose of acquiring friends by acts of beneficence, must remain the centre-point of the parable, for otherwise the selfish, at least, if not deceitful, conduct of the steward would be recommended to imitation. The commendation bestowed upon the steward by his lord, when viewed in connexion with the now supposed righteousness of conduct, will import as much as: My steward, indeed, in the earlier part of his behaviour, showed little conscience, but this last official act of his, an act of beneficence, is of a different character, and I cannot but praise him for having consulted in such a manner for his future entertainment, and made friends to himself at the right time. Schulz finally remarks, that a doctrine is never taught and explained in a parable by being compared to its opposite, but always things only that are similar are set over against and compared to each other, so that the conclusion is often drawn from the small to the great, but never from the opposite. But however true this remark may be, it still does not properly affect the case in question, for even according to Schulz, prudence is the leading idea of the parable,—under the example of the steward, a similar prudence is recommended, and the righteousness or unrighteousness of his conduct *never comes at all into the comparison,* no more than the disobliging conduct of that friend, (Luke xi.,) and the reckless character of that judge, (Luke xviii.) As in these two parables the efficacy of prayer is the only thing that is unfolded by a conclusion from the less to the greater, so here, in that of the steward, prudence by a similar conclusion: If an impure prudence is commended by men, how much more will the Lord commend a holy prudence! Calvin: "The sum of this parable is, that we must deal humanely and kindly toward our neighbours, so that when we stand before the tribunal of God, we may receive the fruit of our liberality."

TRAIN OF THOUGHT IN THE PARABLE.

Of Christian prudence.

I. Obligation to this:

1. Because we are dependent on God; v. 1: Who had a steward.

2. Because we are accountable to him, v. 2.

II. Its proper nature is represented:

1. In the general:

a.) It is provident of the future, v. 3: What shall I do?

b.) It conceals not from itself the true state of matters, v. 3: My Lord taketh away my stewardship from me.

c.) It is inventive of means for its well-being, v. 3: I cannot dig, to beg I am ashamed.

d.) It forms its purpose with greatest determination, v. 4: I am resolved what to do, &c.

e.) It discloses, clearly, who or what can be of service to it for the accomplishment of its purpose, v. 4: That they may receive me into their houses.

f.) It does not content itself with purposes, but goes immediately to action, v. 5: So he called every one, &c.

g.) It employs the time without delay, v. 6: Sit down quickly, &c.

h.) It transacts every thing with careful consideration, v. 5—7, drawn from the questions to the creditors.

2. In particular:

a.) It employs temporal goods in well-doing, v. 9: Make to yourselves friends.

b.) It is mindful of death and the day of reckoning, v. 9: When ye fail.

c.) It has an eye to eternal bliss, v. 9: That they may receive you, &c.

III. The consequences of it:

1. It obtains the approval of the Lord and Judge of all, v. 8.

2. It renders us capable and worthy of receiving greater, truer, abiding goods, v. 10, 11, 12.

V. 1. *There was a certain rich man, who had a steward*—the relation of man to God; every thing that man has, especially in earthly goods, whether it may have come to him by inheritance, industry, or any turn of fortune, is a gift committed to him by God, not a property, with which he can do and act after the will and pleasure of his own heart; he must some time give in an account, as is implied in his dependent relationship. The person here mentioned is a steward, to whom the Lord had committed the charge of his land-goods, and who only used to possess a knowledge of husbandry,—hence at his removal from office, nothing remained for him but hard labour or begging, v. 3. As he was put into the office by his master, and consequently held it in right and justice, we might here, on this ground, conclude, that what is afterwards meant by the *unrighteous mammon* cannot be money acquired by unrighteousness.—*The same was accused unto him*,—an accusation accordant with truth: nothing is concealed from God,—*That he had wasted his goods;* in this the steward showed just as much levity, unfaithfulness, and want of conscience, as the publicans, avaricious pharisees, and the rich man in the next parable. For avarice, as well as extravagance, is nothing else than a waste of the earthly goods committed to one by God. Gnomon: "The parable does not bear respect to all stewards, who ought rather through the whole period of their stewardship, to exercise fidelity, 1 Cor. iv. 2, but to those who, through a long period of their stewardship, have behaved ill. The general course of the world is a dispersing of outward goods, inasmuch as these are brought to places not properly their own, although some unrighteous persons appear to *gather* them."

V. 2. *And he called him, and said unto him, How is it that I hear this of thee?* An intimation of the abuse of the confidence that had been placed in him, to which he had so ill responded, and in which he had showed ingratitude, and inconsiderate forgetfulness of his obligations. Gnomon: "God is represented as *hearing*, as if he did not *see;* thus the steward was left to himself." *Give an account of thy stewardship;* in this is expressed God's holy zeal against all unfaithfulness, and that the application made by men of earthly goods, is far from being a matter of indifference to him. But, in the threat—*thou mayest be no longer steward*—his righteousness shines forth, while it is intimated, that the steward must presently be removed from his place. A short respite, however, was still allowed him, which he might employ, and which is to be referred to the period of life granted to every one, always uncertain, and never long in continuance.

V. 3. *What shall I do?* The first trait that indicates his prudence; in a moment, without the least delay, he enters into consideration, how he can well secure his deliverance under so pressing a danger; he is now no longer careless and secure about his future state, but takes the matter into serious contemplation; the rich man did not so, and hence his irrevocable condemnation, v. 25, 26.—*My lord taketh away from me the stewardship*—second trait. He does not conceal from himself the greatness and nearness of the danger, sees his whole criminality, together with the just zeal and righteousness of his master, believes also the word spoken to him, that he could no longer be steward. Such faith the rich man had not, v. 29.—*I cannot dig, to beg I am ashamed*—third trait. He casts about for other means and ways of doing for himself, but throws them away as not suitable. He could not dig, for, if he had the power, his indolence would not let him give the application; he was ashamed to beg, his pride not permitting him. To understand by the digging, a seeking of salvation through desert of works, and by begging, through the grace of God—is contrary to the design of the parable, and inconsistent with its leading idea. In these traits we must think only of the prudence they serve to manifest, by much thoughtfulness and consideration.

V. 4. *That they may receive me into their houses*—fourth trait. He is inventive, and knows with the greatest determination what he desires, namely, an easy, agreeable securement of his prosperity and future support. *Houses*, (οἴκους,) properly, families. Fifth trait—seeing he manifestly discerns who can help him to his object, on whom he has to lean, namely, the debtors of his lord—this the rich man did not perceive, v. 20.

Ver. 5. *So he called every one of his lord's debtors*—sixth trait. He does not stand with mere resolutions and purposes; what he has prudently conceived, he executes without loss of time, and with determination; his eagerness is also marked by the little word, *quickly*, in v. 6; and that he rightly understood and employed his short time, constitutes the seventh trait, through which his prudence was displayed. *How much owest thou to my lord?*—Eighth trait. He knew right well, but puts the question in order that the debtor, by his answer, might be made to acknowledge the greatness of his debt, (rent,) and consequently afterwards the greatness of the part remitted to him, the greatness of the favour shown him; that he might also feel himself the more distinctly bound to a grateful requital. When he says, *owest thou to my lord*, he recognises now, that all good is a trust, not a property.

V. 6. *Take thy bill*—thy bond, thy lease, which demonstrates the strictness of this obligation, and the largeness of the sums remitted. *Write fifty*—the new act of unrighteousness flows from the earlier; the sinner will help himself by sin, and thus sinks always the deeper, for every sin becomes the seed of another, while the moral feeling always gets more hardened, conscience less tender.

V. 7. Similar conduct in regard to the other debtors. Whether this deceiver was again deceived by his accomplices in guilt, whether he actually attained his end or not, whether the deceit practised by him, and discovered by his lord, v. 8, was punished so as to disappoint him of his design, these are things we must not inquire into, as the parable is here left unfinished, like that of the unfruitful fig tree. Enough that there is here shown what was to be shown, a conduct throughout prudent, though shameful, and the consequence is here given only on one side, in regard to the praise obtained from the lord, so that this is the sole conclusion we can draw from the whole: How much must a holy prudence be commended by God, since, &c.

V. 8. *And the lord commended the unjust steward;* that the lord of the steward is here meant is manifest from the manner in which Christ distinguishes himself, *And I say unto you;* but as that lord only commended prudence, so he also only commends and exhorts to this, v. 9. The commendation which was here accorded by the lord to his steward, notwithstanding the injury thereby sustained by himself, has nothing improbable in it. He might have said something to this effect: "It is true he is a shameful cheat, but he certainly has conducted his affairs prudently, has cunningly employed the time for his own benefit, and we cannot deny him, amid all his worthlessness, the credit of having craftily done his best." One might say the same of a merchant, who, for his own profit, plays a false bankruptcy.

For the children of this world are in their generation wiser than the children of light. These are not the words of the lord of the steward, but of Christ, which are thrown out before as a general experimental truth, and from which afterwards the admonition in v. 9 is drawn, so that the connexion is to be taken only thus: As we see it to have been in this steward, so is it constantly, that the children, &c., and therefore I admonish you, &c. These words obviously point to the design of the parable, setting forth an example of prudence, and thus forming a sort of key to the right understanding of it. Gnomon: "The comparative is used, and that in a diminutive way, for the prudence of the world does not deserve to be called prudence in the positive—the force of the comparative is besides in the proposition υπερ." Luther, House-Pos. 4. 412, 413: "Christ here utters a very frightful word; it needs not profound thought, we see it daily before our eyes, more a great deal than is proper, that the world every where seeks after that, in which it espies an advantage, and in the pursuit grudges no pains or labour. How much labour, care, and danger do vagabonds undergo? They have rest neither day nor night, and they are besides in constant danger of the axe or the halter; still they have such a liking to their wicked life that they cannot grow weary of it. So also the thief, the rake, the adulterer, lead a troublesome life, and submit to hard laws, use all sorts of trick and cunning shifts and advantages, that they may carry on their villanous and profligate schemes, insomuch that they shrink from these till they have paid the devil his tribute. But, on the other hand, we see the children of light, that is, true Christians, how lazy, backward, unprofitable, and slow they are in the things of God, although they know that God looks with satisfaction on what is done therein, and that they shall reap the fruit of it in eternity. So that it goes according to the common proverb, that the wicked do more to deserve hell, by diligently and laboriously serving the devil, than the righteous heaven—and it is well spoken, if it were but rightly understood. Therefore must God draw and pull his people, as with cords, that they may do what they should. Here learn what thou shouldst do in good toward God and his word and thy salvation, and take to thyself a profitable lesson and example from such wicked persons. Think, since the builder, citizen, merchant, servant, &c. serve the devil with so much diligence, and grudge no trouble, wherefore should I not serve, in like manner, my Lord, whom I shall enjoy in eternity? They run, as if they were irrational, after what makes for their eternal hurt and perdition, and how then should I be so dull and sleepy in what concerns my soul's salvation, that God should need to draw me as with ropes?"

The children of this world—in Scripture a person is called the child of any thing, the nature and properties of which he has in himself: the children of this world, therefore, are those who possess the nature, feeling, mode of thinking and acting of the world, in so far as that is opposed to God, consequently unrighteous and sinful,—whose thoughts are all engrossed with what is earthly, visible, perishable, only love and are conversant with that, and endeavour, by all possible, even disallowed means, to obtain possession of it. *Light*, in Scripture, designates divine truth and purity, moral worth; the children of light, therefore, are those who already, in part, possess a state of mind in accordance with that, and partly also are striving and wrestling after a meetness to be partakers of the inheritance of the saints in light. *In their generation;* γενεα, according to Wahl, progenies, familia, stirps, pro socii, genus, kindred; the children of this world are toward their fellows, with whom they have to do, therefore manifestly in the business, transactions, &c., of a worldly nature, more prudent, foreseeing, and careful, show more zeal, thought, concern, than the children of light toward their spiritual kindred, (all the faithful being brethren in Christ,) in regard to those cares, labours, and employments, which concern the work of salvation; the former think far before them, calculate, work, not so the latter.

V. 9. *And I say unto you.*—I give you the following counsel and advice. Since it is the case that the children of light are not as zealous as they should be in striving for salvation, this admonition of Christ should be the more laid to heart, and especially since riches and covetousness are such formidable hinderances to salvation, so readily withdraw the eye from it, so completely entangle the heart and render it cold and indifferent towards the higher interests of its being, 1 Tim. vi. 9, 10. Grotius: "By connecting in this manner his admonition with what precedes, Christ intimates that we are not so much proprietors as dispensers of the good things we possess."

Make to yourselves friends of the mammon of un-

righteousness, or unrighteous mammon. Luther, Church-Pos. 13. 223: "Mammon is, in German, wealth, and not an improper wealth, but superabundant, beyond what nature and necessity require; if we were to take our measure from God and truth, we should find many such, but if we take our measure from men and the world, then (from the greed and avarice of the human heart) we should find but few. He, however, is properly said to have mammon, who has more than he needs, with which he ought to help others and not injure himself." Mel.: "The exhortation obviously enjoins us to use well the means with which we have it in our power to make friends, viz., Christ and the saints. Concerning the legitimate use of riches, we are often told elsewhere, and it is in substance that we should first of all apply them to our own necessities, then to support the cause of the gospel; thirdly, to the necessities of the state; lastly, to the relief of our poor brethren, and especially those of them who are members of Christ." Lavater, Considerations, 2. 184: "How many are there who call themselves children of light, yet never think of making to themselves out of what they term their property, friends to receive them into everlasting habitations! In these words there appears to me a deep thought, a sort of hint, intimating the possibility of the salvation of some, otherwise very faulty men." The mammon is called *unrighteous*, not because it has been acquired in an unrighteous manner, for this was not the case with the goods committed to the steward, and the exhortation given concerning it is not applicable to those merely who have become rich in such a manner, but is quite general. Were it indeed unrighteously acquired goods that were spoken of, it could not possibly be beneficence alone that was recommended, for the first obligation, in such a case, would be restitution, Luke xix. 8. Hence, Luther says, House-Pos. 4. 408: "Unrighteous gain must be restored, and not applied in the way of doing good to others with it, or giving alms, according to Isa. lxi. 8, which declares, that whosoever would give a burnt offering, or bestow charity, or do a service to God with money, he must do it of his own, and with what has been acquired in righteousness, or else be free. For with the wealth of others nothing must be done, but what has been unrighteously gotten must be restored." Mel.: "Isaiah testifies, that God abhors sacrifices offered from goods unjustly obtained. Christ therefore by no means intends that alms should be given of such things as have been unjustly obtained, but speaks of the riches of the saints. Even these he calls the unrighteous mammon, not because unrighteously obtained, or held without a good conscience, but because of the manifold abuses which, through human infirmity, are wont to grow out of them—for what a misapplication is there of talents, what a multitude of needless extravagances!" The opinion, that mammon is called unrighteous, because the unequal division of earthly goods is a consequence of the fall, and great riches are hence unrighteously possessed, is partly artificial, partly untrue, as the distribution of all God's gifts, even spiritual ones, is very unequal. Neither is the mammon called unrighteous, because of its being put to an improper use, as in the case of the unjust steward, for it would still be a strange thing to apply as a predicate to the mammon what properly belonged to its possessor; we must rather consider it to be called unrighteous, on account of its own nature and properties—and as αδικια (unrighteousness) according to Wahl, means also fraud, perfidy, deceit, faithlessness, unrighteous mammon is as much as faithless, unstable, insecure, what does not abide, what appears to promise to its possessor continued happiness, while yet it cannot always remain with us. The soundness of this exposition is not only confirmed by v. 11, where the opposite to the *unrighteous*, is the *true*, the *certain* good, and by v. 12, where the *unrighteous* is identified with *another's* and the opposite is *your own*, but also by the parable itself; for the steward disposed of the goods of his lord as if they were his own, while still they were not,—held the stewardship as if he were always to hold it, though soon to be displaced. Now, as mammon of itself cannot make blessed, as both the covetous man and the spendthrift cheat themselves with delusive imaginations, presently to be exemplified in the case of the rich man, the Saviour therefore gives to the possessors of it the admonition, so to use it that it may be the means of bringing him to the enjoyment of a true and abiding happiness, since that must soon be taken away; and it is so used when by acts of beneficence we make friends to ourselves.

When ye fail,—properly, *die*, for εκλειπω, according to Wahl, means precisely morior, lit.: I leave, namely, life. Death is for the temporal life and its cares, obligations, and labours, the same that the dismissal from office was to the steward, a termination of the calling hitherto maintained. Others have supplied mammon to the leaving, and Luther has with that view adopted the sense of *deprived*, but the comparison is not then so pointed.

They may receive you into everlasting habitations, with reference to v. 4, to which it stands in opposition. Gn.: "Σκηνας, so called, on account of the security, pleasantness, and convenience of the mode of life pursued in tents. *Their* is not added here, as in v. 4, because the tents or mansions are God's." Luther, House-Pos. 4. 409: "We shall find friends there for the good deeds we have done, the kindness and beneficence we have shown to the poor, these shall not only be witnesses of our brotherly and Christian behaviour, but shall also be commended and recompensed. Then one shall come and say, Lord, here is a person who gave me a coat, a little money, a piece of bread, a cup of water in the time of need. Yea, as Christ tells us, Matth. xxv., he himself shall come forth and testify before his heavenly Father, angels and saints, what we have done for him, and how we have thereby approved our faith. Those friends will stand up for us and help us into heaven." That all salvation comes from Christ, does not hinder that men should there, as well as here, be instruments, through whom he makes his grace to flow to us, and it is not therefore to be considered contrary to the analogy of scripture and this life, that those who have been benefited by us on earth, should in eternity be the instruments and agents of our well-being: this is also countenanced by v. 24. Lavater, Considerations, 2. 183: "The supported poor man, who makes a good use of the kindness shown him, has some power also of recompensing in the future world. He can make friends for the friend-makers, and receive into his everlasting habitations those who received him into their earthly houses." Mel.: "A promise is added to the precept concerning alms as elsewhere: Give, and it shall be given to you. Here two questions arise, shall the saints receive? And shall we be received on account of our good deeds? The answer is very easy to the righteous. There are two synecdoches. The saints receive, that is, Christ and the church; Christ as the Saviour and giver of salvation,—the church as a witness, celebrating the gift bestowed through this deliverer, and giving thanks to a remunerating God. And for the second synecdoche, whether we receive on account of our own works, the answer is short; for in all discourses concerning good works, it is necessary to suppose a faith going before and believing, that the obedience to be rendered shall be accepted through a Mediator according to the Word: Through him we have access to God." However, as Luther remarks, it is not works which gain heaven for us, but Christ freely grants eternal life to those who believe and give evidence of their faith in works of love, and the right employment of their earthly goods. This the rich man did not do, therefore he wanted faith, and hence the whole parable, v. 19—31, is directed against unbelief as a warning in regard to its fearful consequences.

V. 10—12. Luther, House-Pos. 4. 425: "This is merely a proverbial saying, taken from the economical management of domestic and worldly concerns. Our Lord applies it to what is spiritual, to rebuke the pharisees, who were covetous, and means by it: Whosoever is not faithful in temporal goods, but seeks his own honour and advantage, he will never be faithful in spiritual goods, as in preaching and handling gospel privileges." *Faithful*, Gnomon: "The Lord now commends, not prudence, but *fidelity*, for fidelity begets and directs prudence." Duvernoy, Extracts from Zinzendorf's Discourses, vol. 5, p. 48: "There is much more art in being faithful in small, than in great things, because the small are not so easily preserved as the great, because the small are much more numerous than the great—because in great concerns, pride, self-love, a regard to character, can go much farther in making one faithful and diligent. Small things, on the other hand, are not seen or noticed, are very easily overlooked, and if attended to with care and diligence, these are seldom recognised. So that it certainly requires more principle to be faithful in small things than in great,—requires a heart more deeply grounded in what is good, in order to take pains about things which might be more slightly passed by, and deal with them as matters of importance. But to draw the conclusion: Whosoever is faithful in great, would also be faithful in small things, would not hold, for many things might conspire to produce fidelity in what is great, which might not be found in what is small. To be faithful in the chamber, will argue more than to be faithful on the theatre of the world; to be faithful to the Saviour in a cellar, is more than to be so on a balcony before the eye of the world. The reason why it is more difficult to be faithful in small things than in great, is, that the great have more advantages and opportunities for leading one to be so than the small." Mel.: "A useful rule is added. The saying may be understood either way, of debt or of reward. It is due, that whatever may be our vocation, whether great or small, we should regard it as a divine appointment, and exercise ourselves in it with fear and diligence. David, in his calling as a soldier, recognised it as a divine appointment, and for the sake of God rightly discharged it, much more therefore did he afterwards regard his royal calling as held of God. But, secondly, the saying: To him that hath shall it be given, and from him that hath not, shall be taken away even that which he hath, may also be understood of rewards. He who uses well the gifts of God, deserves to have these increased, as Augustine says: *Dilectio meretur incrementum dilectionis*, that is, if it be rightly used." Grotius: "Masters are wont to scrutinize the fidelity of their servants in matters of small moment, and thus to form their opinion in regard to larger ones."

V. 11. *The true*, Gnomon: "Jesus speaks from a heavenly point of view."

V. 12. "Mammon, (says Luther,) is called, by our Lord, not unrighteous merely, but also a strange thing, (another man's,) intimating that it is a temporal good, and not always abiding, like that which is spiritual. Eternal life is ours, that is, the Christian's good, the true good, which remains eternally ours." It is appointed to us by God for an everlasting possession and property, but only can be attained by those who exercise, during their time of trial and preparation, the necessary prudence and fidelity in smaller, in temporal things, and manifest, thereby, their capacity and fitness to receive, of undeserved grace, the heavenly, the true, and perpetually abiding riches. Verse 10th contains a general truth; v. 11, 12, the application of that truth to the relation of time and eternity, with respect to the use of earthly goods. Hence these three verses draw the very natural conclusion, from the smaller to the greater; and intimate, at the same time, the mournful consequences of an imprudent use of earthly goods to purposes of avarice or extravagance, which shall only be felt in eternity, as is strikingly exemplified in the case of the rich man, who found himself, at once, bereft of all temporal and eternal good. Calvin: "Though the unrighteous should gorge themselves with the riches of the world, they still can call nothing *their own,* because they take what they have by a sort of theft, and possess it under the curse of God. But it is a great consolation to the pious, that, by living moderately, they take nothing which is *another's;* and they receive, from the hand of their heavenly Father, a due allowance, until they reach the possession of their inheritance, while all the creatures minister to their glory. For to this end shall the heaven and earth be renewed, that they may contribute, according to their measure, to the lustre of the divine kingdom."

V. 13. In case, now, a heart, given either to greed or extravagance, should think, that possibly it might reconcile the criminal employment of temporal riches with the attainment of eternal life and the true honouring of God, our Lord anticipates this vain refuge, and declares the impossibility of uniting the service of God and mammon, because the heart can only, in earnest, attach itself to one,—it ever has but one God; and the delusion of being able to love both God and mammon, to belong to both at the same time, while it is combated in v. 13, is also exposed in the following parable; for the outwardly righteous and legal pharisees, (supposed servants of God,) but inwardly given to the lusts of the world, (actually servants of mammon,) who are there depicted, must have seen, in the fate of the rich man, whom they resembled, how irreconcilable the love of the world is with the true fear of God; so that here again the connexion between the two parables, and the relation of one to the other, forces itself upon us.

XXXIII.

THE RICH MAN AND LAZARUS.

Luke xvi. 16—31.

We have already spoken of the connexion between this parable and that of the unjust steward. Many expositors have thought they discovered, in this story, a real history, and referred it to the family of Annas and his son-in-law, Caiaphas, whose sadducean unbelief, in regard to a future state, and Epicurean mode of life, are here delineated and reproved; but by far the greater number regard it merely as a parable, and with more judgment. Gnomon: "This parable, (for it is a parable, although it may have been grounded on a history,) exposes not only an abuse of earthly goods, through avarice and pride, but also a supercilious contempt of the law and the prophets. The rich man is an example of the pharisees; Lazarus, of those who are poor in spirit; the state of each is disclosed, both in this life and in that which is to come." Calvin: "It is not to be doubted that, by this example, Christ confirms his last discourse. For he shows what sort of fate awaits those who, neglecting the care of the poor, abandon themselves to fleshly pleasure." Grotius: "Here Christ returns to the argument, with which he began, concerning the use of riches, and shows that the law of Moses was plainly violated, in this respect, by many adherents of pharisaism, as if he had said; There is no need that the law of my new kingdom condemn you, since the law of Moses is amply sufficient for your condemnation." Luther, House-Pos. 4, 186: "Here it is not necessary to dispute whether there is a real history or only a parable, for, since Christ names the two persons, and says what sort of life they both lived, and what befell them after death, we must believe that such was actually the case; and further believe, that the same portions shall be appointed to all who, on earth, resemble the rich man and Lazarus." That the main object of the parable is the chastisement of unbelief, Luther, in another place, has expressly declared: "Our Lord, in this passage, holds up before us an example of faith and of unbelief, or a godless condition, that we might be scared from a course of life which is contrary to faith and love, and apply ourselves to these with the more diligence. For here we see the judgment of God upon the believing and unbelieving, how frightful it is in the one case and how consolatory in the other." It is perfectly consistent with this view of the parable to say, as Luther does elsewhere, that "Christ spake this parable especially against the pharisees, who were covetous, and has here rebuked their covetousness." For their covetousness was the fruit of their unbelief on God's word, as the want of love here represented, v. 19, 20, sprung from the same evil root. And Luther is quite right, also, when he says, further, that "our Lord presents to us this example of the rich man, that he might drive us from being careful only about temporal things, and might lead us to be concerned for what is eternal; but that we might so conduct ourselves, in regard to the present and temporal, as not to bring ourselves into eternal condemnation." For all anxiety about eternal things springs from faith, and all indifference from unbelief.

Vitringa gives a quite inadmissible interpretation of the several parts of the parable, when he says: The rich man represents the rulers of the Jews; Lazarus, the Lord Jesus, who had not where to lay his head, and is called Lazarus, because God helped him; his lying before the gate of the rich man, denotes the rejection of Christ by the Jews;—full of sores, the reproaches of the Jews, or also the sins of men, which he bore;—his desiring the crumbs to satisfy himself, his satisfaction with his state on earth, or his fellowship with the despised;—the licking of the dogs, the conversion of the heathen;—the bearing into Abraham's bosom, Christ's ascension into heaven;—the death of the rich man, the overthrow of the Jewish state;—the entreaty to send Lazarus, the desire after a Messias;—the five brethren, the Babylonian Jews.

TRAIN OF THOUGHT IN THE PARABLE.

Of unbelief.

I. The manifestations of unbelief in this life are:—

A. Insatiable thirst for enjoyment, v. 19.

a.) Unbelief seeks all sorts of enjoyment; *clothes* itself with purple, *lives* sumptuously.

b.) It seeks in these perfect satisfaction; *all day*, &c.

c.) It regards the temporal as its only and highest good.

B. Cold-hearted uncharitableness, v. 20, 21.

a.) Unbelief despises the poor as worthless, v. 20.

b.) It hardens itself against the daily sight of others' misery, v. 20; Lay before his gate, full of sores.

c.) It extends no relief, v. 21: The dogs came, &c.

II. The fate of unbelief in the life to come.

A. It is fearfully undeceived, v. 22, 23.

a.) In regard to the worth of earthly goods and enjoyments, v. 23: In hell he lifted up his eyes, being in torments;

b.) In regard to the salvation, once hoped for, the true nature of which he now, for the first time, though still imperfectly, apprehends: Saw Abraham afar off.

c.) In regard to the relations respectively held by him and Lazarus, toward God: Lazarus in Abraham's bosom;

B. It continues, in its sinful state of mind, v. 24:

a.) As to its fleshly confidence upon the descent from Abraham: Father Abraham.

b.) As to its imaginary pretensions to salvation: Have mercy on me;

c.) As to its unholy lusts, which only torment it the more from the want of all means of satisfying them: That he may dip the tip of his finger, &c.

C. It is self-condemned, by an evil conscience, v. 25—31.

a.) As being dealt with after the strictest justice, v. 25;

b.) As being incapable of deliverance, on account of its state of mind, v. 26.

c.) As being without all excuse,

1. Because there had been no want to it of the means of grace, v. 27—29.

2. Because these means of grace were quite sufficient for the attainment of salvation, v. 30, 31.

V. 19. *There was a certain rich man, &c.* Luther, Church-Pos. 13. 2: "We must not conceive of the rich man according to his outward walk; the gospel does not describe him as an adulterer, a robber, a murderer, a criminal, or as having done any thing which the world or reason might condemn, so that he must have led externally a holy life, and, according both to his own and his neighbours' thoughts, kept the whole law like him in Luke xviii. 12. We must look into his heart, and view his spirit, and there we shall discover a heart and a tree of unbelief. For he is not punished because he had such rich apparel and sumptuous food, since many holy persons, kings and queens, had before him used these, such as Solomon, Esther, David, &c. but because his heart was bent on those things, sought after them, clave to them, and chose to have all its joy, pleasure, delight, and its very God, as it were, in them. This Christ intimates by the word *every-day;* for it is thereby manifested, that he pursued such a life with eagerness, was not constrained to adopt it from his official standing, or for doing service to his neighbours, but his object therein was merely to satiate his own lust, and he lived to himself and for himself. In this, as a bad fruit, we can trace the secret sin of his heart, unbelief."

Purple and fine linen.—Expressive of his love of pomp and effeminate luxury, which clothes itself in the softest and most delicate apparel. Grotius: "The rich man here is not accused of rapine, nor that he needlessly hoarded up his wealth, but that he pampered himself with delights, while others were consumed with want, and he is charged with the violation of an ancient, not of a new, and that a more perfect law. How then shall the great part of Christians escape the punishment inflicted upon this rich man?"

V. 20, 21. Luther, Church-Pos. 13. 4: "Here now appears the other sin, that he neglected the love he owed to his neighbour. For faith has the art of looking to God for all good, and perceives him to be so good and gracious. And whosoever feels God's goodness, he feels also his neighbour's necessities; whosoever does not feel God's goodness, neither does he feel his neighbour's necessities. Therefore we see in this example of the rich man, that it is impossible to love where there is no faith, and impossible to believe where there is no love, for they will and must be in each other."—*Named Lazarus*, Gnomon: "Lazarus by his own name known in heaven; the rich man not distinguished by any name, v. 25: he had only a genealogy in this world, v. 27. Even in a parable admission may be given to a proper name, Ezek. xxiii. 4. It is possible, however, that a person of the name of Lazarus may have existed at that time in Jerusalem, and Theophylact mentions a tradition of the Hebrews to that effect."

Before his gate, Gnomon: "The antithesis to v. 22, *bosom.*" Grotius: "In sight of the rich man, that he might not have ignorance to plead." Luther, Church-Pos. 3. 6: "We must not look at poor Lazarus in his outward condition, with his sores, poverty, and wretchedness; we must look into his heart, and seek the treasures which his sores have made so precious, which is undoubtedly his faith and love, for without faith no one can please God, Heb. xi. 6. He must, therefore, have been in such a state of mind, that in the midst of his poverty and wretchedness he viewed all good as in God, and found consolation in the gifts and graces which he had been permitted so richly to enjoy, and had such delight therein, indeed, that he could heartily have suffered still more, if the will of his gracious God had so ordered. Here then is a really living faith, which has softened his heart through the knowledge of divine grace, so that nothing is too much for him to suffer and to do. Such a state of mind is produced by faith, when it apprehends the grace of God. But that Lazarus had such thoughts (he says again, House-Pos. 4. 189,) and experienced such consolation in his sufferings his name first of all testifies. For Lazarus is the Hebrew name Eleazer, and means as much as God helps, intimating that he had placed all his confidence upon the eternal sufficiency of God, not upon men. The same thing is afterwards signified in his being said to be in Abraham's bosom: which simply means, that Lazarus had placed his confidence upon the promise which was made to Abraham, that in his seed all the families of the earth should be blessed. By such a promise could Lazarus support and console himself, although the whole world might hold him for an outcast, because so poor and miserable, assured that he should be of the blessed seed of God, and should not come into condemnation, but be for ever a subject of grace. And such faith it was which sustained him." From faith springs hope, patience, devotedness, and resignation. What a contrast between the condition of the rich man and Lazarus! There every thing which seems worthy of desire, here a fulness only of poverty and wretchedness. Mel.: "Law and reason judge from the event; this man is wretched, therefore he is neglected. Thus always does human reason judge, while it remains in its native darkness. But the gospel teaches, that distresses are not signs of the wrath of God, nay, that we are afflicted for the purpose of being brought to God, and that the righteous under affliction are under the special care of God. Thus, from the beginning of the world, the saints have suffered affliction, Abel, prophets, Christ, apostles. Therefore, whenever we are in affliction, let us learn that we are consoled by this doctrine of the gospel, and stir ourselves up to prayer; this is the warfare of the saints, to stand in such faith and wait for help."

V. 21. *And desiring to be fed with the crumbs*, &c. Grotius: "Two things are here intimated, both the inhumanity of the rich man, who, from a store so rich, from a table so well replenished with dainties, could spare nothing in mercy to Lazarus; and the great patience of the latter, whose highest wish was to receive only what was given to the dogs." The greatness of Lazarus's misery is marked by his poverty and sickness, a poverty so deep, that he earnestly desired to be fed with the offals of the rich man's table, which were cast to the dogs. The following expression: *Moreover, the dogs came and licked his sores*, connected with the preceding by αλλα και, obviously contains an elliptical contrast to something understood. Scholten supplies this in the following manner: ου' μονον ʻοι κυνες ειασαν, vel μη διεκωλυον, scil. αυτον χορτασθηναι, αλλα και ερχομενοι, &c.) As it is manifestly the aim of the whole representation, v. 19—21, to exhibit in the strongest manner the want of compassion on the part of the rich man by the contrast between his prosperity and the wretchedness of Lazarus, the sentence beginning with αλλα και must also do this by way of an addition, implying a comparison between the behaviour of the dogs and the conduct of the rich man; and the defective sentiment might perhaps be supplied thus: Lazarus desired to be fed with the crumbs, &c., (but although the rich man was so devoid of compassion as not to be at all concerned for the poor man who lay at his gate) the dogs came, &c. Irrational creatures put to shame the rich man, while they alleviated the pains of Lazarus by licking his sores,—they were more compassionate than he, and, as Luther says, deserved better at the hands of Lazarus. The foregoing construction is favoured by the circumstance, that many codices have, after *fell from the rich man's table—and no man gave to him.* Some expositors, however, are of opinion, that by the licking of the dogs can only be intimated the nakedness of Lazarus, his weakness, as not able to defend himself from the dogs, and consequently a deeper aggravation of his wretchedness; but apart from the circumstance, that such licking was in point of fact an alleviation of the pain, there would, according to this view, only be a representation of the necessitous case of Lazarus by itself, which, however, is only designed as the means of bringing out the heartlessness of the rich man, who neither satisfied the hungry, nor soothed the distressed. And though we grant what Olshausen says, that in scripture dogs appear always with a bad character, and are never taken as symbols of fidelity and compassion, we are not thereby necessitated to think that lust and rapacity are here meant, but rather compassion, as the natural character of the dogs, coupled with what they did, serves but to bring out more strikingly the cold-hearted indifference of the rich man. Calvin: "The rich man had already been convicted of huge barbarity, since so miserable a spectacle could not move him to compassion; but now this mass of wicked and more than beastly ferocity was not able to learn mercy even from dogs. What more prodigious, than that a man should be cared for by dogs, and neglected by his immediate neighbour? Nay, that not even a crumb of bread should be given by a servant, to him whom the dogs attempted to soothe with their tongues?" Brower: "We behold a poor mendicant, covered with sores, whom dogs presently approach, lick his sores, and afford some solace and refreshment to a man abandoned by his fellow-men; so that brute animals surpass such men in humanity."

V. 22. This verse forms merely the transition to the other part of the parable, and connects both parts with a noble greatness and simplicity. *By the angels*, see Heb. i. 14. Ps. ciii. 20. Calvin: "It is not in vain that Christ assigns this office to the angels, whom we know to be given as ministers to the faithful, to aid and co-operate with them in the matter of their salvation." Grotius: "Lo, a sudden change. He who lately was the sport, not only of man but of dogs is presently honoured by the ministry of angels." Luther, House-Pos. 4. 207: "The rich man also dies, and is buried, doubtless with the greatest pomp, but other angels wait on *him* and bear him into hell. There every thing is reversed. The poor Lazarus, in the judgment of the pharisees, is condemned and accursed, and according to them also, the rich man inherits the blessing of God. We must judge, however, not as the pharisees did, but as it is written here. But we must be careful to distinguish rightly, and say not that the poor man attains to heaven because he is poor, and the rich man goes to hell because he is rich, but that the one did well in his poverty, and acted rightly in regard to it, while the other did quite otherwise in regard to his riches. Poverty in itself is not good, but evil; it saves no one, neither does wealth condemn any one." Grotius: "The *also* here is significant; as if it had been said, riches avail nothing against death. Nor was it improperly taken notice of by the fathers, that the goodness of God is marked in the circumstance of Lazarus dying first, and the rich man afterward; the one being removed from the trials of life, the other permitted long time to repent."

Abraham's bosom.—Luther understands this of the word of God, on which the fathers all believed, and through which they attained to salvation. But to go to Abraham's bosom is a figurative expression, which, like that used in Matth. viii. 11, denotes nearness to that holy patriarch, the highly-honoured friend of God, and this local nearness is again the image of participation in Abraham's blessedness, intimating that it was well with Lazarus in eternity, and that he was treated as a true descendant of Abraham, Rom. ii. 28, 29. Gnomon: "As a genuine son, he becomes the fellow heir and companion of Abraham reclining in the heavenly kingdom. It is a concise mode of speech, for bosom presupposes a feast; a feast, the kingdom of heaven. Lazarus is admitted to the kingdom of heaven, nay, to the feast, nay, into the bosom of Abraham. So that Lazarus is in closer fellowship with Abraham, and is hence said to be εν τοις κολποις αυτου the plural." Mel.: "The bosom of Abraham is the rest of the pious, who, from the promise made to Abraham, have attained to faith, comfort, and eternal life. This promise is more fully opened up in the gospel, for there it is expressly said, that every one who believes upon the Son has everlasting life. But as now we should sustain ourselves when departing by faith on this promise given us in Christ, and through such faith enter into life eternal; so then the saints of God sustained themselves on that word to Abraham, and leaning thereon in faith, they entered into life eternal. Therefore the bliss of heaven is called the bosom of Abraham, because it is the blessing promised to Abraham, on account of the seed, that is, Christ." Grotius: "Here the highest honour is ascribed to Lazarus, as having a place next to Abraham in that happy region, whom he resembled in his exalted faith and constancy in enduring trials."

V. 23. *And in hell he lifted up his eyes, being in torments.* Grotius: "As persons in prison are wont to be tormented before they receive condemnation; so disembodied spirits (laden with sin) cannot but be afflicted with severest agony, forewarned by conscience of their coming doom." Luther, Church-Pos. xiii. 11: "Hell here cannot mean hell, properly so called, which is to begin at the last day. For the rich man's body was certainly not in hell, but buried in the grave. It must, however, be a place where the soul can be, and finds no rest; there can be nothing corporeal about it; and we must therefore understand by this hell an evil conscience, which is without faith and the word of God, and with which the unbelieving are racked even till the day of judgment." The word rendered hell, is properly hades, the region of the dead; and

Bauer remarks here, according to the Jewish doctrine, paradise is removed from hell only by a hand-breadth, so that one could see from the one place to the other, though between them there was still a deep gulf.

In regard to the conversation between the rich man and Lazarus, Luther: Church-Pos. 13. 11, makes the following remarks: "There could, indeed, be no bodily speech, since the bodies of each were lying in the grave, therefore there could just as little be a corporeal tongue, which the rich man felt to be scorching in the fire, as there could be a corporeal finger or water, which he sought from Lazarus. So that all must be understood of the conscience after this manner. When conscience is awakened at death, or beyond death, what is here said is true of its unbelief, and it then for the first time sees the bosom of Abraham. Then such thoughts arise in the conscience as would have expressed themselves in the manner the rich man did to Abraham, could they have spoken, and cause help to be sought from the word of God, and all who have believed therein, with so much eagerness, that the smallest consolation would be taken from the smallest things, and still it cannot be found." Again, in his Sermons: "No, it is not corporeal, all is transacted in the conscience, as he perceives that he has acted against the gospel. Nothing was actually spoken by him, but only internally felt. He knows in his conscience that he must be for ever there, (v. 26,) and therefore he has no rest. He seeks help at all hands, in heaven and in hell, but there is no help for him, no more than there was with the foolish virgins. He thinks: gracious God! had I but believed, or were there but a believer who could communicate his faith to me! And this thought which I have attributed to him, was simply present to his conscience." Gray: "This circumstance—the conversation between Abraham and Lazarus—is evidently fictitious, contrived merely to enforce and illustrate the moral of the parable. It is similar to that between

God and Satan in the book of Job, and to be viewed in the same light, as contrived to convey the intended instruction, through the help of the imagination, in a more lively and forcible manner." It is, therefore, the most probable way, not to regard that as a real conversation, but only a form for embodying certain thoughts, and feelings, which were most painful to the unbelieving and cold-hearted rich man after death; so that the utterance merely serves to remove the covering, and present the truth in the liveliest manner. Calvin: "Souls are not possessed of eyes and fingers, neither can they be affected by thirst, or hold conferences one with another; but the Lord here delineates a picture, which represents to us the state after death in a manner suited to our senses. The meaning is: The wicked are dreadfully tormented by a sense of their own misery, catch at some consolation, but with disappointed hope suffer double anguish; the more oppressed with pain also, that they are constrained to remember their past crimes, and to compare the present bliss of the faithful with their own miserable and lost condition."

Lifted up his eyes—like a man awake from a dream and a state of unconsciousness, and again restored to sound thought; it displays the fearful delusion of the rich man in regard to the continuance, worth, and sufficiency of temporal goods, which could neither guaranty nor bestow the possession of happiness in eternity, as he had supposed. Grotius: "As corporeal acts are customarily ascribed to God, so are they by a like figure ascribed to disembodied spirits."—*Saw Abraham afar off*,—this intimates that he had now obtained an idea, though still a very dark one, of the happiness which was enjoyed by Abraham in the world of spirits. Grotius: "Abraham is here mentioned as the chief of the blessed; then as the person in whom they were accustomed to glory as the head of the family. But how different from this man was Abraham, who so kindly entertained strangers!"—*And*

Lazarus in his bosom,—this points to another delusion of the rich man, who had formerly considered Lazarus as an outcast from God, and could not now see him so highly honoured without envy and astonishment. Luther, House-Pos. 4. 213: "We may therefore hold this to be the occasion of bitterest grief, that the rich, and others who suffer condemnation, must see heaven occupied by the poor, whom they treated with contempt on earth, as is also written in the Book of Wisdom, chap. v."

V. 24. It is signified by the figurative expressions of this verse, that the rich man's perversity of heart continued also in eternity, and that death brings not the smallest moral change upon man; they contain partly a prayer for mercy, partly a description of his condition.—*He cried, and said, Father Abraham;* his pride, on account of his fleshly descent from Abraham, and his Judaism, had gone with him; he thinks of laying claim to salvation as a right wholly standing in himself, and is quite blinded in regard to his unfilial state of heart, Matth. iii. 8. Rom. ix. 6, 7, though he recognises Abraham as his father. In such a state of mind his condition must be doubly painful to him, Matth. vii. 22, &c. *Send.* Gnomon: "This voluptuary still treats Lazarus as of little account, as afterwards Moses, v. 30." Grotius: "From this it appears probable, that those are always present to the thoughts of the wicked, whom they remember to have been ill treated by them."—*Cool my tongue,* &c.—marking the continuance of his lusts and desires, which were now without any means of satisfaction, and consequently increased his torment; the thirst bespeaks a longing desire after an absent good; the suffering of pain a present feeling of distress; the flame is an image of the highest degree of pain; he begs, not for entire deliverance, but only for alleviation; he sues for mercy, who himself had been so unmerciful. Grotius: "He compares the torture of conscience to a burning flame; and suitably to this the other things are feigned, for they who are burned feel thirst especially in their tongue; thirst is relieved by water; the least portion of water is what adheres to the finger. The meaning is, that the rich man who had formerly despised Lazarus, would now willingly supplicate him, if only he could obtain the slightest alleviation of such tortures."

V. 25, 26. Abraham's answer is the reply of an accusing conscience, which was once disregarded in its admonitions and warnings, but must now be heard in its condemnatory judgment. The first part of the answer in v. 25, points to the righteousness of God,—that he was dealt with just as he deserved, in accordance with his earlier state and conduct. Olshausen: "The *jus talionis*, which serves as a basis to the whole of the Old Testament, is that through which Abraham convinces the rich man of the righteousness of his sufferings; so that Moses, upon whom the pharisees hoped, appears as their accuser, John v. 45—47." It is from his connexion with Moses' writings, that the accusing conscience of the rich man, who is painted as a pharisee, draws his self-condemnation. The other part of the answer in v. 26, refers to the impossibility of his now, when it was too late, obtaining help, Matth xxv. 11, 12.

Son, remember,—an affectionate address; without figure: To me also, as a descendant of Abraham, was salvation granted, and God's goodness besides afforded me so many benefits for my earthly life. Upon the propriety, beauty and truth of this form of address, Brouwer makes the following remarks: "The reply is void of every thing like harshness, cruelty, or wrong; the patriarch softly addresses a wretched man. Nor is there any thing more envious or hurtful to human f. eling, than when those, who are rejoicing in the highest felicity, treat with scorn and contumely the miserable, though they may have become so through their own misconduct, and thus embitter their sorrows. In all the discourses of our Lord, there is manifest that regard for what is honourable and becoming, which cannot but make the perusal and reperusal of them pleasant." Luther, House-Pos. 4. 212: "*Thou in thy lifetime receivedst thy good things,* now thou must suffer for it pain and torment; and, as thou wouldst have it so, no injury is therefore done to thee. Thou wouldst have thy heavenly kingdom upon earth; gold and treasure were thy salvation, rich apparel and fine living were thy paradise," Gal. vi. 8. Jas. ii. 13. Of Lazarus it is not said, that he had received his evil things, as if in these he had met with the just punishment of his transgressions, but simply that they were the appointments of heaven. Calvin: "*Thy* is emphatical; as if Abraham had said: Though thou wast created for immortality, and the law of God again sought to raise thee to the meditation of a divine life, yet, forgetful of so noble a calling, thou hast preferred being like a sow or a dog; therefore thou receivest the just reward of such brutal pleasures." So also Grotius: "*Thy* good things—those, namely, which thou didst reckon truly, nay mainly good, which thou didst use, not as intrusted to thee after a certain law and manner, but as properly thine own, in which, in short, thou didst place thy confidence."

But now he is comforted, &c.—All is, therefore, done in righteousness, I desired only an earthly good, and despised the heavenly, hence this is now denied me. Grotius: "That expression, *but now*, intimates the strongest resolution. It happens indeed very often, that those who fare best in this life, fare worst in the next. On the other hand, those who have been oppressed here with all sorts of evil, enjoy there the highest felicity." Lavater, Considerations 2. 189: "Thou hast already had enjoyment, and in the midst of thy fulness didst not care for human misery—now therefore the eternal order of things brings it to pass, that waste is succeeded by indigence, misery by bliss."

And besides all this, &c.—Luther, House-Pos. 4.

213: "If we would befriend thee, and go and cool thy tongue, yet we cannot. We act not according to our own will, but God's; what he wills, that we also will; we have no power to do what you ask. When Lazarus and thou wast together, were in a sense neighbours, he lay before thy gate, one could have helped another, thou hadst no gulf to pass over." And again! "These are the thoughts of despair, when conscience feels that the word of God is for ever withdrawn from him, and can never help him."—*They that would*, Grotius: "They that would, that is, if they would." Lavater, as above: "Now thou must miserably bear thy fate! No deliverance or alleviation is to be thought of now, no refreshing or consolatory visit of Lazarus to thee. Upon earth every thing is mixed—in eternity there shall be a complete separation. Here the good must be conversant both with good and evil; but in the world of spirits the good are associated with the good, while the evil shall have the irreversible fate of being united only to the evil. Now every one is preparing himself for his destiny, hereafter he shall find it. The nature of things and the eternal laws of the Creator change not," Gal. vi. 7—9.

Ver. 27—31. After the rich man had in v. 25, 26, given utterance to his own condemnation, there is represented from v. 27, the attempt of his wicked heart to justify itself. He first of all, v. 27, 28, tries it on the ground, that he had not been sufficiently warned or made aware of the mournful consequences of a life given to worldly lusts—the refutation of which is found in v. 29. Then he seeks to excuse himself by falling foul of the ordinary and regular means of grace, as if they were neither sufficient nor powerful enough for salvation, and asks for extraordinary methods, v. 30,—the exposure of this refuge is given in v. 31. Olshausen: "But the parable does not conclude with this (v. 25, 26.) The rich man, giving himself up to his fate, appeals from justice to grace, and begs that

Lazarus might be sent to his brethren, and warn them, but they also are left by Abraham to Moses and the prophets. It is certainly matter of wonder, that what Abraham here put away from him, has been fulfilled by God in Christ, so that in this parable we have at once a representation of the nature of the law, and an intimation that something higher than that was possible."

Ver. 27. *That thou wouldest send him*, Grotius: "Send him, namely, restored to his body, lest any one should imagine reference were here made to spiritual apparitions. That it is, as we have said, appears from the expression farther on: though one should rise from the dead."

Ver. 28. Luther, House-Pos. 4. 215: "This is, however, a pious reprobate, who would fain that others do not come into condemnation and torment. But it is not written because the damned actually feel so, but for a warning to others." As the whole is only a colloquy of the lost man with himself, we must neither say, that he begged this out of regard for his brother's well being, nor affirm that he did it out of self-love, that his agonies might be increased by the reproaches of those who had been misled by him. The five brethren stand for persons of the same temper and mode of life with himself; the prayer for them is only a cover for the thought: I was not sufficiently warned.

That he may testify to them, διαμυρτυρομαι, Wahl: "I testify and affirm, by God and the faith of men; when used of exhortation: I seriously admonish;"—it denotes, not the first communication or report of a thing, but rather its confirmation by an irrefragable testimony.—*Lest they also come into this place of torment;* it might therefore have been possible, through faith upon earth, to have been kept from condemnation; but this faith is the free act of the mind; the rich man had not used his opportunities so as to attain to faith, and would shove the guilt off himself upon the evidences.

V. 29. He must still further say to himself, that in Moses and the prophets a testimony had been given to him, which he himself recognised for divine, and which was sufficient for faith to rest upon—but which, though well enough known to him, he had failed to receive in true faith, Acts xiii. 15; xv. 21. Calvin: "Christ tells us, that when a certain rule of life is prescribed to us, it is not at all to be expected that the dead should rise up to teach and admonish us. For Moses and the prophets, while they lived, were such proficient teachers to the men of their own age, that from their writings the same benefit may be derived to posterity. And since God wishes us in this manner to be furnished for a godly life, there is no reason why the dead should be sent as witnesses to testify of the punishments or rewards of a future state; nor will any excuse be found for the indolence of those who take up with this pretext, that they know not what is to happen hereafter, Deut. xxx. 12. If we would handle sacred history in a pure and pious manner, let us remember that it must be so handled as that we shall derive from it the fruit of sound instruction. And its design indeed is partly to direct our life, partly to confirm our faith, partly to excite us to the fear of God."—Luther, House-Pos. 4. 195: "Here, indeed, the office of preaching is lauded, and people are truly admonished to attend on it, since there is no other way through which they can provide against the frightful danger of eternal condemnation. But Moses and the prophets preach chiefly these two articles. The first is, that they point to the seed of the woman as the great object of faith—so that according to them, faith in Christ Jesus is the only and the true way whereby sin and death can be escaped and salvation attained. The other is, that we must also be obedient to God, and in this present life do and cleave to that which he commands us, shun and forsake that which he forbids us, for this is to fear God and keep him before us." Gnomon: "The scope of this passage is to commend scripture, which the pharisees despised. Moses and the prophets are here considered, especially as testifying concerning Christ, v. 16, whom they mocked, v. 14." Grotius: "They have Moses, whose words are still extant, plainly commanding help to be given to the needy; and the prophets, as Isaiah, who told the Jews boasting of their fasts, that the best fast was to feed the hungry, to bring the outcast into the house, to clothe the naked, chap. lviii. 7."

Let them hear them. Gnomon: "This is said severely, no one is compelled; men are saved by faithful hearing, not by apparitions. Herod, unwilling to hear the word, sees no miracle. Very little is openly and plainly said in the New Testament concerning the states after death, which ought at least to suffice for repentance."

V. 30. Luther, House-Pos. 4. 215: "They are now, he means to say, accustomed to Moses and the prophets, so that these will not do; but this would be a great and uncommon thing, and would command regard, if one from the dead should appear to them, and testify of my anguish in these flames." Without a figure: he demands extraordinary means, as if the ordinary ones were not sufficient.

V. 31. Luther, House-Pos. 4. 216: "He whom God's word cannot of itself move, will not be moved by any one, whether it were a dead man from hell, or an angel from heaven. For it is not the person who brings a man to believe right, but the word of God must bring him thus far, at least that he shall know it for certain to be the word of God, who is the greatest person." Lavater, Considerations, 2. p. 192: "Whose bones and marrow do not tremble at this discourse of the most merciful and compassionate of teachers? One can hardly believe, that he, who had just so lately spoken of grace and kindness, of forgiveness and mercy, should by such a representation cut off all hope—should place between salvation and condemnation such an impassable gulf, that he despairs of a man's recovery, who has no relish for the truth spoken by Moses and the prophets. At this fearful warning one cannot but tremble for the consequences of that carnality which neglects the cultivation of the understanding and the heart. We have learned much from this discourse of our Lord, if we have only learned that our whole eternal fate depends upon our so formed or misformed internal state—ultimately, and strictly speaking, nothing of our future destiny depends upon the arbitrariness of our judge, but that this arbitrariness merely determines itself according to our real state of mind, according to our religious or irreligious, our tender or hardened disposition." The mightiest testimony of God, the most convincing work, THE GLORIOUS RESURRECTION OF JESUS CHRIST, which is here manifestly pointed at, and whatever else God has appointed to move men to repentance and faith, all this will fail of its design and prove powerless, if the blinded heart *will* not believe; for faith depends much more upon a moral bent of mind, than upon the kind and character of the testimony. Gnomon: "The rich man had said: If one *were sent to them they would repent*, now (as it is affirmed, that they would not be *persuaded*, though one *rose from the dead*,) the antecedent hypothesis is increased, but the consequent decreases. There are many proofs to be drawn from the invisible world, (Matth. xxvii. 53,) but not in regard to this particular point, that men will repent. Another Lazarus was raised up, but they did not believe, John xi. 44, 53. Πειθεσθαι, as well as απειθειν, sometimes refers to the understanding, sometimes to the will; often to both." Grotius: "Christ restored to life another man, called Lazarus (nor is it improbable that Christ had respect to this when he uttered these things.) Did the Pharisees on that account more heartily yield to the admonitions of Christ? Nay, they did but strive the more to kill him, and Lazarus too. Christ himself returned from death, and not a few, of blameless life, and corrupted by no bribe, were witnesses of the fact. Yet, so far from being moved to repentance, they only sought to suppress their testimony by force." The certainty of a life after death, the connexion between that life and the present, by the continuing of the same state of mind hereafter, and still farther development of the consequences of our conduct upon earth—that the space given for repentance shall have an end—that repentance may come too late—that there is to be a righteous and irrevocable judgment—that unbelief in God's word is the source of condemnation and of all misery; these truths are plainly brought to light in the preceding parable, and if the parables in the 15th chapter speak of the mercy of God toward the penitent, this presents in the clearest light the righteousness of God toward the impenitent, Rom. i. 18, as it uplifts the veil which conceals the future world from our view.

XXXIV.

THE WORKING SERVANT.

Luke xvii. 7—10.

After our Lord had spoken to his disciples of inevitable offences, that is, of the wicked and malicious opposition of the world to his gospel and the professors thereof, and had also alluded to the singular guilt of those from whom these offences proceeded, (v. 1, 2,) he admonishes them in v. 3, to cherish a loving and placable disposition, which is ever ready to receive again and pardon, however often it may have been injured, v. 4: which doctrine is still farther illustrated and enforced in the 18th of Matthew, by the parable of the wicked servant. Upon this the apostles spoke to him, doubtless under a lively sense of the difficulty which there was to human hearts in fulfilling such a command, and said: *Lord, increase our faith.* The feeling, however, of their own impotence, and their conviction of the necessity of having an increased measure of faith for the fulfilment of what was enjoined, might not be the only occasion of this prayer, in which something more than what was expressed appears to have mingled, as we may gather from the small parable delivered by our Lord on this occasion, in which, as in so many others, some error or failing is evidently combated. The prayer for an increase of faith seems here to point to the error, which supposes faith capable of being increased without any thing further—by an arbitrary manifestation of grace on the part of the Lord, without respect to the spiritual condition of those whose faith is to be strengthened. And as they pray: Increase (add to) our faith, there appears to have existed in the deepest underground of their hearts a certain self-sufficient confidence and respect to the faith they already possessed, of which they perhaps thought the more, that so many others did not believe in Jesus. So, looking upon their faith as meritorious, they thought that they had good grounds for claiming an increase to it. But when the Lord meets them in v. 6, with the declaration; If ye had faith as a grain of mustard-seed, &c.; he means to tell them, that if they really had right, true, living faith, existing as a divine power in the soul, they would not be in the least afraid of the difficulties and hinderances in question, they would be able to overcome them as small and inconsiderable; and if they were called to contend with opposition, and perform what was difficult, they might still do so though they had faith but as a grain of mustard-seed, which even when so small can overcome the world. Upon this follows the parable of the working servant, in which, as the only way of attaining to an increased faith, an unmoved persevering obedience is recommended, and that grounded, in v. 9, 11, upon humility. Through these two the heart is prepared for growing in faith, and so for receiving the desired strengthening or increase of faith. Grotius: "Many of the fathers extend this similitude to the most approved deeds of Christians, teaching, that even in these there is nothing on account of which we should boast or presume before God. For, as Chrysostom says, an humble mind without works will more readily bring a man to salvation, than pride along with works. There are many considerations which ought to prevent us from seeking a reckoning with God." Calvin: "The sum of this parable is, that since God can by an absolute right challenge every thing to himself, and hold us for his own property, however zealously we may apply to any duty, we cannot bind him to us by the obligation of our merits, because since we are his, he can be in nothing indebted to us. But the argument is from the less to the greater, for if such power is yielded to one man over another, that day and night he may urge him to incessant labour, and yet may lie under no obligation to compensate him, as if he was his debtor: how much more may God, &c. We see, therefore, that all are condemned of sinful arrogance, who imagine that they deserve something at the hands of God, as if they had laid him under contribution to themselves." Olshausen: "To the (foregoing) commendation of faith, which naturally includes within itself an advice to strive earnestly for its increase, succeeds now a parabolical representation of the relation of disciples to their Lord, which manifestly grows out of what precedes. The prevailing sentiment in the minds of the apostles which led them to ask for an increase to their faith, and our Lord to deliver this parable, was a mournful feeling in regard to the difficulties of the warfare to be maintained, and a thirsting for future rest and reward. In reference to these, Jesus reminds them of the relation in which they stood; they were as servants to their Lord, and the calling of a servant is to work for the interest of his master, and in obedience to his will. To work thus, however, can bring no desert, it is matter of obligation. So that the humble Son of Man appears here as a commander, whom all must serve; and the point of the parable is, to press it on the apostles, and through them on all the members of the church, that man can acquire no merit in the service of God—that the highest fidelity is nothing but fulfilled obligation, and that he must consequently seek all his consolation in grace."

TRAIN OF THOUGHT IN THE PARABLE.

The necessity of Humility.

It is necessary,

1. Because in all matters we depend on God (are his *servants*,) v. 7;
2. Because we are bound to employ all our powers in his service, v. 8;
3. Because, in such circumstances we have no claims for any special praise or recompense from obedience, v. 9;
4. Because an unpretending disposition is expressly demanded of us, v. 10.

V. 7. *Servant*, a body slave.—*Ploughing or feeding cattle.*—Olshausen: "Images of spiritual labour, to which the apostles were called." *Go and sit down to meat*—in one thing or another to have been obedient, and to have laboured for the Lord, is not enough to warrant our expecting from him an immediate refreshment and recompense.

V. 8. The Lord properly regards what the servant has already done, as a matter of obligation, and demands from him further obedience, additional labour. *Gird thyself*, that you may wait upon me without hinderance.

V. 9. The Lord is not in the least bound to give particular thanks to his servant, and the servant must not lay claim to this as his due; the ground of its being so lies in the mutual relationship. Grotius: "In this respect *reward* differs from *grace;* that reward looks mainly to the work done, grace to the state of mind; so that reward becomes due according to agreement, although the slave or hired labourer has not done willingly the required work. But they are proper subjects of grace who work with a ready mind, and would do even what they cannot accomplish. Elsewhere, however, the word *reward* in a looser sense imports any sort of recompense, even though much beyond what the deed merits, as an expression of kind feeling. Luke, therefore, after his custom, opposes grace to reward."

V. 10. This verse contains the application of the similitude to the disciples of our Lord. *When ye shall have done all*, by the powers both of nature and of grace, which have been conferred on you; it is spoken by way of concession, and must not be understood, contrary to the doctrine of scripture, as importing that man actually can yield a perfect obedience to what the law requires in respect to God and Christ. Gnomon: "There was among the apostles an overweening regard to the obedience they had hitherto rendered, strengthened by what they saw of the shameful obstinacy of others, xvi. 14; the Lord here calls them away from such a line of reflection."

Say, we are unprofitable servants—confess, in a spirit of deep, unpretending humility, that they can build nothing upon their own worth. Olshausen: "Ἀχρεῖος is used in Matth. xxv. 30, in a positive sense, denoting worthless, punishable; here it is used rather negatively, of one, who brings no (special) gain, but does only what is commanded, and hence can obtain blessings only through grace. It therefore involves ταπεινός, indicating a consciousness of one's own want of desert and worth, in reference to the divine being." —*We have done that which it was our duty to do*, no more than our duty. Gnomon: "Every slave should confess himself to be unprofitable, on the account that he is a slave, owing every thing, and liable to be beaten with stripes, if he is a delinquent; if he does all, he deserves nothing; he ought to esteem nothing *done*; no thanks are due to him, as it is not for him to expect any thing great either in employment or in reward. God, who alone is good, can want our services," Rom. xi. 35. Matth. xix. 17. Calvin: "Christ speaks here concerning the perfect observance of the law, which is nowhere to be found; for even he, who is nearest perfection, is yet very far from the righteousness which the law requires. The question, therefore, is not discussed here, whether we are justified by works, but whether the observance of the law deserves any reward from God. This last is denied, and because we all come short, not only is an obedience defective, but no part of it exactly corresponds to the judgment of God. He does not wish that his faithful people should be slothful, but only forbids them to be mercenaries, who may demand any thing of God, as if it was their legal right." Luther, Church-Pos. 7. 176: "We have said enough to show that our works are nothing before God, and we have never in any work fulfilled the least command, how much less could we attain to his righteousness, so as to deserve his grace! Still, if we even were so powerful as to keep his commands, and walk up on all hands to his righteousness, we should not thereby be deserving of his grace and salvation; he should not be obliged to give us these, but might demand the whole of us, as service due to him from his own creature. What he gives, therefore, is pure grace and mercy." Duvernoy: "This is an important inquiry, why we yet get so little thanks for what we do. We have done it with a willing heart, but still it is accounted as nothing: we are conscious of pain, if others make much of it. The ground of this is that virtue of modesty which springs from a sense of our misery and guilt. For who can say, that he has done every thing which he was bound to do? This is not the modesty which is found among the fair pretences and hypocrisies of the world." Apolog. Aug. Conf. iii. De dilect. et implet.

legis 34: "These words plainly declare that God may save through his own mercy, and because of his promise, but not because he owes it on account of the excellence of our works. Christ condemns all confidence in our works, accuses these works of being unworthy. Ambrose clearly teaches the same: Agnoscenda est gratia, sed non ignoranda natura, promissioni gratiæ, confidendum est, non naturæ nostræ. Unprofitable servants mean insufficient ones, because no person so much fears, so much loves, so much trusts God, as he ought. It is manifest, that confidence in one's own works is reprehended."

XXXV.

THE UNJUST JUDGE AND WIDOW.

Luke xviii. 1—8.

This parable, the design of which, according to v. 1st, is to excite to zealous and persevering prayer, stands in close connexion with chap. xvii. 20—37, where our Lord discourses of the mournful times which were to accompany the destruction of Jerusalem. He manifestly wishes, by the help granted to the importunate widow, and the promise therewith connected in v. 8, to console his disciples, to whose view he had disclosed those troublous times, and to assure them that they would not be involved in the fearful overthrow of the enemies of his kingdom, if they faithfully followed his guidance and instruction in other things, for the mighty help of God should then be manifested for their deliverance. In regard to their conduct amid those dismal calamities, our Lord gave them direction in v. 23, 31; and the parable was added to stir them up to continued and fervent prayer before God, as the most powerful means for preserving them from faint-heartedness, sustaining them in immoveable confidence, invincible patience, and the requisite cheerfulness of spirit. Lavater, Considerations, 2. p. 205: "Great, alone interpreter of God and of human nature! What friend of man or of God, what poet or orator, can come as thou dost into the human heart, and make it believe what to the worldly wisdom, which knows neither God nor man, is so hard, so impossible to be believed:—THE RESISTLESS POWER OF IMPORTUNATE PRAYER!"

The history of the hard-hearted, unfeeling judge, is admirably fitted to set forth the zeal and perseverance which Christians must exhibit in their supplications to God—for the begging widow gains her object only by persevering in her entreaty; without such perseverance she had found as little success as had been given to the man pleading for his friend in Luke xi. As, therefore, in the parable circumstances are represented most unfavourable for the widow, on account of the reckless character of the judge, the conclusion must, according to v. 7, stand thus: If this woman moved an unfeeling judge, and prevailed upon him to fulfil her urgent prayer, how much more may not we reckon upon a gracious hearing from God to our supplications; since he holds the faithful so indescribably dear to him, and ever desires their welfare! And in this conclusion there is contained a most powerful admonition to continued prayer, even when the wished for result does not immediately follow, and relief is withheld. The history of the Canaanitish woman in Matth. xv. 21—28, and of Jacob in Gen. xxxii. 22—31, afford real illustrations of this parable. Olshausen: "The parables of the Redeemer are sometimes drawn from that point of view, which is, not absolutely, but only relatively true. In the former, God could never have been compared to such a judge, let men labour as much as they please to soften the representation;—but considered in the human, subordinate point of view, the comparison speaks a profound truth, for the experience of those, who have to contend with the necessities of a life on earth. In the struggle with the world and sin, without them and in them, under a sense of the desertion of God (as is delineated in the book of Job,) bereft of all support and consolation, the soul appears like a widow, who implores in vain an unrighteous judge. But assiduity in prayer overcomes at last the severity of heaven." Calvin: "We know how rare and difficult a virtue is perseverance in prayer; and in this appears our want of faith, that, if we succeed not with our first supplications, we presently relinquish our endeavours, together with our hope. But we then only manifest a becoming confidence, when, though disappointed in our desires, we still do not sink into despondency. Wherefore it was not without cause, that Christ here commends to his disciples perseverance in prayer." Gnomon: "Two parables treat of prayer. The first dissuades from indolence, the other from confidence in ourselves; the two extremes are remarkable. For indolence and improper confidence are opposed in v. 1, 9; as proper confidence and indolence in 2 Cor. iii. 4; iv. 1, Eph. iii. 12, 13."

TRAIN OF THOUGHT IN THE PARABLE.

Motives to persevering prayer.

I. The greatness of the necessity is represented,

1. In our own helplessness; v. 3: There was a widow.

2. In the evil inflicted; v. 3: Avenge me of mine adversary.

3. In the delay of help; v. 4: And he would not for a while.

II. The ultimate success; v. 4: But afterward he said within himself, &c.; and in this success is certainly to be expected:

1. From the goodness of God; v. 7: And shall not God—as opposed to the unprincipled judge.

2. Who wills our salvation; v. 7: His elect.

3. If we continue with confidence in prayer; v. 7: Who cry to him day and night.

4. Notwithstanding the long delay in the promised help; v. 7: Though he bear long with them.

5. On account of the sure word of promise; v. 8: I say unto you, &c.

6. Although the help vouchsafed may at first be concealed from our view; v. 8: Nevertheless, when the Son of Man cometh, &c.

V. 1. *Always to pray, and not to faint,*—εκκακειν, is to flag or to be remiss, because one is apt to let the spirit sink before threatening dangers, here in particular on account of deferred help. Gnomon: "*Crying* is befitting, v. 7; *exemplified* in v. 39." The widow did not remit her entreaties, neither must believers. Olshausen: "In the New Testament, prayer appears not as a work or piece of service restricted to hours, but as the internal abiding condition of the higher life, Luke xxi. 36. Eph. vi. 18. 1 Thes. v. 17. Suitable prayer, accordingly, is not to be regarded as a repetition of certain forms, but as an internal direction of the soul toward God, as a lively longing after manifestations of him, as the breath of the inner man. In this constant internal flux and reflux of the spiritual life, we find the Redeemer standing, John i. 51; v. 19: but as in his life, which might be termed a prayer, there were not wanting seasons in which he especially applied himself to prayer with his heavenly Father, so the command *always to pray* does not exclude from the life of the believer periods of a more special and elevated exercise of a prayerful spirit, in which this pours itself out before God in the words of a direct address. But since the preservation of this higher life presupposes a contest, inasmuch as it has constantly to labour with the oppression of earthly things, Jesus subjoins the admonition, that we should not now tire of this internal warfare."

V. 2. The character of the judge is so marked, that one could look for no good from him, for he has neither the fear of God, nor the fear of men, who are too feeble to injure one that is in the possession of power.

V. 3. That the suppliant here is a widow, conveys the idea of perfect helplessness, and gives a still more frightful idea of the hard-heartedness of the judge, which continued unmoved by the circumstance of a desolate woman pleading, not for revenge, but only for her just and righteous claims against the wrongs of her oppressor. Εκδικεω, Wahl: "I defend any one, by pleading his cause," to obtain justice. Calvin: "Christ's proposing to us a widow in the parable, teaches us, that however wretched and despised they may be who entreat his favour, let them only not cease from their continued supplications, and they shall at length be regarded by him, and have their necessities supplied." Grotius: "A *widow*, bereft, despised, and one whom this cruel monster valued not a rush." Lavater, Considerations, 2. p. 208: "We must not create for ourselves arbitrary wants, and go with these before God. The poor widow went not to her judge for the purpose of making a trial. She had to concern herself simply with help and deliverance. Help and deliverance must be the object of thy prayer. Thy circumstances must lie upon thy heart, as the widow's lay upon her heart. She could find no rest, day or night, until she obtained the ear of the judge. Amid all other things, the oppressed situation in which she was, continually forced itself back upon her. This burdened, vexed, afflicted her unceasingly, and drove her to the only person from whom, if at all, deliverance was to be hoped for. Without the constraint of such a necessity it is folly to beg, and folly to expect deliverance. The feeling of necessity must even burn as an inextinguishable fire in the bosom. We must have grace to believe in God, as in an ever-present almighty agent. We must renounce every other help, and throw ourselves back upon God alone. But our necessity, our prayer, our faith, our courage, must not be a matter of contrivance and artificial constraint. Suffering and faith are the only two essential conditions of prayer. Suffering produces humility, faith, boldness. And humility and boldness in proper measure, constitute the perfection of men and Christians."

V. 4. *And he would not for a while,*—how unrighteous is this delay of the judge, bound as he was to exercise justice. *But afterwards he said within himself, &c.,*—he is so shameless, as not to be ashamed of his ungodly state, yea, rather takes pleasure in proclaiming this. Here he negatively confesses what did not move him to fulfil the prayer of the widow,—it was neither the fear of God, nor a sense of duty.

V. 5. Now are the true efficient motives of his conduct given. It is unpleasant and painful for him to be ever and anon met with the entreaty of the unfortunate widow,—therefore self-love, regard merely for his own ease, was what moved him to help her; he wished simply to get rid of her. *Lest she weary me,* rather, *dun me,* υπωπιαζω, 1 Cor. ix. 27. Wahl: "From υπωπιον, that part of the face which is immediately below the eyes, and properly signifying to be struck there so as to have lurid marks, to be made black and blue." Luther's note: "That is, that she might not plague and torment him, as one says of forward, intrusive persons,—How troublesome this man is to me!"

V. 6. Here the application made by our Lord begins. *Unjust judge*—properly, godless, reckless, as in Luke xvi. 8.

V. 7. The question implies a very strong affirmation: yes, God will certainly do it. Grotius: "Every word has a stronger meaning and emphasis. God, the just one, as opposed to that miserable judge, will he not repel violence, not from those whom he contemns, but from those whom he loves—not from those who trouble him, but from those whose prayers are greatly esteemed by him?" *Shall he not avenge,* as in v. 3; procure justice, defend against the oppressions of the enemy in times of distress; from him who is love itself, certain help is to be expected. *His elect,*—a new ground of confidence in regard to the help of God, as what could not fail to come, though it might be delayed,—he wills the salvation of those who trust in him. The elect,—according to Matth. xxiv. 22, 24, where it is said, that for the elect's sake, the days of trouble should be shortened, and that if it were possible the elect should be deceived by false Christs and false prophets—are undoubtedly the avowed friends and followers of Jesus, who recognised and acknowledged him for the Messias. Olshausen: "The elect are named as the objects of divine care (εκδικησις;) these are constantly, until the manifestations of the Son of Man, exposed to the attacks of sin on the part of the kingdom of darkness, but shall be delivered by the Lord in his own time with a strong arm, while they continue in faith, of which persevering prayer is a necessary manifestation. Persevering prayer, therefore, is not strictly the condition of the εκδικησις, this rather lies in the being elected; the elect are in their nature the steadfast believers, whom their Father in heaven will infallibly deliver."

Who cry to him day and night,—another ground for expecting unfailing help as the elect fall in with the divine arrangement, and manifest their faith in his power and love by continuing instant in prayer.

Though he bear long with them. Olshausen: "The help from above is expressly represented as deferred according to God's counsel, with reference to v. 4; in which there is at the same time an intimation given, that the apparent injustice (αδικια) of God is always but a wise manifestation of his love." Μακροθυμεω, Wahl: "I am tardy in bringing help to any one, or in vindicating him from the wrongs of another." Gnomon: "The long-suffering of God is here extolled, which so regards the injuries of the bad and the sorrows of the good, that it does not immediately put an end to both, although men may think that their indignation against the bad, and their compassion toward the good, demands a speedy termination." Grotius: "This word is expressive of a delay, which, as it is beneficial to the debtor, so is it grievous to him who suffers wrong." Olshausen: "As used of God, this word presupposes his relation to the sins of men. The elect themselves are to be thought of as in part also belonging to sinful humanity, and the delay of redemption is to be regarded, not as an accidental, but as an intentional thing, designed for the purification of the elect; so that the bearing long carries a very fine reference." Although God delays long in bringing help, yet for the reasons just mentioned, we must not lose heart and cease praying. For this is introduced to remove an objection and a depressing mistrust, as if the help which is only delayed were not to be granted, and so the expression corresponds to that in v. 4: He would not for a while. Other expositors think that the divine patience and long-suffering must intimate that he, the merciful Jehovah, is not annoyed by the continued prayers of his elect, as the judge in question was by the prayers of the widow; but this view does not appear to suit the context so well. Calvin: "If at any time God winks longer than we would like at our wrongs, let us consider, that he does so with the fatherly design of training us to endure. Were we allowed to look into his hidden counsels, we should learn that his aid is always prompt and seasonable, and is never indeed a moment delayed, but is ready for every emergence." Lavater, Considerations, 2. p. 207: "Whoever calls persevering prayer a powerless thing, he calls Jesus a deceiver. Whoever calls the expectation of an answer to the persevering prayer of an elect man, *i. e.* of an approved, righteous worshipper of God, enthusiasm, he calls Jesus an enthusiast. Indeed, we must pray repeatedly and perseveringly. We must begin, continue, and finish; we must wait and tarry; we must continue as steadfast as if we saw him who is invisible, and as if we received the word directly from the mouth of the Lord. The word of the Lord: *Shall not God,*—must be to the soul of the supplicant as clear and certain, as the sun shining at noon-day. Whoever can believe and pray on account of this unfailing, ever-abiding word of God, he belongs to the elect." But divine wisdom sometimes postpones the deliverance of his suffering people on other grounds, which accord well with its goodness toward them, and with its fidelity and its promises. In part, such delay must serve for the trial and increase of their faith and piety, and produce in them a much livelier sense of the goodness experienced in the deliverance after great calamities; they must thereby be trained to a more humble resignation to the will of God, to patient continuance in well-doing, and to a firmer confidence in his almighty power and protection. In part also, when the Lord delays the rescue of his people to the time of greater necessity, he seeks to render his power and his glory more brightly conspicuous.

V. 8. *I tell you that he will avenge them speedily*—last ground of confidence and continued prayer: the true and faithful promise of divine help. He is to interpose speedily, *i. e.* suddenly, unexpectedly, before they, with their weak faith, and under their heavy formidable trials, looked for it. Grotius: "He will speedily deliver them, which is opposed to μακροθυμειν (the bearing long;) nor are we called to depart from this very plain interpretation by the fact, that God sometimes suffers his people to be for a time oppressed by the wicked; for that period, though it may seem long to the sufferers, is yet of very short continuance, only momentary, and hence Paul speaks of the season of tribulation as but for a moment, 2 Cor. iv. 17. Besides, the delay itself is fraught with much good to those who have to suffer, although often not apparent. But it will tend much to encourage us to diligence in prayer, if we can rest in confidence, not only that we shall be delivered, but that we shall be quickly delivered, although it may still be delayed."

Nevertheless, when the Son of Man cometh—namely, to fulfil the promise just given, to deliver his own people. "Every special interposition of the Lord in behalf of his own is a coming of him; and he comes most unexpectedly when prayer and faith are well-nigh extinguished. But the discourse here is more particularly of his coming to his kingdom, as the season of mightiest deliverance to his people, when little faith shall be found remaining in the earth." (Meier's Bible.)—*Shall he find faith on the earth?* The beginning of help at the coming of Christ, is so concealed, that even his elect recognise it not as such, because the power of evil and the weight of tribulation has pressed on them so heavily. The question bespeaks a strong negative, that this should not be the case, and that even the faithful should be found faint and desponding. Grotius: "Christ complains that many will not persevere in patient trust, and thence in the exercise of prayer, until the time of deliverance comes, which is not far distant." Calvin: "Faith, therefore, ought not to regard one's own weakness, misery and shortcomings; but with all diligence should wait upon the alone efficacy of God. For if we lean upon our own righteousness or glory, we shall never rise to think of the power of God."

XXXVI.

THE PHARISEE AND THE PUBLICAN.

Luke xviii. 9—14.

When our Lord delivered the parable of the unjust judge, and there admonished to steadfastness in prayer, there might be among the hearers persons with pharisaical hearts, who complacently flattered themselves in the inmost sentiments of their mind, with being zealous in the discharge of this duty, and hence not only conceived themselves to be distinguished by great piety, but also looked with contempt upon others, to whom they did not ascribe the same fear of God and diligence in prayer. Against people of this sort the following parable of the pharisee and the publican, according to v. 9, is directed in which our Lord describes, under the publican and his prayer, the proper character of a prayer which is acceptable to God, and the spirit of true piety as exemplified in prayer, contrasting it also most strikingly with the deportment and prayer of a pharisee, with the view of admonishing to genuine godly fear, and warning against all conceit in pretences of piety, which is an abomination before God. The connexion, therefore, between the two parables may be thus stated, that the first recommends generally the duty of prayer, and the second gives us to understand the property of a right prayer, which alone can obtain the blessing—for the publican only is heard, whilst the proud pharisee, who properly asks nothing, receives no grace, and in his prayer is not accepted before God. Calvin: "Now Christ gives instruction concerning another virtue, which is necessary for praying rightly, that believers may come into the presence of God in a simple and lowly state of mind. No distemper is more deadly than arrogance, which yet is so deeply inherent in the nature of all, that it can scarcely be expelled and rooted out by any means." Mel.: "There are two examples; in the one Christ condemns confidence in our own righteousness; in the other, he holds up the pattern of true righteousness." Grotius: "Luke wisely annexes to the admonitions concerning constancy in the faith, the discourse concerning lowliness of mind, which, as it is of service in every part of life, is especially so in prayer." Luther, House-Pos. 5. 20: "Here our blessed Lord teaches us how we must be true and humble Christians, for it is only through this virtue that we can attain to grace. Where this virtue of humility is not, there God can take no pleasure in men, nor be gracious to them." Lavater, Considerations, 2. p. 211: "It appears to have been one of the chief designs of Jesus to oppose the dead-legal, the cold-religious piety of the pharisees. Why did our Lord do so? For the sake of the heart, the internal sense, the inward life of man, as far before external punctilios and legal exactness. He desires humble hearts toward God, and loving hearts toward men. He delights more in lost sons, who return to their father's love, than those never-lost, heartless, self-righteous—in humble labourers, sin-stricken publicans, than in outwardly blameless, but proudly self-righteous, pharisees."

TRAIN OF THOUGHT IN THE PARABLE.

Of the conceit of being Pious.

I. Its nature is delineated:

A. In the pharisee, with respect to what belongs to this conceit:

1. It is inclined to stand aloof from others, v. 11: The pharisee stood by himself;

2. It ascribes all good to self as its own desert; v. 11: God, I thank thee;

3. It thinks the worst of other men: v. 11: That I am not, &c.;

4. It judges of neighbours in a heartless way from appearances; v. 11: Or even as this publican;

5. It elevates itself above all, taking itself for perfect, v. 11;

6. It extols its own works, v. 12.

B. In the publican with respect to that which is wanting, where this conceit fails;

1. In a lively feeling of guilt; v. 13: Smote upon his breast;

2. In a confession of this and of deserved punishment; v. 13: Said, God, be merciful to me, a sinner;

3. In desire after God's favour; v. 13.

II. The consequences of it are unfolded, v. 14.

1. It loses the favour and approbation of God, v. 14: This man went down, &c.

2. It shall be humbled, v. 14: For every one, &c.

Ver. 9. *Who trusted in themselves that they were righteous*—they had confidence in their own selves, and the ground of their confidence stood in the conviction, that they were righteous, in possession of the divine favour. The expression, as illustrated by what follows, evidently marks a groundless persuasion, a vain imagination, a mere conceit. The state of mind described is that of him, who fancies himself to be perfectly righteous, and grounds upon that supposed righteousness a proud self-confidence. Calvin: "Christ reproves and condemns two sins, improper confidence in ourselves, and pride in despising others—the one of which springs from the other; for whoever deceives himself by a false confidence, cannot fail to magnify himself above others. Nor is it wonderful that he should despise his equals, who deals proudly toward God himself. But every one, who is puffed up by such self-confidence, avowedly wars with God himself, as his favour can no otherwise be gained, than by an entire renunciation of ourselves, and a simple dependence upon his mercy." Olshausen: "To the pharisee there is certainly ascribed a righteousness, but one only that is external, legal; to the publican an unrighteousness. The relation of the heavenly kingdom, which manifests itself to the penitent and needy, must accordingly be brought out here, as in Luke xv. in connexion with a legal standing. The endeavour to regard the law as something merely outward, must lead to a flattering self-righteousness, which removes us farther from God, than transgression of the law, in the event of this leading to a desire for salvation. A rampant profligacy, in which transgression of the law is coupled with no repentance and no thirsting after salvation, is certainly worse than both." Grotius: "As righteous, that is, as if they were righteous, or because they were righteous, namely in their own estimation; for the words are capable of either interpretation, and the meaning is substantially the same. For as the eye that is suffused with humour sees all things, not as they are, but according to the quality of the humour, so he, who is full of self-love, foolishly dreams, and judges of every thing, not according to the truth, but according to his own desire."

And despised others, properly lessened them, thought little of them, not giving them credit for so much good as themselves, and less indeed than actually belonged to them. This despising of others is always inseparably connected with that immoderate self-elation, for the conceit, let its object be what it may, is perpetually as to its nature an error of the understanding, the man conceiving too highly of his own worth, and also a perversity of heart, taking one's self to be better than others. The judgment of the pharisee, v. 11, 12, shows it to be so. Luther, House-Pos. 5. 21: "These were the two leading views of the pharisees, that they were persons who not only thought highly of themselves, which had been sin enough, for it is a devilish one, but also despised others."

Ver. 10. *Pharisee and publican*—two sorts of people most widely apart from each other, as well in their manner of life, as in the opinion publicly entertained of them. Olshausen: "The representatives of the two classes—of the self-applauding, arrogant law-keepers, and the abased law-breakers, are set forth in their common relation to God, in prayer, and the thoughts which occur to them in this relation are to be regarded as the expression of their state and character." Luther, House-Pos. 5. 21: "The pharisees were among the Jews just like the monks in the papacy; they had a peculiar dress, set days for fasting and prayer, and prosecuted the work of righteousness so diligently, that other men were but poor sinners in comparison of them. Hence were they called pharisees, which in Hebrew signifies as much as a separatist, one who separates himself from the common herd, and seeks to be something singular."

Ver. 11. *The pharisee stood, and prayed thus with himself;* according to Luther, he spoke for himself, that is, for his own satisfaction, and with much complacency of heart, the following congratulatory prayer. It may, however, be more naturally understood as meaning that he stood by himself alone, walked to a side from others, that they might observe him and hear him pray; he wishes to be seen of men, Matth. vi. 5.—*God, I thank thee*, Luther, House-Pos. v. 28: "Whoever would judge merely by the words, must confess it was not unrighteously spoken what was here said by the pharisee. For such words are uttered by the truly pious in their prayers, but with a different spirit. For when they thank God for any thing, they acknowledge that it is his work and gift, they have it not of themselves. But this was not the pharisee's meaning, else would he have said: That I am no adulterer, &c. Lord, I have no one to thank but thee. Of myself, apart from thy grace, I would have acted even as other men, for we are all alike; one must not glory over another. This pharisee, however, did not think thus, but entirely reverses it, finds all his virtues in himself, as if he had all of himself and not of God, and so he properly thanks not God, but himself, his own reason, his free-will and strength, that he had done so much." Calvin: "Although in giving God thanks he confesses that all he has of good works were merely of grace conferred, yet, as he rests his confidence in works, and prefers himself to others, he is rejected with his prayer. A remarkable passage; for to some it appears sufficient, if they take from man the glory of good works, on the ground of these being the gifts of the Holy Spirit; and thus they understand that we are justified freely, because God finds no righteousness in us, excepting what he has himself conferred. But Christ proceeds much farther, not only ascribing the virtue of acting righteously to the grace of the Spirit, but emptying us of all confidence in our works; for the pharisee is not reproved for having arrogated to himself what properly belonged to God; but because he trusted in his own merits, that he might have a gracious God, as far as he deserved it." Olshausen: "The first half of the prayer put into the mouth of the pharisee might be the expression of sincere piety, if in this, *I thank thee*, there were a real acknowledgment, that his superior moral condition was a work of divine grace, and that to God alone the honour consequently belonged. But then such a confession of what was done by God could not have been made, without an expression of regret at his own unfaithfulness, which is always most distinctly recognised where the power of God most powerfully works. To beget this acknowledgment of sin, is always the proper design of the law, which, with the pure, it must of necessity accomplish. It was only the pharisaical impurity which occupied itself with the form, without laying open the inner man to the working of the law, that could thence arrogate the vain and self-pleasing distinction of observing the law." Mel.: "The first image presents to us a secure man, without repentance, without the fear of God, without faith and without prayer. He has, however, the works of the law, and thinks them to be righteousness, on account of these he conceives that God is his debtor. Therefore he does not supplicate, that is, does not ask pardon of God or other good things. But why does he give thanks, since the giving of thanks is a part of true worship? I answer: This giving of thanks was feigned, like that of wicked men, who, when they abound in riches, also use words of gratitude, and yet in reality do not feel that riches are the gift of God, but have either been gotten by their own industry, or thrown in their way by chance. Thus the pharisee apprehends that he has made a law by his own efforts, and soothes himself by the thought of that adorning, whereby he excels others, and has confidence toward God. Had he truly given thanks, he would have trusted in mercy alone, and not have said, I am not as other men; but would have acknowledged, that he also, if left to himself, would have been incited to robberies and other crimes, and would have declared it to be the goodness of God that he had been preserved. Hence it may be sufficiently understood, that these words of the pharisee were not a real giving of thanks."

That I am not as other men. Gnomon: "The pharisee forms two classes, into the one of which he throws the whole human race; he himself appears to constitute the other and better one." Grotius: "He twice errs; first, in that he reckons it matter of great praise not to be among the most depraved, then in judging so harshly of other men, the greater part of whom were not known to him." What shameful calumny, to declare the whole world besides to be wicked and abandoned wretches, and what pride! And is it virtue, genuine fear of God and true piety, if a man is only free of the grossest vices and misdemeanors! Heartlessly he both judges and condemns. Luther, House-Pos. 5. 23: "So does the hypocrite; O God, says he, thou seest that thou hast in me a very pious man." He recounts before God his virtues and moral excellencies, that God might know how to recompense him, as his like was not to be found in the world. Mel.: "Here consider how rash the worship of hypocrites is—they approach God without fear, without repentance, and oppose their own righteousness to the judgment of God. But what can be more absurd, than to approach such majesty without fear!"

Or even as this publican! how arrogantly he pretends to judge of hearts, and judges of them after the appearance, guided by prejudice. With slighting and contempt he looks upon the publican, with self-satisfaction and delight upon himself. Grotius: "If there had been any principle of love in him, he would have believed that the publican had come to the temple for the purpose of repenting, which his very gesture indicated. But if, believing this, he threw out the taunt against him on account of his former life, that was still more atrocious."

Ver. 12. As he had already spoken well of his person, so now he praises his works, his extraordinary good deeds, through which God had become, as it were, his debtor. *I fast twice in the week;* according to Lev. xvi. 29—31, and Numb. xxix. 7, a yearly fast only is enjoined, but the Jews, and especially the pharisees, from peculiar sanctity and regard to the service of God, observed two fast days every week, the second and fifth days, for reflecting on the ascent of Moses to Mount Sinai, when he went to receive the law, and on his return thence. *And give tithes of all that I possess*—according to the command of God, it was only the fruits of the earth, and the produce of cattle and flocks, that were to be tithed. Numb. xviii. 21. Deut. xiv. 22. Lev. xxvii. 30. The pharisees extended the obligation to the whole of their possessions, and thereupon grounded a certain claim to distinction and reward, Matth. xxiii. 23. Luther, House-Pos. 5. 23: "To fast is right, to pray is right, to give tithes is right, so also to preserve chastity, and abstain from robbery and injustice,—all right and good in itself. But the pharisee bespatters himself with proud pretensions to such a degree, that all became, as it were, pollutions of the devil. How can God be well pleased with sanctity, when men vaunt and talk proudly against him?" Duvernoy, Extracts 5. p. 26: "The error of the pharisee stood in his thinking that he was righteous, and the goodness or happiness of the publican, that he acknowledged himself to be a sinner. It belongs then to the heart, and must be sought in the state of the pharisee's and publican's hearts, if the one is named righteous and the other not. The pharisee thought not only that he was better than a robber, adulterer, &c., but that he was entirely different from, and not at all as, a robber, an adulterer, or ungodly person. The poor man did not bethink himself of his heart, how it stood with him in regard to the fountain-head, from which every thing proceeds, and therefore he is quite unconcerned. It occurred not to him, that so long as the evil was not subdued in its deepest root, it would avail a poor man little if he did a few imperfect good works. The pharisee thought not of the state of his heart, the publican saw that his heart was worth nothing. Therefore the publican stood before God better than he regarded himself; he looked upon himself just as he was." Lavater, Considerations, 2. p. 212: "In fact, it was impossible to be more self-righteous, more an egotist, more legal and contemptuous. Who is contemptuous, if he is not, who despises every one but himself? He, who recounts his deserts before God, has, methinks, few deserts. The most white-washed grave was still full of dead men's bones. The pretension destroyed all good, or showed rather, that every thing, which bore externally the appearance of good, was internally rotten and lifeless."

V. 13. *The publican, standing afar off*—far from the holiest, which, from his deep sense of sin, and painful consciousness of guilt, he would not approach, because he did not think himself worthy.—*Would not lift up so much as his eyes unto heaven,* because he was ashamed—a manifestation of deep humility; *smote upon his breast,* as an indication of his keen remorse and melting of heart on account of sin. Gnomon: "In repentance, either fear or shame predominates. Shame is more ingenuous than fear, chap. xv. 18, 21. Ez. xvi. 52. Better is a melting heart, than one merely contrite through terror and fear of punishment. The particles rubbed from a sandy stone still retain their hardness; a heart become flesh from one of stone pleases God as his workmanship, and gives glory to him."—*God, be merciful to me, a sinner.* In this short prayer there are three things—I am a sinner—I am liable to punishment—I beg for grace, for pardon of sin, for remission of deserved punishment, that thou mayest again visit me with thy favour. So this publican shows himself to be a repenting and believing sinner, for prayer for the pardon of sin presupposes faith in God's mercy; and he is rightly informed, both in regard to his own condition, and in regard to God, as the proper and only helper. Calvin: "That he should obtain favour, he confesses himself unworthy; and, certainly, as the remission of sins alone can conciliate God to us, it is necessary to make our commencement here, if we desire that our prayers should be acceptable to him. In fine, no one will attain to the righteousness of faith, excepting he who will be unrighteous in himself. This tenet then is to be held, that we are justified, not by our own excellence, but by the mercy of God." Lavater, as above, "We have here a short, simple, warm speech from the heart, which, before God and man, is infinitely more valuable than all pompous eloquence. The heart prays in the publican. The poor sinner begs. The wounded oppressed conscience in him supplicates; and there proceeds now a great internal change and revolution. This internal work upon his soul, this judgment upon himself opens within him a new spring of strength and satisfaction; he returns justified to his house." Mel.: "In the other character we have set before us a man exercising himself to repentance, terrified by the conviction of his sins and the apprehension of the wrath of God. For his not daring to lift his eyes to heaven, betokens his apprehension of the wrath of God, his still fleeing from God and struggling with distrust; but by and by faith gains the victory in him, through which he returns to God, casting himself on divine mercy, crying and begging for pardon. Therefore he truly becomes righteous and acceptable to God, because in the midst of fears and repentings he is raised up through faith. This is an example of true justification. Nor are good works wanting, for we have here repentance and prayer." The publican longs after God's grace, but sees nothing in himself on account of which he deserves it; for the measure of good which was in him was to him as nothing, and he therefore placed his entire confidence upon the sovereign mercy of God, and the sole ground of his hope was, that God is gracious, though he himself was poor and miserable. This is the nature of humility. It stood essentially, not in the publican's deportment, but in his state of mind. The humble man knows his wants, his sins, his imperfections, knows that he might and should have been better, feels before God only for his guilt, and his endeavours are consequently directed simply upon the favour and grace of God.

V. 14. This verse contains the judgment of Christ upon the relation of these two men of prayer to God. *This man went down to his house justified, rather than the other*, that is, the publican was justified, but not the pharisee; the one received what the other did not, and as the former had sought the pardon of sin, so he obtained this for his portion—God received him into favour—gave him the consoling testimony and the blessed assurance, that his sins were forgiven him, Psl. l. 15; li. 3—5, 19. Isa. lvii. 15. By the being justified is manifestly to be understood, not a moral change of heart, but only his altered relation toward God. As the full and rich pharisee has asked nothing, so he received nothing, for the best gifts and bounties of Heaven can be possessed only by those who first desire, and then beg for them. And this justification is always, as in the case of the publican, obtained no otherwise than through humility, repentance and faith. It is not amendment of life, nor preceding good works, which are the ground of acceptance, but simply the free grace of God, which the sinner lays hold of by a firm faith. Wherever there is any confidence in one's personal and individual merits, there the foundation of the heart is not pure; but God gives his grace only to those who, while they wholly and entirely renounce themselves, trust in him with undivided hearts, Rom. iii. 24. Eph. ii. 8, 9. Calvin: "This passage tells, distinctly, what it is properly to be *justified:* namely, to stand before God as if we were just or righteous; for the publican is not said to have been justified on this account, that he had suddenly acquired some new quality, but, because his guilt being cancelled, and his sins abolished, he found favour; whence it follows, that the being just is made to stand in the remission of sins. As the pharisees spoiled their virtues by a vicious confidence, so that their righteousness, however lauded by the world, was of no price before God, so the publican, without any merits of his own, obtained righteousness simply by entreating pardon, because it is to be looked for only in the free mercy of God. If any one would seek to obtain peace of conscience by his works, (which is seen to be the case with profane and brutish men,) he will labour in vain. For either his bosom has been lulled to sleep through contempt or forgetfulness of divine judgment, or else it is full of fear and trembling, until he has gone to repose in Christ; for he alone is our peace. Therefore, peace of conscience means the security which comes from apprehending that God is reconciled. *That* neither the pharisee has, who is elated with false confidence in his works, nor the stupid transgressor who, intoxicated with the pleasure of sin, is conscious of no disquiet."

For every one that exalteth himself, &c. In this sentiment, often repeated, and on very different occasions announced by our Lord, there is contained a general fundamental principle of the divine kingdom, according to which God regulates his procedure; here, in particular, it forms the ground why the publican, but not the pharisee, was justified. The haughtiness of the latter excluded him from the enjoyment of the divine favour; the humility of the former rendered him capable and worthy of receiving grace. What is meant by exalting one's self, the pharisee's prayer shows to be an overvaluing of real or only fancied excellencies. He who exalts himself, shall receive a treatment from God quite opposite to the judgment of men, whereby he shall be humbled. The prayer, as well as the entire behaviour of the publican, springing from the deepest feelings of the heart, and not merely so in appearance, is the self-humiliation which pleases the Lord; and whosoever so humbles himself, shall elicit both from men and from God a judgment and dealing, which is accordant with his graces, Luke xiv. 7—11. Mel.: "A terrible maxim is added concerning pride in general. *Humility* is indeed to fear God, and to acknowledge that gifts are bestowed by him, that we may be of service to others, not that we may oppress them; likewise, that they are not capable of making us happy without God. On the other hand, *pride* is to admire one's self without the fear of God, to trust in personal gifts, and by such confidence to attempt much without word and calling, as Saul against the word of God endeavours to hand down the kingdom to his posterity."

XXXIV.

THE TEN POUNDS.

Luke xix. 11—27.

THIS parable was delivered by Jesus in the house of Zaccheus the publican, when he was on his last journey to Jerusalem, therefore earlier than the similar parable recorded in Matth. xxv. 14—30, which was spoken after his arrival in Jerusalem, on the Mount of Olives, and only to the twelve, whereas, when the one before us was spoken, other hearers were also present. The occasion of this parable was the error which even the disciples of Jesus held in common with the mass of the people, that he was going to establish an earthly and visible kingdom, from which they promised to themselves, as partakers, and especially as friends of Jesus, honour, power, and great glory. This error might have been confirmed by a misunderstanding of the words of our Lord in ver. 10, which they did not apprehend in their true spiritual meaning, and would still farther be strengthened by certain dark expectations, that at the approaching feast something great and decisive in regard to the kingdom would happen. The occasion, then, which gave rise to the parable, intimates the object it has in view, viz. to correct erroneous views and expectations regarding the Messiah's kingdom, to lead to the proper knowledge of its true nature, and to disclose how men would stand related to it. Two false hopes in particular are pointed at in v. 11; the first, that this kingdom should be *immediately*, without any further delay, set up, against which the intimation in the parable is directed, that it should necessarily be a long time before the return of the nobleman; and the second, that the kingdom should *appear*, should stand forth as a visible institution, against which it is taught, that the kingdom was to be received in a far country. Calvin: " But a twofold error prevailed, in that they imagined they should enjoy a blessed rest without suffering, and then conceived of the kingdom of God after their own carnal mind; from which it appears how weak and unenlightened their faith was. In this respect also Christ's disciples were much deceived, as they thought that he would now have a fixed place for his kingdom, and would come to Jerusalem that he might presently establish its happy condition. So that by taking away the hope of a present kingdom, he exhorted them to hope and patience; for he informs them that many labours must be long and faithfully discharged by them, before they inherited that glory, after which they too eagerly grasped." Grotius: " Christ, indicating future things covertly, as was his custom, declares indeed that a kingdom was appointed to him, and that not in respect to the Jews only, but in respect to all nations, as had been predicted concerning the Messiah; but that, before the full and blessed establishment of that kingdom, many labours were to be undergone by his people, and much opposition raised on the part of the Jews." There were two other perverted expectations concerning this kingdom, of a more latent form, springing from the conviction of its earthly nature, and which are also combated in the parable before us. It was thought that every one would most joyfully close with this kingdom, and submit themselves to the king; this error is opposed in v. 14. And then men hoped that they should attain to the blessed enjoyment of the kingdom, altogether apart from their state and disposition of mind, in opposition to which we are told, that the nobleman required activity of his servants, v. 13; that he rewarded them after the measure of their proved fidelity, v. 16—19, while he punished the faithless, v. 20—24, and dealt still more severely with the avowed enemies, who set themselves up against his sovereignty. The blessedness of the members of Messiah's kingdom is, therefore, made to depend on their previous state of mind and manner of acting—Bauer agrees with us in regarding this parable as a different one from that recorded in Matth. xxv., and remarks on its peculiarity: "Jesus could not just plainly say to his disciples, that they were deceived in expecting that his kingdom would *now* be established with outward pomp and splendour. Their prejudices, which had been imbibed with their mother's milk, were too deeply rooted. He, therefore, chose the agreeable method of the parable, to tell them, under covert of a figure, what, on account of their prejudices and limited capacities, he could not plainly and openly declare: that he was indeed the Redeemer (σωτηρ, with reference to v. 9, σωτηρια, and v. 10, σωσαι, comp. Luke ii. 68,) the Messiah, and was going away to receive from God the kingdom prepared for him; but still that he would not shine forth with splendour, glory and majesty. The royal state and glory of his kingdom were only to be manifested then, when he should return again. Meanwhile, his servants must employ the goods committed to them, because he will some time call them to a reckoning, reward the faithful, humble the slothful, and severely punish all his enemies."

To me it always appears the proper plan to take each parable by itself, just as it stands, to search into its main subject and illustrate it. Though it have a greater or less resemblance with some other, as is the case here, yet there is no sufficient ground for denying its individuality, and finding out for it a proper aim and subject. While it is the part of the critic to fix, as far as he can, the probable position, the occasion and relative connexion of each parable, it is always the duty of the practical expositor to treat what was delivered just as it stands in the gospels, according to the precise form and structure given to it there, and, in particular, when it is a parable, to investigate its chief object and design, as it stands before him. Hence I cannot at all agree with what Unger says, p. 129, upon this parable, in its relation to that of Matthew, maintaining that in Matthew we have the parable in its simple and proper form, and that Luke has by a sort of incongruous mixture, joined to it another parable, spoken at another time, and for another purpose. I agree with what is said by Starke, in his Synopsis of the New Testament, "That this parable is different from the one in Matthew is manifest from all the circumstances. It contains, as it were, the testament of Jesus, wherein he shows what was the nature of his kingdom, also his death, resurrection, glory, and future advent."

TRAIN OF THOUGHT IN THE PARABLE.

The kingdom of Christ is a heavenly one.

I. The proper nature of the kingdom:

1. The Son of God from heaven is king; ver. 12: A nobleman;

2. He has received the kingdom in heaven; ver. 12: Went into a far country to receive to himself a kingdom:

3. He will give full manifestation of it from heaven; 12: And return.

II. The present state of the kingdom; although

Christ's is a heavenly one, it yet stretches over the whole human race upon earth; for on earth he has;

1. Servants, as stewards of intrusted gifts, v. 13;

2. Enemies, who grudge his heavenly glory, v. 14.

III. The future manifestation of the kingdom shows it to be a heavenly one, from the manner in which rewards and punishments are to be distributed; which is,

1. Righteous and beneficent in the gracious apportionment of reward to those of approved fidelity, as exemplified in the case both of the first, v. 15—17, 24—26, and of the second servant, v. 18, 19.

2. Just and righteous in the punishment,

a.) Of the faithless, v. 20—24;

b.) And of avowed enemies, v. 27.

V. 12. *A nobleman*—a man of noble birth, ευγενης, through his birth, family, ancestry, distinguished from the rest of the people, ver. 14. This was the case with Jesus, who being descended from Abraham and David after the flesh, was of kingly origin, and, besides, was the Son of God. This noble one lived for a long time among his fellow-citizens, as one of their equals, until at last the time came when he attained to a power and a glory, which belonged to him from his birth, was appointed to him, and raised him far above all those among whom he had first lived. Grotius: "A nobleman, to whom the kingdom among his citizens was, by birthright, due."

Went into a far country to receive for himself a kingdom—a reference to the death and ascension of Jesus Christ, which must mean that he has his kingdom in heaven, and from thence he exercises his power, Matth. xxviii. 18. Phil. ii. 9—11. Eph. i. 17, 20—22; until he comes again at the last day to the judgment, Matth. xxv. 31. Von Brunn: "This kingdom is an invisible kingdom, and can only be known from its operations; and if there must always be something visible in this kingdom, it is only the power which may be seen and felt in the actings of the Christian church, in the exercises of individual souls, and in the exalted visions of a John. The possession of the kingdom consists mainly in the execution of the great plan of the Father in Jesus Christ—in the deliverance of the whole of humanity by degrees from the power of darkness—in opening up to them more and more an entrance into the kingdom of light, and at last entirely translating them into it. But the chief development of this great work takes place in the kingdom of spirits, and but rarely manifests its influence in the great transactions of the world in a manner fitted to strike the eyes of men grovelling in the dust. As soon, however, as it is accomplished, the nobleman shall return again." This image has, besides, an historical reference, for Josephus informs us, (Antiq. B. xiv. ch. xxv.) that Archelaus and his brother Agrippas, durst not take possession of the kingdom, which came to them by inheritance from their father, until they had sent to Rome, and in a certain way had been invested by the Roman emperor, as their proper sovereign, with kingly dignity.

V. 13. The distribution of the gifts points to a relation of dependence, and lays the ground of the future reckoning and judgment, v. 15, &c. At the same time, this image gives instruction upon the conscientious employment of what is committed to us in the kingdom of Christ.—Von Brunn: "The calling of the ten servants was fulfilled in the choice of the disciples, whom Jesus appointed for his ambassadors in the kingdom. The number ten appears to have indicated no other purpose on the part of our Lord, than that he chose as many labourers in the kingdom as were necessary for making known the gospel to all nations. Moreover, this calling of the servants must certainly be referred, not only to the disciples, who were singled out by Jesus for his service during his personal ministry, but to all whom he at any time calls, to point out to his brethren the way of salvation, and press them to yield themselves to him. The former received not the call till they had received the gifts which fitted them for accomplishing the object of the Lord; the latter, on the other hand, find this call in the gifts which he confers upon them at their birth, or which he afterwards imparts to them through his Spirit. The pounds which the Lord gave to the servants whom he left behind him, are partly the lessons which they received from the mouth of Jesus, and which have been handed down through the writings of the Evangelists to Christians of later times; partly, also, the extraordinary gifts which were conferred on the disciples of Jesus at the outpouring of the Holy Spirit, and through imposition of hands on those who, by receiving their word, believed on Jesus; and finally, those gifts which even to the present time, adorn through God's grace so many teachers in the church as servants of the Lord."

Ten Pounds, minae, about twenty dollars (between three and four pounds sterling;) the distribution of the pounds is here made equally, in Matthew unequally; and both alike true, for the measure of the gift is different with different persons, but in all it is so far equal, as the Lord gives to each one precisely what he is able to employ, Matth. xxv. 15.—*Occupy;* Gnomon: "The charge is of one meaning with that well known saying, γινεσθε καλοι τραπεζιται."—Von Brunn: "He therefore gave them to recipients, not that they might enjoy themselves therewith, but that, through application, they might increase them and give employment to others, Matth. x. 27; v. 14, 15. 1 Cor. xii. 4—11." Grotius: "Since the gifts which we receive from Christ are partly common, such as the word of the gospel, and things immediately connected therewith, and partly peculiar, such as ministerial gifts and the miraculous powers, which Christ bestowed after his ascension upon whom he pleased; Christ appears to me to have had the former in view while pursuing his course on earth, but the latter when drawing near to his death. Therefore, in Luke, the gifts conferred are equal, in Matthew unequal; Rom. xii. 6. 1 Cor. xii. 7, 11, 29. Eph. iv. 11.

Ver. 14. This enmity of the nobleman's fellow-citizens has its primary fulfilment in the hostile procedure of those who would not regard Jesus as their Lord and Saviour. Von Brunn: "The citizens of the nobleman are doubtless in the first instance the Jews, who even to this day cannot deny their deep and rooted enmity. They are here named his citizens, as by John they are called his own (property,) for according to the oldest predictions he was the king of Zion. They sent messages enough after him to show that they would not acknowledge him as their king, when they incited the heathen to persecute the followers of him whom they crucified. They still send after him such messages, because they pronounce the curse over all their members who venture to receive the Christian faith. With these citizens, however, of the nobleman, we are certainly to class those also, who, while they bear the Christian name, will only recognise Jesus as an enlightened teacher, but not as their Lord and Saviour." For this part of the image also there exists an historical ground, in that the Jews sent messengers to Rome, who protested against Archelaus being made king of Judea; but in vain, and he did not leave their opposition unpunished.

Ver. 15. The return of Christ, and the general judgment which is to be held upon all who have been his servants, and have received gifts from him, and have known his will. *That he might know*—as the omniscient he knows all things; but the conduct of one and all must be made known before the whole world, as also the righteousness of the Lord be acknowledged in rewarding and punishing.

Ver. 16. A speech of humility—he gives to the Lord all the glory; he attributes his success, not to his own diligence, his fidelity, his application, but to the goodness of the Lord in having given to him.

V. 17. *Have thou authority over ten cities*—glorious recompense of grace, which stands in exact accordance with his past performances, with his approved fidelity, and his acquired capacity—but still far surpasses his desert.

Ver. 18, 19. The same substantially as with the former servants, in v. 16, 17. Rev. iii. 21; iv. 6. Mat. xix. 28. 1 Cor. viii. 2, 5.

V. 20—24. Von Brunn: "This servant is an image of those Christians who employ not their powers, lest they should, in doing so, hurt either themselves or others; and of those who withhold teachers that would labour for the salvation of others, from the fear of a negligent use being made of them; and also of such as having obtained the pardon of sin and an interest in grace, from fear of falling again under the power of temptation, shut themselves up in cloisters, or withdraw themselves from the society of men." See Matth. xxv. 24—28. Grotius on v. 23: "Lest you should say that you could find no one who was in need of money. The bankers take money from all with interest. The meaning is: You cannot plead the risk of laying out the money; it was mine; and I should have exacted it not at your, but at my risk. For they are safe who manage the affairs of others, as long as they give credit to those who have the public confidence."

V. 25. The men could not perceive the wisdom and righteousness of the divine procedure.

Ver. 26. Hence the Lord unfolds the deep ground of his procedure, which, so far from being arbitrary, consists in the highest righteousness, Matth. xxv. 29.

V. 27. The judgment extends also to those who would not acknowledge the nobleman for their Lord. The immediate fulfilment of this threatening was to be found in the destruction of Jerusalem; death, unutterable and eternal death, is the fate of those who despise the glorious riches of Christ's kingdom; but to be enabled to enjoy the eternal blessings of his kingdom, there is needed a faith that worketh by love.

Calvin: "In this second part, Christ appears to aim chiefly at the Jews; comprehending, however, all who during his absence take up the weapons of rebellion. But Christ's object was not only to terrify such persons by the denunciation of fearful punishment, but also to keep his own disciples in the faith of obedience. For it is not a small temptation to see the kingdom of God wasted by the perfidy and rebellion of multitudes. Therefore, that we may continue steadfast amid the disorders, Christ admonishes us that he will return, and at his arrival will execute vengeance upon those who have impiously rebelled against him." The punishment figuratively threatened in v. 27, was, in plain language, delineated, v. 43, 44, in the literally fulfilled prophecy upon Jerusalem, which the Lord spake, when he saw the city lying before him, and, by not knowing the time of its merciful visitation, preparing itself for overwhelming destruction.

THE END.

www.ingramcontent.com/pod-product-compliance
Lightning Source LLC
LaVergne TN
LVHW020107110826
845151LV00001B/84

9781425544201